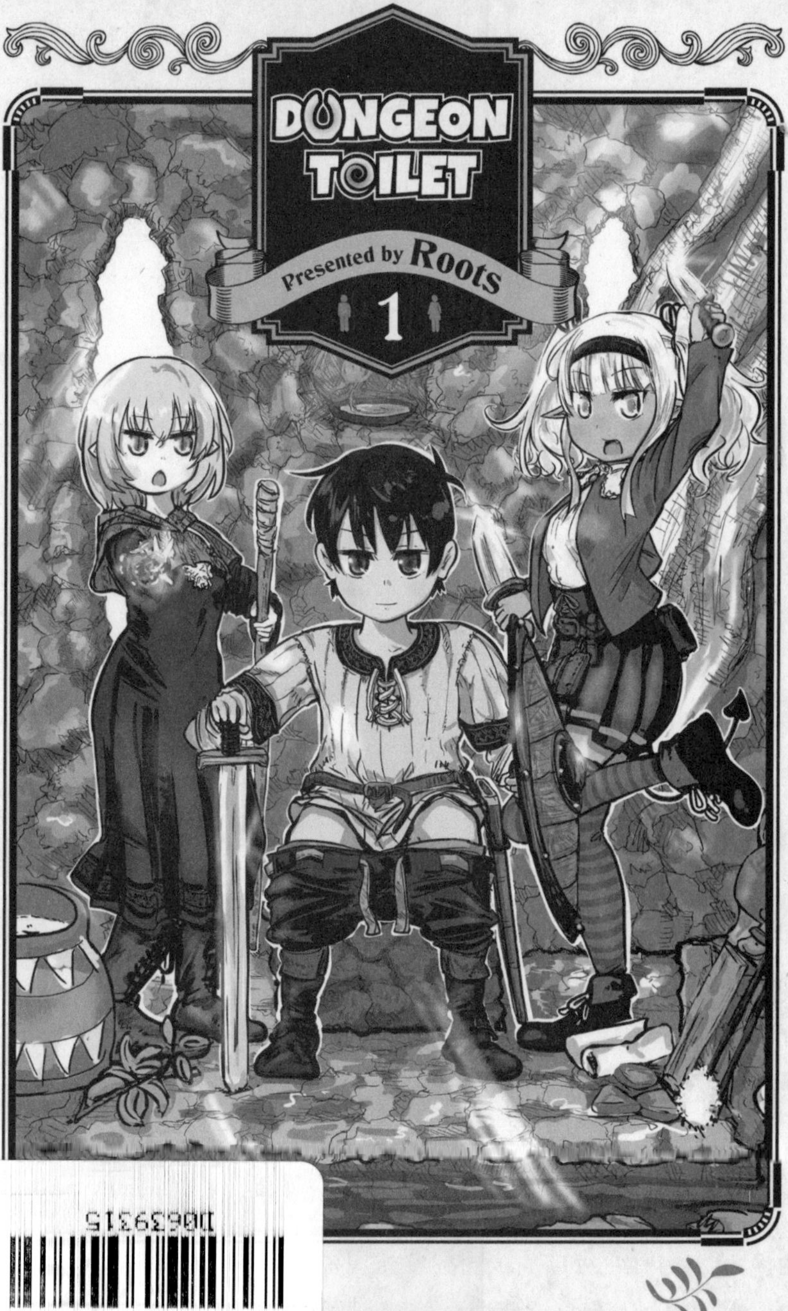
DUNGEON TOILET
Presented by Roots
1

CONTENTS

1

FIRST FLUSH —→ 3

SECOND FLUSH —→ 17

THIRD FLUSH —→ 27

FOURTH FLUSH —→ 37

FIFTH FLUSH —→ 45

SIXTH FLUSH —→ 55

SEVENTH FLUSH —→ 63

EIGHTH FLUSH —→ 73

NINTH FLUSH —→ 81

TENTH FLUSH —→ 91

ELEVENTH FLUSH —→ 99

TWELTH FLUSH —→ 109

THIRTEENTH FLUSH —→ 117

FOURTEENTH FLUSH —→ 127

FIFTEENTH FLUSH —→ 135

SIXTEENTH FLUSH —→ 145

SEVENTEENTH FLUSH —→ 153

EIGHTEENTH FLUSH —→ 163

COLUMN

PEOPLE WHO DON'T VALUE TOILET TIME ARE NO GOOD.

❖ SHORT VERSION: TOILET TIME

FIRST —→ 25

SECOND —→ 35

THIRD —→ 53

FOURTH —→ 71

FIFTH —→ 89

SIXTH —→ 107

SEVENTH —→ 125

EIGHTH —→ 143

NINTH —→ 161

BONUS CONTENT —→ 172

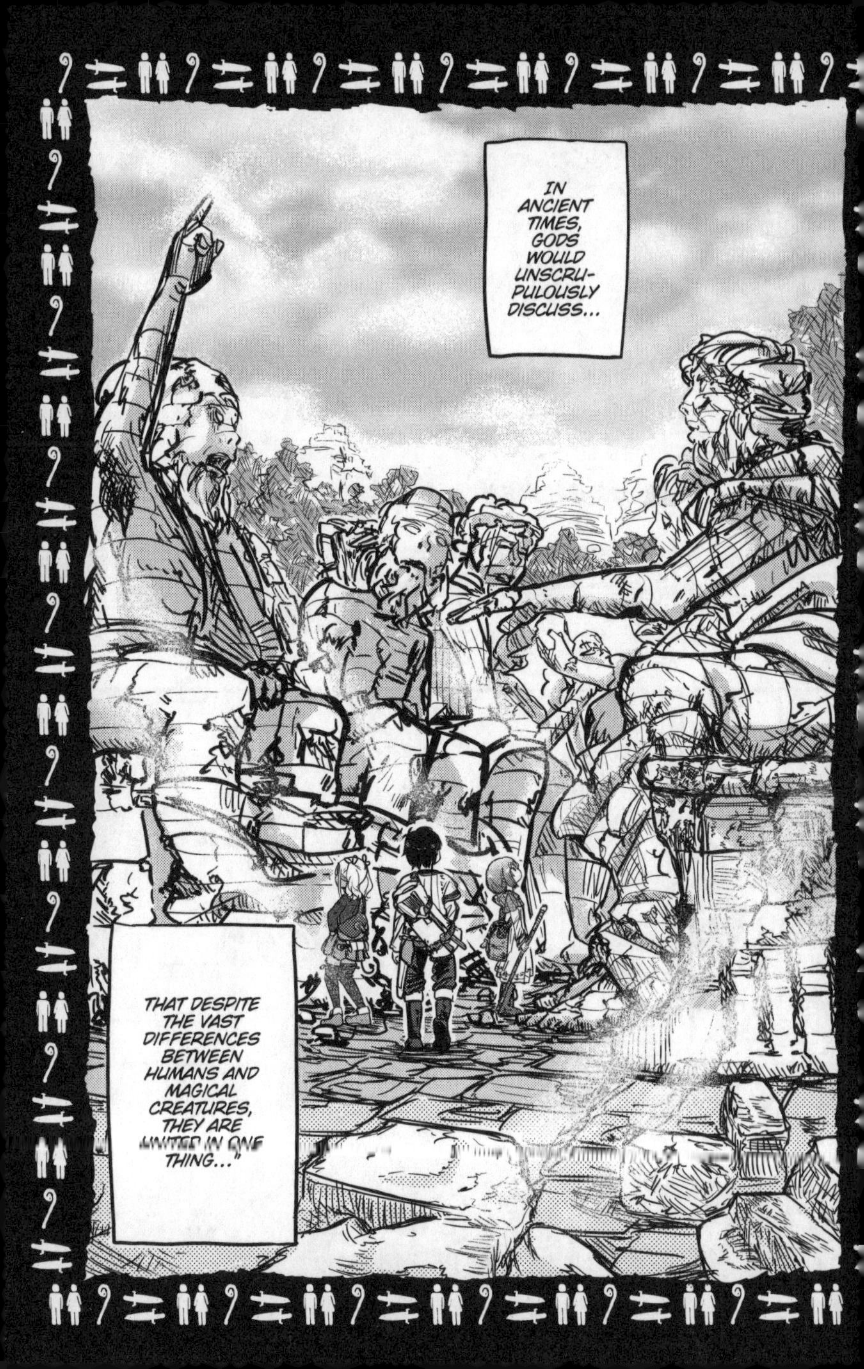
IN ANCIENT TIMES, GODS WOULD UNSCRU-PULOUSLY DISCUSS...
THAT DESPITE THE VAST DIFFERENCES BETWEEN HUMANS AND MAGICAL CREATURES, THEY ARE UNITED IN ONE THING..."

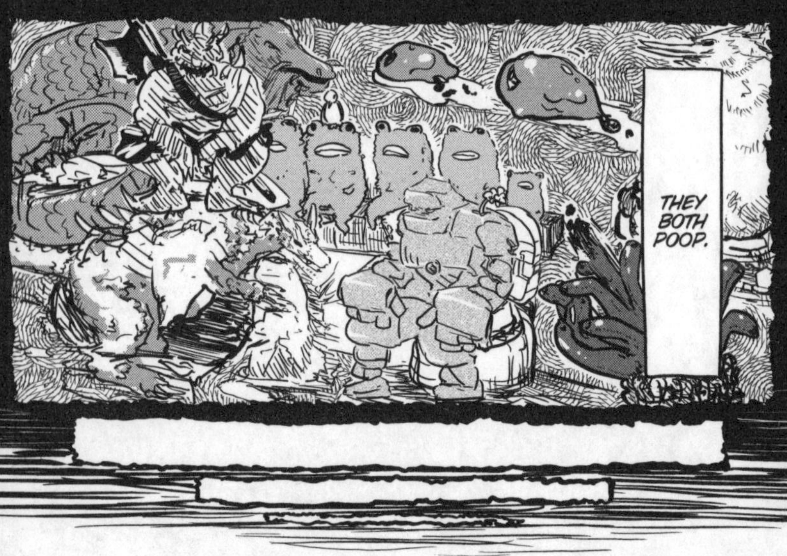
THEY BOTH POOP.

MANY YEARS HAVE PASSED SINCE THEN.

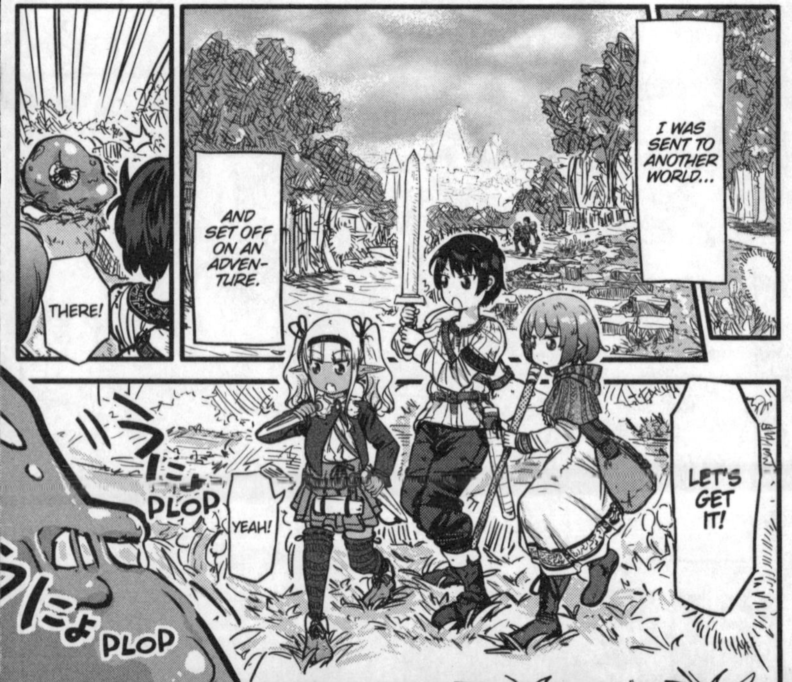
I WAS SENT TO ANOTHER WORLD...
AND SET OFF ON AN ADVEN-TURE.
THERE!
LET'S GET IT!
YEAH!
ぷにょ
PLOP
ぷにょ
PLOP

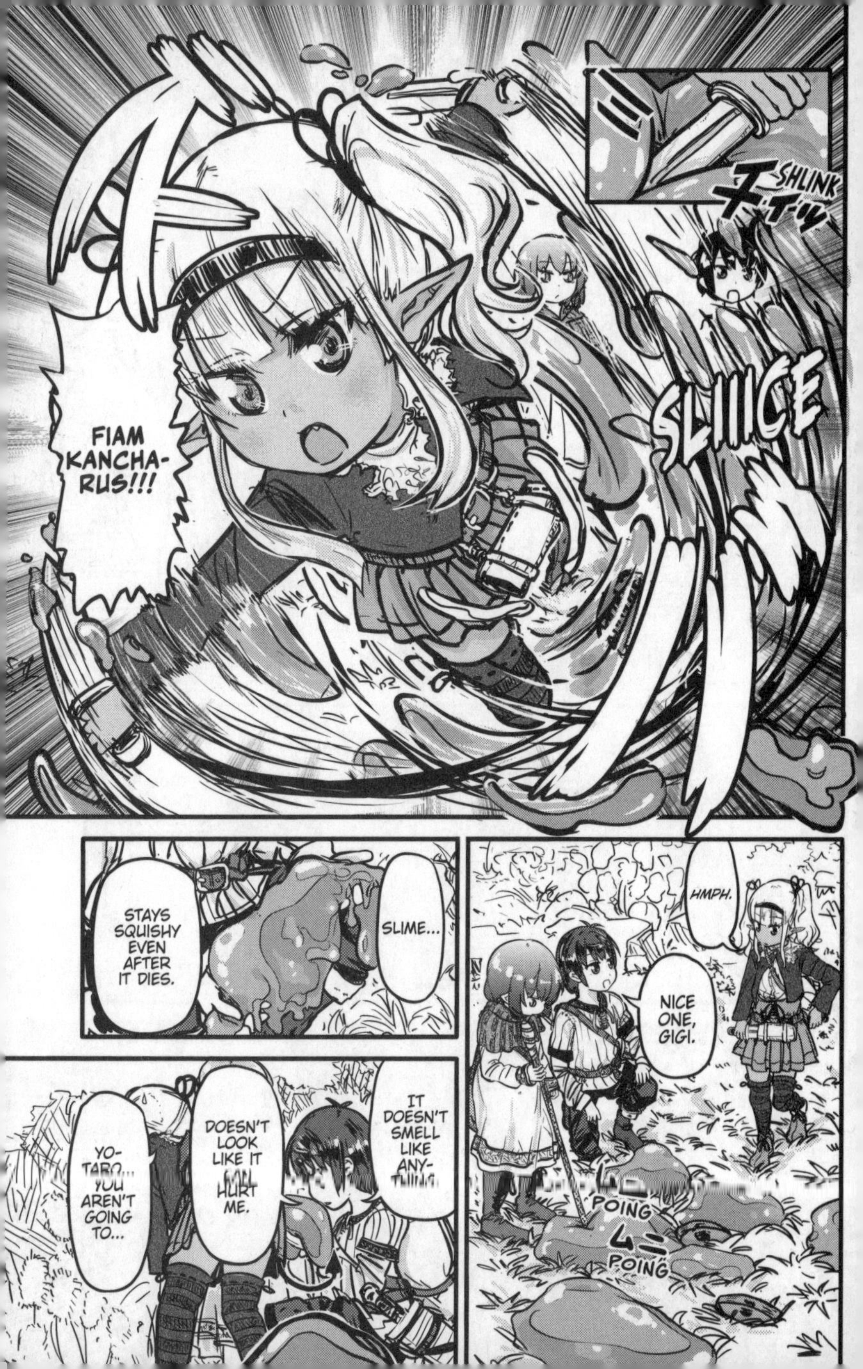
SHLINK
SLIIICE
FIAM KANCHARUS!!!
HMPH.
NICE ONE, GIGI.
POING
POING
SLIME...
STAYS SQUISHY EVEN AFTER IT DIES.
IT DOESN'T SMELL LIKE ANY-
DOESN'T LOOK LIKE IT CAN HURT ME.
YO-TARO... YOU AREN'T GOING TO...

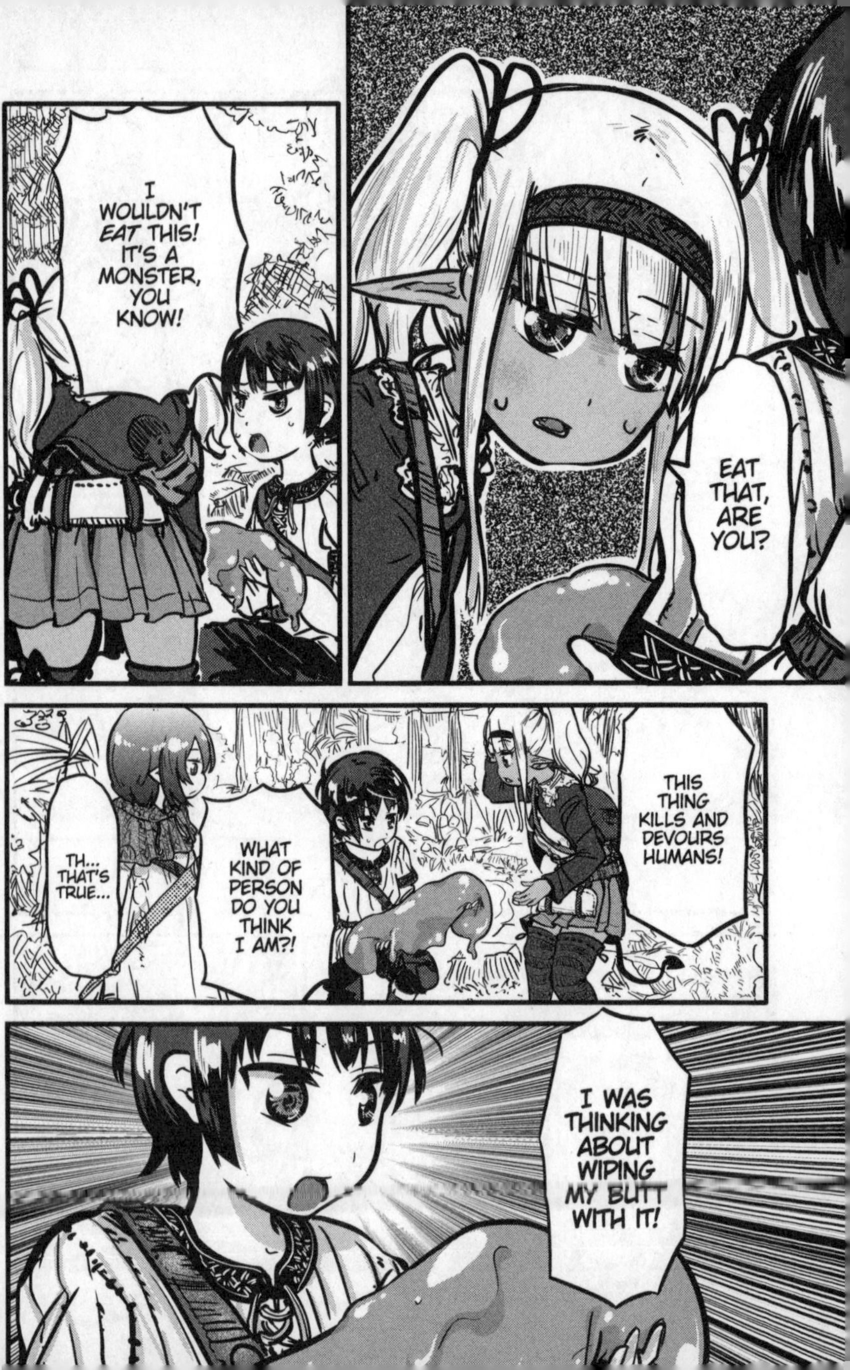
EAT THAT, ARE YOU?
I WOULDN'T EAT THIS! IT'S A MONSTER, YOU KNOW!
THIS THING KILLS AND DEVOURS HUMANS!
WHAT KIND OF PERSON DO YOU THINK I AM?!
TH... THAT'S TRUE...
I WAS THINKING ABOUT WIPING MY BUTT WITH IT!

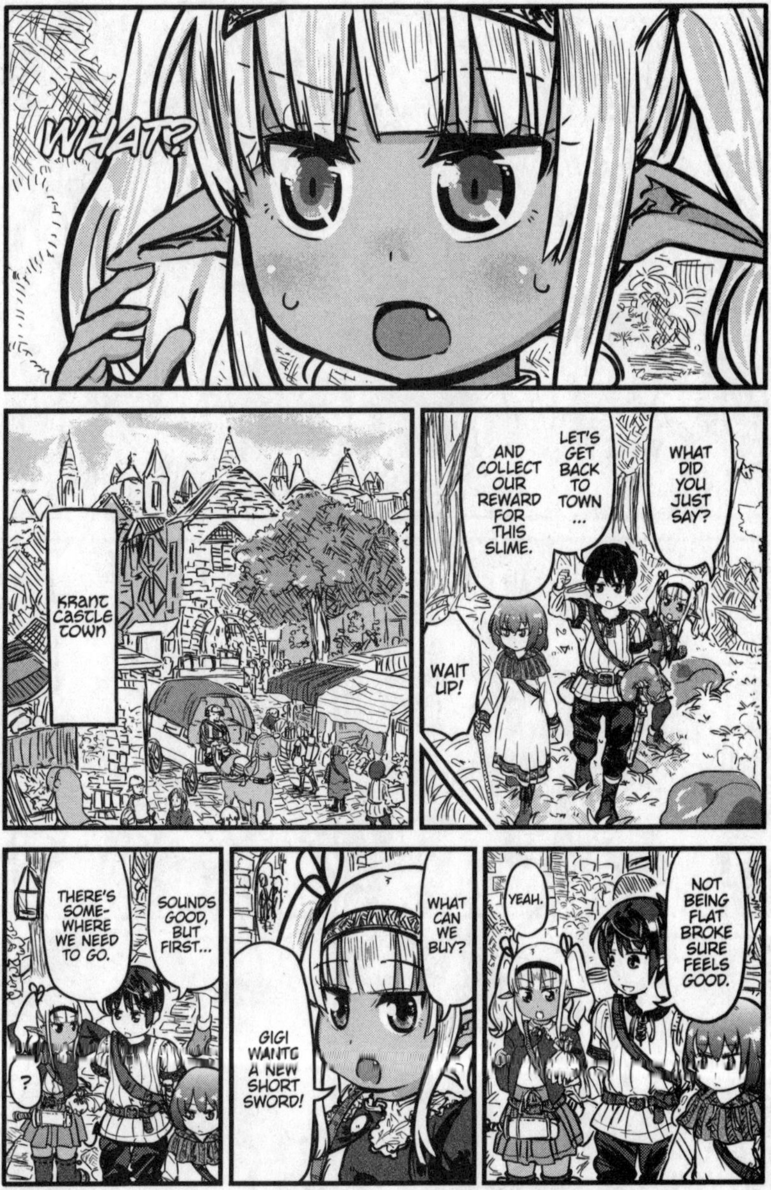
WHAT?
WHAT DID YOU JUST SAY?
LET'S GET BACK TO TOWN ...
AND COLLECT OUR REWARD FOR THIS SLIME.
WAIT UP!
KRANT CASTLE TOWN
NOT BEING FLAT BROKE SURE FEELS GOOD.
YEAH.
WHAT CAN WE BUY?
GIGI WANTS A NEW SHORT SWORD!
SOUNDS GOOD, BUT FIRST...
THERE'S SOME-WHERE WE NEED TO GO.
?

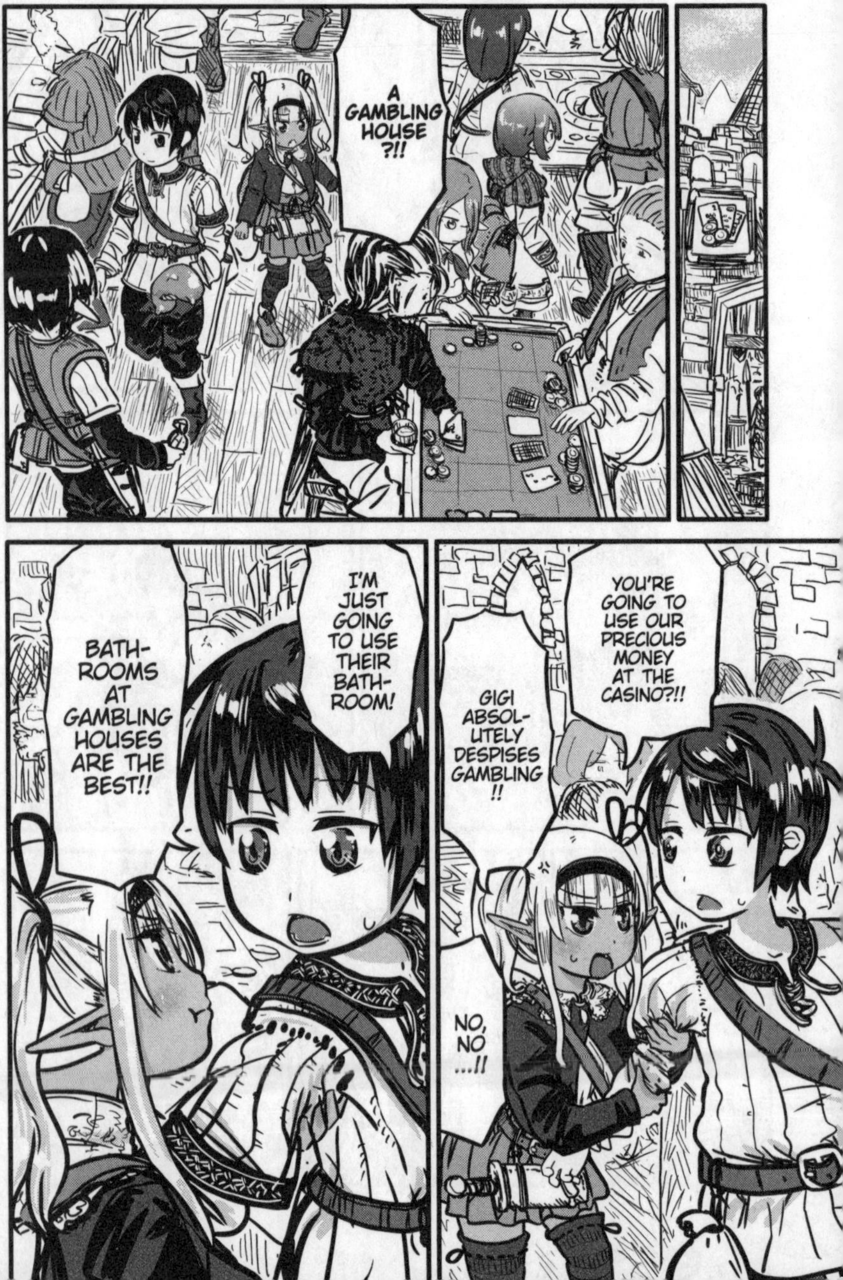
A GAMBLING HOUSE ?!!
YOU'RE GOING TO USE OUR PRECIOUS MONEY AT THE CASINO?!!
GIGI ABSOLUTELY DESPISES GAMBLING!!
NO, NO ...!!
I'M JUST GOING TO USE THEIR BATHROOM!
BATHROOMS AT GAMBLING HOUSES ARE THE BEST!!

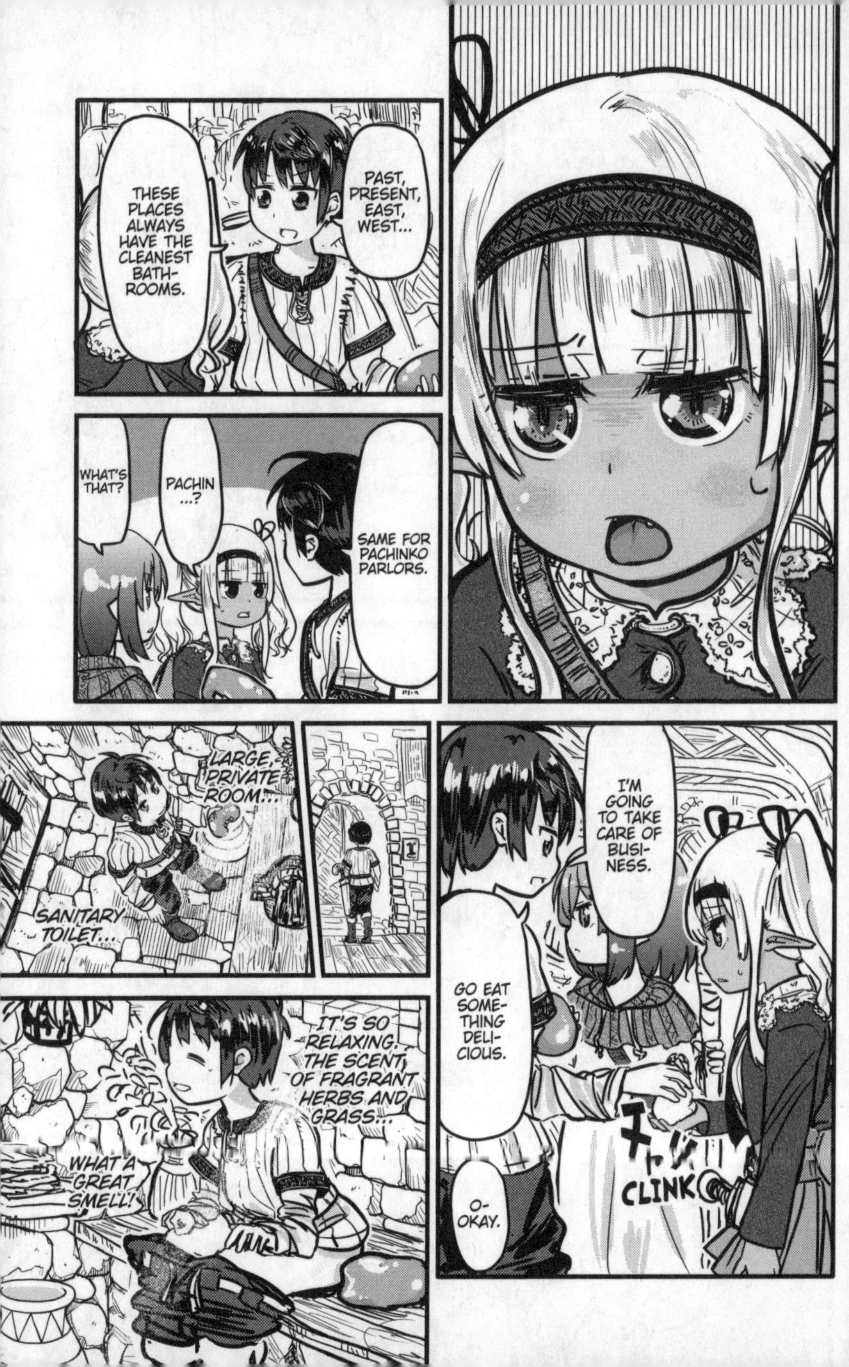
PAST, PRESENT, EAST, WEST...
THESE PLACES ALWAYS HAVE THE CLEANEST BATHROOMS.
SAME FOR PACHINKO PARLORS.
PACHIN...?
WHAT'S THAT?
I'M GOING TO TAKE CARE OF BUSINESS.
GO EAT SOMETHING DELICIOUS.
CLINK
O-OKAY.
LARGE, PRIVATE ROOM...
SANITARY TOILET...
IT'S SO RELAXING. THE SCENT OF FRAGRANT HERBS AND GRASS...
WHAT A GREAT SMELL!

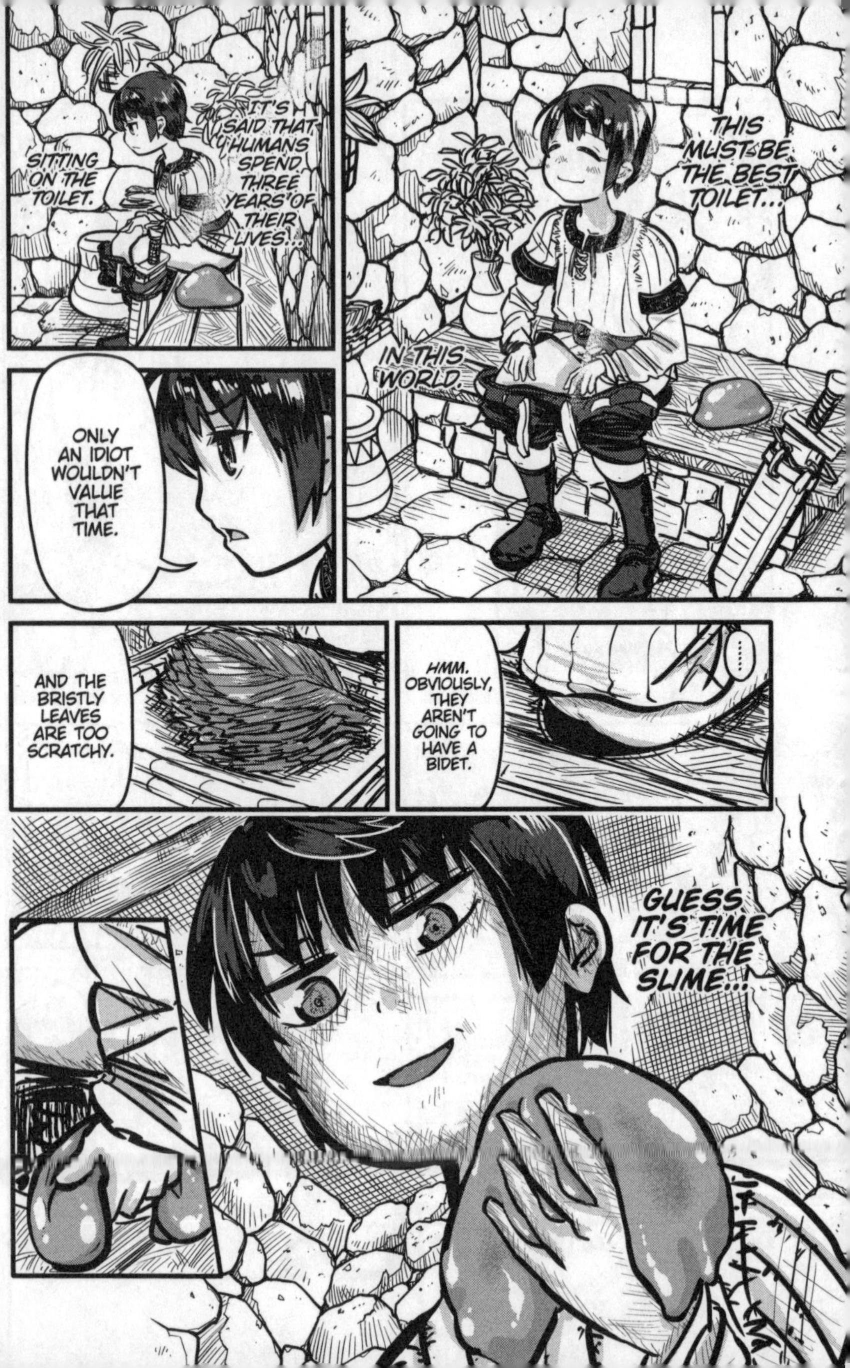
THIS MUST BE THE BEST TOILET...
IN THIS WORLD.
IT'S SAID THAT HUMANS SPEND THREE YEARS OF THEIR LIVES...
SITTING ON THE TOILET.
ONLY AN IDIOT WOULDN'T VALUE THAT TIME.
...
HMM. OBVIOUSLY, THEY AREN'T GOING TO HAVE A BIDET.
AND THE BRISTLY LEAVES ARE TOO SCRATCHY.
GUESS IT'S TIME FOR THE SLIME...!

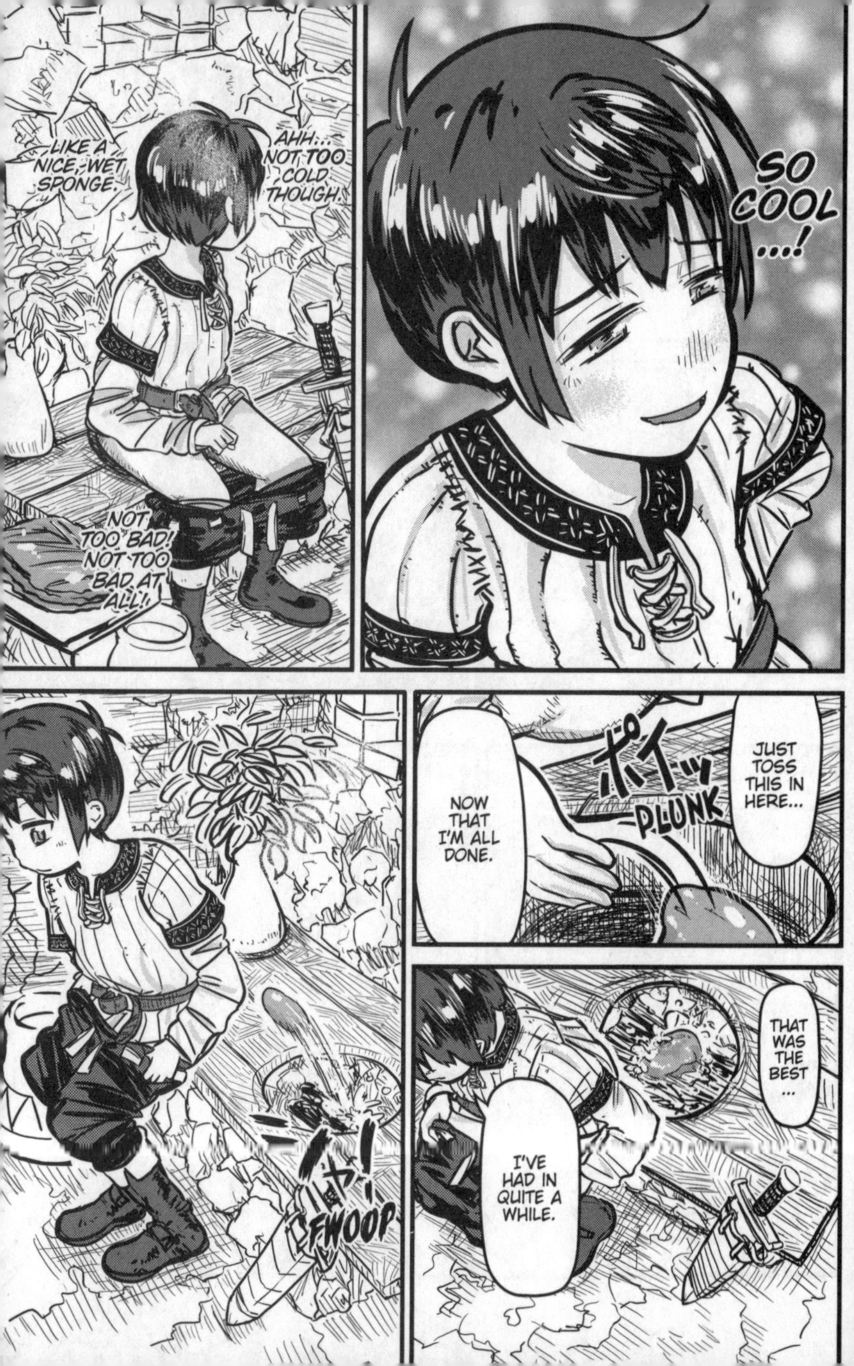
SO COOL...!
AHH... NOT TOO COLD THOUGH.
LIKE A NICE, WET SPONGE.
NOT TOO BAD! NOT TOO BAD AT ALL!
JUST TOSS THIS IN HERE...
ポイッ
PLUNK
NOW THAT I'M ALL DONE.
THAT WAS THE BEST...
I'VE HAD IN QUITE A WHILE.
FWOOP

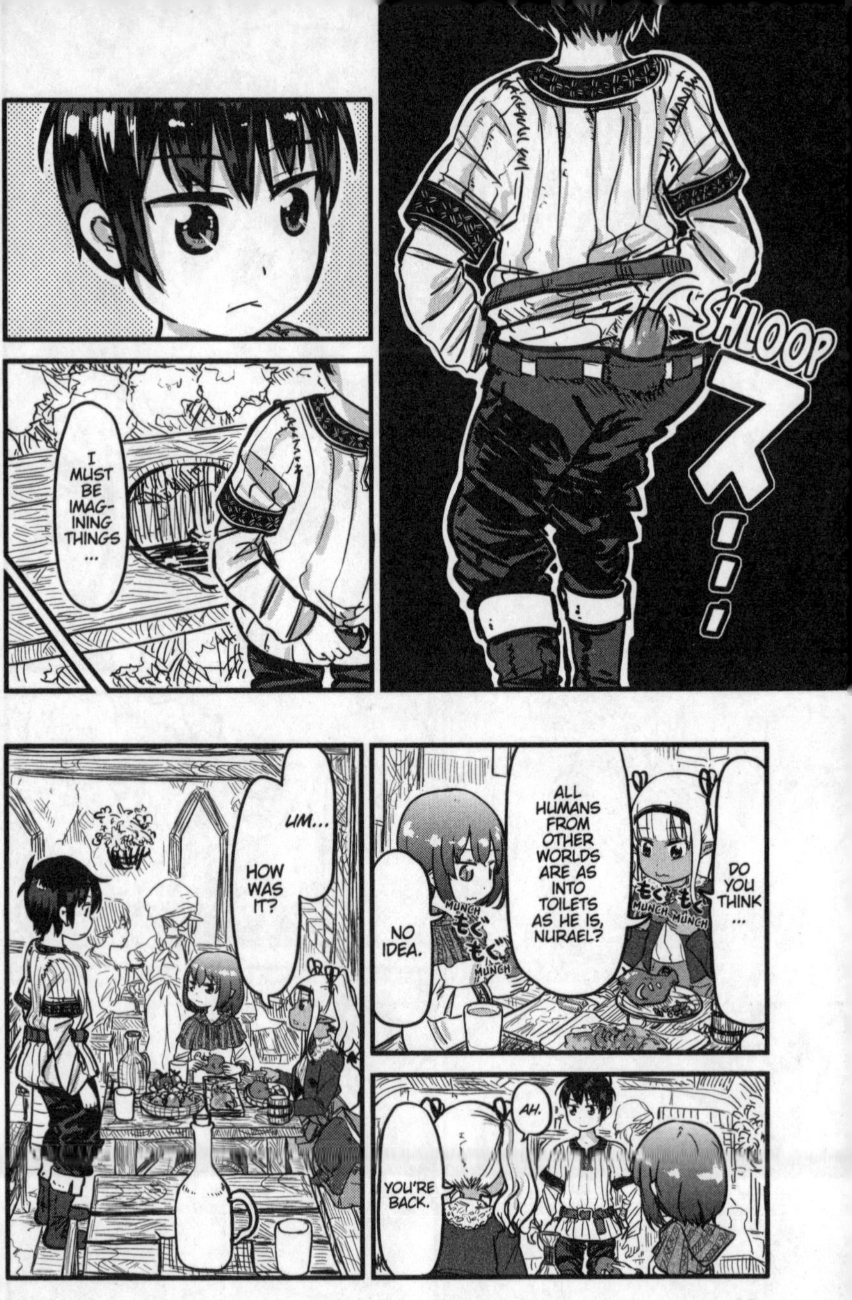

SHLOOP
ス・・・
I MUST BE IMAGINING THINGS...
DO YOU THINK...
ALL HUMANS FROM OTHER WORLDS ARE AS INTO TOILETS AS HE IS, NURAEL?
もぐもぐ MUNCH MUNCH
もぐもぐ MUNCH MUNCH
NO IDEA.
AH.
YOU'RE BACK.
UM...
HOW WAS IT?

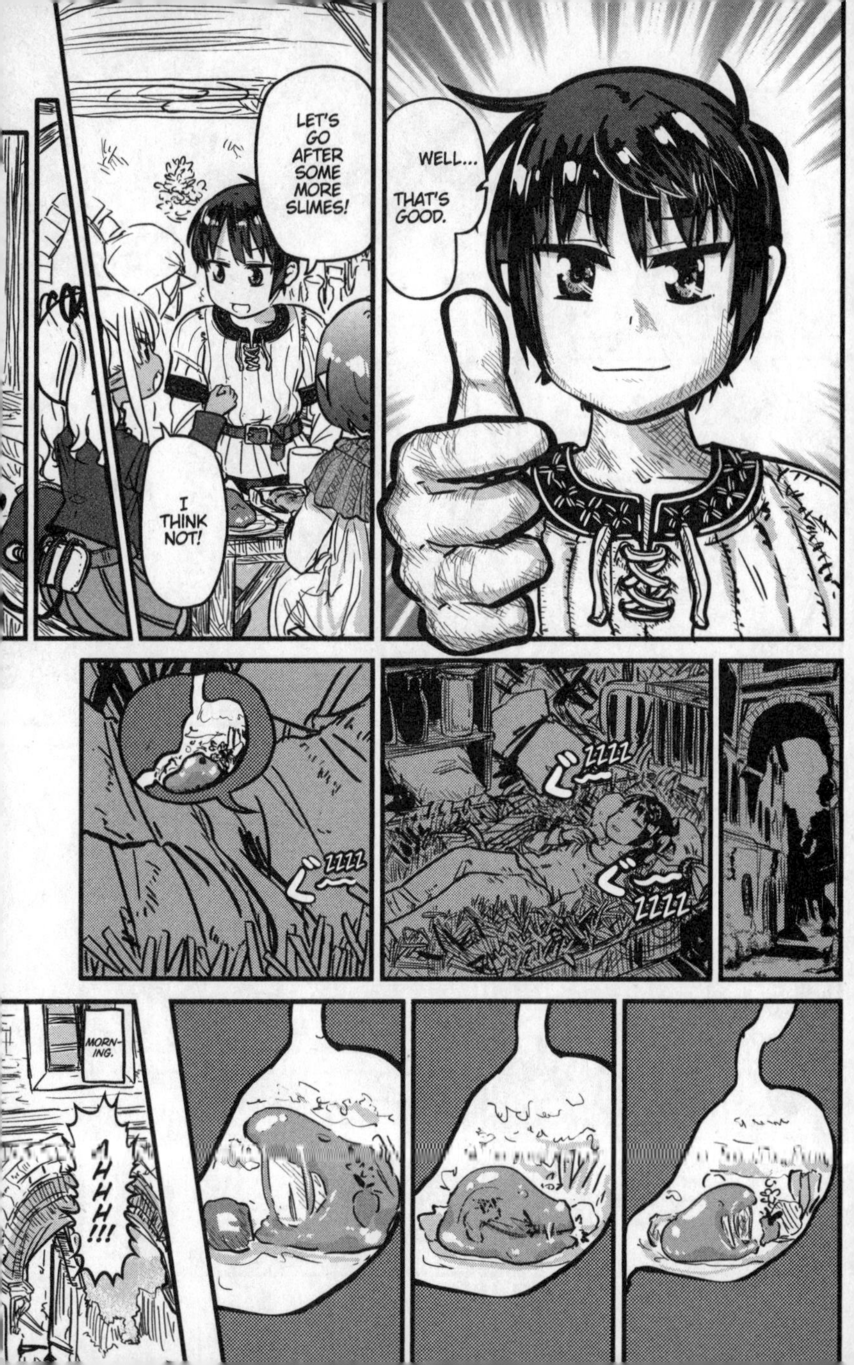
WELL...
THAT'S GOOD.
LET'S GO AFTER SOME MORE SLIMES!
I THINK NOT!
ぐ～ ZZZZ
ぐ～ ZZZZ
ぐ～ ZZZZ
MORN-ING.
AHHH!!!

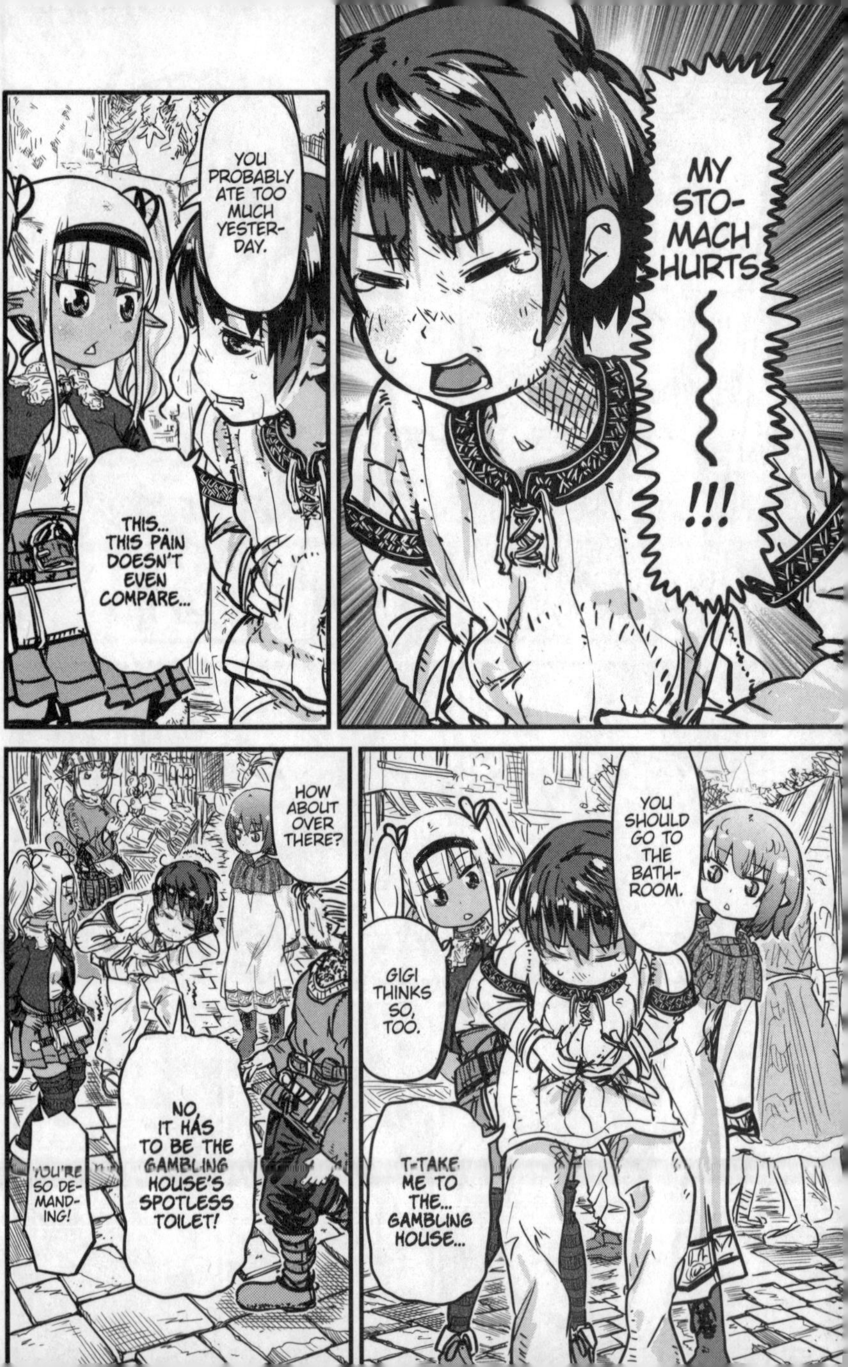
MY STO-MACH HURTS ~~~!!!
YOU PROBABLY ATE TOO MUCH YESTER-DAY.
THIS... THIS PAIN DOESN'T EVEN COMPARE...
YOU SHOULD GO TO THE BATH-ROOM.
GIGI THINKS SO, TOO.
T-TAKE ME TO THE... GAMBLING HOUSE...
HOW ABOUT OVER THERE?
NO, IT HAS TO BE THE GAMBLING HOUSE'S SPOTLESS TOILET!
YOU'RE SO DE-MAND-ING!

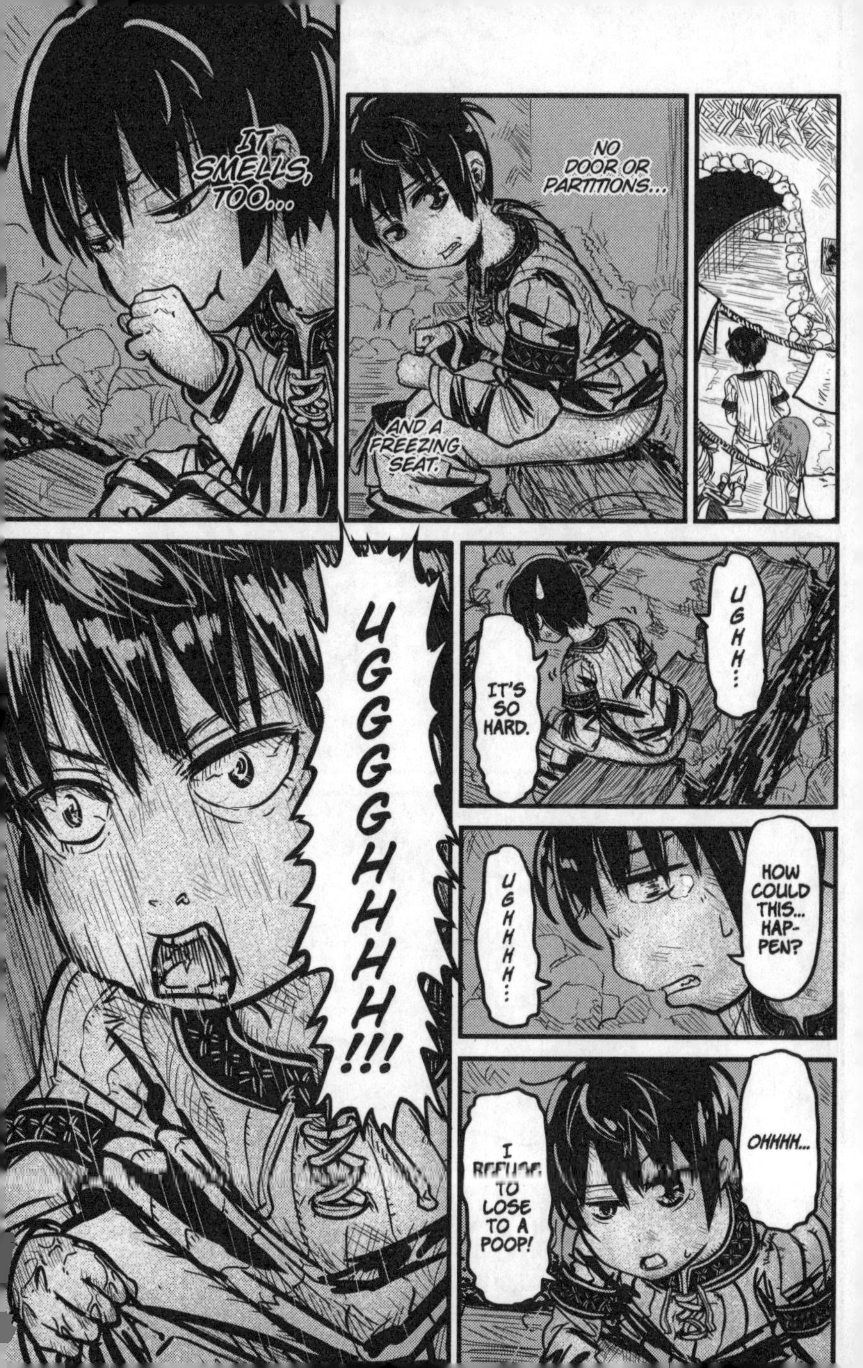
NO DOOR OR PARTITIONS...
AND A FREEZING SEAT.
IT SMELLS, TOO...
UGHH...
IT'S SO HARD.
HOW COULD THIS... HAP-PEN?
UGHHHH...
OHHHH...
I REFUSE TO LOSE TO A POOP!
UGGGGHHHH!!!

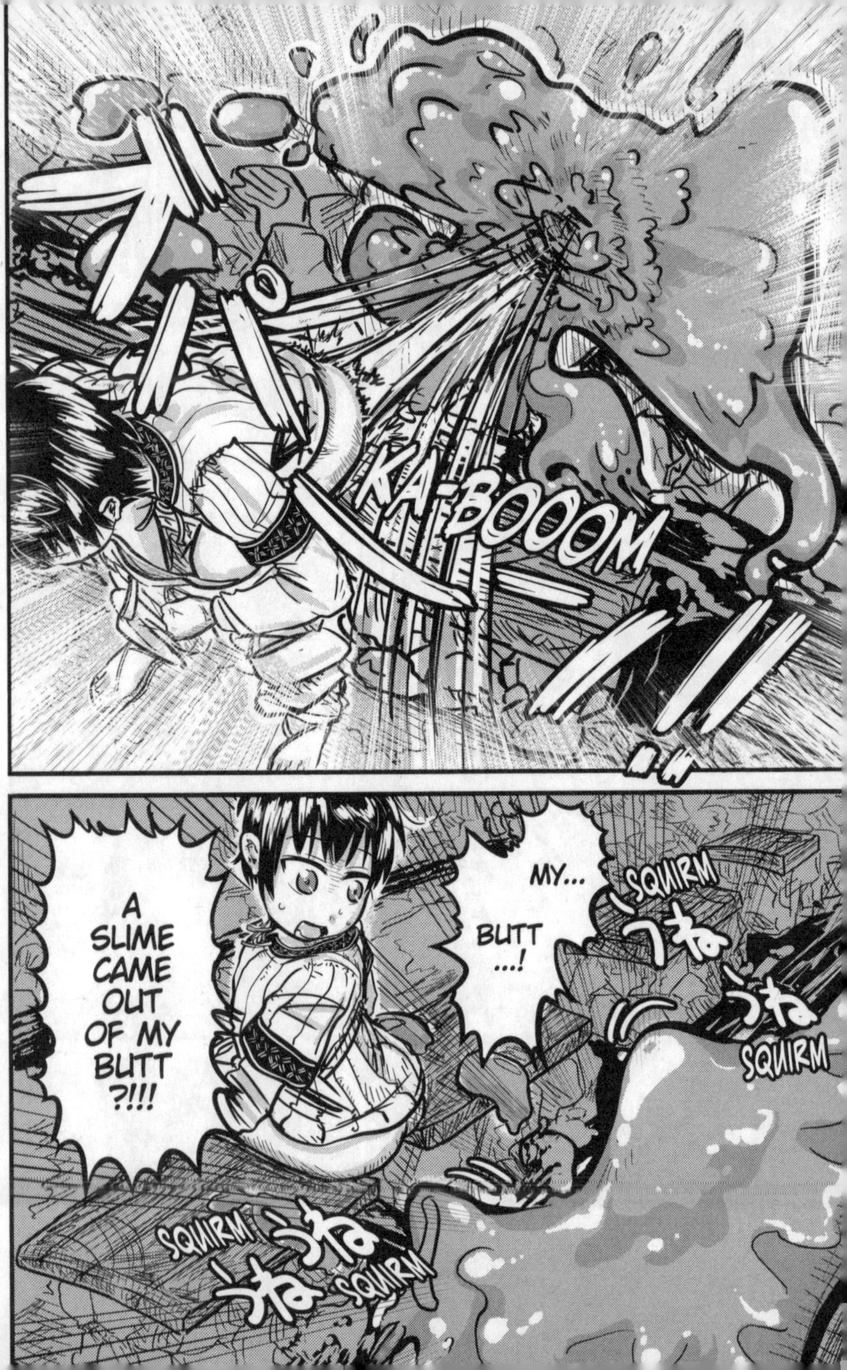
KA-BOOOM
SQUIRM うね
うね SQUIRM
MY... BUTT ...!
A SLIME CAME OUT OF MY BUTT ?!!!
SQUIRM うね
うね SQUIRM

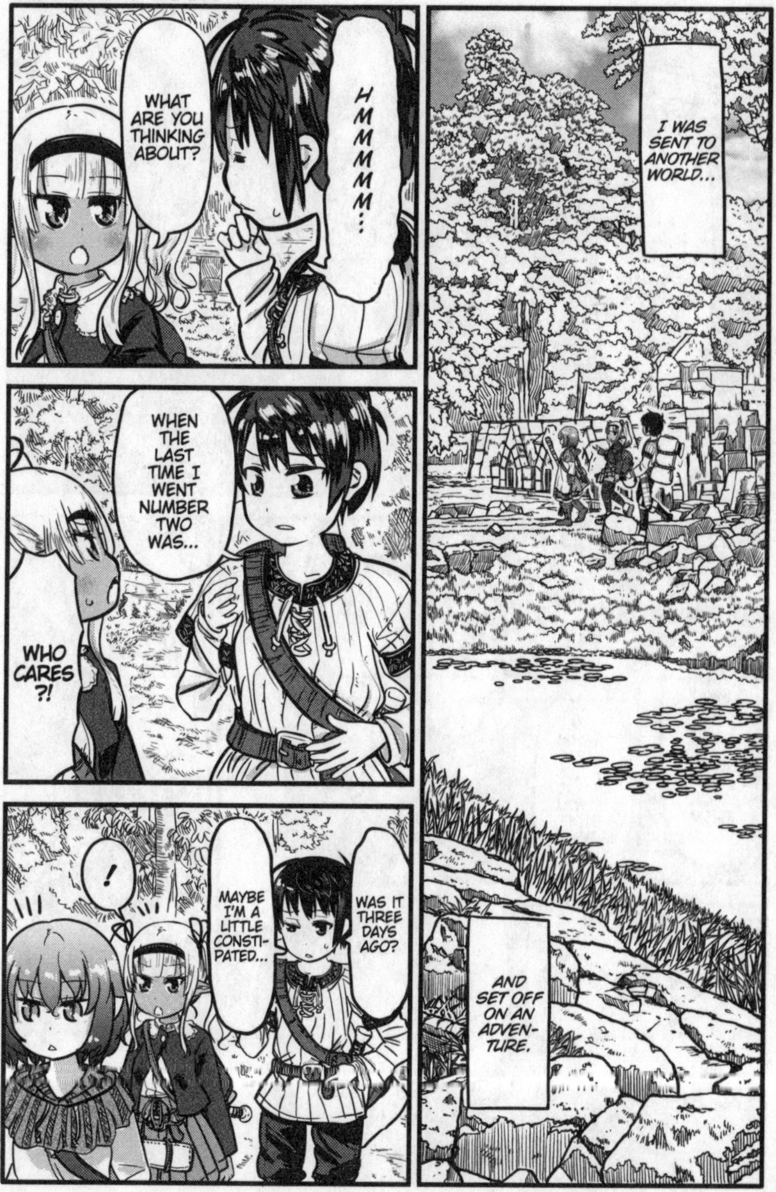
I WAS SENT TO ANOTHER WORLD...
AND SET OFF ON AN ADVENTURE.
HMMMMM...
WHAT ARE YOU THINKING ABOUT?
WHEN THE LAST TIME I WENT NUMBER TWO WAS...
WHO CARES?!
WAS IT THREE DAYS AGO?
MAYBE I'M A LITTLE CONSTIPATED...
!

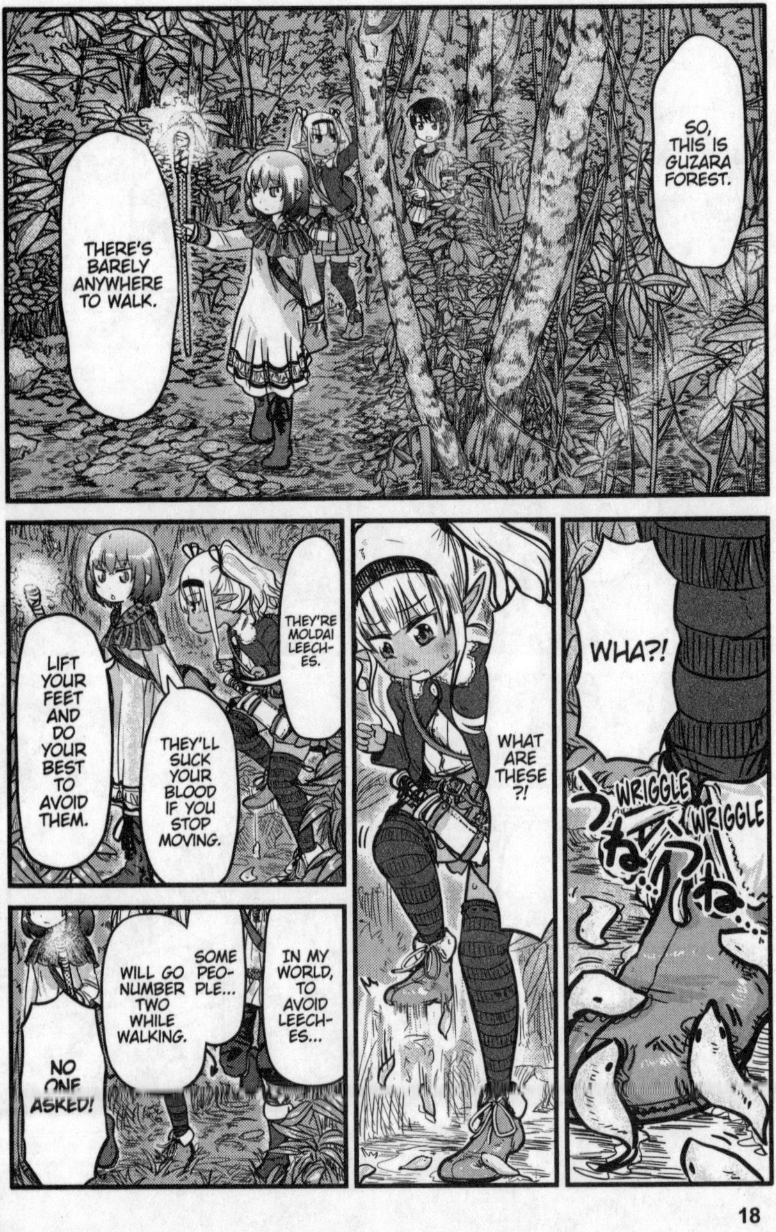
SO, THIS IS GUZARA FOREST.
THERE'S BARELY ANYWHERE TO WALK.
WHA?!
WRIGGLE WRIGGLE
うねうね
WHAT ARE THESE?!
THEY'RE MOLDAI LEECHES.
THEY'LL SUCK YOUR BLOOD IF YOU STOP MOVING.
LIFT YOUR FEET AND DO YOUR BEST TO AVOID THEM.
IN MY WORLD, TO AVOID LEECHES...
SOME PEOPLE...
WILL GO NUMBER TWO WHILE WALKING.
NO ONE ASKED!

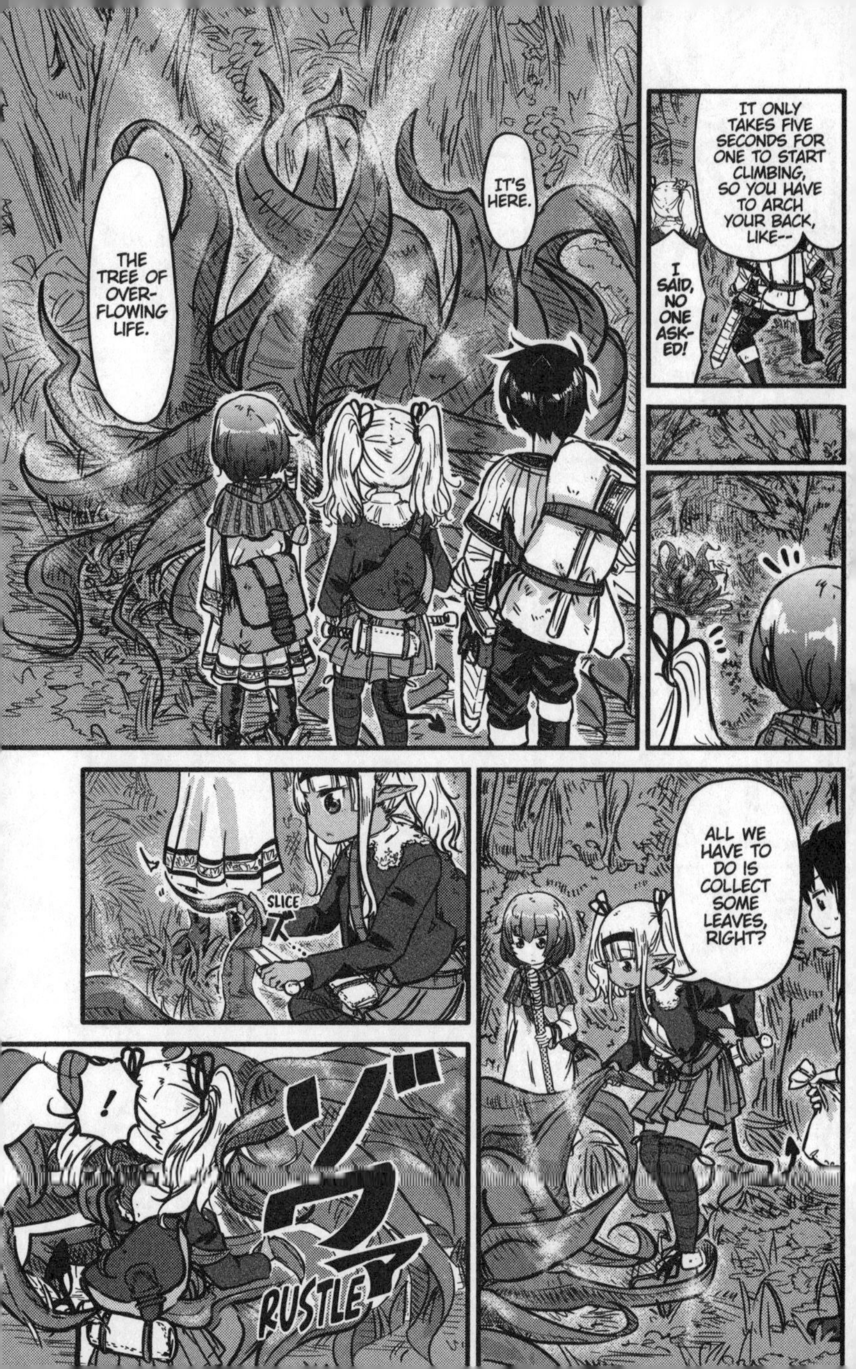
IT ONLY TAKES FIVE SECONDS FOR ONE TO START CLIMBING, SO YOU HAVE TO ARCH YOUR BACK, LIKE--
I SAID, NO ONE ASK-ED!
IT'S HERE.
THE TREE OF OVER-FLOWING LIFE.
ALL WE HAVE TO DO IS COLLECT SOME LEAVES, RIGHT?
SLICE
!
ゾワ
RUSTLE

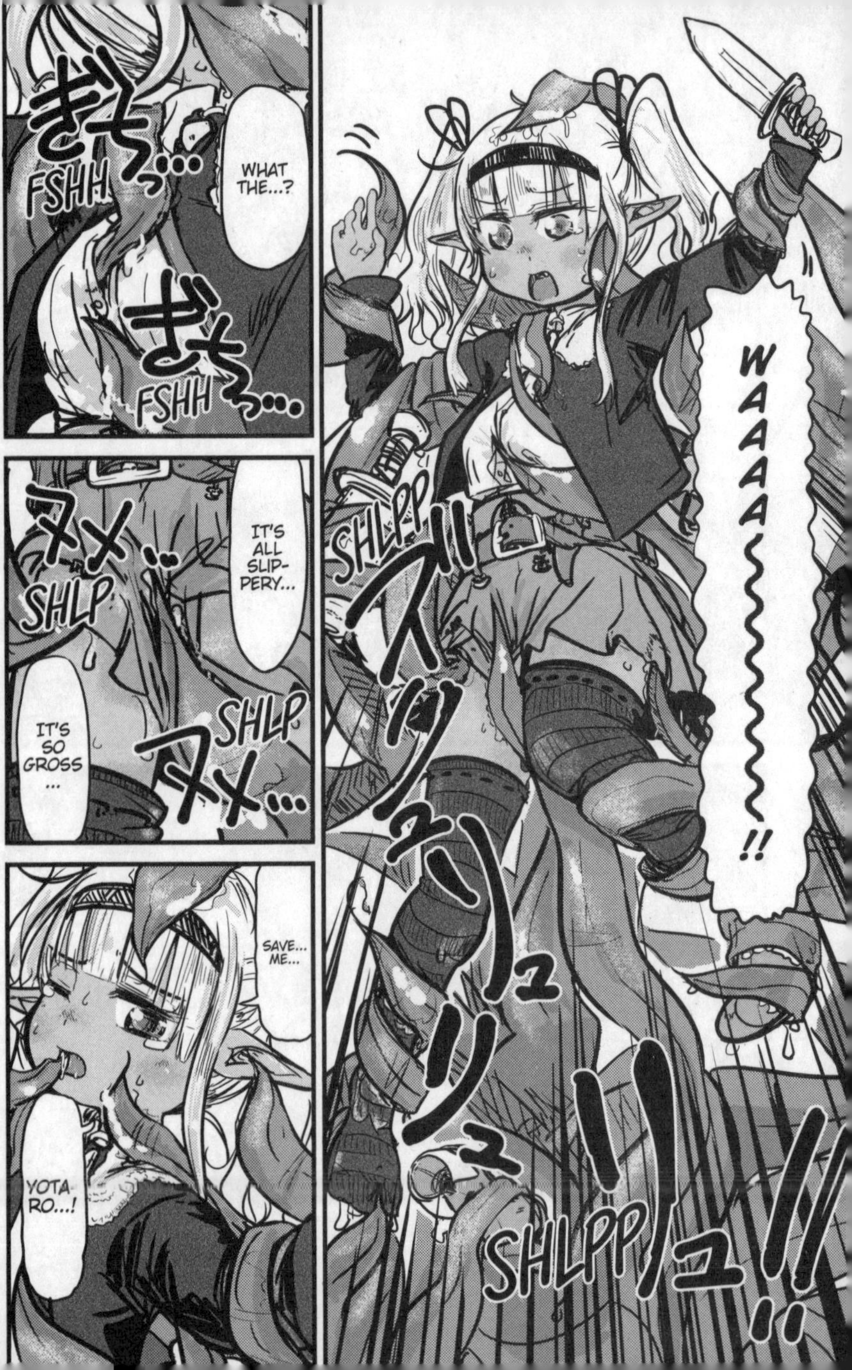

WAAAAA~~~~!!
SHLPP
SHLPP!!
WHAT THE...?
FSHH
FSHH
IT'S ALL SLIPPERY...
SHLP
SHLP
IT'S SO GROSS...
SAVE... ME...
YOTARO...!

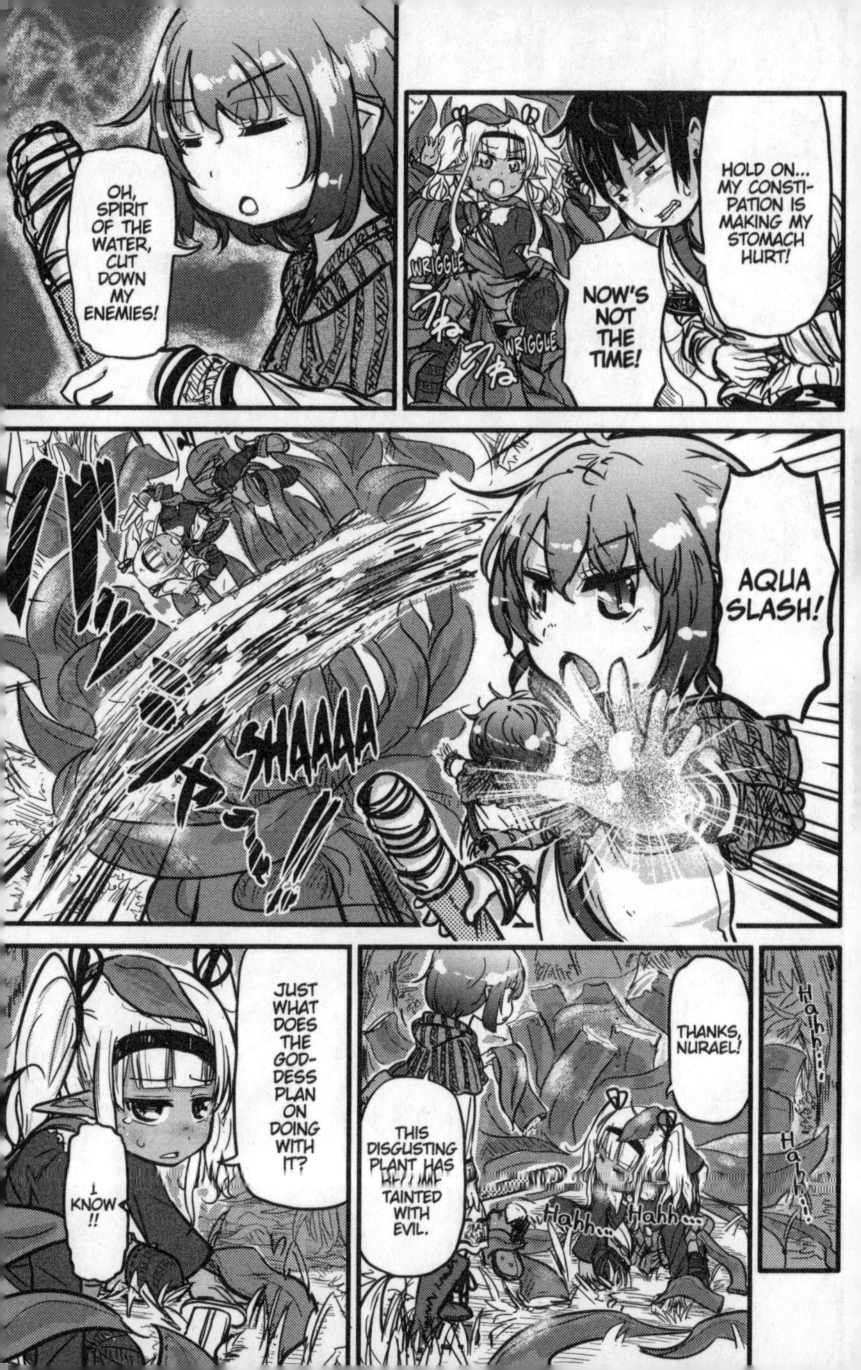
HOLD ON... MY CONSTIPATION IS MAKING MY STOMACH HURT!
NOW'S NOT THE TIME!
WRIGGLE
WRIGGLE
OH, SPIRIT OF THE WATER, CUT DOWN MY ENEMIES!
AQUA SLASH!
SHAAAA
Hahh... Hahh...
THANKS, NURAEL!
THIS DISGUSTING PLANT HAS TAINTED WITH EVIL.
Hahh... Hahh...
JUST WHAT DOES THE GODDESS PLAN ON DOING WITH IT?
I KNOW!!

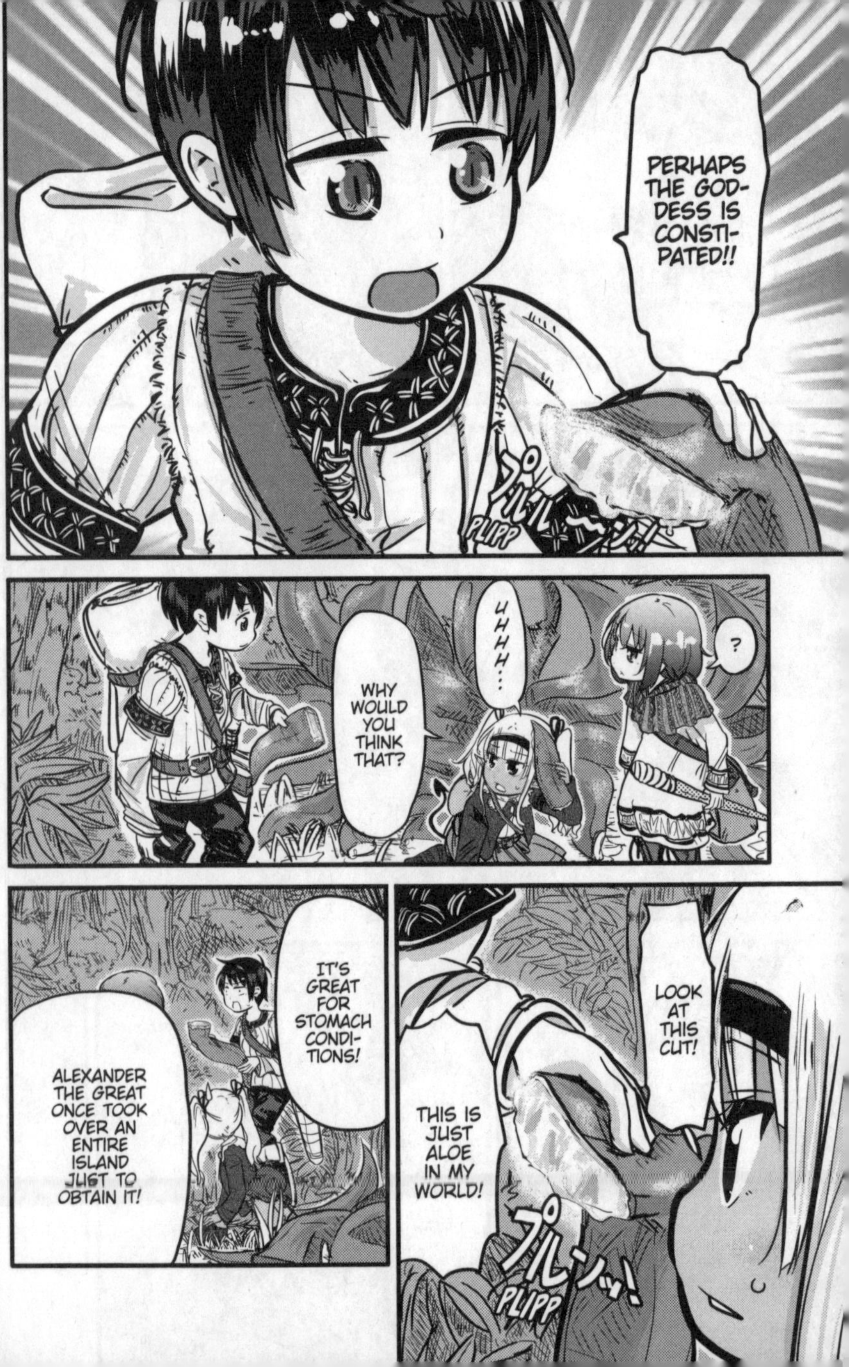
PERHAPS THE GOD-DESS IS CONSTI-PATED!!
PLIPP
?
UHHH...
WHY WOULD YOU THINK THAT?
LOOK AT THIS CUT!
THIS IS JUST ALOE IN MY WORLD!
プルーンッ!
PLIPP
IT'S GREAT FOR STOMACH CONDI-TIONS!
ALEXANDER THE GREAT ONCE TOOK OVER AN ENTIRE ISLAND JUST TO OBTAIN IT!

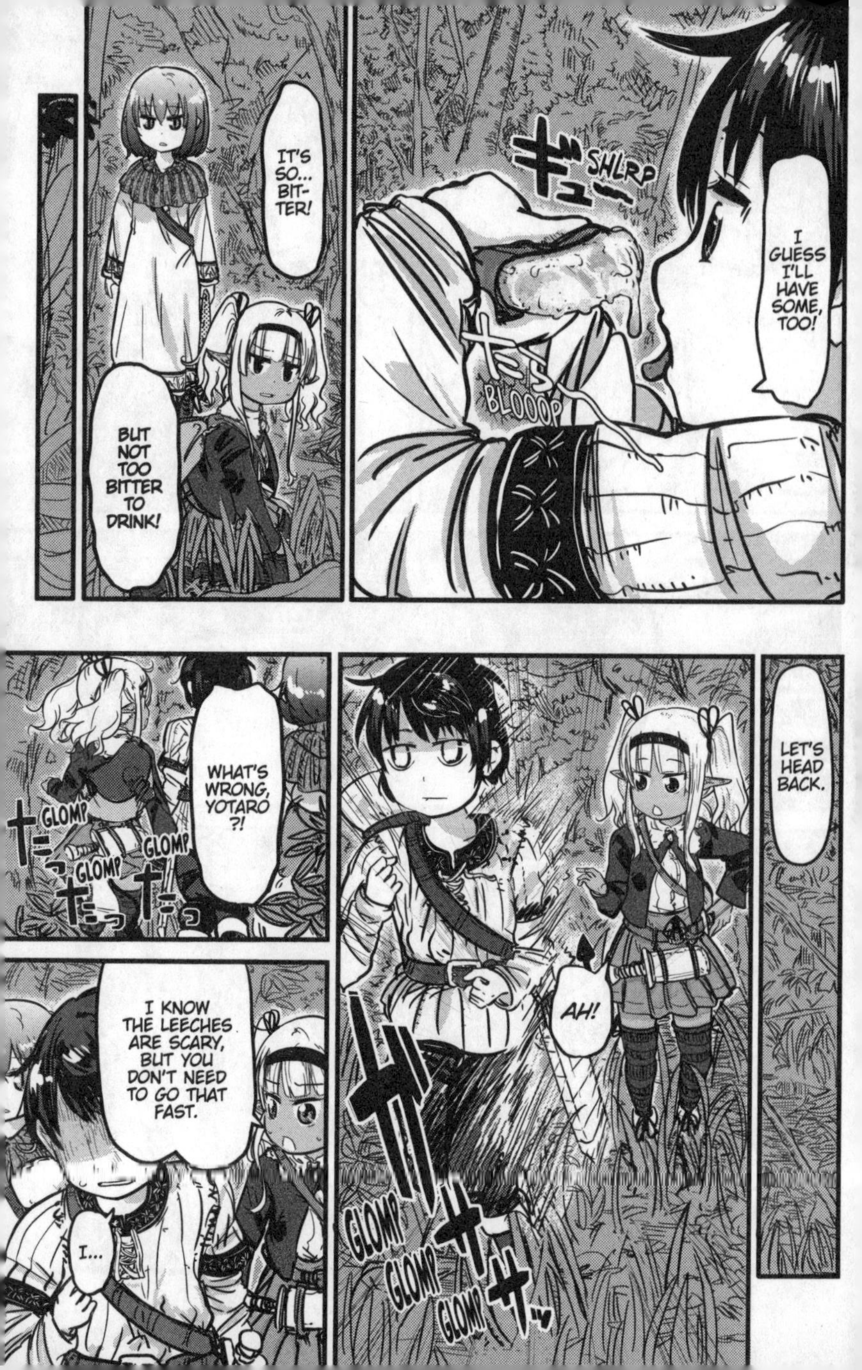
ギュー
SHLRP
BLOOOP
I GUESS I'LL HAVE SOME, TOO!
IT'S SO... BIT-TER!
BUT NOT TOO BITTER TO DRINK!
LET'S HEAD BACK.
AH!
GLOMP
GLOMP
GLOMP
WHAT'S WRONG, YOTARO?!
GLOMP
GLOMP
GLOMP
I KNOW THE LEECHES ARE SCARY, BUT YOU DON'T NEED TO GO THAT FAST.
I...

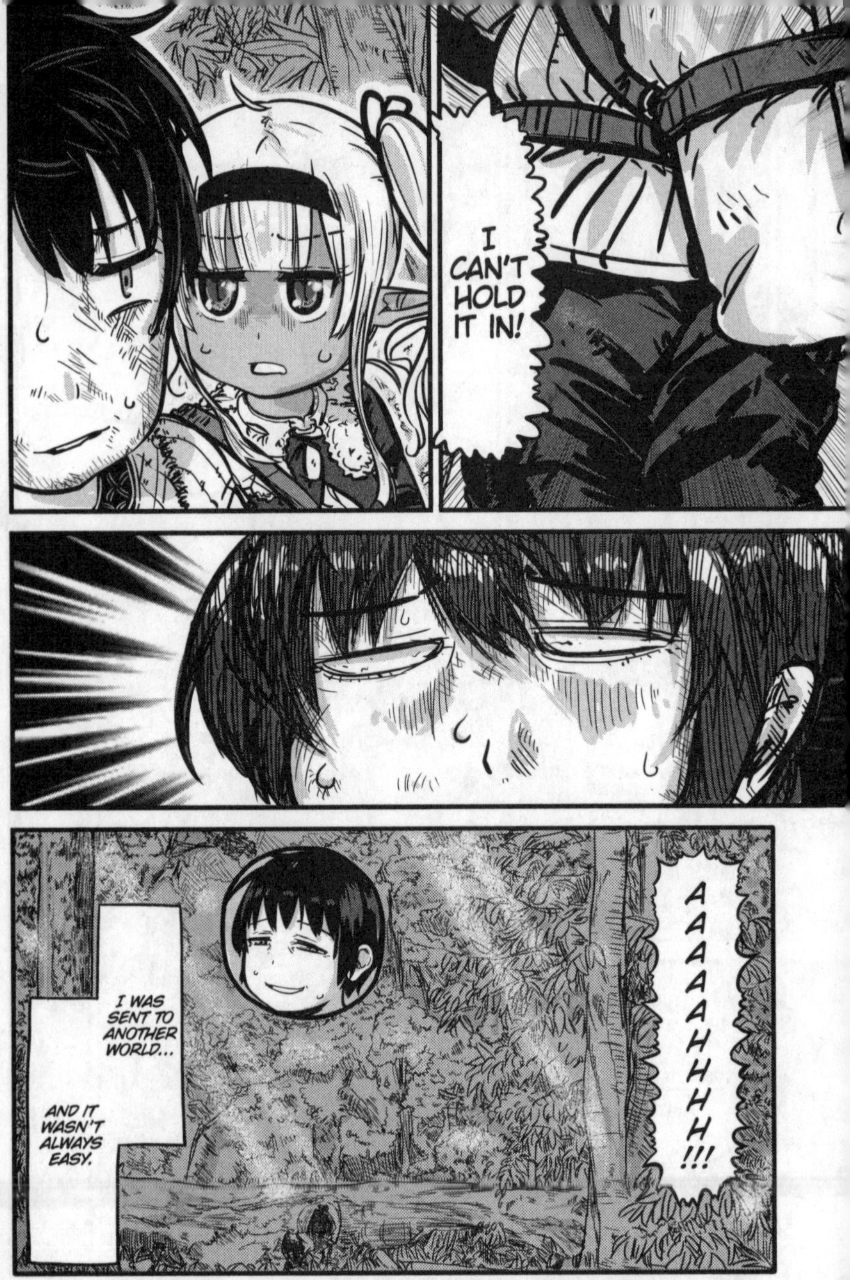
I CAN'T HOLD IT IN!
AAAAAAHHHHH!!!
I WAS SENT TO ANOTHER WORLD...
AND IT WASN'T ALWAYS EASY.

ROOTS

PEOPLE WHO DON'T VALUE TOILET TIME ARE NO GOOD.

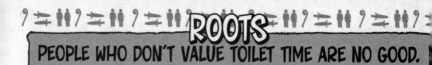

FIRST TOILET TIME

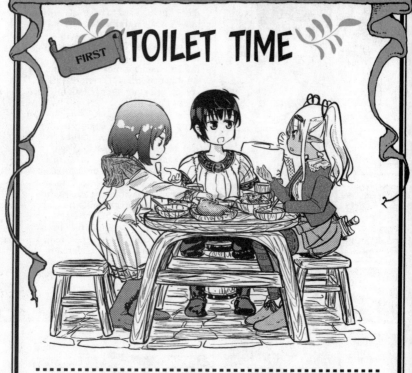

Starting with this chapter, I'll be writing mini-articles called, "People who don't value toilet time are no good," or in short, "Toilet Time." I'll include trivia and fun facts about toilets so you all can live your best toilet-loving lives.

This article's theme is "Island Life," or perhaps, "Island Toilet Life."

It isn't easy to take relaxing number twos on an island. In some places in the world, people without the accommodations we're used to would release their bowels while walking through the forest. If they'd squatted, leeches would have climbed up their legs. On an island, before you can have a satisfying bowel movement, you must be able to protect yourself.

Since I'm not used to releasing my bowels while walking, I can only imagine how difficult it must be. However, on an island with meager food, where a nutritional diet is difficult, perhaps most movements would be diarrhea. Therefore, this style of releasing one's bowels might not be an issue.

For people who have slightly harder movements, I recommend the perfect remedy: aloe. Since long ago, aloe has been a precious medicinal item. It was one of the most prized imports of Ancient Greece. Primarily used for diarrhea, it's also useful for stomachaches and sunburns.

The legendary Alexander the Great, during his conquest of Persia, took over the island of Socotra, famous for its aloe beds. Perhaps he was such a powerful leader because he cared so much about bowel movements.

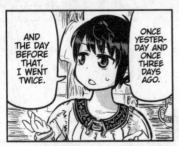

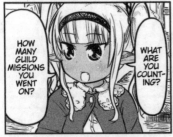

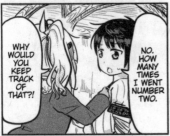

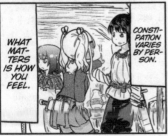

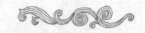

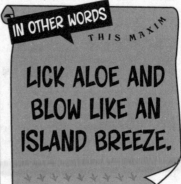

IN OTHER WORDS

THIS MAXIM

LICK ALOE AND BLOW LIKE AN ISLAND BREEZE.

ONCE YESTERDAY AND ONCE THREE DAYS AGO.
AND THE DAY BEFORE THAT, I WENT TWICE.
WHAT ARE YOU COUNTING?
HOW MANY GUILD MISSIONS YOU WENT ON?
NO. HOW MANY TIMES I WENT NUMBER TWO.
WHY WOULD YOU KEEP TRACK OF THAT?!
CONSTIPATION VARIES BY PERSON.
WHAT MATTERS IS HOW YOU FEEL.

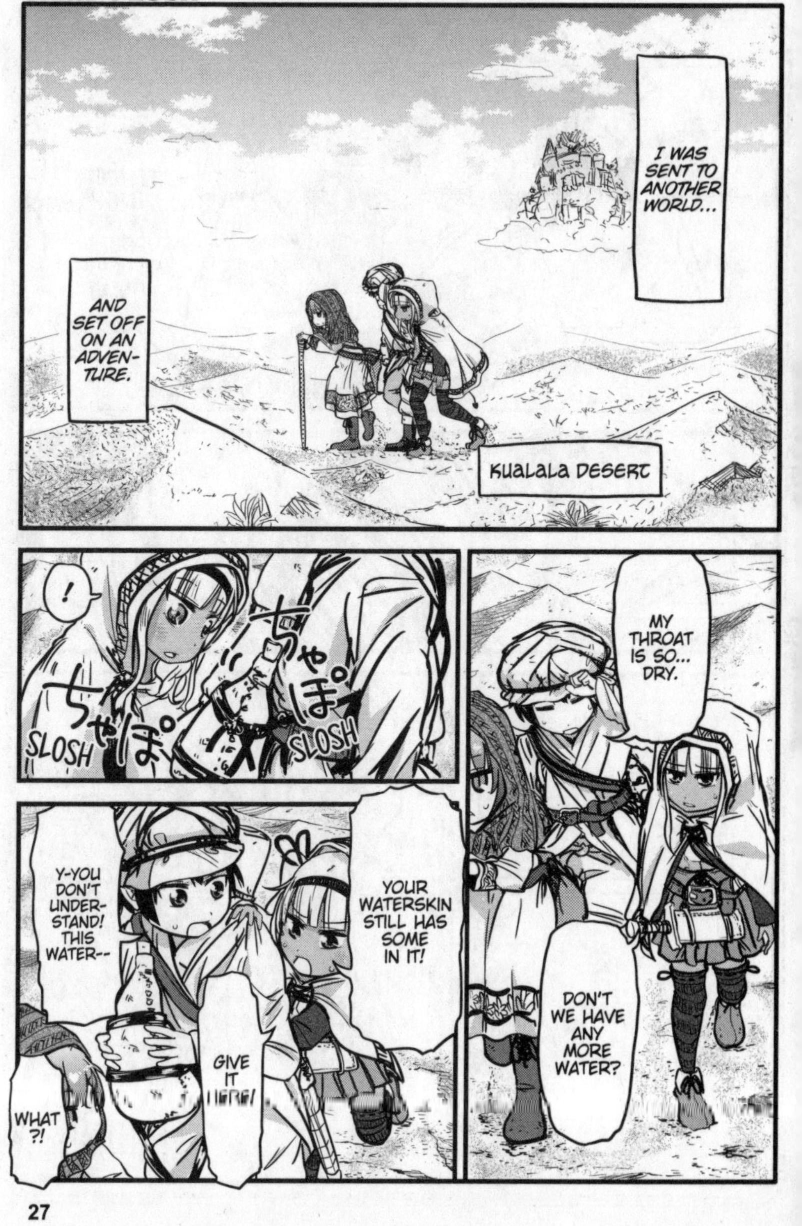
I WAS SENT TO ANOTHER WORLD...
AND SET OFF ON AN ADVENTURE.
KUALALA DESERT
MY THROAT IS SO... DRY.
DON'T WE HAVE ANY MORE WATER?
!
ちゃぽ
SLOSH
ちゃぽ
SLOSH
YOUR WATERSKIN STILL HAS SOME IN IT!
GIVE IT HERE!
Y-YOU DON'T UNDERSTAND! THIS WATER--
WHAT?!

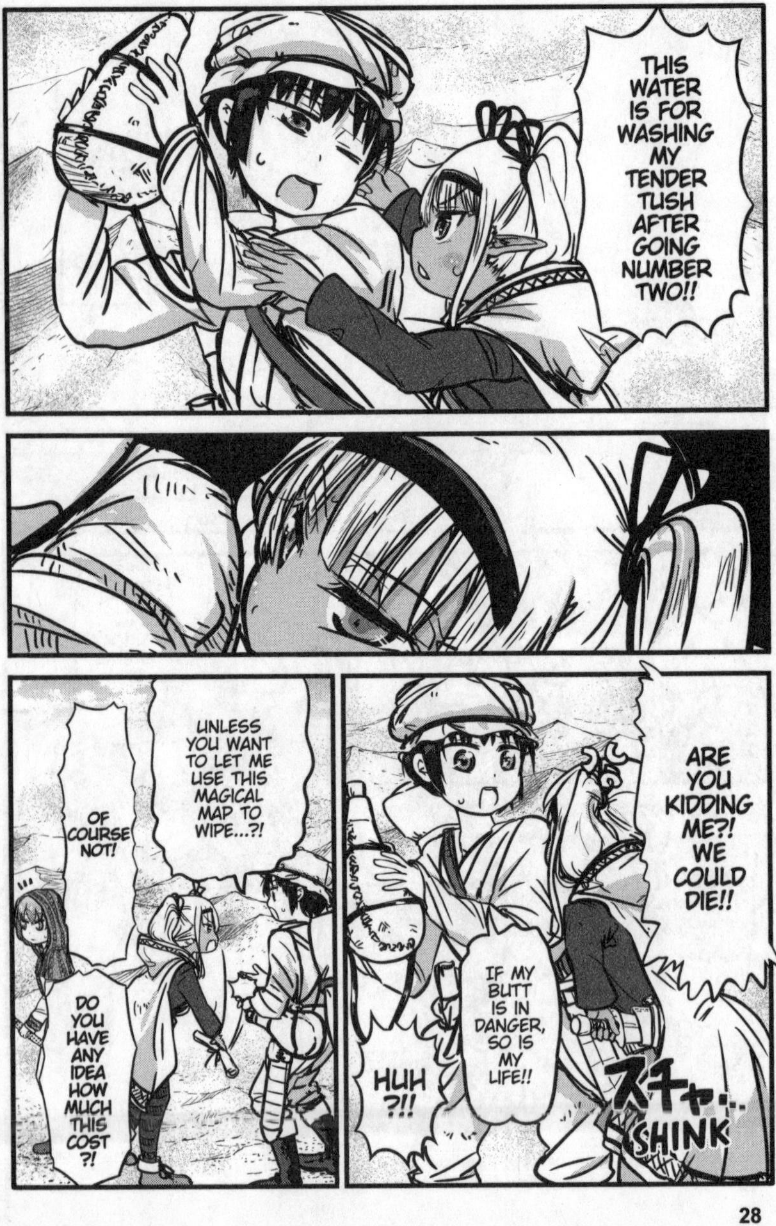
THIS WATER IS FOR WASHING MY TENDER TUSH AFTER GOING NUMBER TWO!!
ARE YOU KIDDING ME?! WE COULD DIE!!
IF MY BUTT IS IN DANGER, SO IS MY LIFE!!
スチャ…
SHINK
HUH ?!!
UNLESS YOU WANT TO LET ME USE THIS MAGICAL MAP TO WIPE...?!
OF COURSE NOT!
DO YOU HAVE ANY IDEA HOW MUCH THIS COST ?!

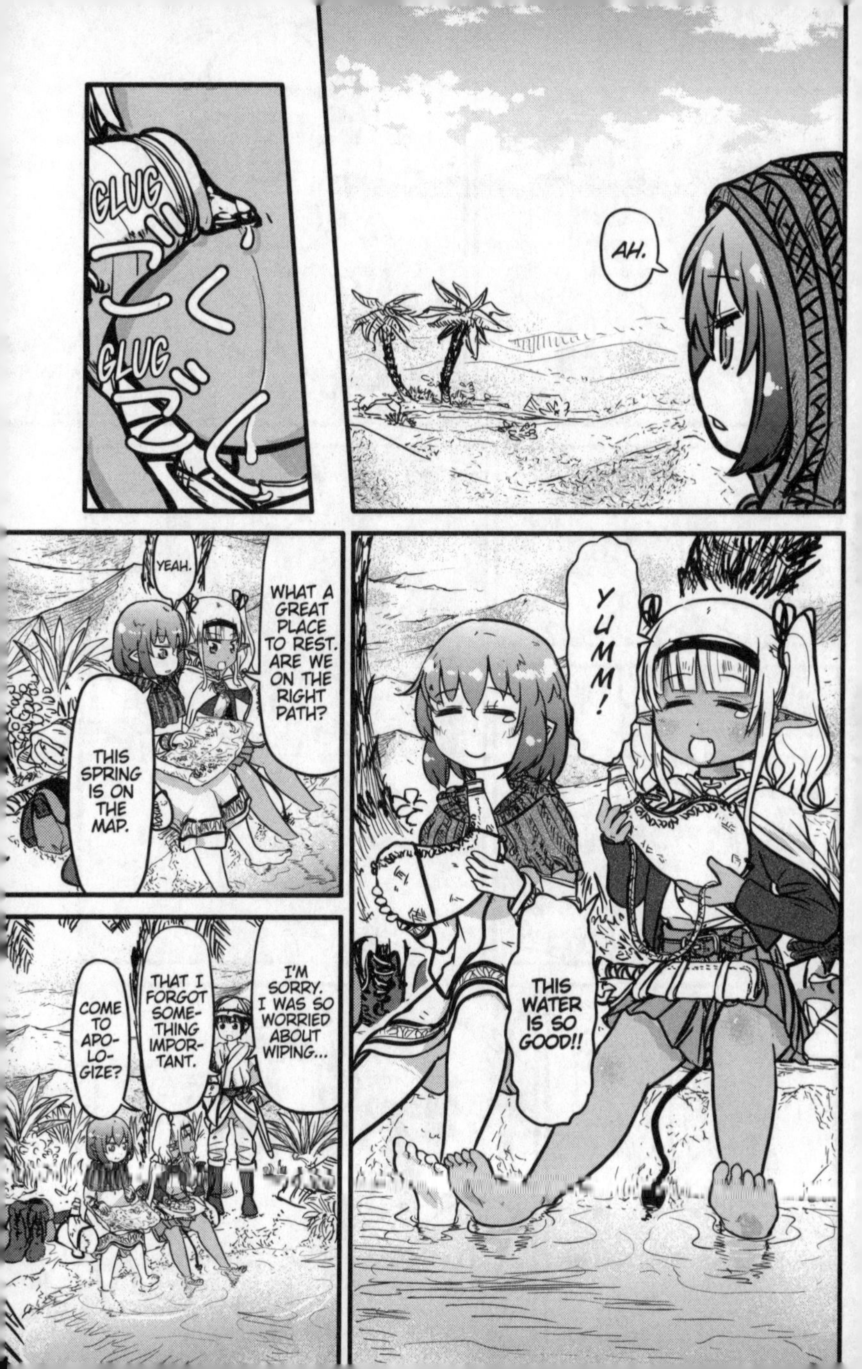
AH.
GLUG
GLUG
YUMMM!
THIS WATER IS SO GOOD!!
WHAT A GREAT PLACE TO REST. ARE WE ON THE RIGHT PATH?
YEAH.
THIS SPRING IS ON THE MAP.
I'M SORRY. I WAS SO WORRIED ABOUT WIPING...
THAT I FORGOT SOMETHING IMPORTANT.
COME TO APOLOGIZE?

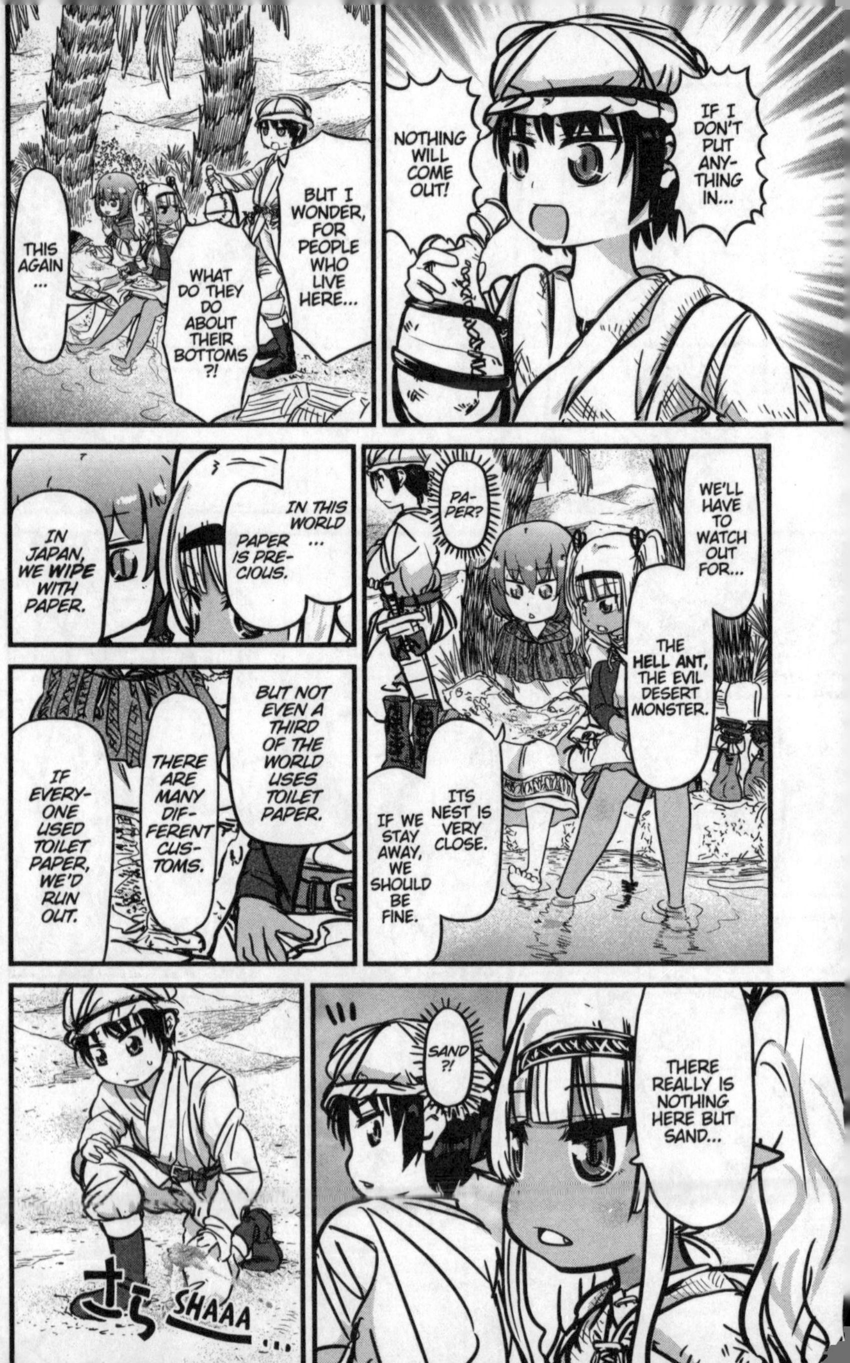

IF I DON'T PUT ANY-THING IN...
NOTHING WILL COME OUT!
BUT I WONDER, FOR PEOPLE WHO LIVE HERE...
WHAT DO THEY DO ABOUT THEIR BOTTOMS?!
THIS AGAIN...
WE'LL HAVE TO WATCH OUT FOR...
PA-PER?
THE HELL ANT, THE EVIL DESERT MONSTER.
ITS NEST IS VERY CLOSE.
IF WE STAY AWAY, WE SHOULD BE FINE.
IN THIS WORLD... PAPER IS PRE-CIOUS.
IN JAPAN, WE WIPE WITH PAPER.
BUT NOT EVEN A THIRD OF THE WORLD USES TOILET PAPER.
THERE ARE MANY DIF-FERENT CUS-TOMS.
IF EVERY-ONE USED TOILET PAPER, WE'D RUN OUT.
THERE REALLY IS NOTHING HERE BUT SAND...
SAND?!
さら
SHAAA

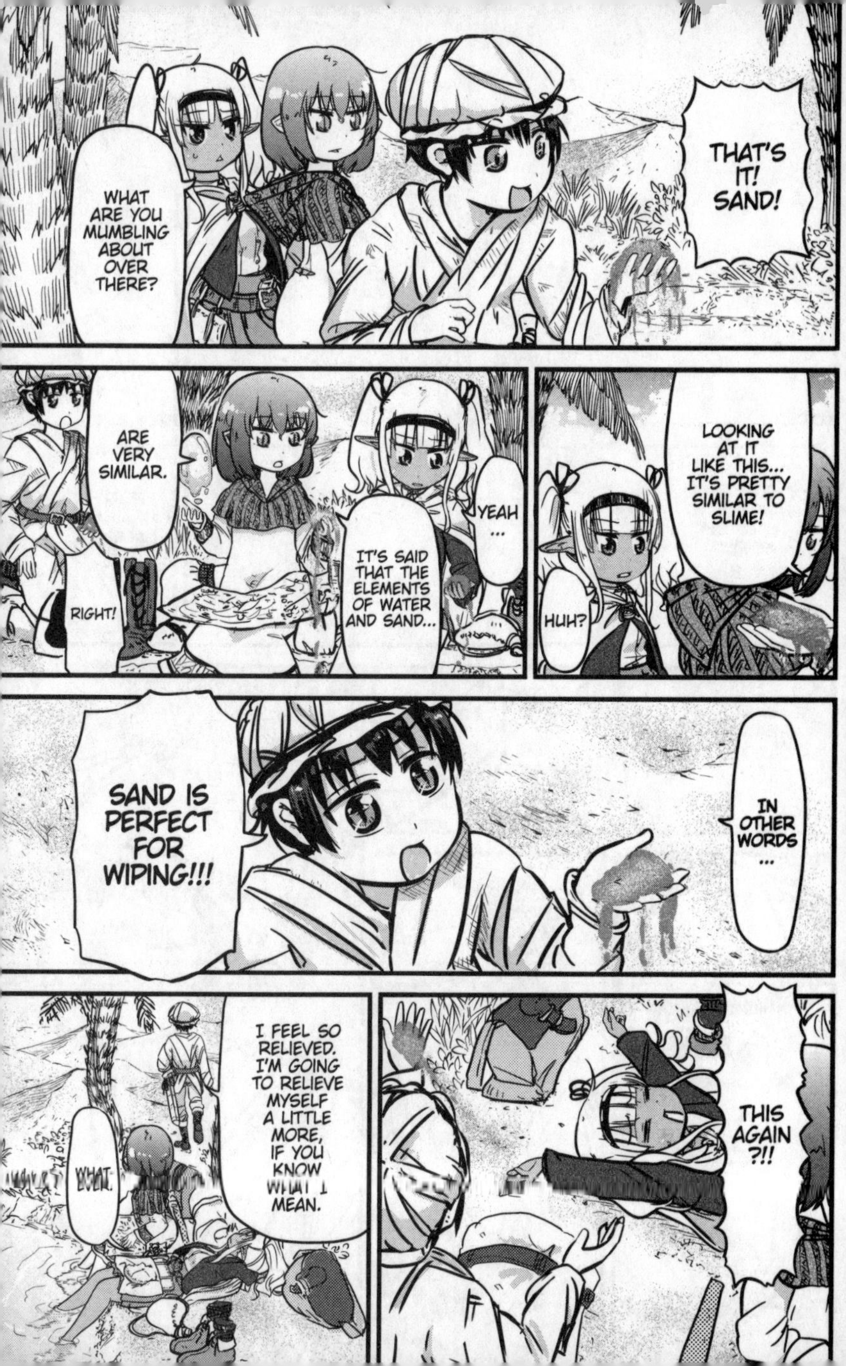
THAT'S IT! SAND!
WHAT ARE YOU MUMBLING ABOUT OVER THERE?
LOOKING AT IT LIKE THIS... IT'S PRETTY SIMILAR TO SLIME!
HUH?
YEAH...
IT'S SAID THAT THE ELEMENTS OF WATER AND SAND...
ARE VERY SIMILAR.
RIGHT!
IN OTHER WORDS...
SAND IS PERFECT FOR WIPING!!!
THIS AGAIN?!!
I FEEL SO RELIEVED. I'M GOING TO RELIEVE MYSELF A LITTLE MORE, IF YOU KNOW WHAT I MEAN.
WHAT

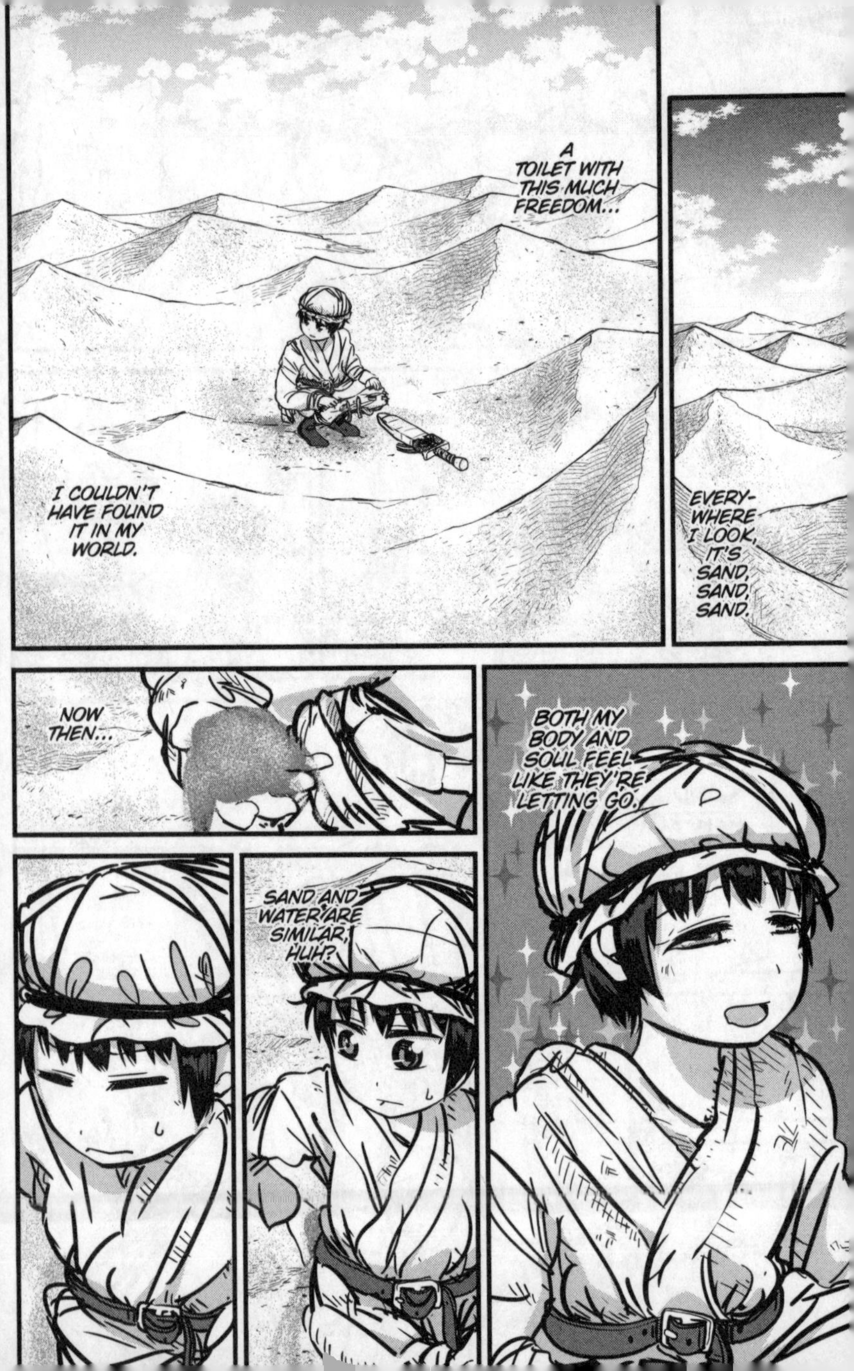
EVERY-WHERE I LOOK, IT'S SAND, SAND, SAND.
A TOILET WITH THIS MUCH FREEDOM...
I COULDN'T HAVE FOUND IT IN MY WORLD.
BOTH MY BODY AND SOUL FEEL LIKE THEY'RE LETTING GO.
NOW THEN...
SAND AND WATER ARE SIMILAR, HUH?

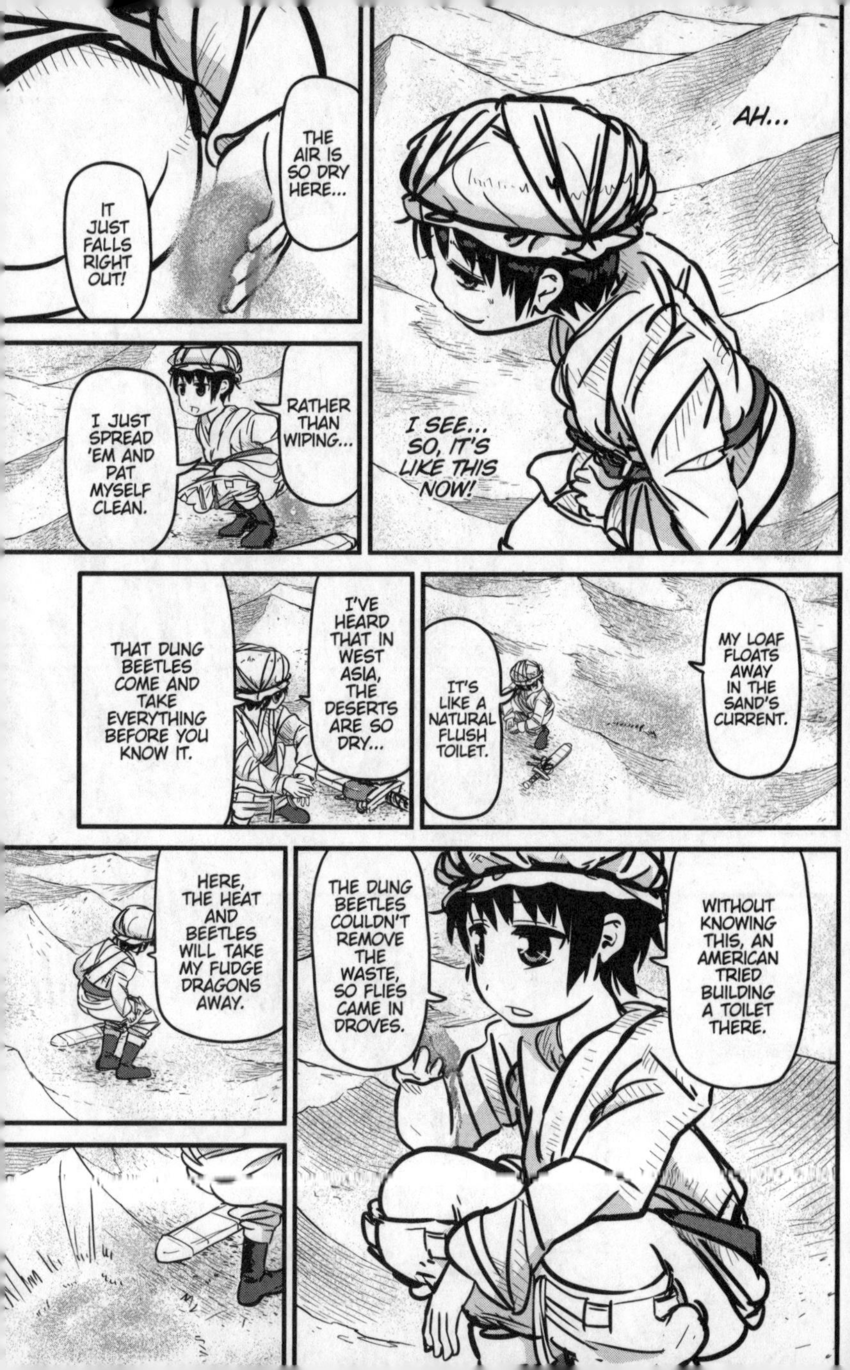
AH...
I SEE... SO, IT'S LIKE THIS NOW!
THE AIR IS SO DRY HERE...
IT JUST FALLS RIGHT OUT!
RATHER THAN WIPING...
I JUST SPREAD 'EM AND PAT MYSELF CLEAN.
MY LOAF FLOATS AWAY IN THE SAND'S CURRENT.
IT'S LIKE A NATURAL FLUSH TOILET.
I'VE HEARD THAT IN WEST ASIA, THE DESERTS ARE SO DRY...
THAT DUNG BEETLES COME AND TAKE EVERYTHING BEFORE YOU KNOW IT.
WITHOUT KNOWING THIS, AN AMERICAN TRIED BUILDING A TOILET THERE.
THE DUNG BEETLES COULDN'T REMOVE THE WASTE, SO FLIES CAME IN DROVES.
HERE, THE HEAT AND BEETLES WILL TAKE MY FUDGE DRAGONS AWAY.

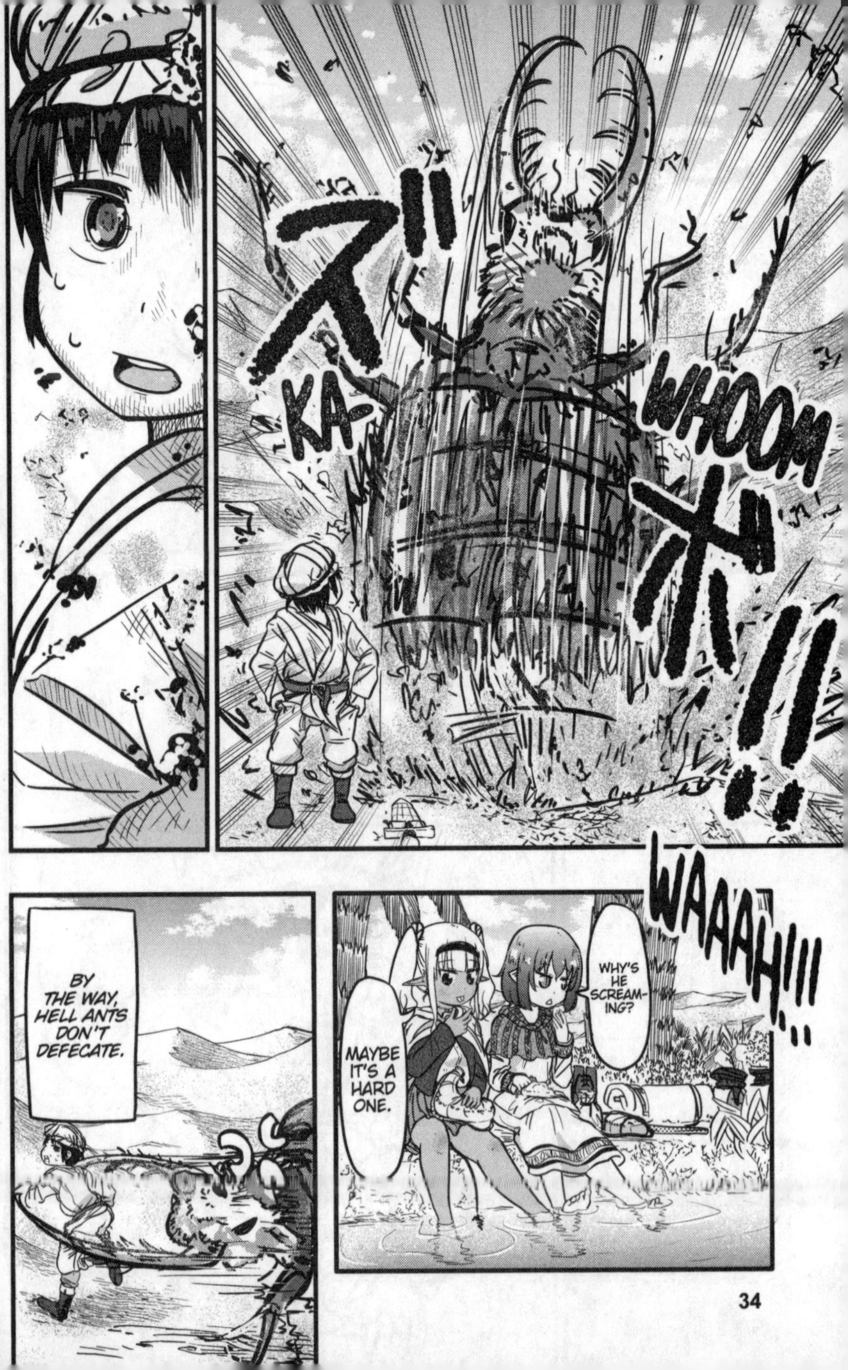
ズ
KA
WHOOM
ボ!!
WAAAH!!!
WHY'S HE SCREAMING?
MAYBE IT'S A HARD ONE.
BY THE WAY, HELL ANTS DON'T DEFECATE.

ROOTS

PEOPLE WHO DON'T VALUE TOILET TIME ARE NO GOOD.

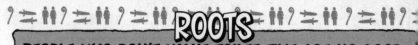

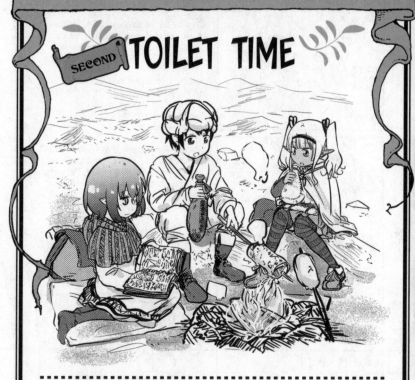

SECOND TOILET TIME

This chapter's "Toilet Time" is about wiping your bottom.

Like Yotaro said earlier, only about a third of the world's population wipes their bottoms with toilet paper. Paper is a valuable commodity, after all.

Japanese people began using paper to wipe themselves around the Edo period. Near Asakusa, there was a place that would break down old paper and remake it anew. This place was famously known as Asakusa Paper.

Asakusa paper was about the size of tissue, and one hundred pieces sold for about a hundred mon (a former currency in Japan). For reference, going to a public bath cost around ten mon, soba from a stand was fifteen mon, and 1.5 kilograms of rice was about a hundred mon.

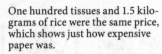

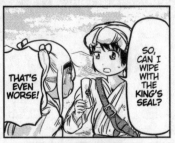

One hundred tissues and 1.5 kilograms of rice were the same price, which shows just how expensive paper was.

Keeping in mind that rice was also an expensive commodity at the time, the price for a pack of a hundred tissues now would be close to $25 or ¥2700, I believe.

Should we rethink how we use toilet paper? Let's be more conscientious and make each wipe count. Perhaps, in turn, our lives will improve as well.

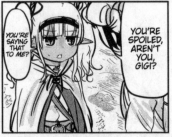

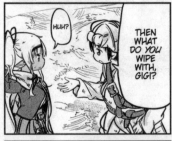

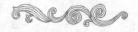

IN OTHER WORDS

THIS MAXIM

PAPER AND RICE, SAME PRICE. AFTER EATING THE RICE, USE THE PAPER TO WIPE.

SO, CAN I WIPE WITH THE KING'S SEAL?
THAT'S EVEN WORSE!
YOU'RE SPOILED, AREN'T YOU, GIGI?
YOU'RE SAYING THAT TO ME?
THEN WHAT DO YOU WIPE WITH, GIGI?
HUH?
NOT TELLING.

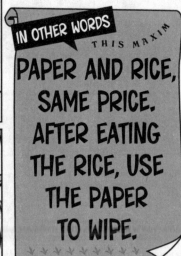

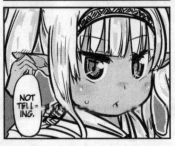

FOURTH FLUSH

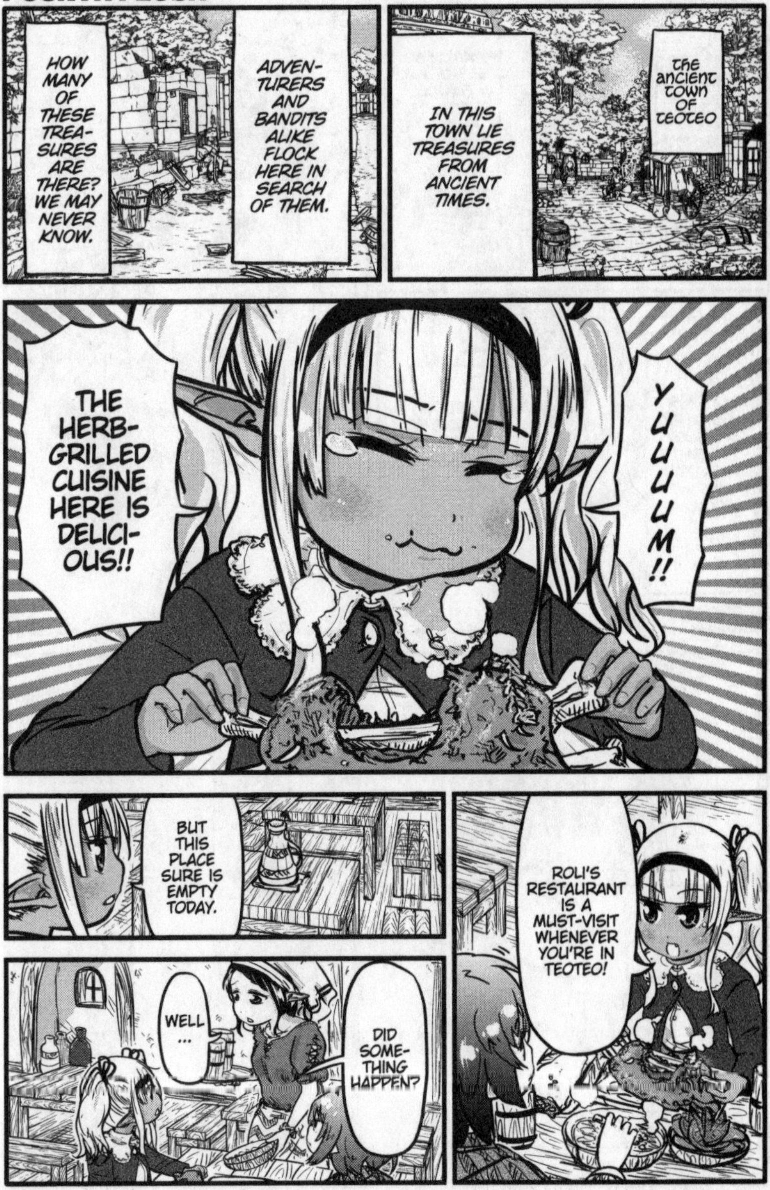

THE ANCIENT TOWN OF TEOTEO
IN THIS TOWN LIE TREASURES FROM ANCIENT TIMES.
ADVEN-TURERS AND BANDITS ALIKE FLOCK HERE IN SEARCH OF THEM.
HOW MANY OF THESE TREA-SURES ARE THERE? WE MAY NEVER KNOW.
YUUUUUM!!
THE HERB-GRILLED CUISINE HERE IS DELICI-OUS!!
ROLI'S RESTAURANT IS A MUST-VISIT WHENEVER YOU'RE IN TEOTEO!
BUT THIS PLACE SURE IS EMPTY TODAY.
DID SOME-THING HAPPEN?
WELL ...

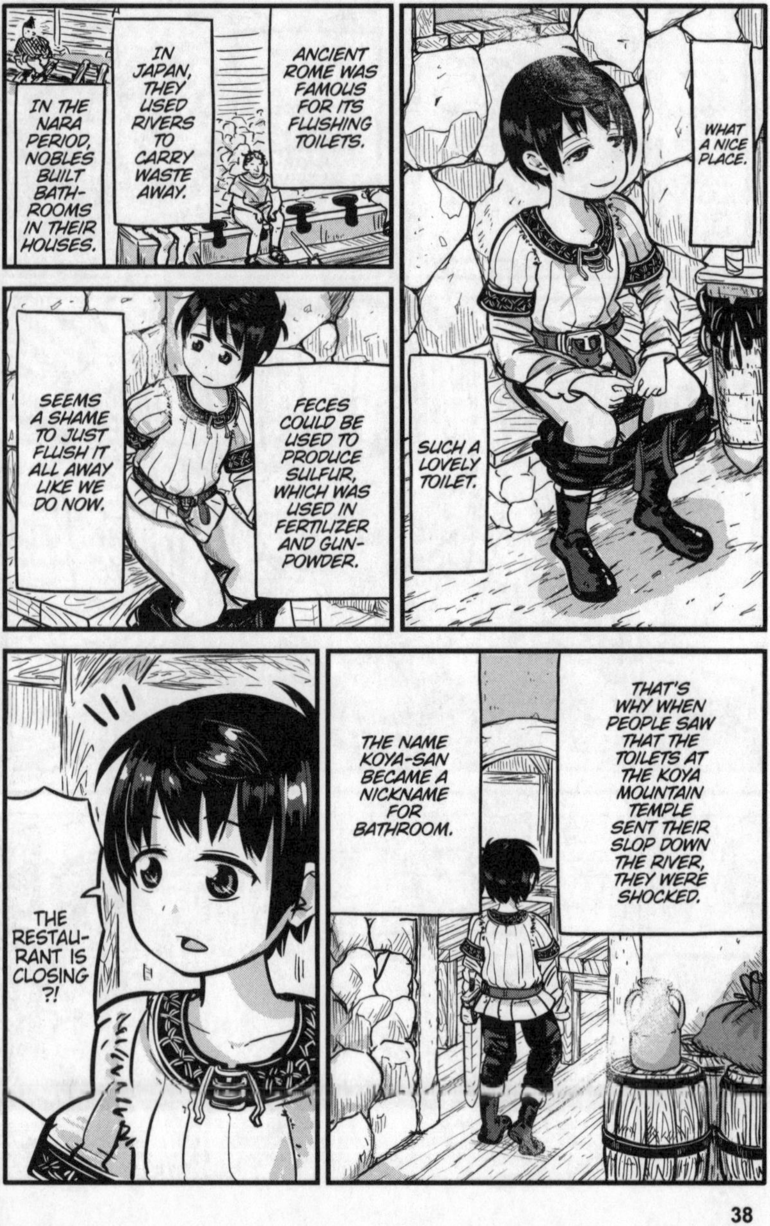

WHAT A NICE PLACE.
SUCH A LOVELY TOILET.
ANCIENT ROME WAS FAMOUS FOR ITS FLUSHING TOILETS.
IN JAPAN, THEY USED RIVERS TO CARRY WASTE AWAY.
IN THE NARA PERIOD, NOBLES BUILT BATH-ROOMS IN THEIR HOUSES.
FECES COULD BE USED TO PRODUCE SULFUR, WHICH WAS USED IN FERTILIZER AND GUN-POWDER.
SEEMS A SHAME TO JUST FLUSH IT ALL AWAY LIKE WE DO NOW.
THAT'S WHY WHEN PEOPLE SAW THAT THE TOILETS AT THE KOYA MOUNTAIN TEMPLE SENT THEIR SLOP DOWN THE RIVER, THEY WERE SHOCKED.
THE NAME KOYA-SAN BECAME A NICKNAME FOR BATHROOM.
THE RESTAU-RANT IS CLOSING ?!

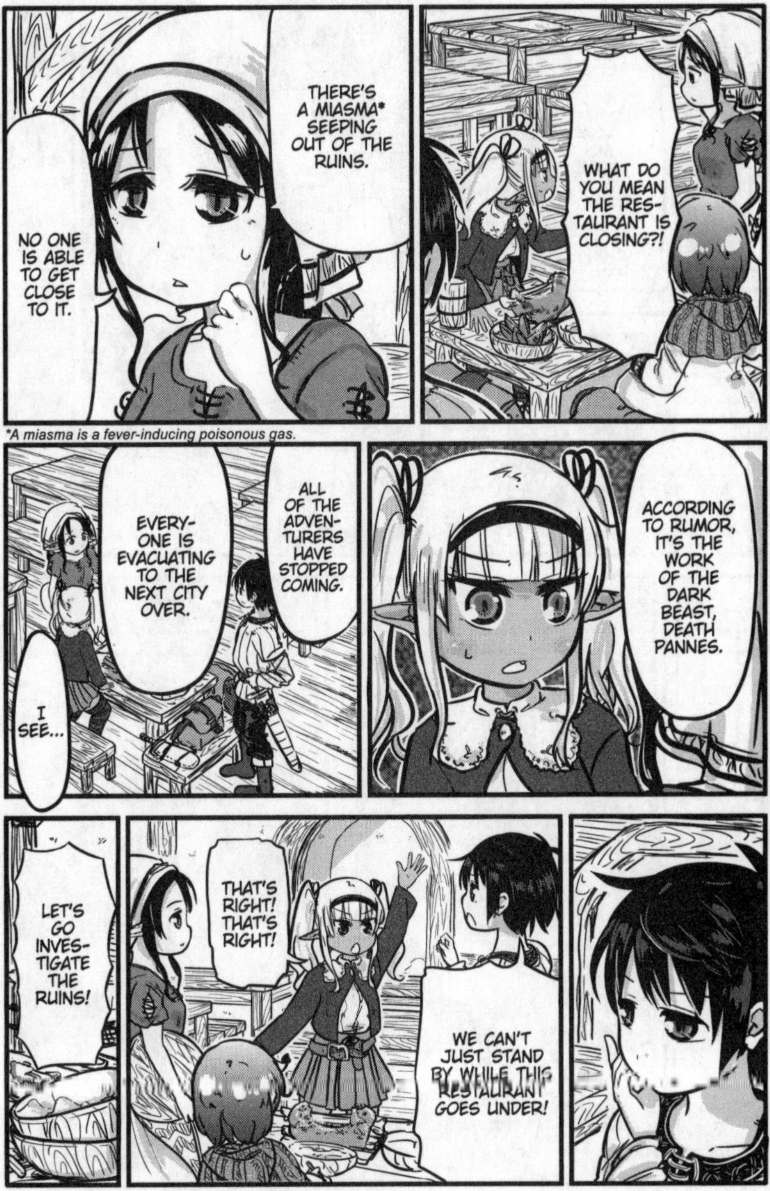
WHAT DO YOU MEAN THE RES-TAURANT IS CLOSING?!
THERE'S A MIASMA* SEEPING OUT OF THE RUINS.
NO ONE IS ABLE TO GET CLOSE TO IT.
ACCORDING TO RUMOR, IT'S THE WORK OF THE DARK BEAST, DEATH PANNES.
ALL OF THE ADVEN-TURERS HAVE STOPPED COMING.
EVERY-ONE IS EVACUATING TO THE NEXT CITY OVER.
I SEE...
WE CAN'T JUST STAND BY WHILE THIS RESTAURANT GOES UNDER!
THAT'S RIGHT! THAT'S RIGHT!
LET'S GO INVES-TIGATE THE RUINS!

*A miasma is a fever-inducing poisonous gas.

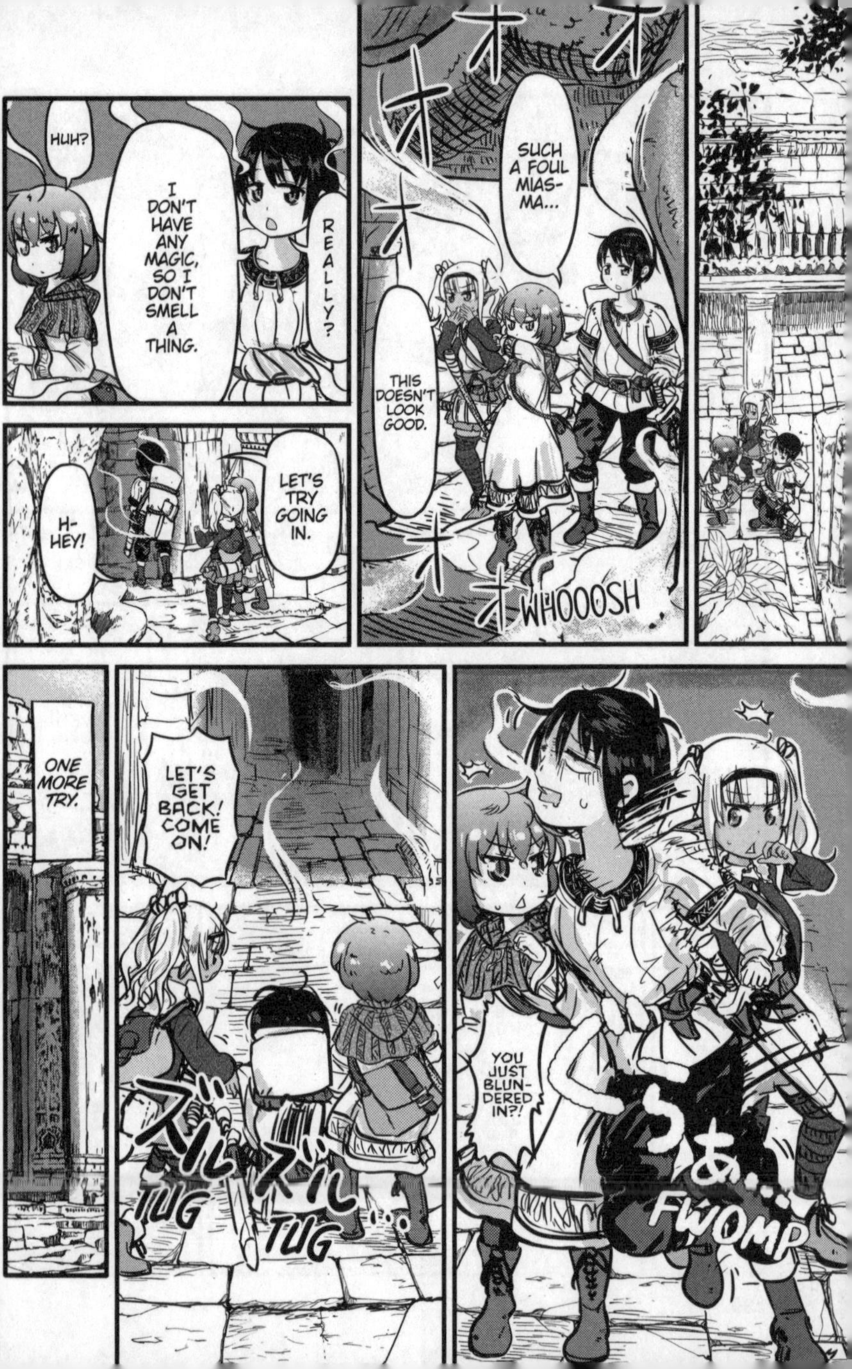

オオオオオオ
SUCH A FOUL MIASMA...
THIS DOESN'T LOOK GOOD.
WHOOOSH
REALLY?
I DON'T HAVE ANY MAGIC, SO I DON'T SMELL A THING.
HUH?
LET'S TRY GOING IN.
H-HEY!
ふぁ…
FWOMP
YOU JUST BLUNDERED IN?!
LET'S GET BACK! COME ON!
ズルズル…
TUG
TUG
ONE MORE TRY.

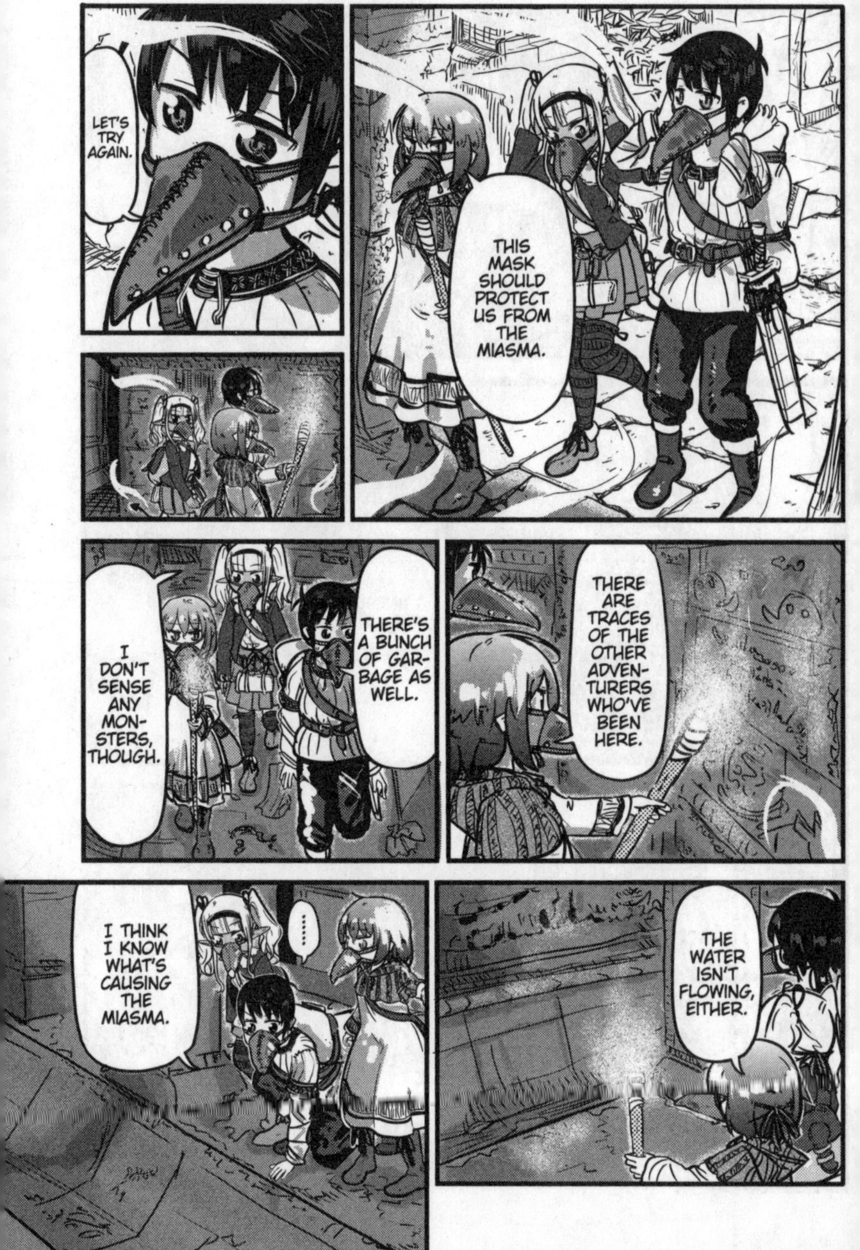
THIS MASK SHOULD PROTECT US FROM THE MIASMA.
LET'S TRY AGAIN.
THERE ARE TRACES OF THE OTHER ADVENTURERS WHO'VE BEEN HERE.
THERE'S A BUNCH OF GARBAGE AS WELL.
I DON'T SENSE ANY MONSTERS, THOUGH.
THE WATER ISN'T FLOWING, EITHER.
......
I THINK I KNOW WHAT'S CAUSING THE MIASMA.

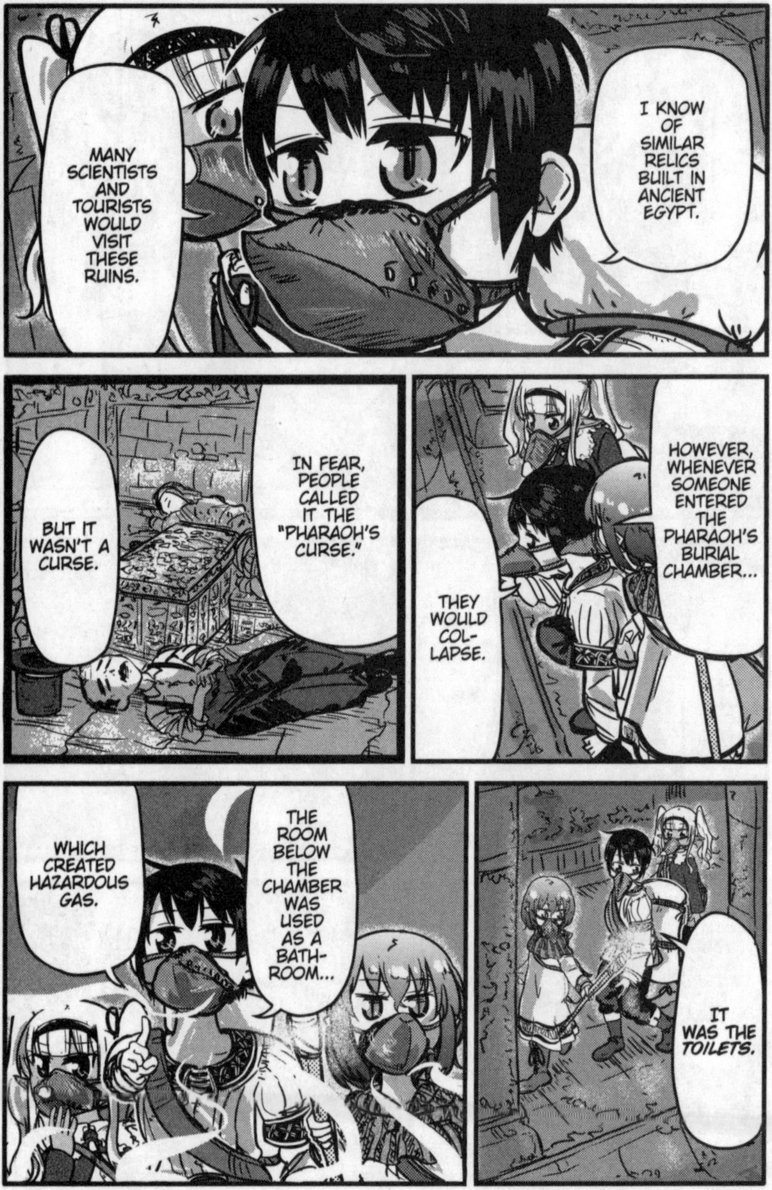
I KNOW OF SIMILAR RELICS BUILT IN ANCIENT EGYPT.
MANY SCIENTISTS AND TOURISTS WOULD VISIT THESE RUINS.
HOWEVER, WHENEVER SOMEONE ENTERED THE PHARAOH'S BURIAL CHAMBER...
THEY WOULD COL-LAPSE.
IN FEAR, PEOPLE CALLED IT THE "PHARAOH'S CURSE."
BUT IT WASN'T A CURSE.
IT WAS THE *TOILETS.*
THE ROOM BELOW THE CHAMBER WAS USED AS A BATH-ROOM...
WHICH CREATED HAZARDOUS GAS.

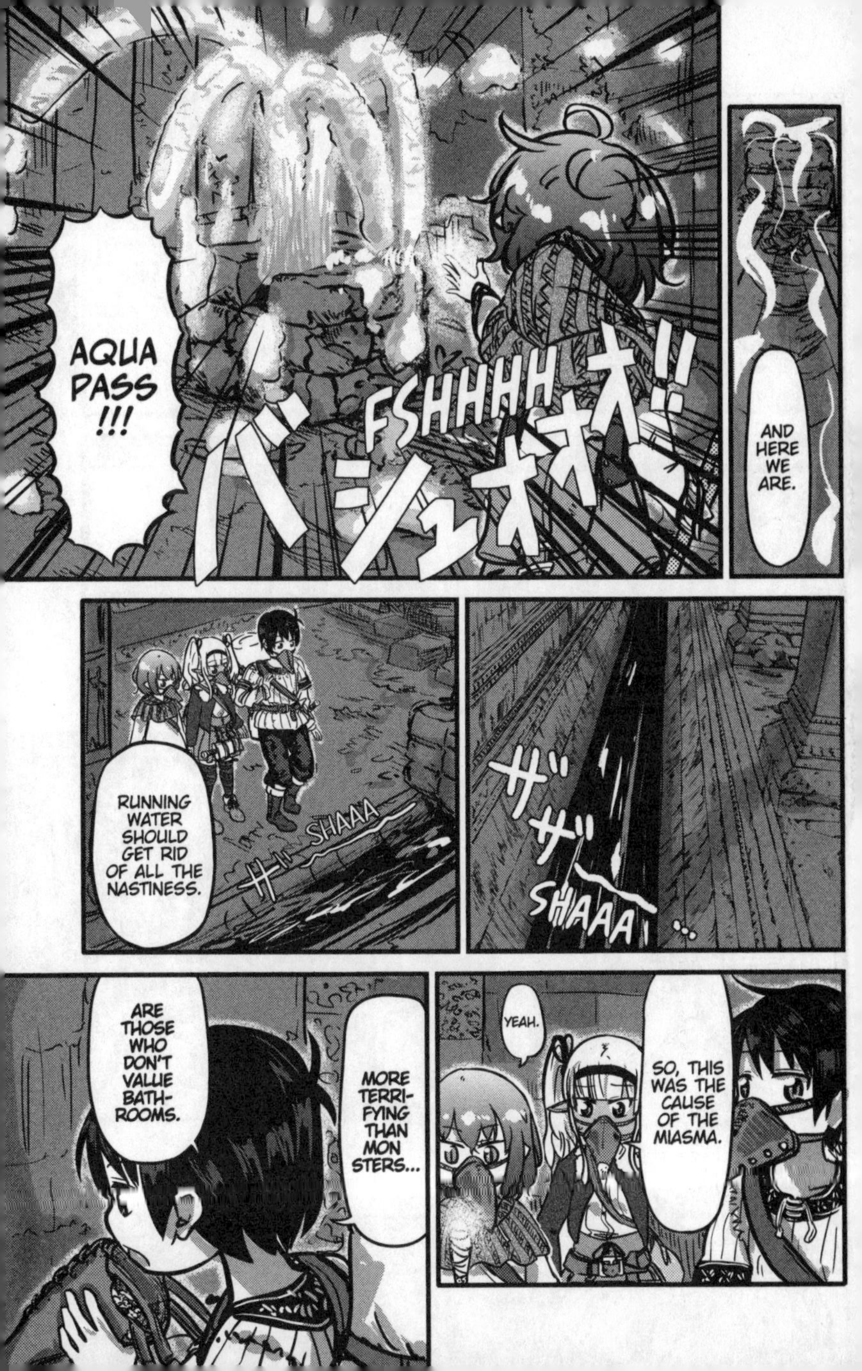
AND HERE WE ARE.
AQUA PASS!!!
FSHHHH
バシュオオオ!!
ザザ
SHAAA
RUNNING WATER SHOULD GET RID OF ALL THE NASTINESS.
SHAAA
SO, THIS WAS THE CAUSE OF THE MIASMA.
YEAH.
MORE TERRI-FYING THAN MON-STERS...
ARE THOSE WHO DON'T VALUE BATH-ROOMS.

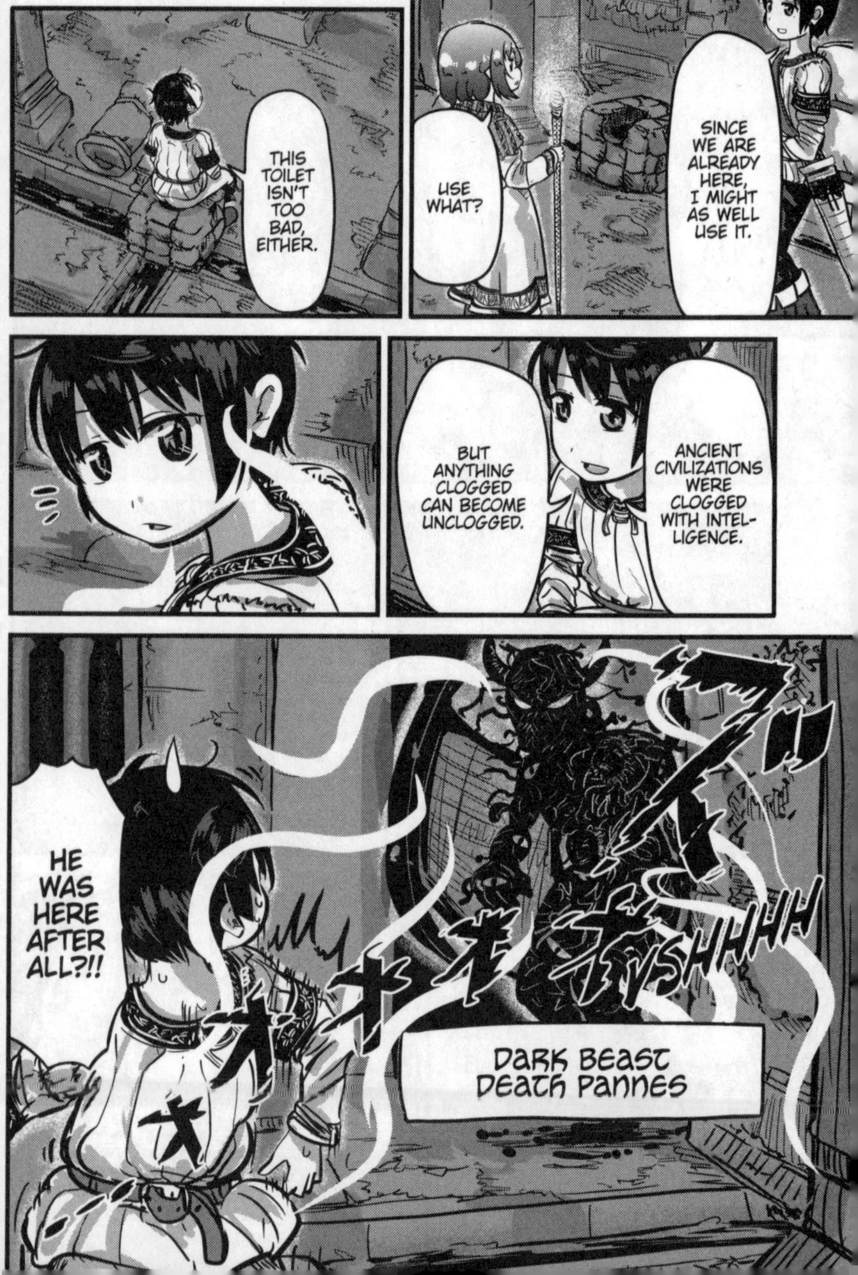
SINCE WE ARE ALREADY HERE, I MIGHT AS WELL USE IT.
USE WHAT?
THIS TOILET ISN'T TOO BAD, EITHER.
ANCIENT CIVILIZATIONS WERE CLOGGED WITH INTEL-LIGENCE.
BUT ANYTHING CLOGGED CAN BECOME UNCLOGGED.
VSHHHH
DARK BEAST DEATH PANNES
HE WAS HERE AFTER ALL?!!

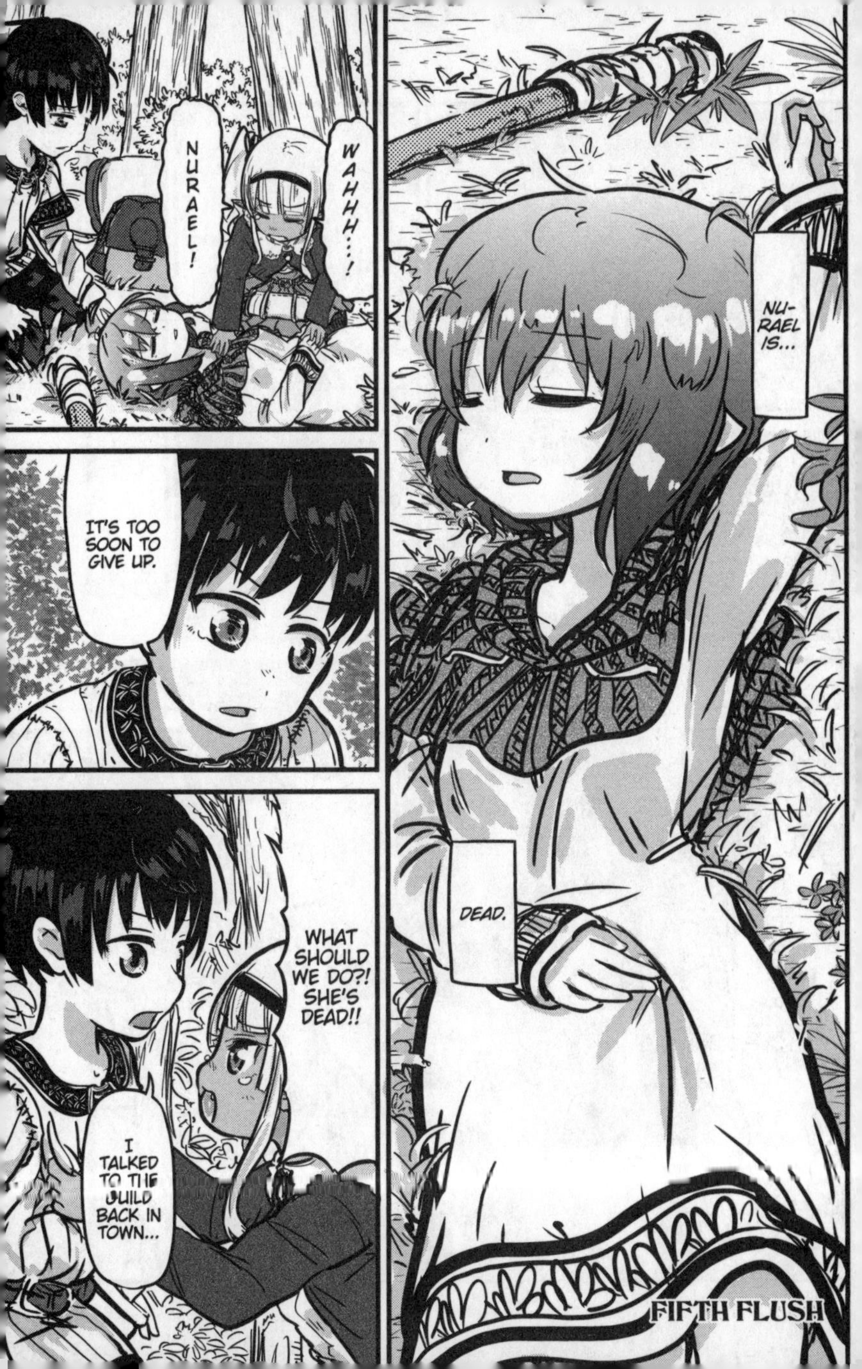
NU-RAEL IS...
DEAD.
FIFTH FLUSH
WAHHH...!
NURAEL!
IT'S TOO SOON TO GIVE UP.
WHAT SHOULD WE DO?! SHE'S DEAD!!
I TALKED TO THE GUILD BACK IN TOWN...

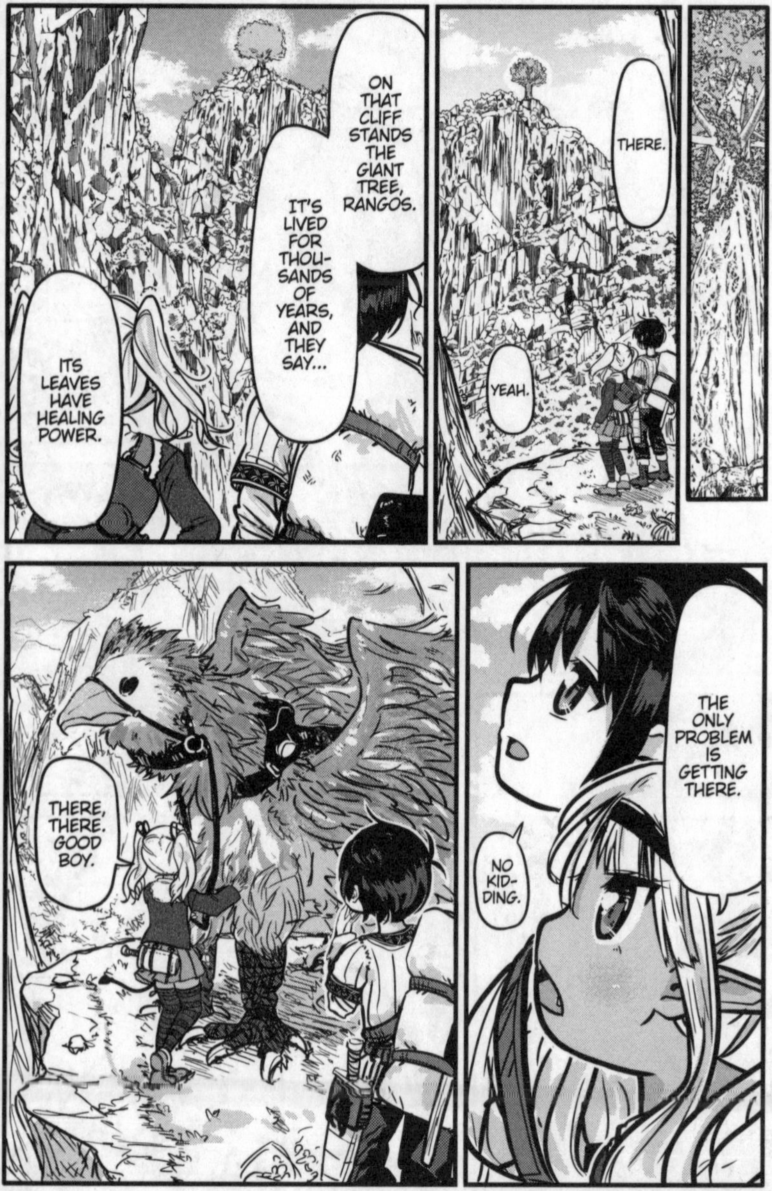
THERE.
YEAH.
ON THAT CLIFF STANDS THE GIANT TREE, RANGOS.
IT'S LIVED FOR THOU-SANDS OF YEARS, AND THEY SAY...
ITS LEAVES HAVE HEALING POWER.
THE ONLY PROBLEM IS GETTING THERE.
NO KID-DING.
THERE, THERE. GOOD BOY.

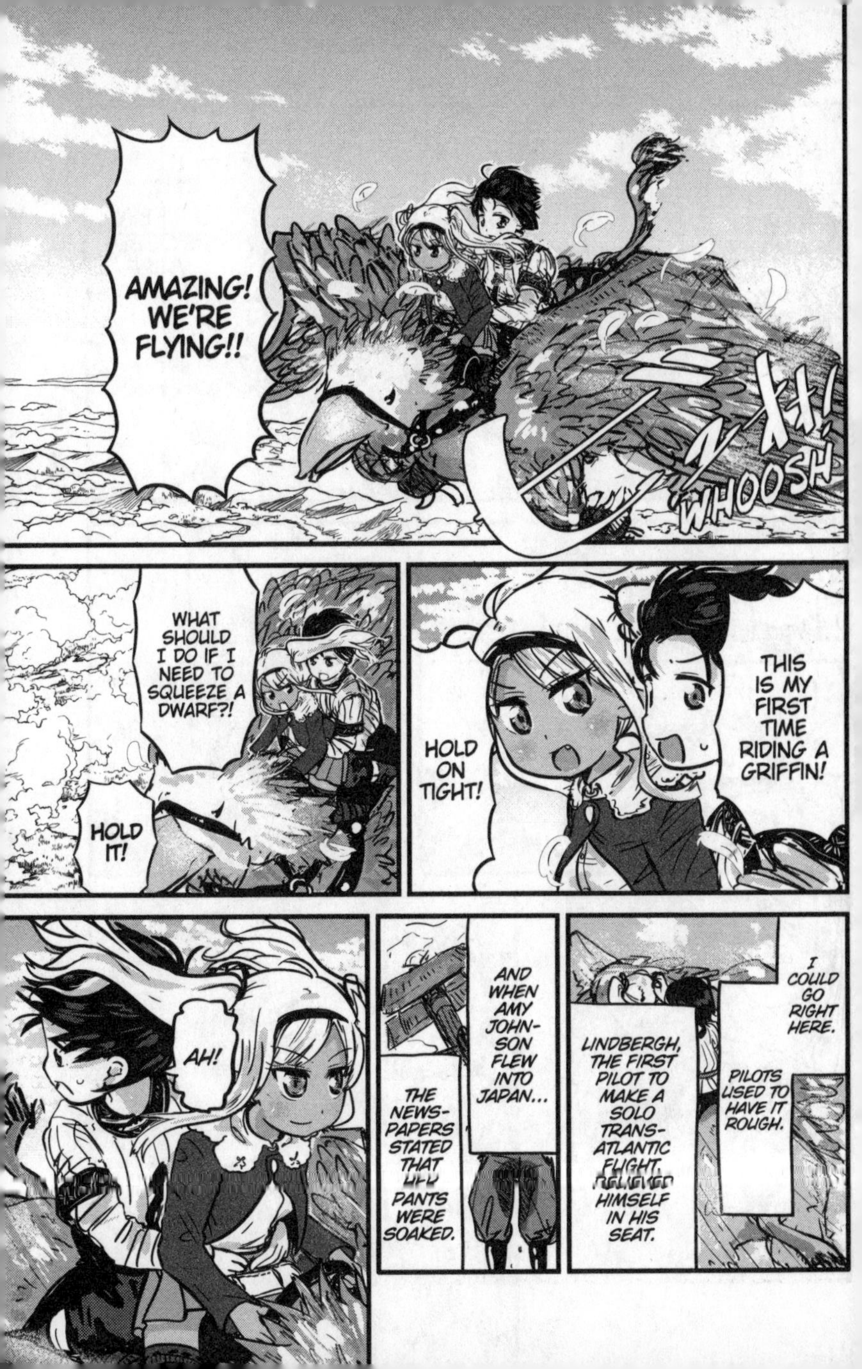
AMAZING! WE'RE FLYING!!
WHOOSH
THIS IS MY FIRST TIME RIDING A GRIFFIN!
HOLD ON TIGHT!
WHAT SHOULD I DO IF I NEED TO SQUEEZE A DWARF?!
HOLD IT!
I COULD GO RIGHT HERE.
PILOTS USED TO HAVE IT ROUGH.
LINDBERGH, THE FIRST PILOT TO MAKE A SOLO TRANS-ATLANTIC FLIGHT, RELIEVED HIMSELF IN HIS SEAT.
AND WHEN AMY JOHN-SON FLEW INTO JAPAN...
THE NEWS-PAPERS STATED THAT HER PANTS WERE SOAKED.
AH!

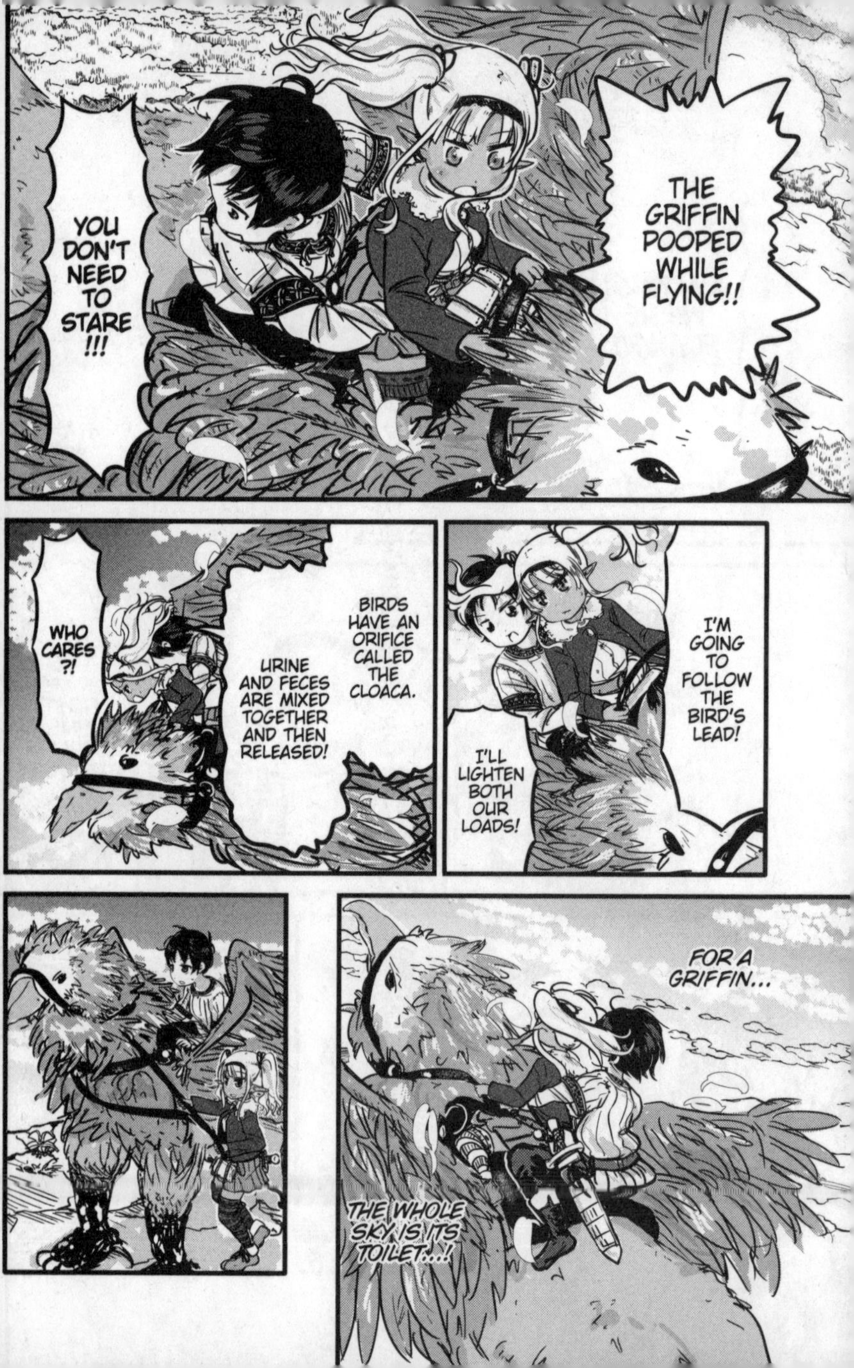
THE GRIFFIN POOPED WHILE FLYING!!
YOU DON'T NEED TO STARE !!!
I'M GOING TO FOLLOW THE BIRD'S LEAD!
I'LL LIGHTEN BOTH OUR LOADS!
BIRDS HAVE AN ORIFICE CALLED THE CLOACA.
URINE AND FECES ARE MIXED TOGETHER AND THEN RELEASED!
WHO CARES ?!
FOR A GRIFFIN...
THE WHOLE SKY IS ITS TOILET...!

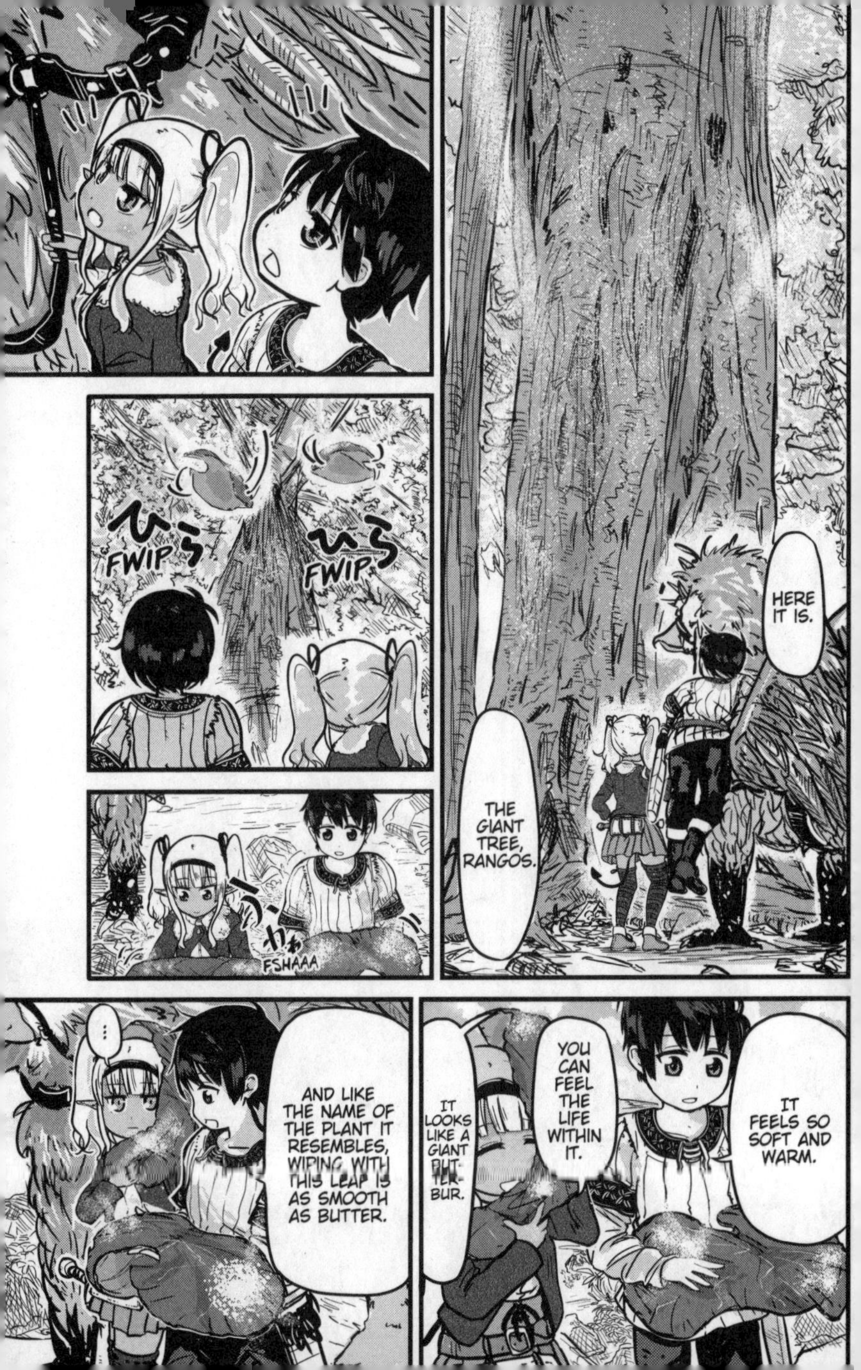
HERE IT IS.
THE GIANT TREE, RANGOS.
ひら
FWIP
ひら
FWIP
FSHAAA
IT FEELS SO SOFT AND WARM.
YOU CAN FEEL THE LIFE WITHIN IT.
IT LOOKS LIKE A GIANT BUTTERBUR.
AND LIKE THE NAME OF THE PLANT IT RESEMBLES, WIPING WITH THIS LEAF IS AS SMOOTH AS BUTTER.
...

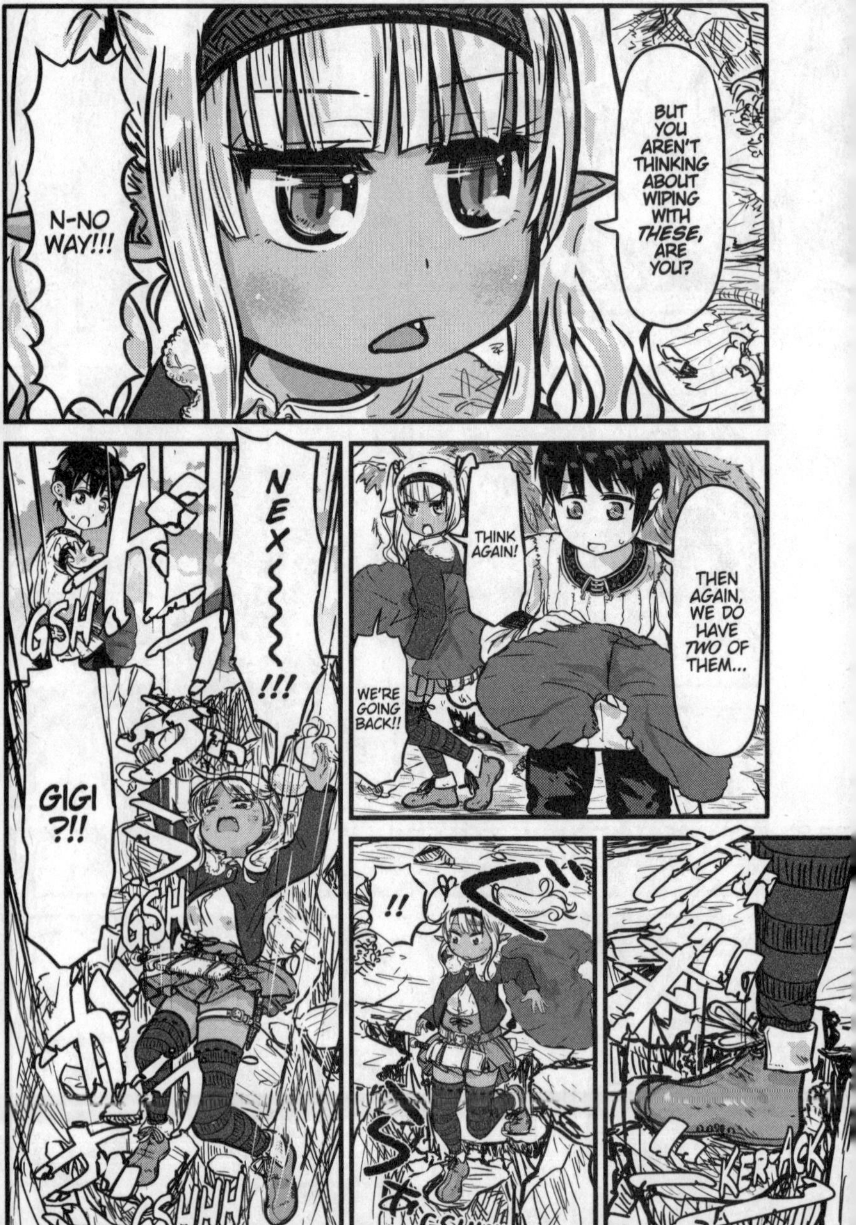
BUT YOU AREN'T THINKING ABOUT WIPING WITH THESE, ARE YOU?
N-NO WAY!!!
THEN AGAIN, WE DO HAVE TWO OF THEM...
THINK AGAIN!
WE'RE GOING BACK!!
KERACK
!!
GSHHH
NEX~~~!!!
GSH
GIGI?!!
GSH
GSHHH

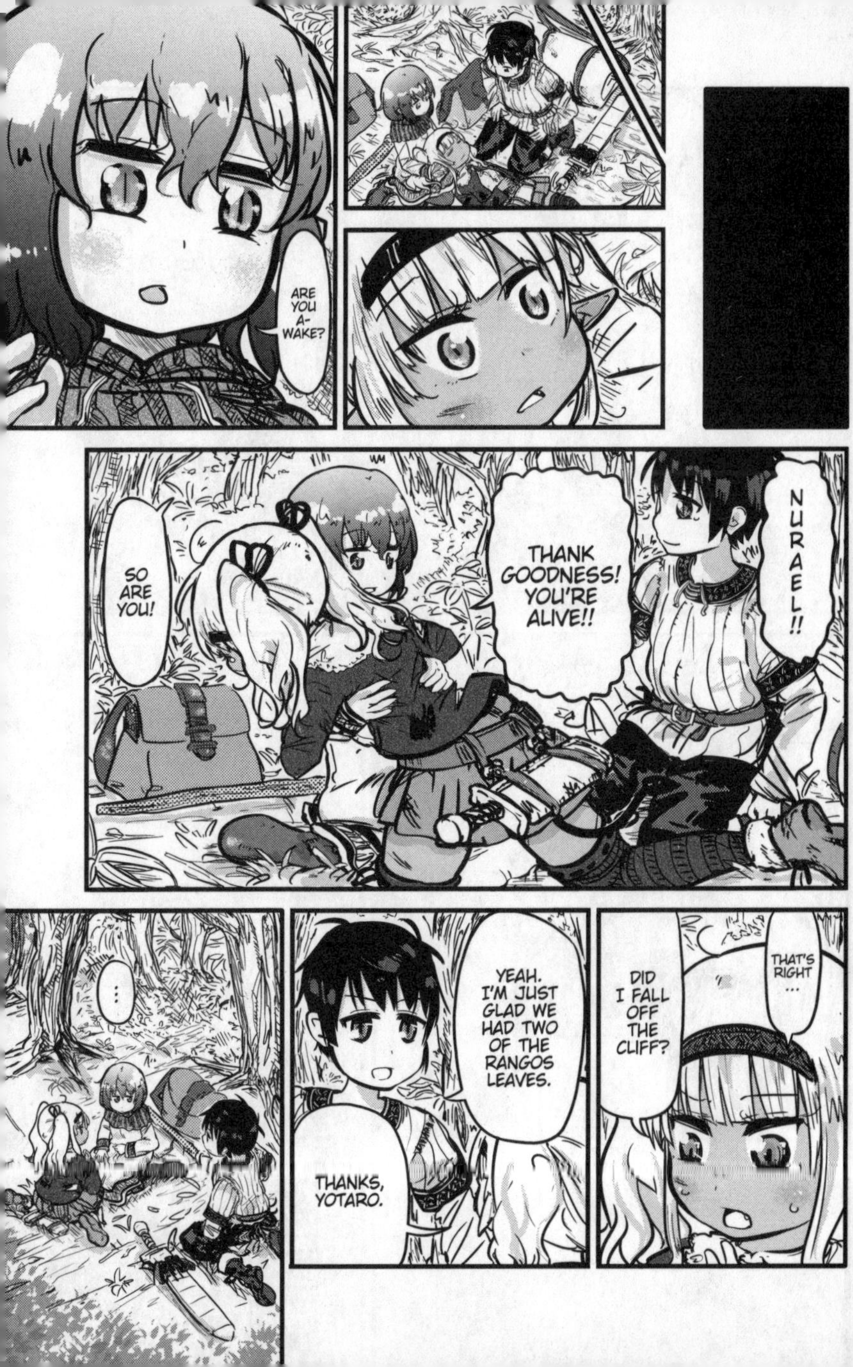
ARE YOU A-WAKE?
NURAEL!!
THANK GOODNESS! YOU'RE ALIVE!!
SO ARE YOU!
THAT'S RIGHT...
DID I FALL OFF THE CLIFF?
YEAH. I'M JUST GLAD WE HAD TWO OF THE RANGOS LEAVES.
THANKS, YOTARO.
...

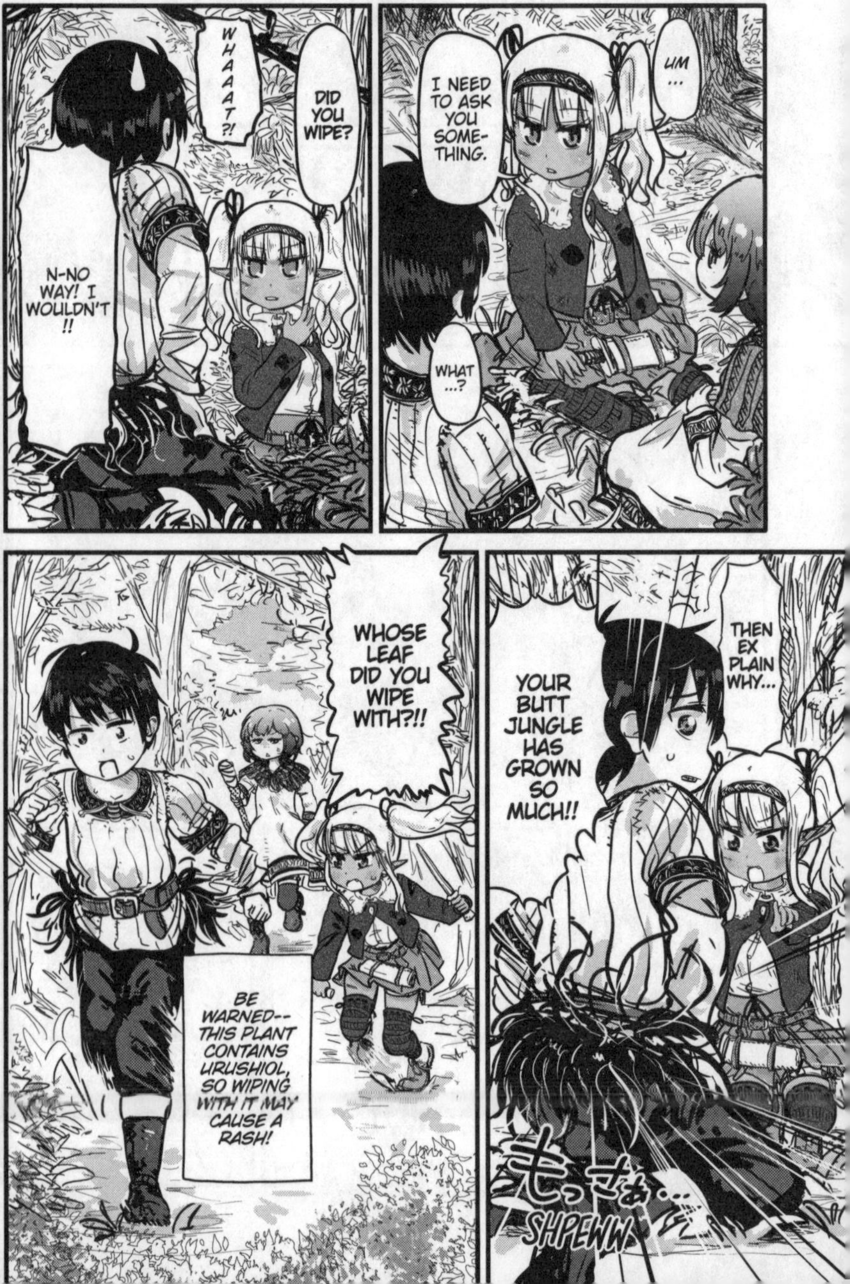
UM ...
I NEED TO ASK YOU SOME-THING.
WHAT ...?
DID YOU WIPE?
WHAAAT?!
N-NO WAY! I WOULDN'T!!
THEN EX PLAIN WHY...
YOUR BUTT JUNGLE HAS GROWN SO MUCH!!
もっさぁ…
SHPEWW
WHOSE LEAF DID YOU WIPE WITH?!!
BE WARNED--THIS PLANT CONTAINS URUSHIOL, SO WIPING WITH IT MAY CAUSE A RASH!

ROOTS

PEOPLE WHO DON'T VALUE TOILET TIME ARE NO GOOD.

THIRD TOILET TIME

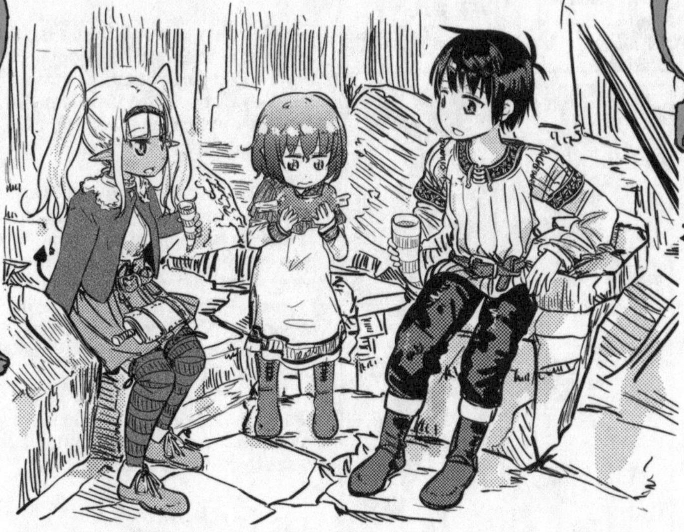

Japan's first flush toilet was invented over 1300 years ago! There were flush toilets even before the Nara period.

However, these weren't the flush toilets you're used to seeing today. These were streams dug out of the side of a river, which took advantage of the current.

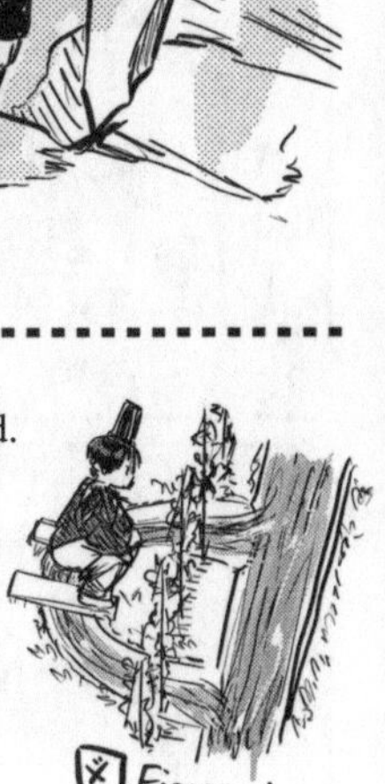

Figure 1

These current toilets can be found throughout history. It was during this time that the word "kawaya" (from "kawa," meaning river, and "ya," meaning room) was born

Long ago, there was a bustling town with a temple at its center, named Koya-san.

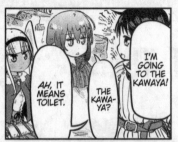

Figure 2

Kitchen
Toilet
To River

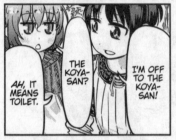

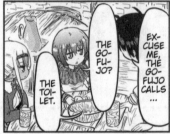

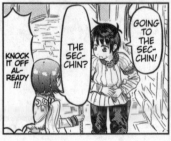

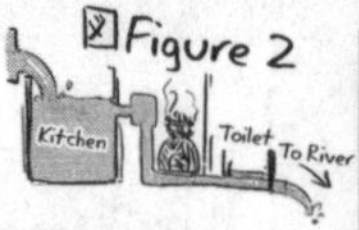

Their toilet was even more developed. Daily water use from the kitchens and baths provided the current for the toilets. (※Figure 2)

This was very economical. In fact, Koya-san's toilet was so popular during the Edo period that "Koya-san" (or "Koya") became a nickname for "toilet." But there was another even more impressive aspect to this.

As Yotaro mentioned, human waste could be used be used as fertilizer, or as an ingredient in gunpowder. However, when it was flushed into the water, the fish downriver were able to ingest important nutrients. And apparently, the Aridagawa River, which fed into Koya-san, was known for housing very large fish.

Next time we go the bathroom, let's take a moment to reflect on the Japanese ethic of efficiency.

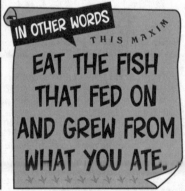

IN OTHER WORDS

THIS MAXIM

EAT THE FISH THAT FED ON AND GREW FROM WHAT YOU ATE.

I'M GOING TO THE KAWAYA!
THE KAWA-YA?
AH, IT MEANS TOILET.
I'M OFF TO THE KOYA-SAN!
THE KOYA-SAN?
AH, IT MEANS TOILET.
EX-CUSE ME, THE GO-FUJO CALLS...
THE GO-FU-JO?
THE TOI-LET.
GOING TO THE SEC-CHIN!
THE SEC-CHIN?
KNOCK IT OFF AL-READY!!!

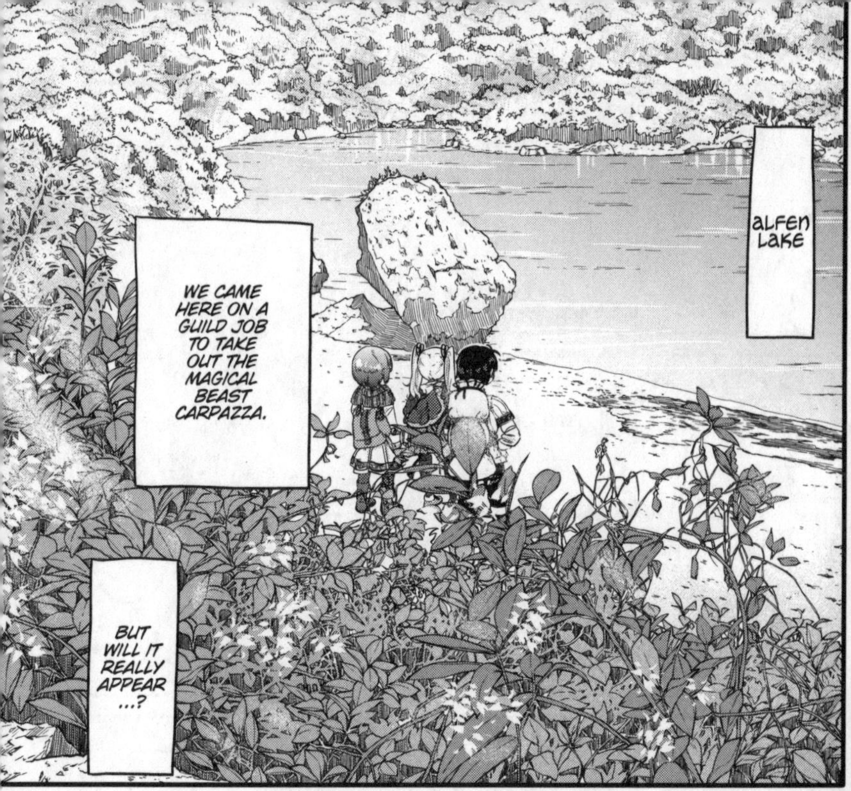
ALFEN LAKE
WE CAME HERE ON A GUILD JOB TO TAKE OUT THE MAGICAL BEAST CARPAZZA.
BUT WILL IT REALLY APPEAR ...?

SIXTH FLUSH

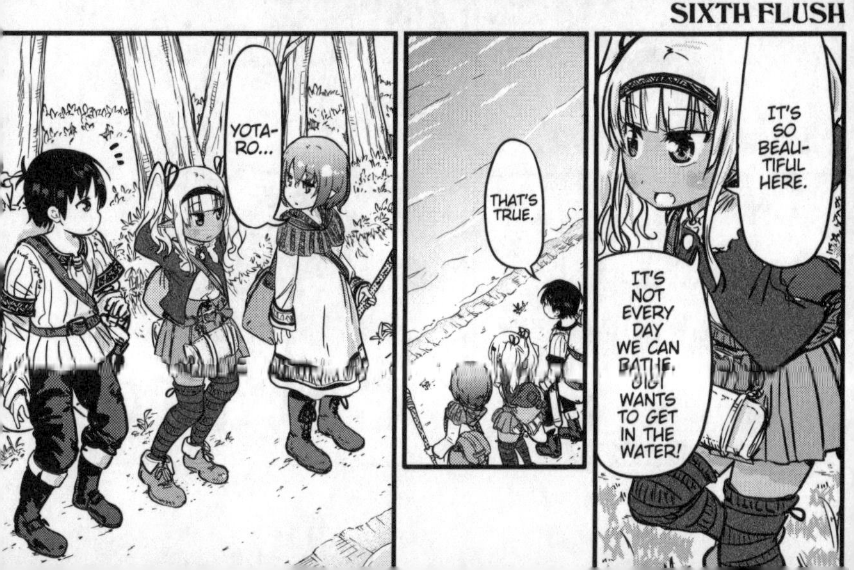
IT'S SO BEAU-TIFUL HERE.
IT'S NOT EVERY DAY WE CAN BATHE. GIGI WANTS TO GET IN THE WATER!
THAT'S TRUE.
YOTA-RO...

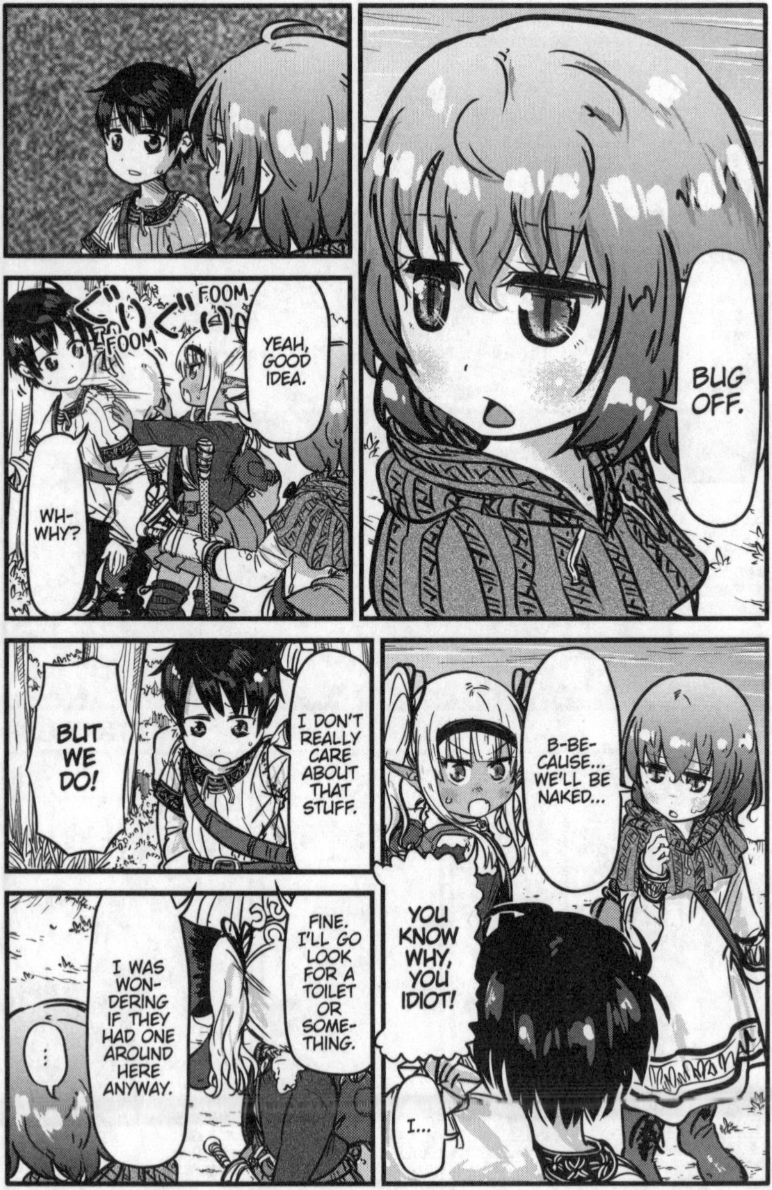
BUG OFF.
YEAH, GOOD IDEA.
ぐい ぐい
FOOM FOOM
WH-WHY?
B-BE-CAUSE... WE'LL BE NAKED...
I DON'T REALLY CARE ABOUT THAT STUFF.
BUT WE DO!
YOU KNOW WHY, YOU IDIOT!
I...
FINE. I'LL GO LOOK FOR A TOILET OR SOME-THING.
I WAS WON-DERING IF THEY HAD ONE AROUND HERE ANYWAY.
...

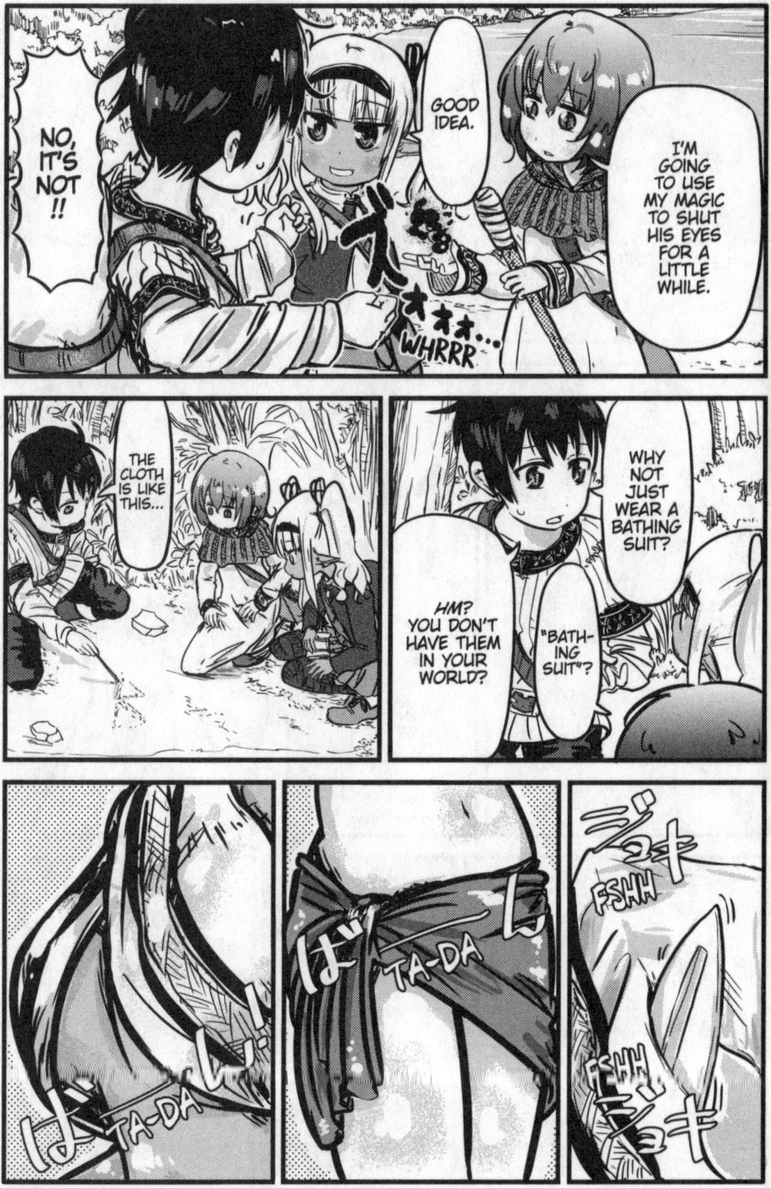
I'M GOING TO USE MY MAGIC TO SHUT HIS EYES FOR A LITTLE WHILE.
GOOD IDEA.
WHRRR
NO, IT'S NOT!!
WHY NOT JUST WEAR A BATHING SUIT?
"BATHING SUIT"?
HM? YOU DON'T HAVE THEM IN YOUR WORLD?
THE CLOTH IS LIKE THIS...
FSHH
FSHH
TA-DA
TA-DA

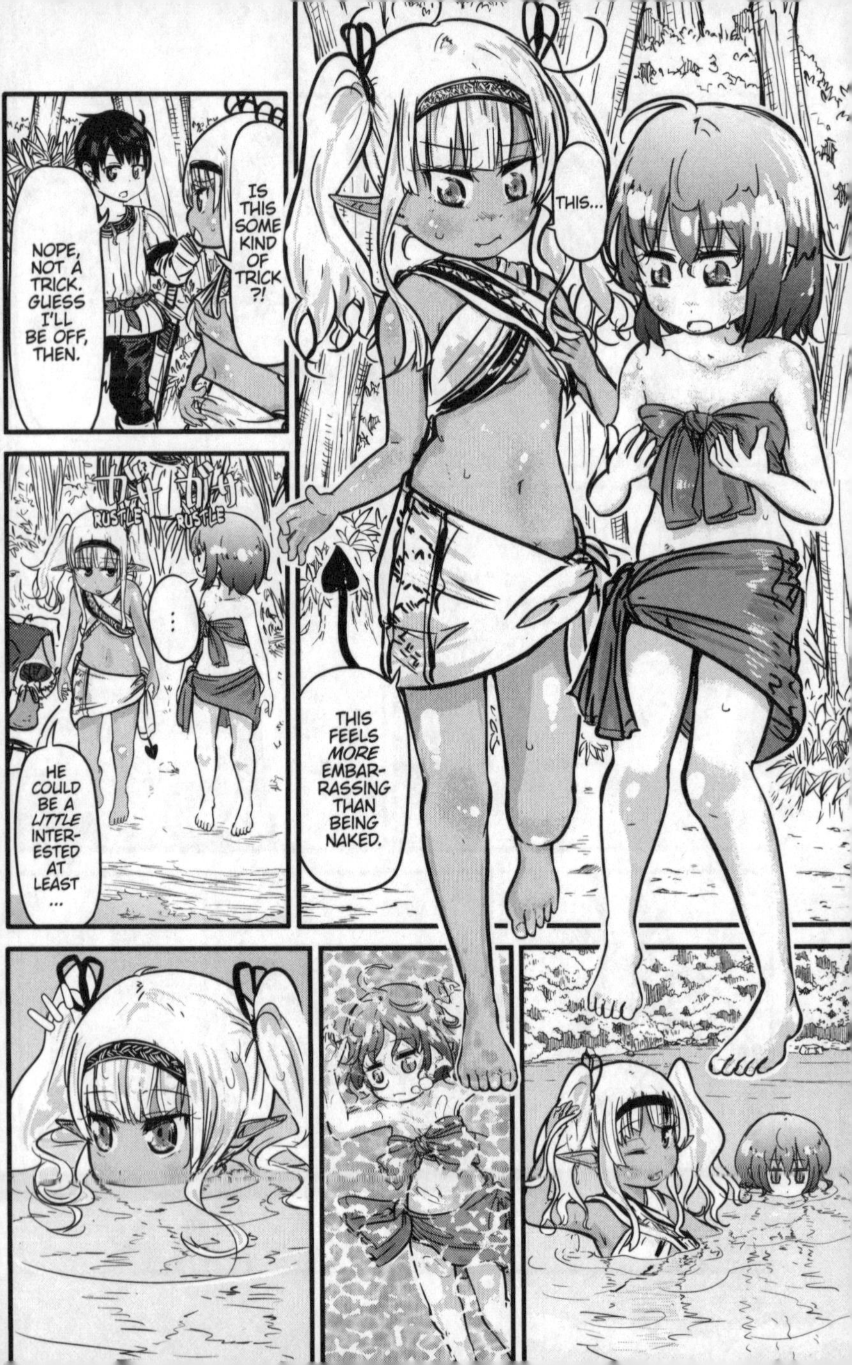
THIS...
THIS FEELS *MORE* EMBARRASSING THAN BEING NAKED.
IS THIS SOME KIND OF TRICK ?!
NOPE, NOT A TRICK. GUESS I'LL BE OFF, THEN.
RUSTLE
RUSTLE
...
HE COULD BE A *LITTLE* INTERESTED AT LEAST ...

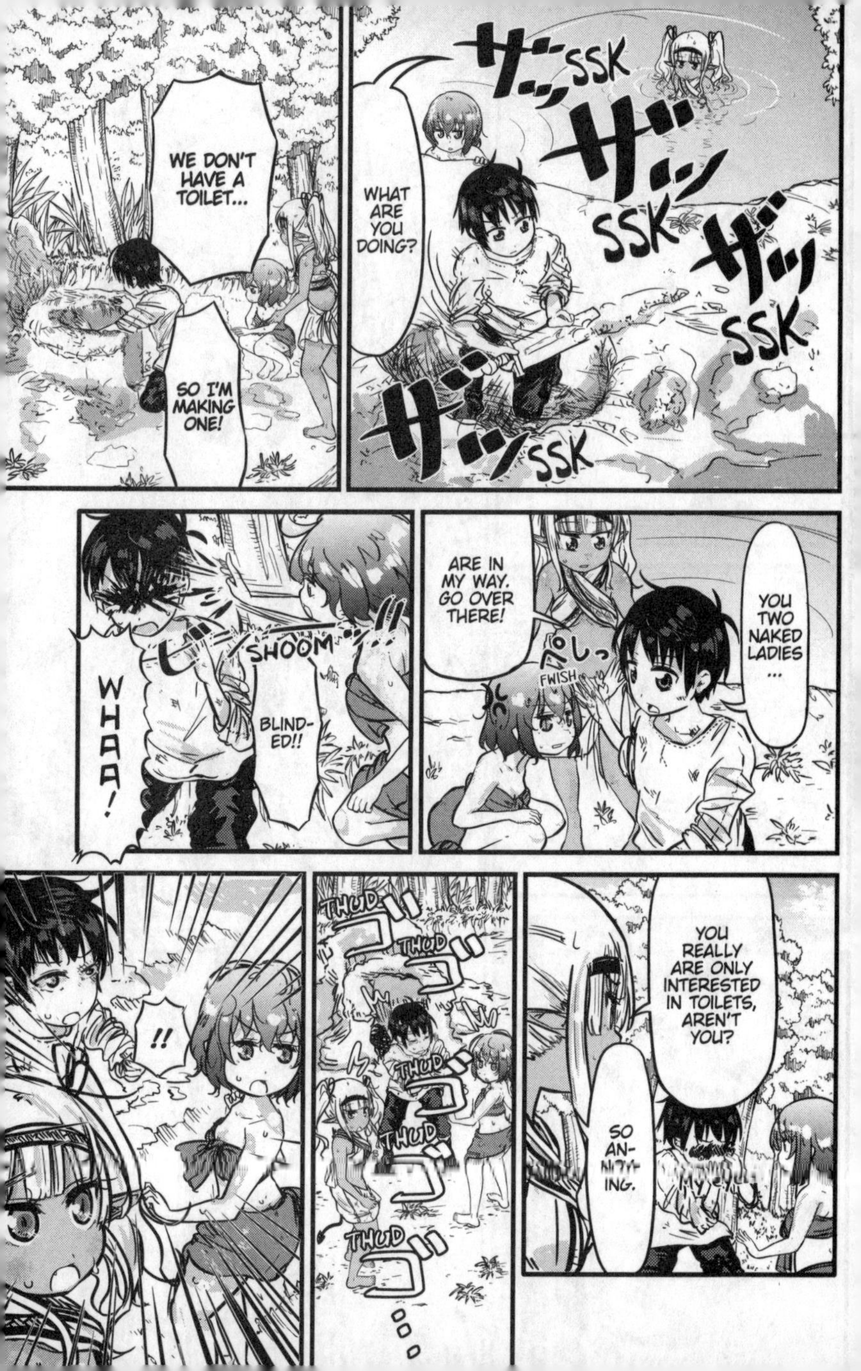

WHAT ARE YOU DOING?
SSK
SSK
SSK
SSK
WE DON'T HAVE A TOILET...
SO I'M MAKING ONE!
YOU TWO NAKED LADIES...
ARE IN MY WAY. GO OVER THERE!
FWISH
SHOOM
BLINDED!!
WHAAA!
YOU REALLY ARE ONLY INTERESTED IN TOILETS, AREN'T YOU?
SO ANNOYING.
THUD
THUD
THUD
THUD
THUD
!!

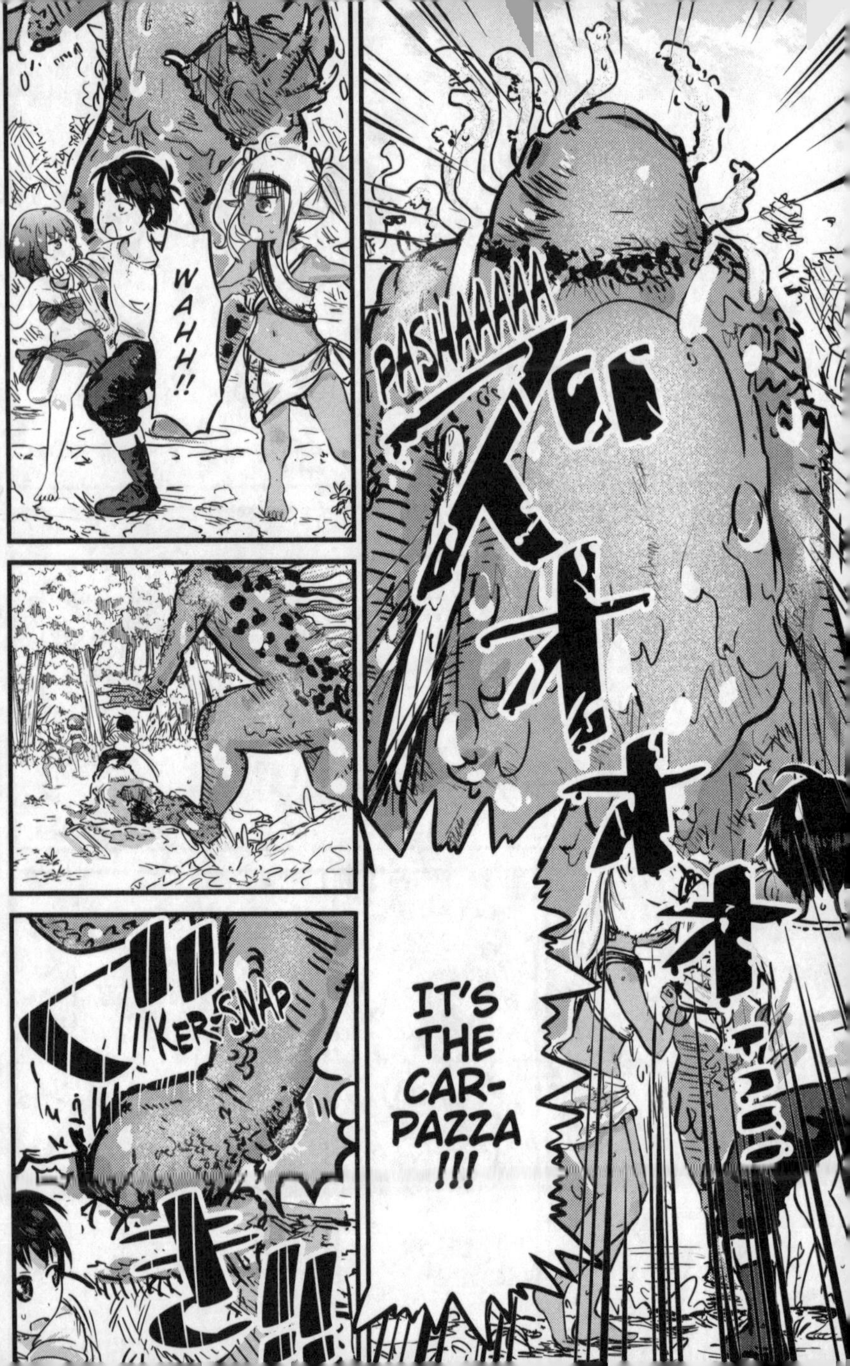

PASHAAAAA
IT'S THE CAR-PAZZA!!!
WAHH!!
KER-SNAP

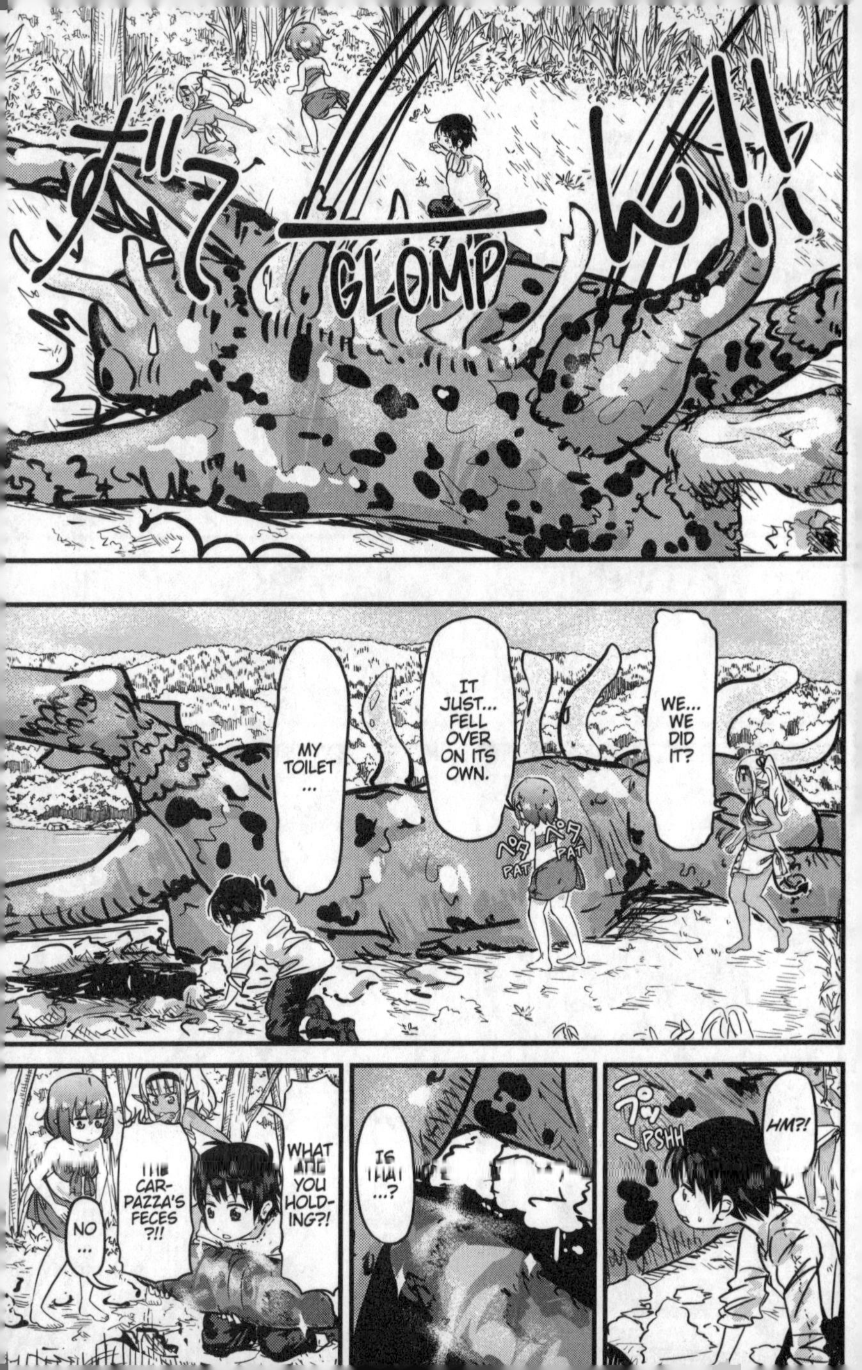
ずでーーん!!
GLOMP
WE... WE DID IT?
IT JUST... FELL OVER ON ITS OWN.
ペタ PAT
ペタ PAT
MY TOILET ...
HM?!
プシュー PSHH
IS THAT ...?
WHAT ARE YOU HOLDING?!
THE CAR-PAZZA'S FECES ?!!
NO ...

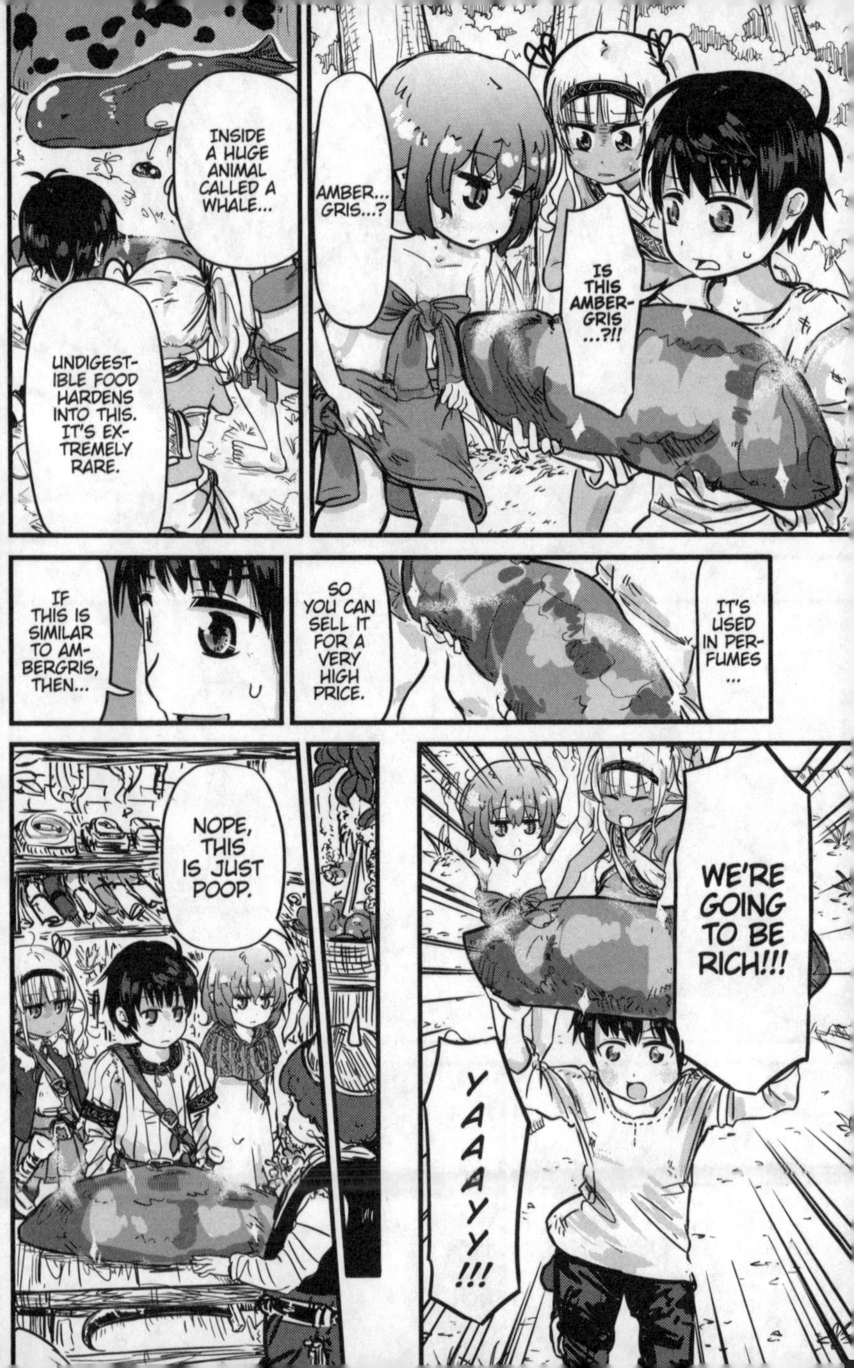
IS THIS AMBER-GRIS ...?!!
AMBER... GRIS...?
INSIDE A HUGE ANIMAL CALLED A WHALE...
UNDIGEST-IBLE FOOD HARDENS INTO THIS. IT'S EX-TREMELY RARE.
IT'S USED IN PER-FUMES ...
SO YOU CAN SELL IT FOR A VERY HIGH PRICE.
IF THIS IS SIMILAR TO AM-BERGRIS, THEN...
WE'RE GOING TO BE RICH!!!
YAAAYY!!!
NOPE, THIS IS JUST POOP.

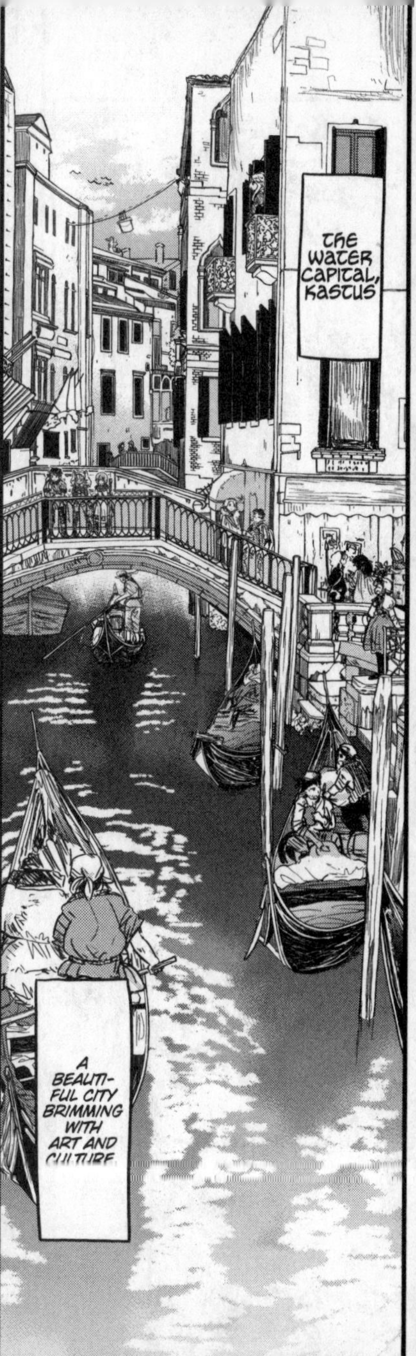
THE WATER CAPITAL, KASTUS
A BEAUTIFUL CITY BRIMMING WITH ART AND CULTURE.

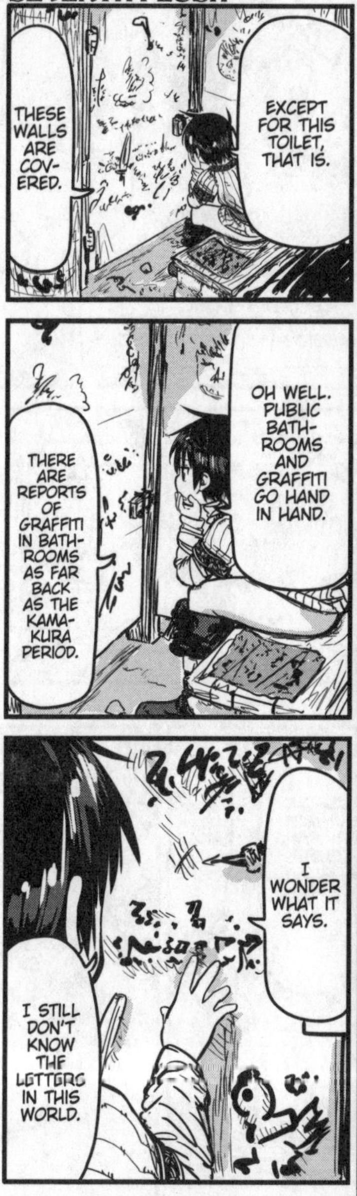
EXCEPT FOR THIS TOILET, THAT IS.
THESE WALLS ARE COVERED.
OH WELL. PUBLIC BATHROOMS AND GRAFFITI GO HAND IN HAND.
THERE ARE REPORTS OF GRAFFITI IN BATHROOMS AS FAR BACK AS THE KAMAKURA PERIOD.
I WONDER WHAT IT SAYS.
I STILL DON'T KNOW THE LETTERS IN THIS WORLD.

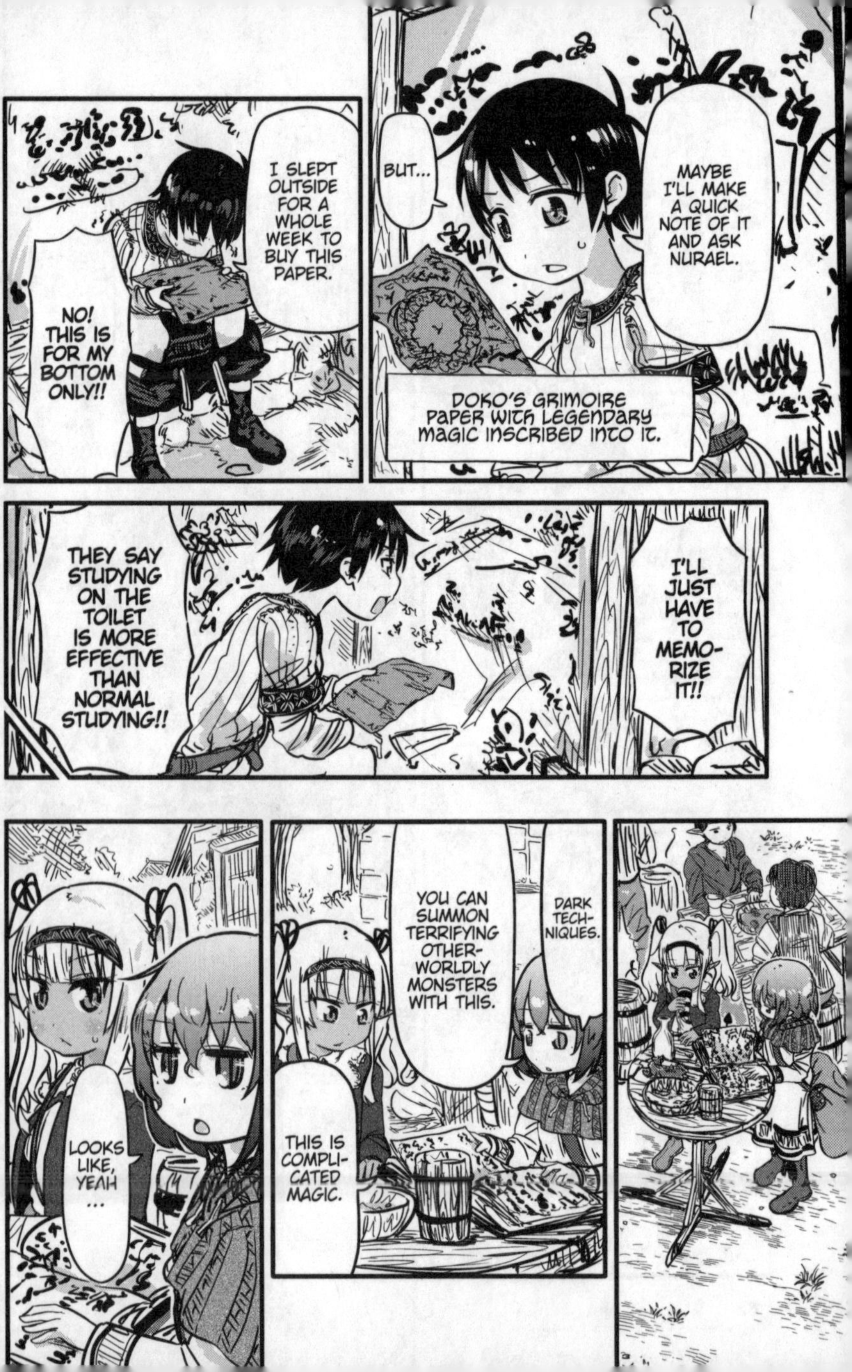
MAYBE I'LL MAKE A QUICK NOTE OF IT AND ASK NURAEL.
BUT...
DOKO'S GRIMOIRE PAPER WITH LEGENDARY MAGIC INSCRIBED INTO IT.
I SLEPT OUTSIDE FOR A WHOLE WEEK TO BUY THIS PAPER.
NO! THIS IS FOR MY BOTTOM ONLY!!
I'LL JUST HAVE TO MEMO-RIZE IT!!
THEY SAY STUDYING ON THE TOILET IS MORE EFFECTIVE THAN NORMAL STUDYING!!
DARK TECH-NIQUES.
YOU CAN SUMMON TERRIFYING OTHER-WORLDLY MONSTERS WITH THIS.
THIS IS COMPLI-CATED MAGIC.
LOOKS LIKE, YEAH ...

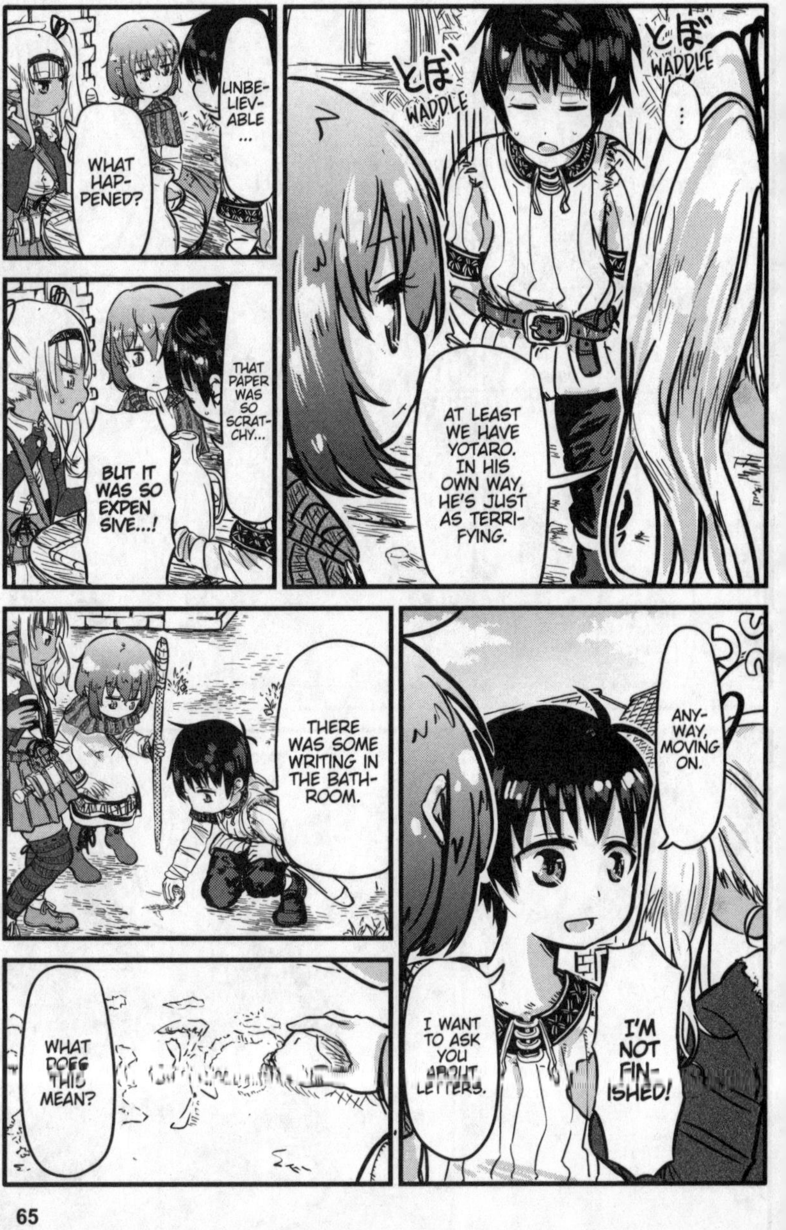

とぼ WADDLE
...
とぼ WADDLE
AT LEAST WE HAVE YOTARO. IN HIS OWN WAY, HE'S JUST AS TERRIFYING.
UNBELIEVABLE...
WHAT HAPPENED?
THAT PAPER WAS SO SCRATCHY...
BUT IT WAS SO EXPENSIVE...!
ANYWAY, MOVING ON.
I'M NOT FINISHED!
I WANT TO ASK YOU ABOUT LETTERS.
THERE WAS SOME WRITING IN THE BATHROOM.
WHAT DOES THIS MEAN?

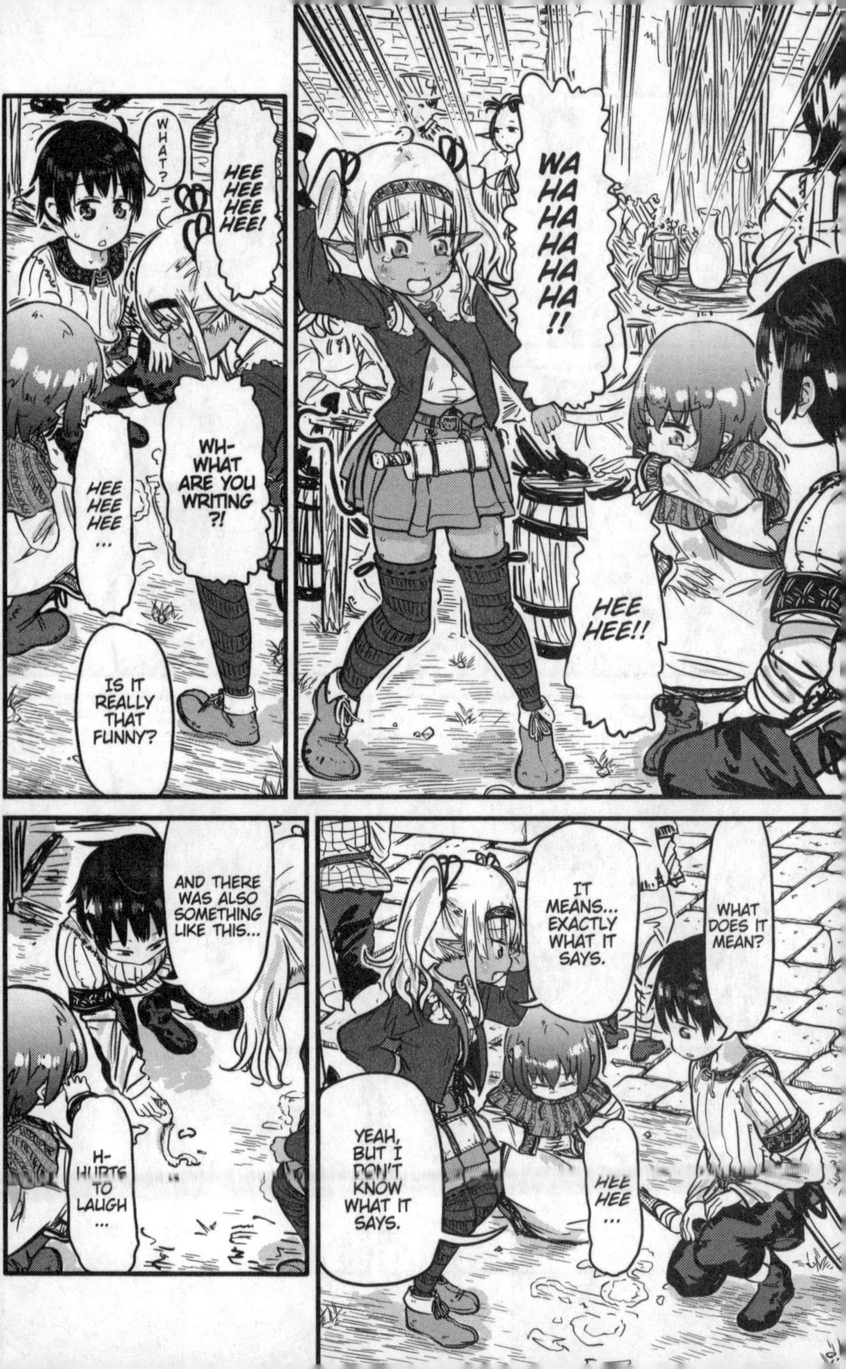
WA HA HA HA HA HA!!
HEE HEE!!
HEE HEE HEE HEE!
WHAT?
WH-WHAT ARE YOU WRITING?!
HEE HEE HEE...
IS IT REALLY THAT FUNNY?
WHAT DOES IT MEAN?
IT MEANS... EXACTLY WHAT IT SAYS.
HEE HEE...
YEAH, BUT I DON'T KNOW WHAT IT SAYS.
AND THERE WAS ALSO SOMETHING LIKE THIS...
H-HURTS TO LAUGH...

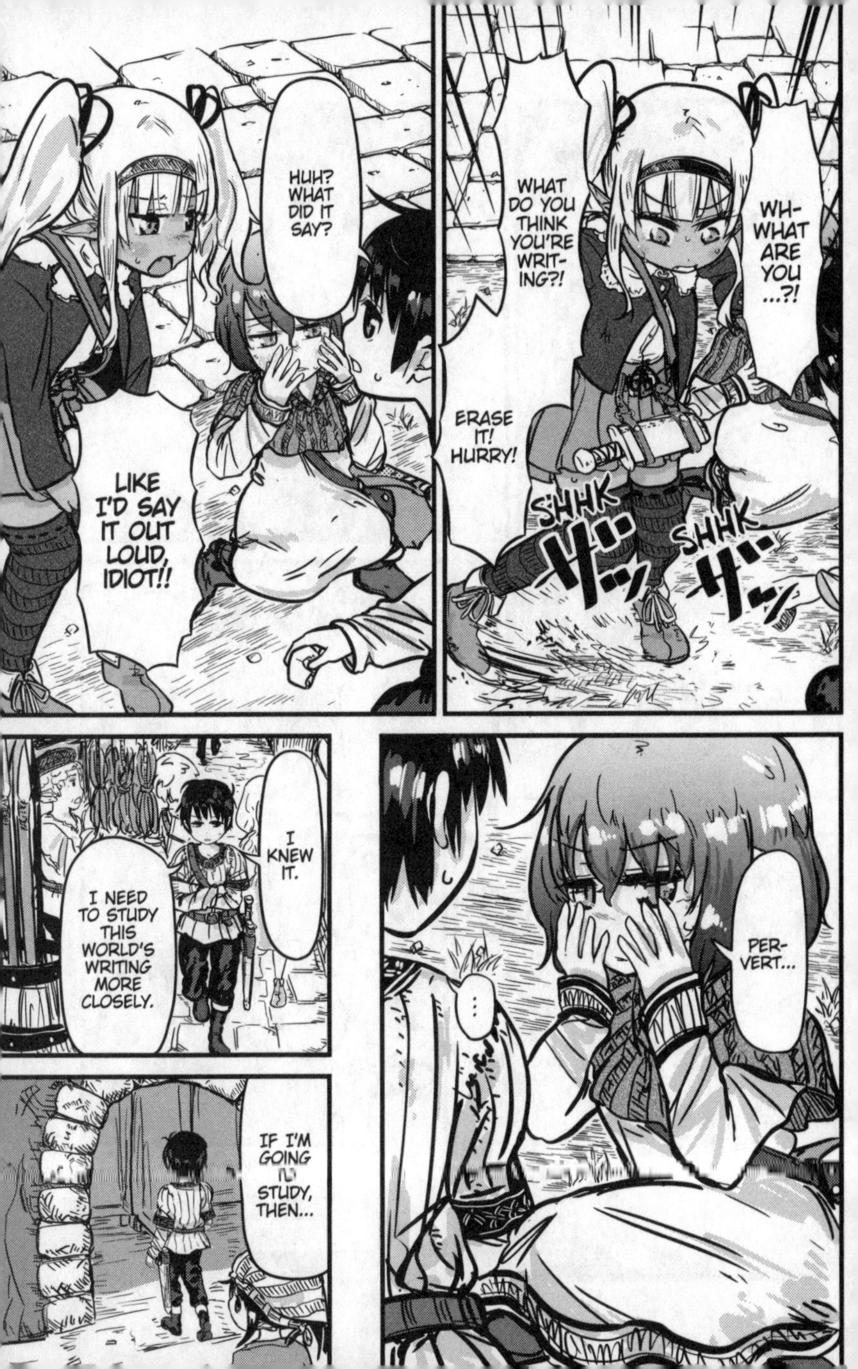
WH-WHAT ARE YOU ...?!
WHAT DO YOU THINK YOU'RE WRIT-ING?!
ERASE IT! HURRY!
SHHK
SHHK
HUH? WHAT DID IT SAY?
LIKE I'D SAY IT OUT LOUD, IDIOT!!
PER-VERT...
...
I KNEW IT.
I NEED TO STUDY THIS WORLD'S WRITING MORE CLOSELY.
IF I'M GOING TO STUDY, THEN...

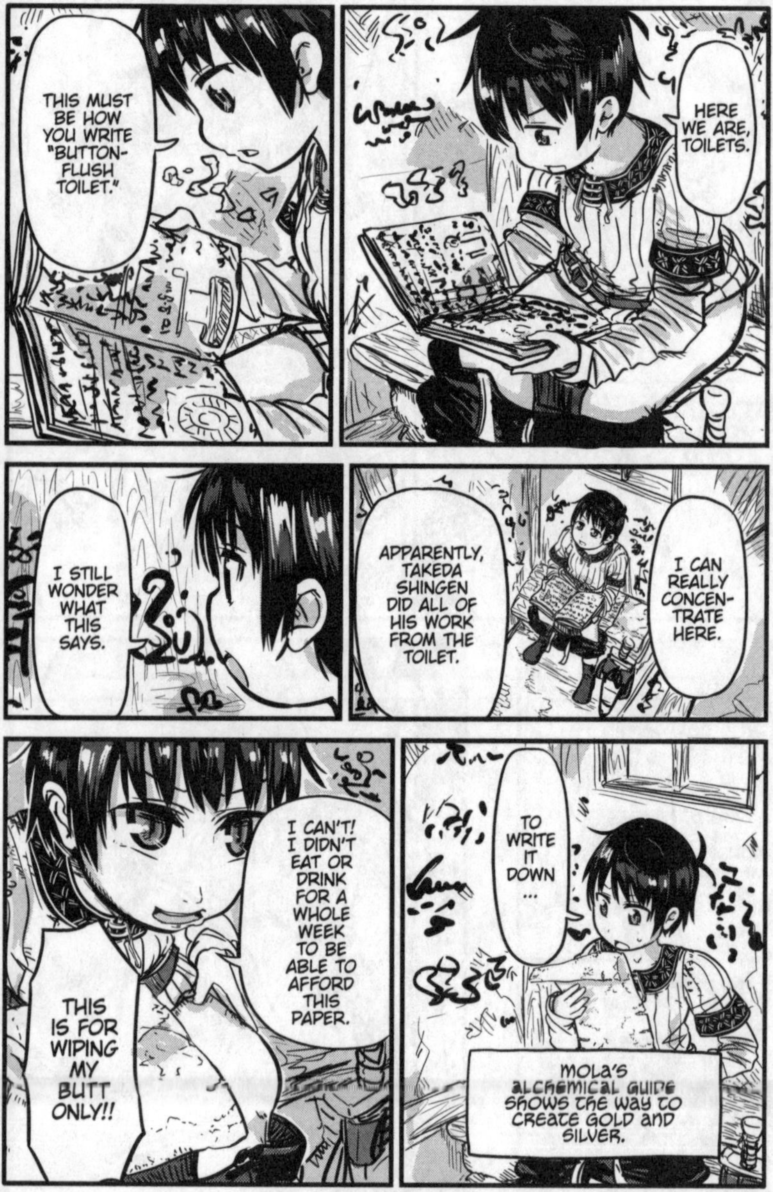
HERE WE ARE, TOILETS.
THIS MUST BE HOW YOU WRITE "BUTTON-FLUSH TOILET."
I CAN REALLY CONCENTRATE HERE.
APPARENTLY, TAKEDA SHINGEN DID ALL OF HIS WORK FROM THE TOILET.
I STILL WONDER WHAT THIS SAYS.
TO WRITE IT DOWN ...
MOLA'S ALCHEMICAL GUIDE SHOWS THE WAY TO CREATE GOLD AND SILVER.
I CAN'T! I DIDN'T EAT OR DRINK FOR A WHOLE WEEK TO BE ABLE TO AFFORD THIS PAPER.
THIS IS FOR WIPING MY BUTT ONLY!!

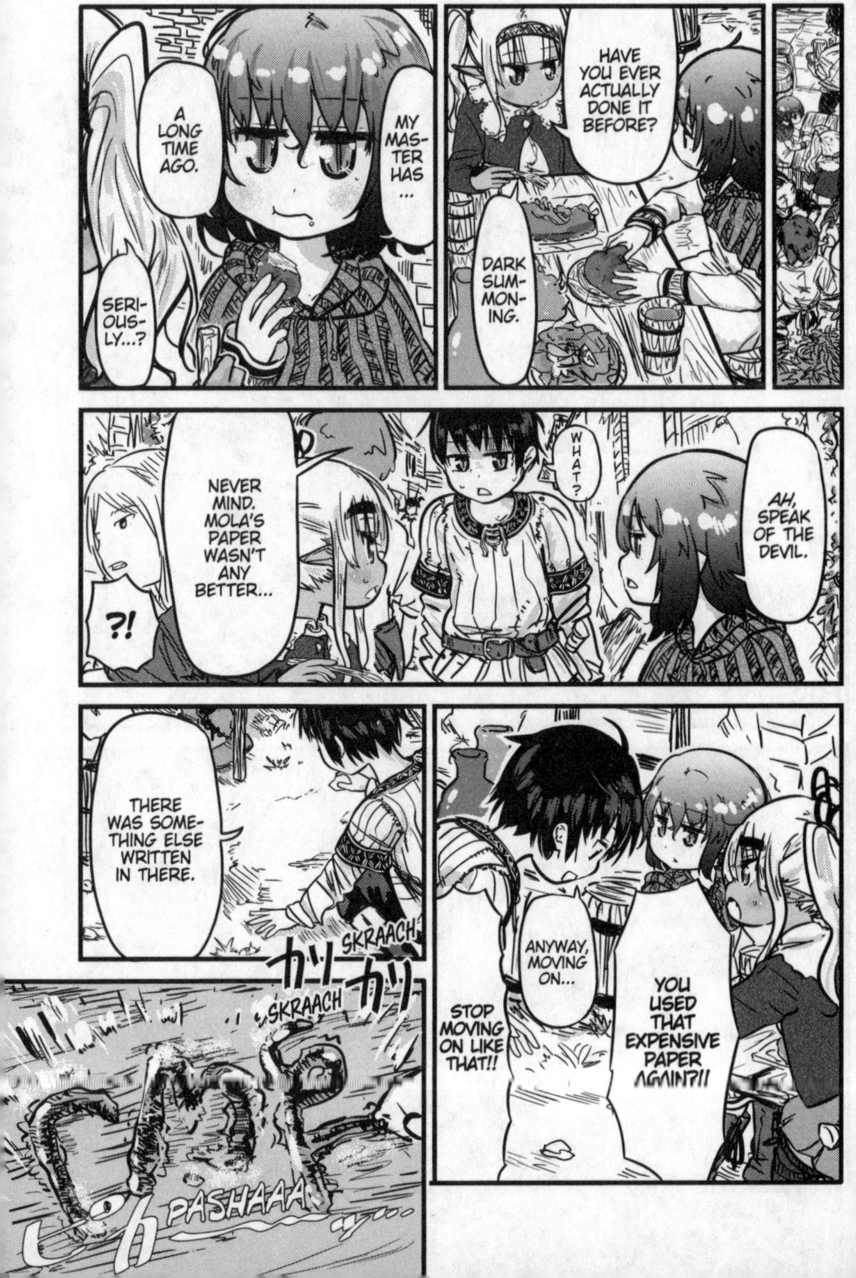
HAVE YOU EVER ACTUALLY DONE IT BEFORE?
DARK SUMMONING.
MY MASTER HAS...
A LONG TIME AGO.
SERIOUSLY...?
AH, SPEAK OF THE DEVIL.
WHAT?
NEVER MIND. MOLA'S PAPER WASN'T ANY BETTER...
?!
YOU USED THAT EXPENSIVE PAPER AGAIN?!!
ANYWAY, MOVING ON...
STOP MOVING ON LIKE THAT!!
THERE WAS SOMETHING ELSE WRITTEN IN THERE.
カリ SKRAACH
カリ SKRAACH
PASHAAA

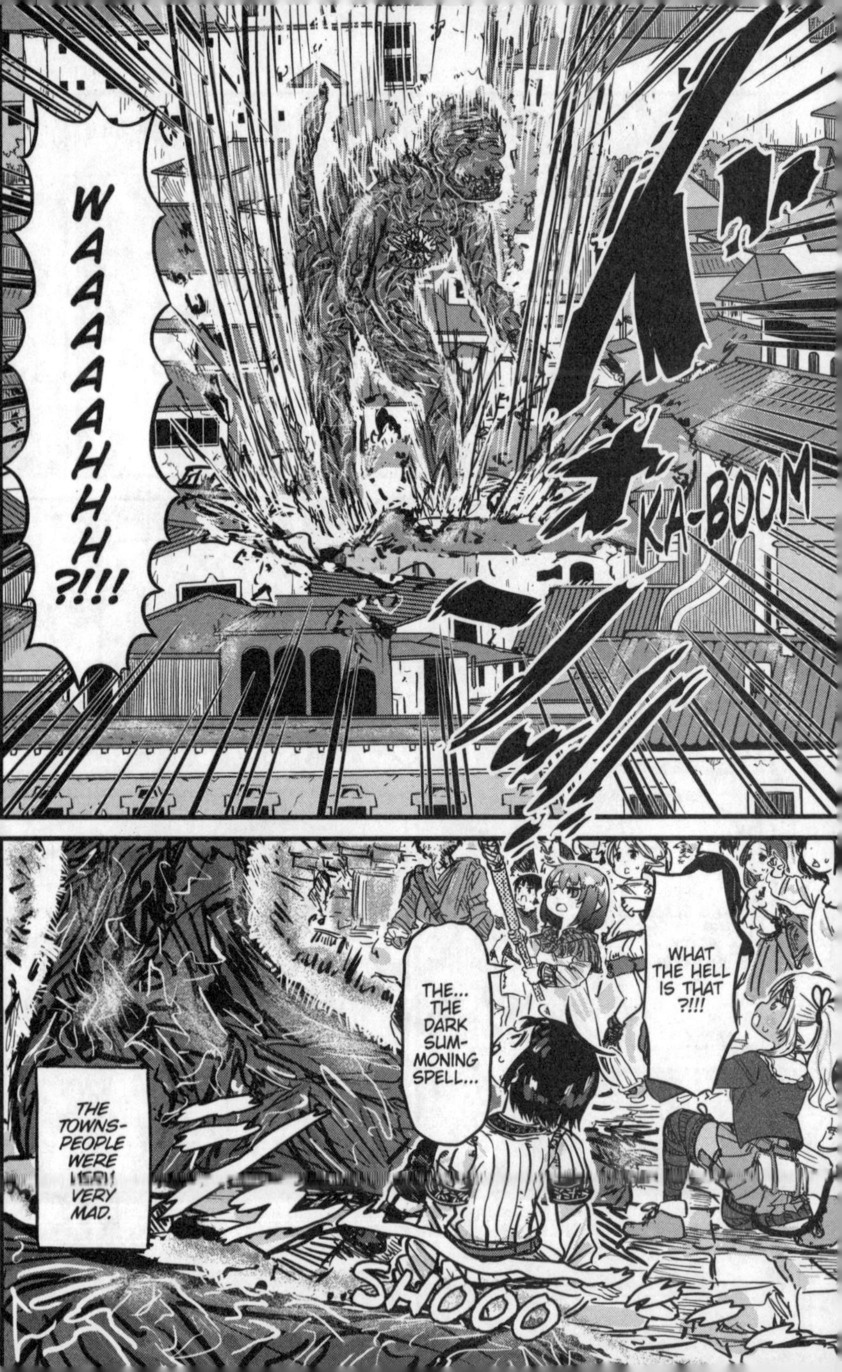
KA-BOOM
WAAAAAAHHHH ?!!!
WHAT THE HELL IS THAT ?!!!
THE... THE DARK SUM-MONING SPELL...
THE TOWNS-PEOPLE WERE VERY MAD.
SHOOO

PEOPLE WHO DON'T VALUE TOILET TIME ARE NO GOOD.

FOURTH TOILET TIME

During the Kamakura period, the renowned Dogen (founder of the Soto school of Zen Buddhism) wrote the *Shobogenzo*, a collection of works also known as *The Treasury of the True Dharma Eye*. Within this collection is a book about toilets, called *Senjo* (Purification).

Senjo describes the way those practicing Buddhism should go about their business. There's a sentence regarding manners, stating that one shouldn't write on the floors or walls of toilets. Dogen also talks about how you should reflect on your feelings when on the toilet, as well as how to wash your hands and clean yourself. He wrote this all out in scrupulous detail.

Of course, there's only one place where you can go to implement these strict teachings.

WHO ...
WHO DOES IT LOOK BETTER ON?!!
EH?!
UH...
...
...
UMM ...
NO NEED FOR THAT!!
I'LL THINK ABOUT IT ON THE TOILET !!

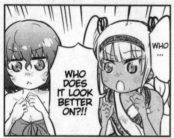

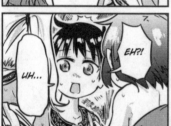

Another famous figure in Japanese history, Takeda Shingen, also loved his toilets. It's said that when he made his war plans, he'd lock himself away in the bathroom. Outside the door, he even had a box to hold different documents he could peruse while taking care of business.

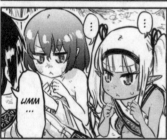

It's said the bathroom was very large, around the size of an average bedroom. But this wasn't just about luxury. The idea was that if someone infiltrated Shingen's toilet, he'd still be able to swing a katana. Even better, since this was during the Sengoku period, Shingen's toilet used recycled water from his bath to flush.

If you're ever worried, why not come up with a plan while you're on the toilet?

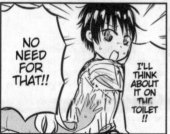

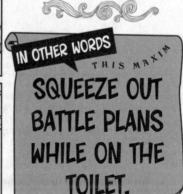

IN OTHER WORDS
THIS MAXIM

SQUEEZE OUT BATTLE PLANS WHILE ON THE TOILET.

EIGHTH FLUSH

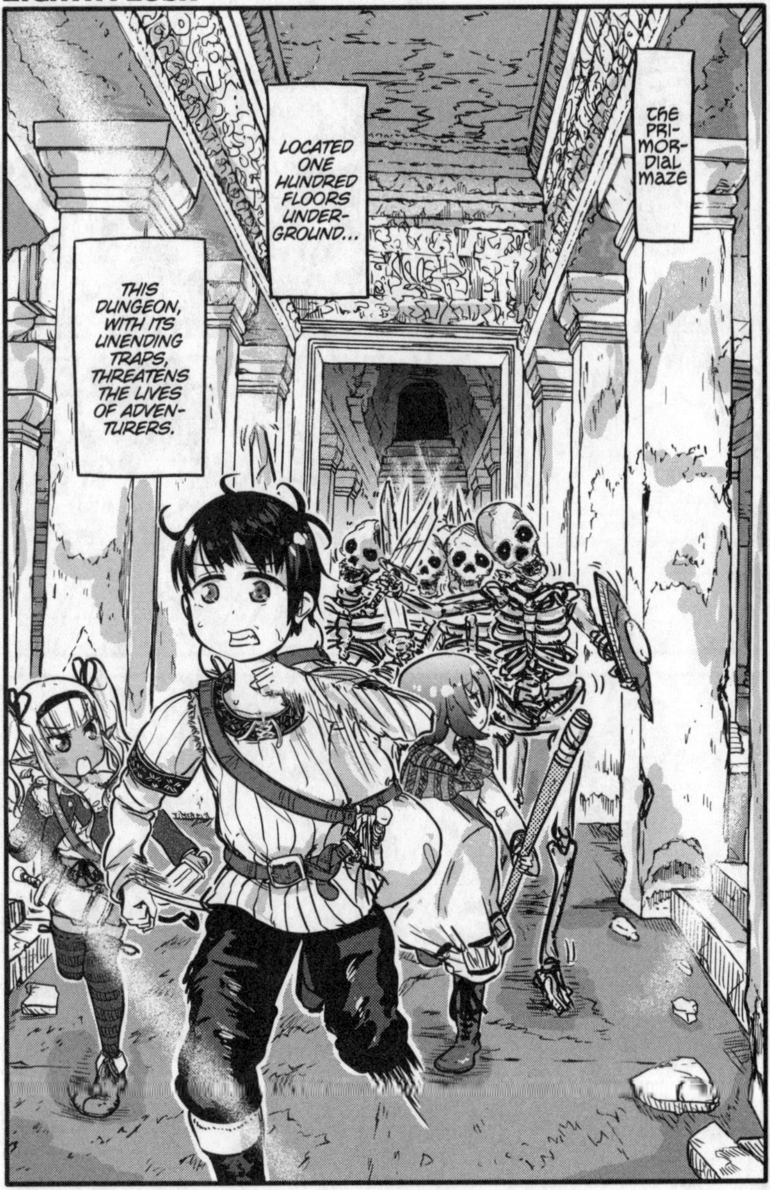
THE PRIMORDIAL MAZE
LOCATED ONE HUNDRED FLOORS UNDERGROUND...
THIS DUNGEON, WITH ITS UNENDING TRAPS, THREATENS THE LIVES OF ADVENTURERS.

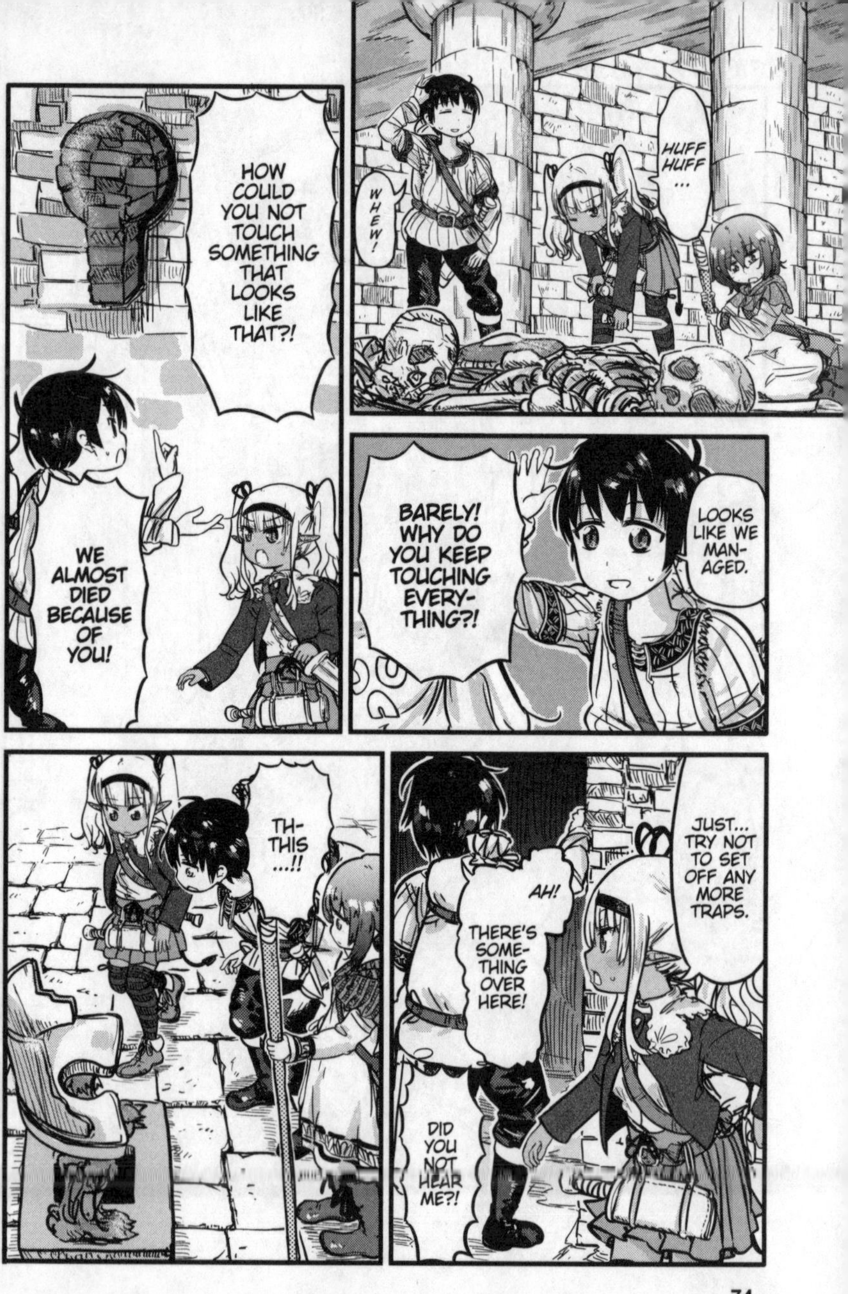
HUFF HUFF ...
WHEW!
LOOKS LIKE WE MAN-AGED.
BARELY! WHY DO YOU KEEP TOUCHING EVERY-THING?!
HOW COULD YOU NOT TOUCH SOMETHING THAT LOOKS LIKE THAT?!
WE ALMOST DIED BECAUSE OF YOU!
JUST... TRY NOT TO SET OFF ANY MORE TRAPS.
AH!
THERE'S SOME-THING OVER HERE!
DID YOU NOT HEAR ME?!
TH-THIS ...!!

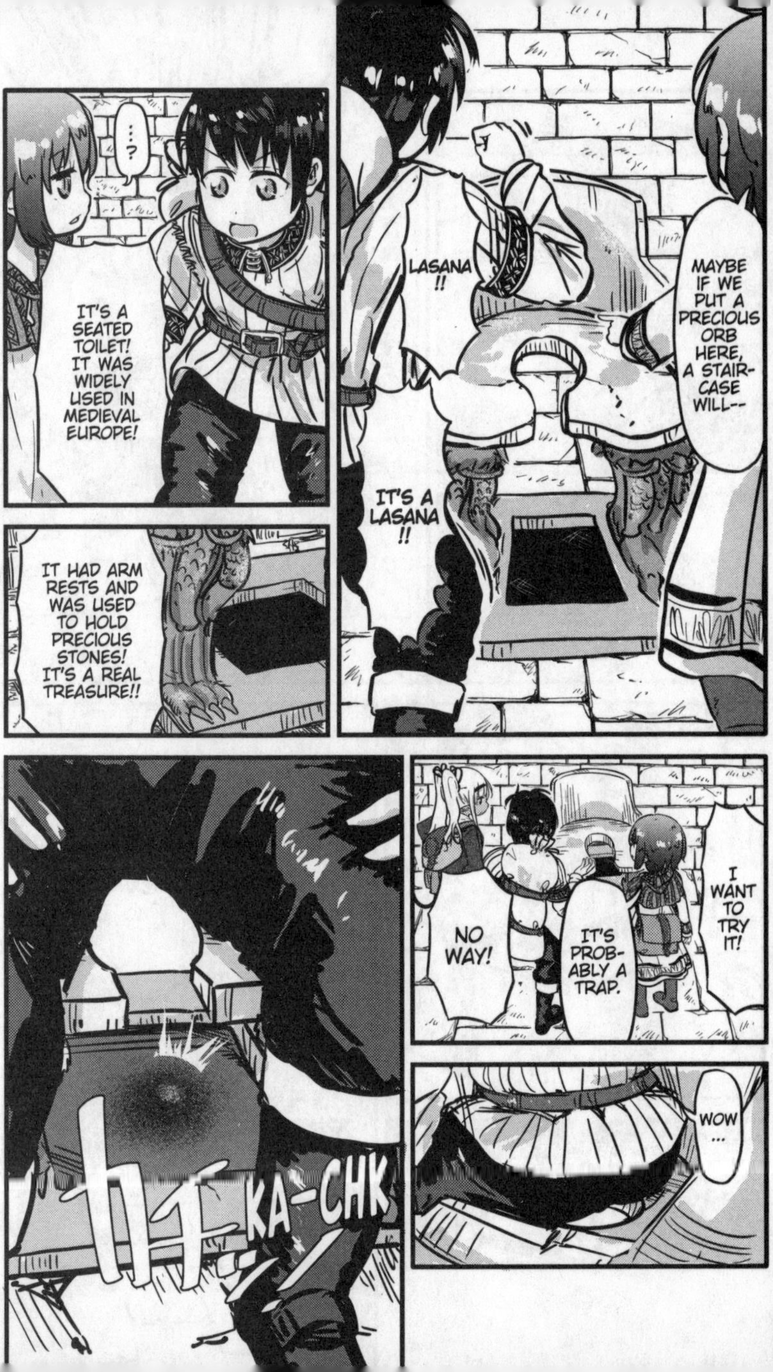
MAYBE IF WE PUT A PRECIOUS ORB HERE, A STAIR-CASE WILL--
LASANA !!
IT'S A LASANA !!
...?
IT'S A SEATED TOILET! IT WAS WIDELY USED IN MEDIEVAL EUROPE!
IT HAD ARM RESTS AND WAS USED TO HOLD PRECIOUS STONES! IT'S A REAL TREASURE!!
I WANT TO TRY IT!
IT'S PROB-ABLY A TRAP.
NO WAY!
WOW ...
KA-CHK

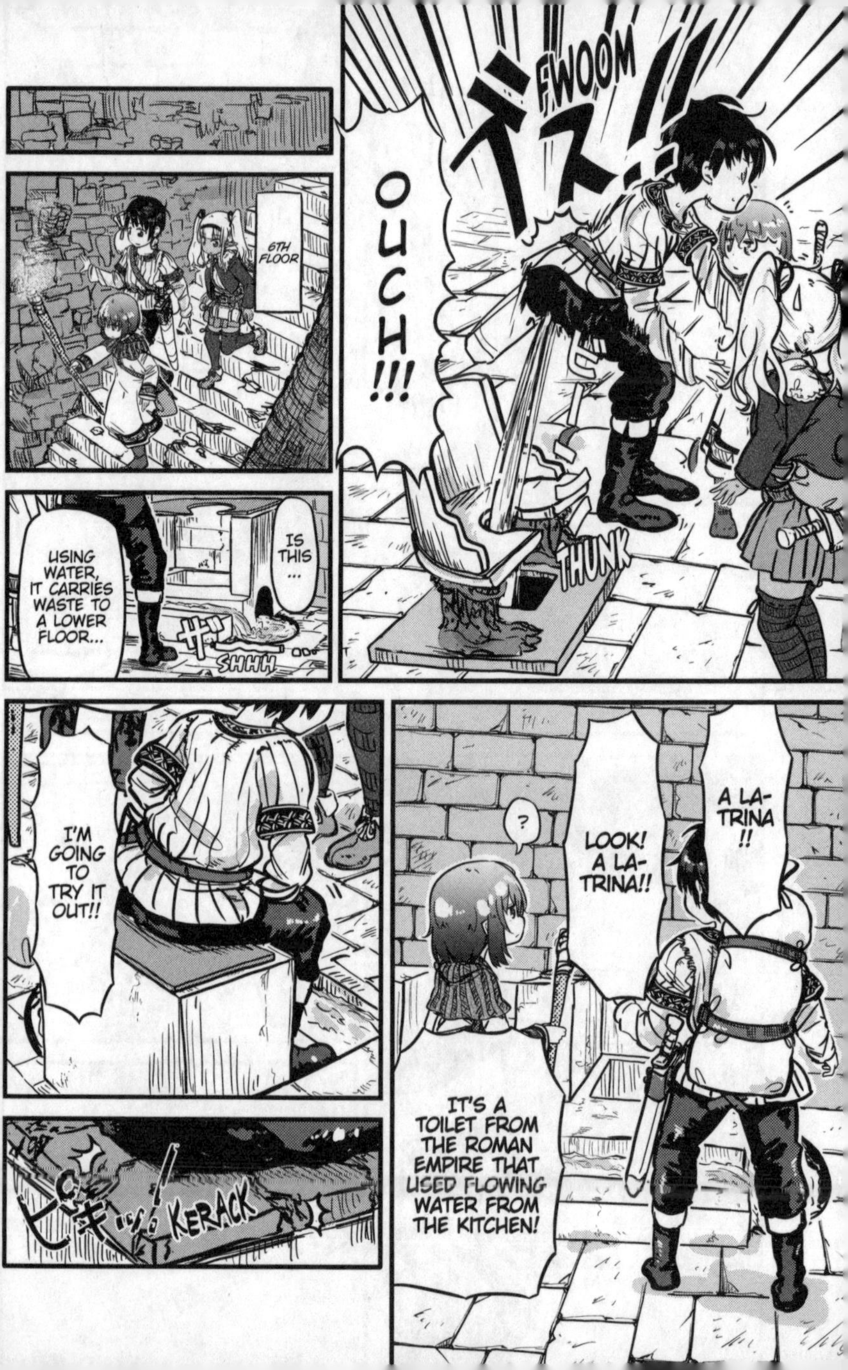
FWOOM
OUCH!!!
THUNK
6TH FLOOR
IS THIS ...
USING WATER, IT CARRIES WASTE TO A LOWER FLOOR...
SHHH
A LA-TRINA!!
LOOK! A LA-TRINA!!
?
IT'S A TOILET FROM THE ROMAN EMPIRE THAT USED FLOWING WATER FROM THE KITCHEN!
I'M GOING TO TRY IT OUT!!
KERACK

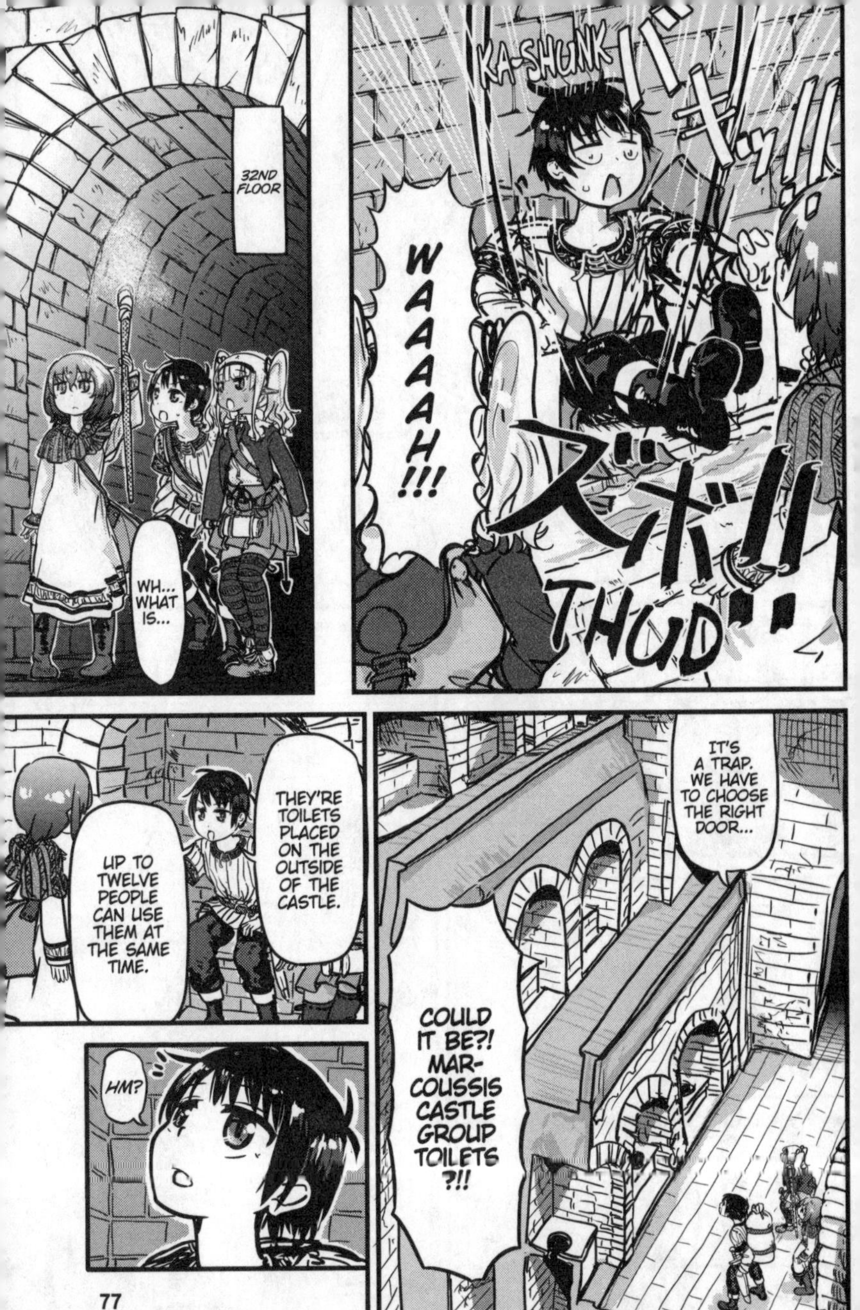
KA-SHUNK
バキッ!!
WAAAAAH!!!
ズボ!!
THUD!!
32ND FLOOR
WH... WHAT IS...
IT'S A TRAP. WE HAVE TO CHOOSE THE RIGHT DOOR...
COULD IT BE?! MAR-COUSSIS CASTLE GROUP TOILETS ?!!
THEY'RE TOILETS PLACED ON THE OUTSIDE OF THE CASTLE.
UP TO TWELVE PEOPLE CAN USE THEM AT THE SAME TIME.
HM?

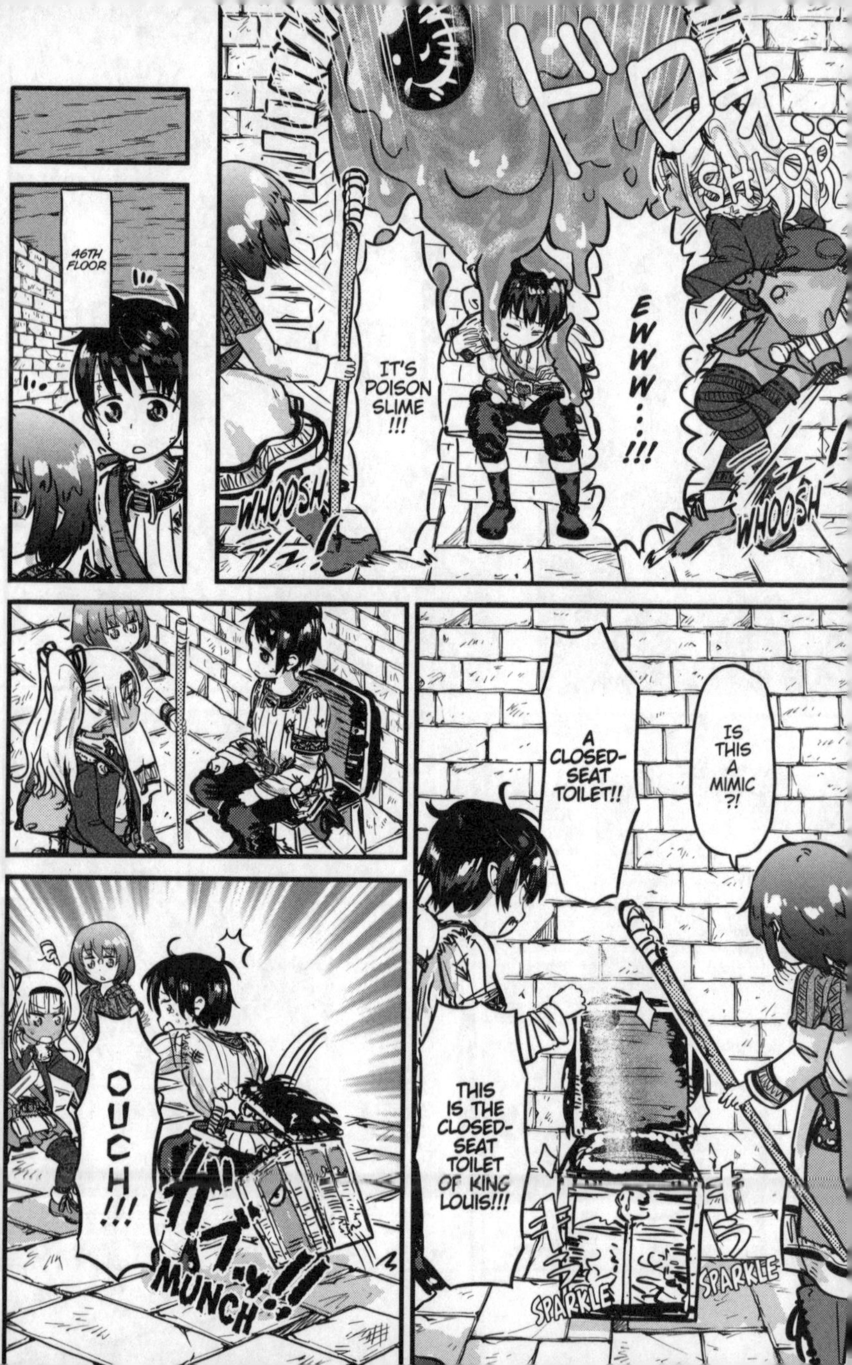

ドロォ…
SHLOP
EWWW…!!!
IT'S POISON SLIME!!!
WHOOSH
WHOOSH
46TH FLOOR
IS THIS A MIMIC?!
A CLOSED-SEAT TOILET!!
THIS IS THE CLOSED-SEAT TOILET OF KING LOUIS!!!
SPARKLE
SPARKLE
OUCH!!!
MUNCH

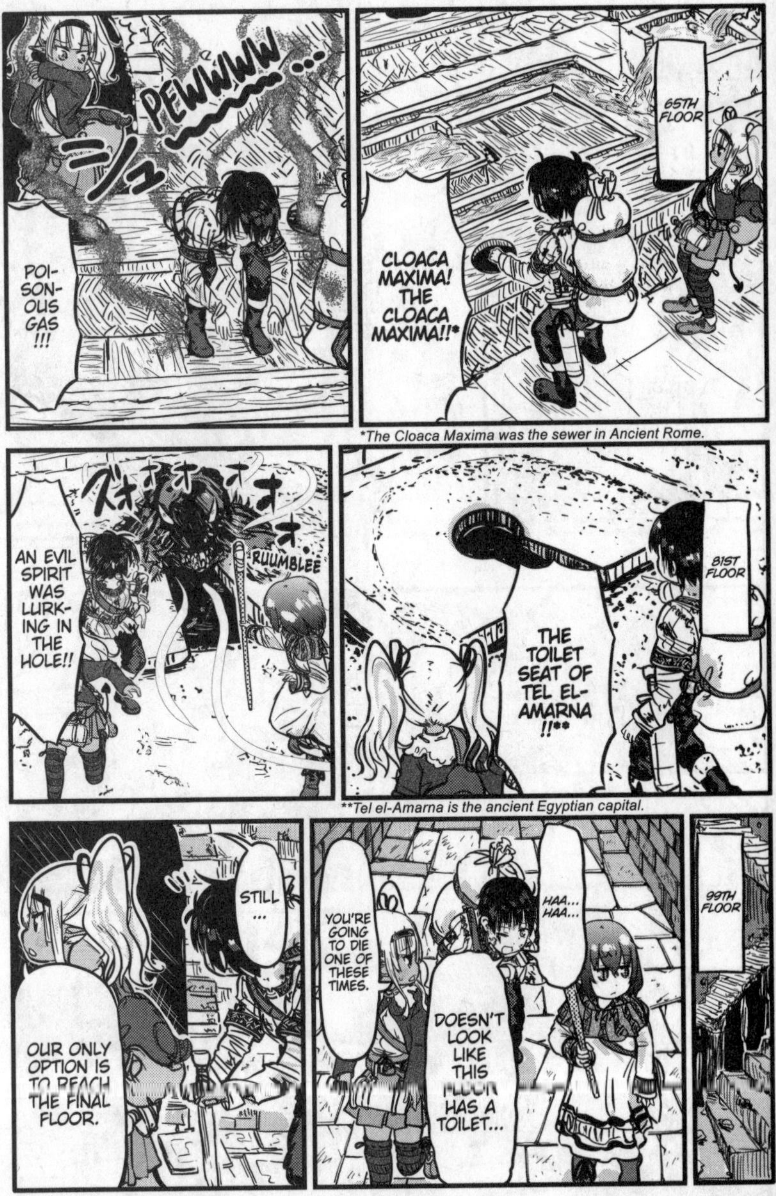
65TH FLOOR
CLOACA MAXIMA! THE CLOACA MAXIMA!!*
PEWWWW~~~...
POI-SON-OUS GAS!!!
81ST FLOOR
THE TOILET SEAT OF TEL EL-AMARNA!!**
RUUMBLEE
AN EVIL SPIRIT WAS LURK-ING IN THE HOLE!!
99TH FLOOR
HAA... HAA...
DOESN'T LOOK LIKE THIS FLOOR HAS A TOILET...
YOU'RE GOING TO DIE ONE OF THESE TIMES.
STILL...
OUR ONLY OPTION IS TO REACH THE FINAL FLOOR.

*The Cloaca Maxima was the sewer in Ancient Rome.

**Tel el-Amarna is the ancient Egyptian capital.

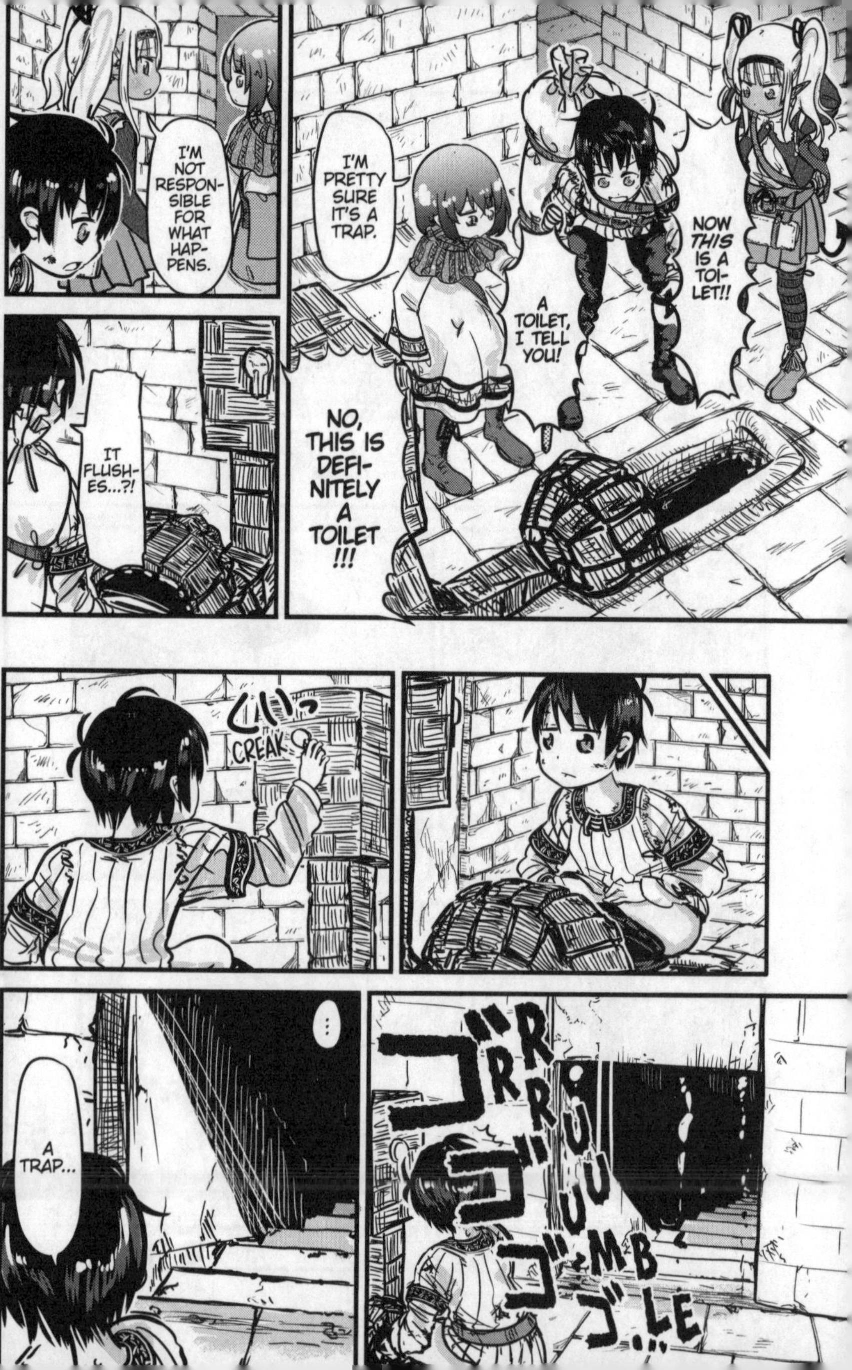
NOW THIS IS A TOILET!!
I'M PRETTY SURE IT'S A TRAP.
A TOILET, I TELL YOU!
NO, THIS IS DEFINITELY A TOILET!!!
I'M NOT RESPONSIBLE FOR WHAT HAPPENS.
IT FLUSHES...?!
CREAK
RRRUUUMBLE
...
A TRAP...

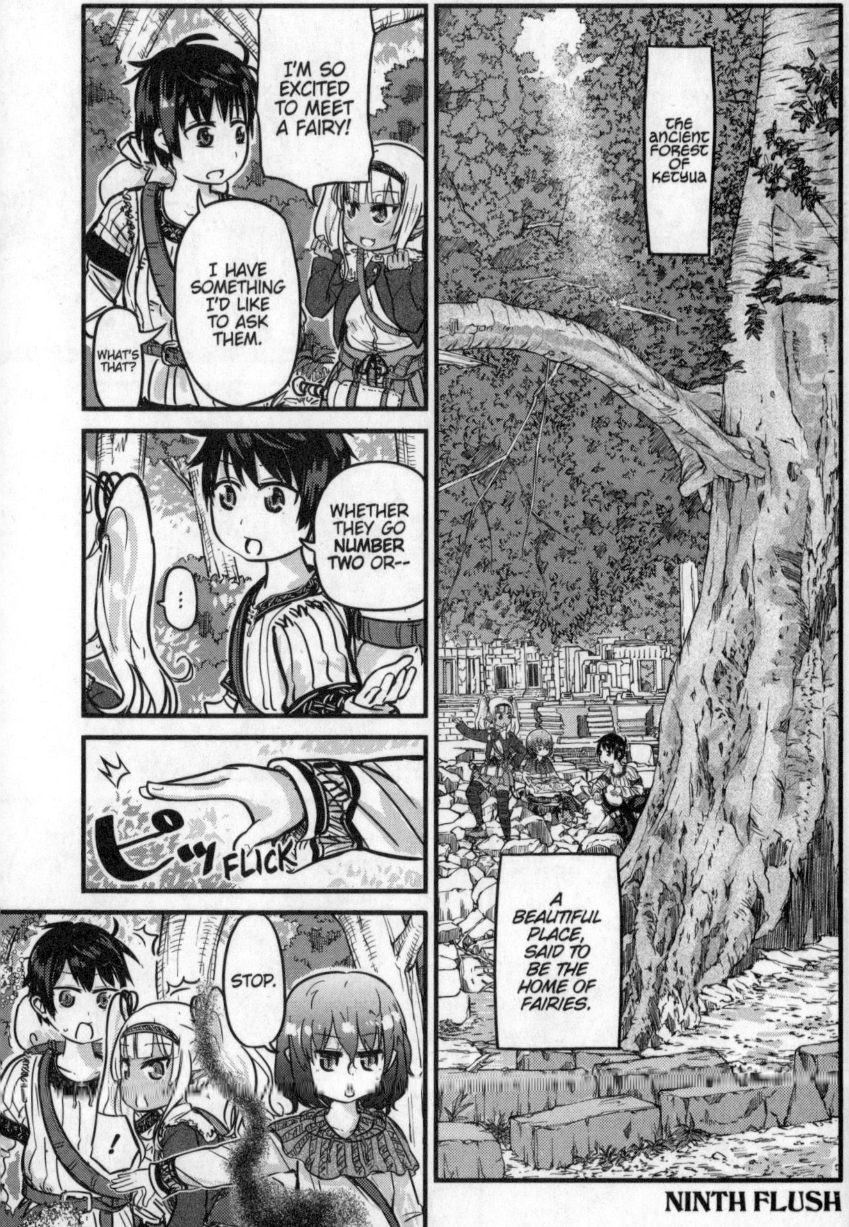
THE ANCIENT FOREST OF KETYUA
A BEAUTIFUL PLACE, SAID TO BE THE HOME OF FAIRIES.
I'M SO EXCITED TO MEET A FAIRY!
I HAVE SOMETHING I'D LIKE TO ASK THEM.
WHAT'S THAT?
WHETHER THEY GO NUMBER TWO OR--
...
FLICK
STOP.
!

NINTH FLUSH

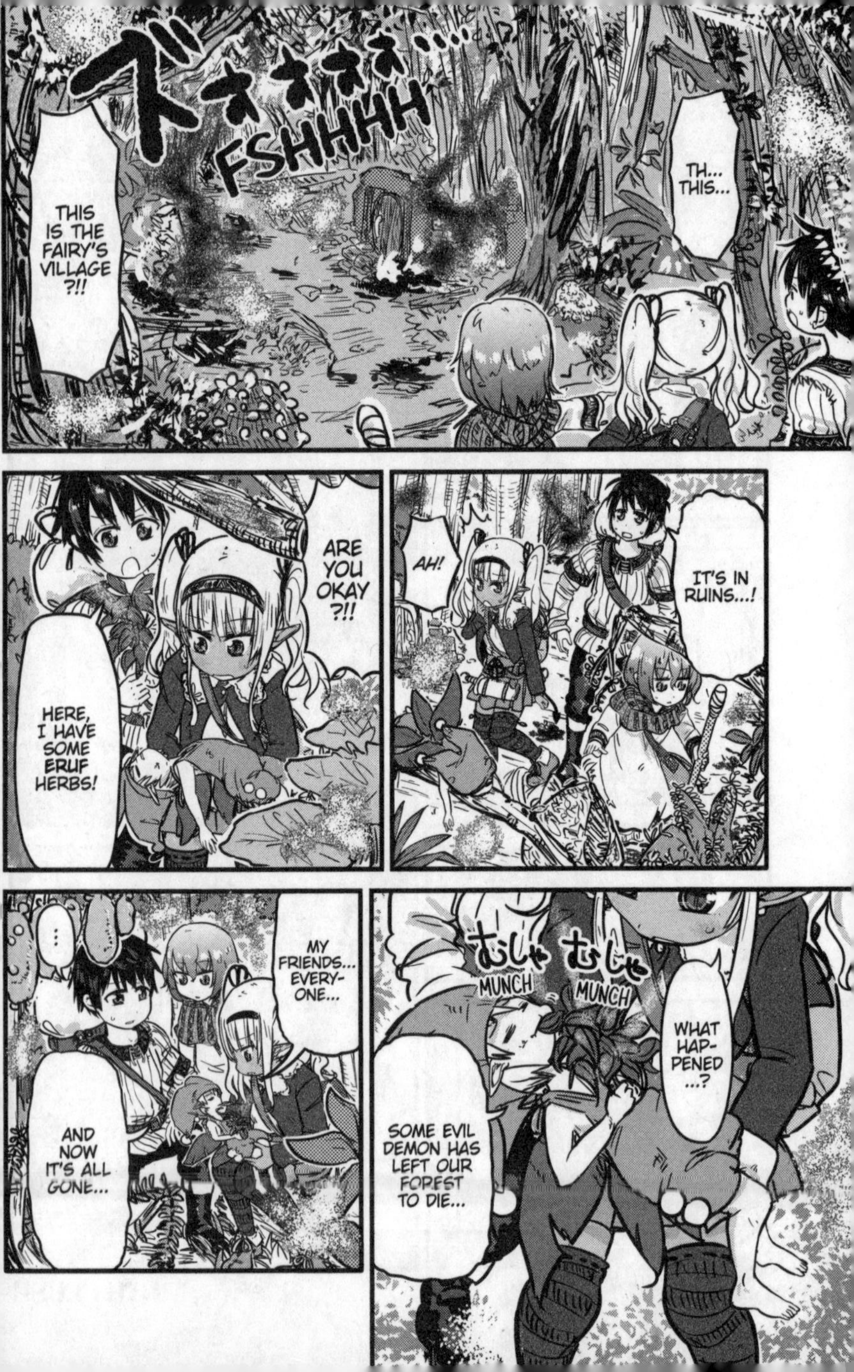
TH... THIS...
ズォォォォ...
FSHHHH
THIS IS THE FAIRY'S VILLAGE ?!!
IT'S IN RUINS...!
AH!
ARE YOU OKAY ?!!
HERE, I HAVE SOME ERUF HERBS!
むしゃ むしゃ
MUNCH MUNCH
WHAT HAP-PENED ...?
SOME EVIL DEMON HAS LEFT OUR FOREST TO DIE...
MY FRIENDS... EVERY-ONE...
...
AND NOW IT'S ALL GONE...

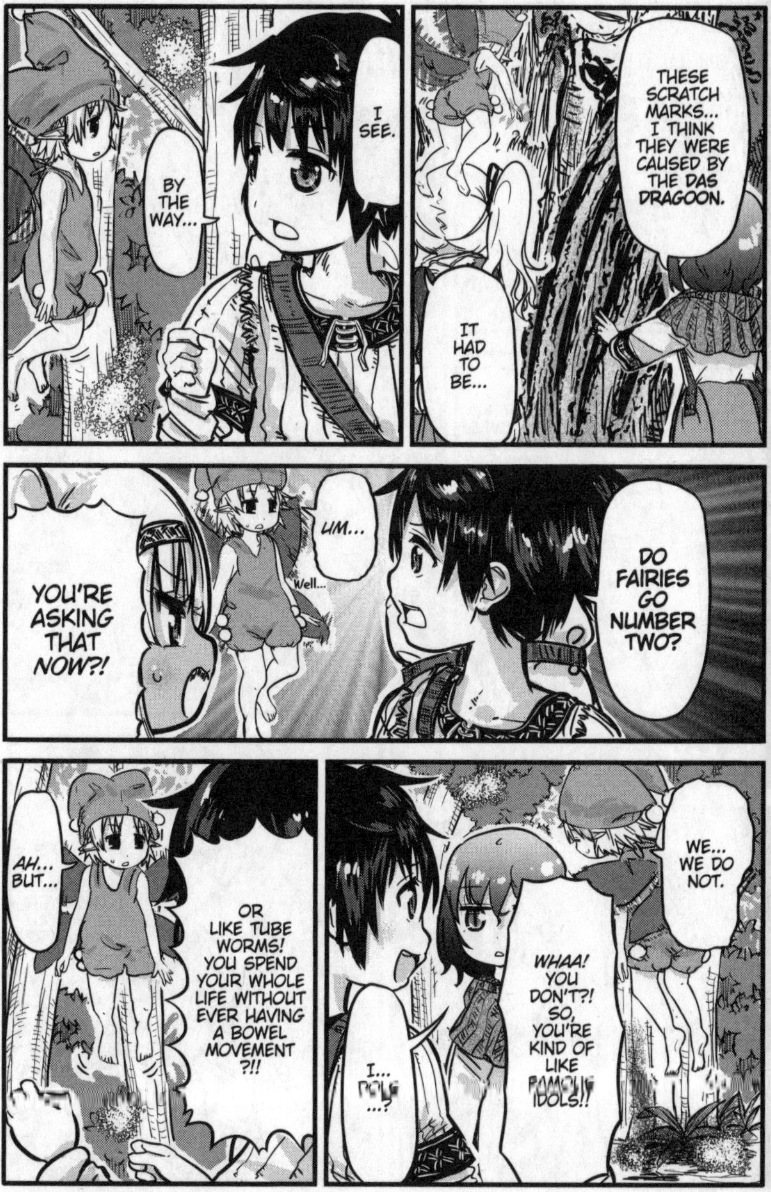
THESE SCRATCH MARKS... I THINK THEY WERE CAUSED BY THE DAS DRAGOON.
IT HAD TO BE...
I SEE.
BY THE WAY...
DO FAIRIES GO NUMBER TWO?
UM...
Well...
YOU'RE ASKING THAT NOW?!
WE... WE DO NOT.
WHAA! YOU DON'T?! SO, YOU'RE KIND OF LIKE IDOLS!!
I... ...?
AH... BUT...
OR LIKE TUBE WORMS! YOU SPEND YOUR WHOLE LIFE WITHOUT EVER HAVING A BOWEL MOVEMENT?!!

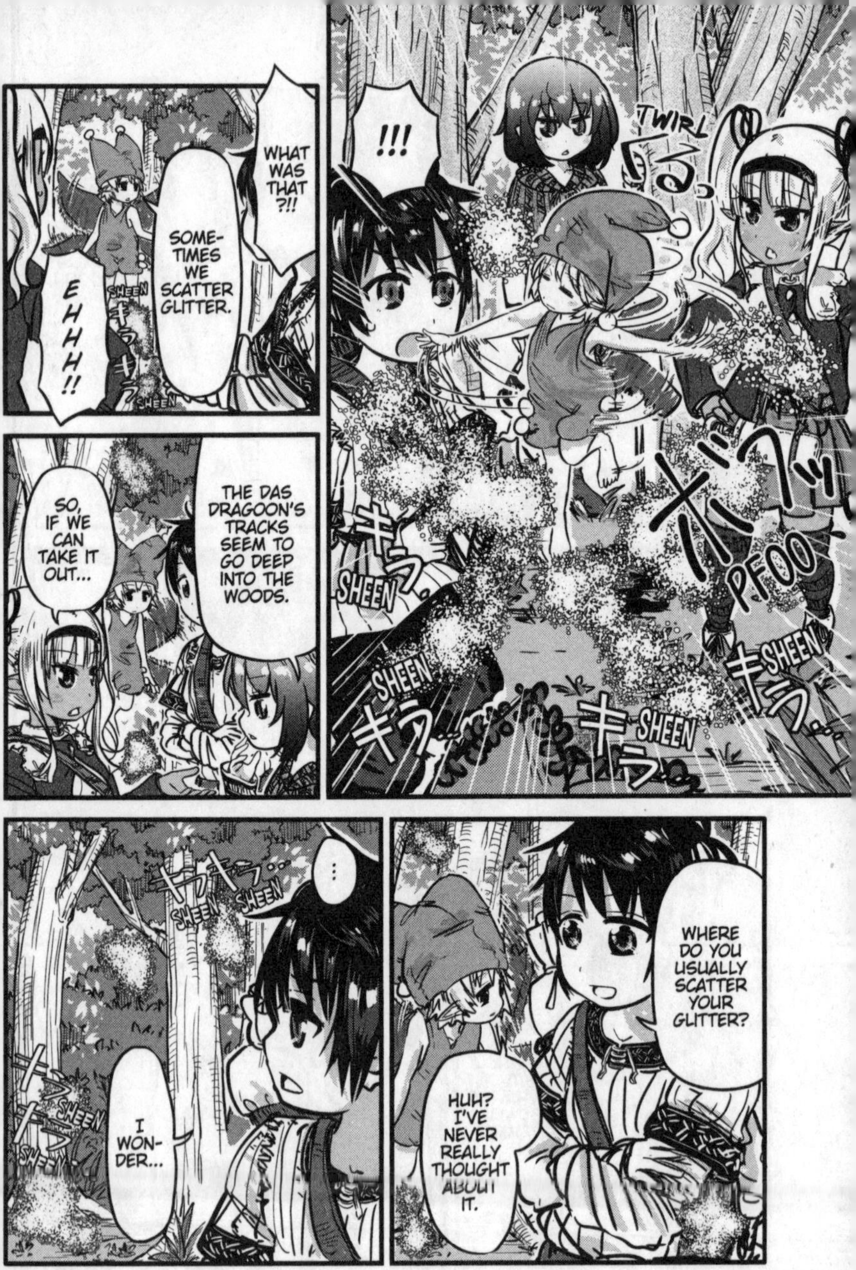
!!!
TWIRL
くるっ
PFOO
SHEEN
SHEEN
SHEEN
SHEEN
WHAT WAS THAT?!!
SOME-TIMES WE SCATTER GLITTER.
EHHHH!!
SHEEN
SHEEN
THE DAS DRAGOON'S TRACKS SEEM TO GO DEEP INTO THE WOODS.
SO, IF WE CAN TAKE IT OUT...
WHERE DO YOU USUALLY SCATTER YOUR GLITTER?
HUH? I'VE NEVER REALLY THOUGHT ABOUT IT.
...
SHEEN SHEEN
I WON-DER...
SHEEN

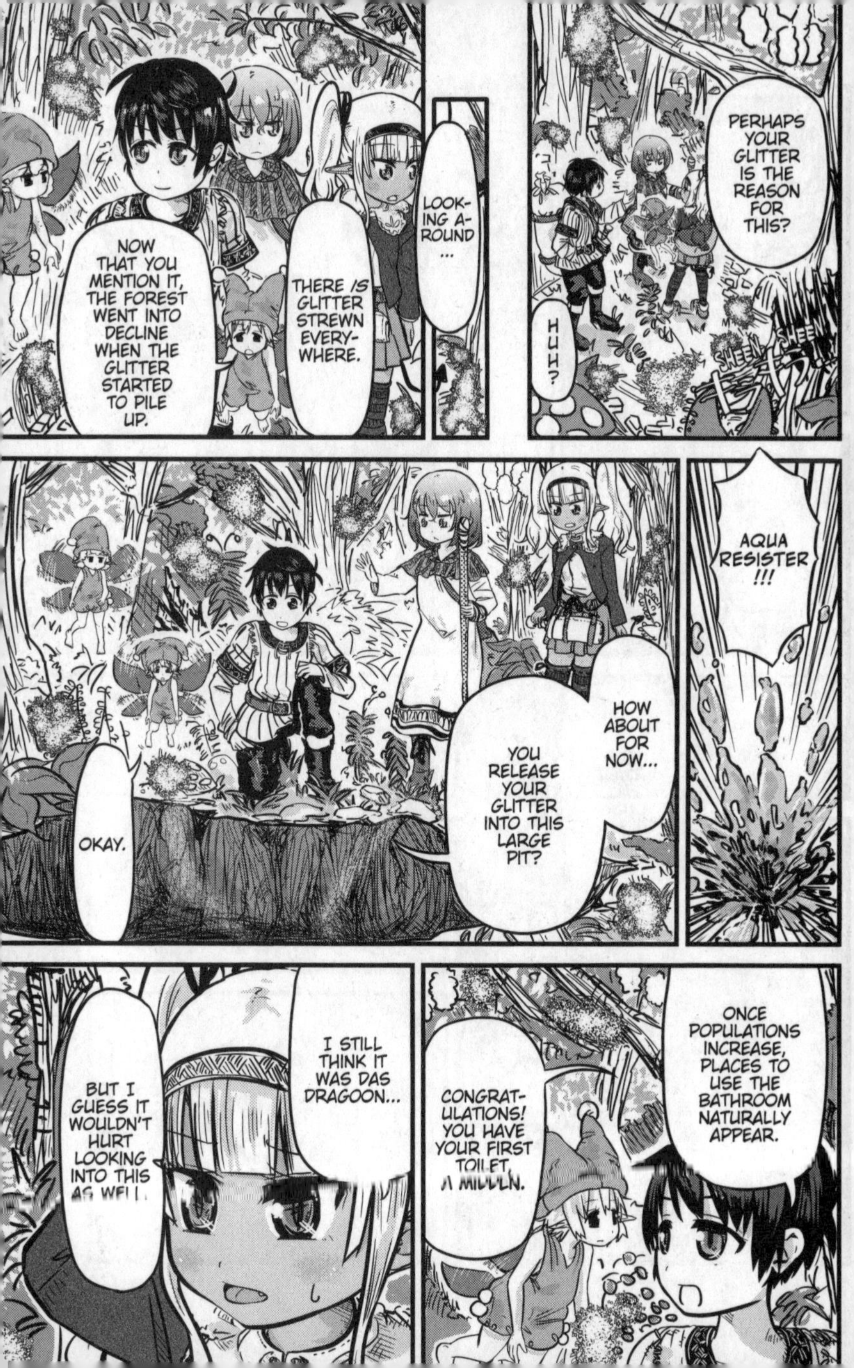
PERHAPS YOUR GLITTER IS THE REASON FOR THIS?
HUH?
SHEEN SHEEN
LOOKING AROUND...
THERE IS GLITTER STREWN EVERYWHERE.
NOW THAT YOU MENTION IT, THE FOREST WENT INTO DECLINE WHEN THE GLITTER STARTED TO PILE UP.
AQUA RESISTER!!!
HOW ABOUT FOR NOW...
YOU RELEASE YOUR GLITTER INTO THIS LARGE PIT?
OKAY.
ONCE POPULATIONS INCREASE, PLACES TO USE THE BATHROOM NATURALLY APPEAR.
CONGRATULATIONS! YOU HAVE YOUR FIRST TOILET, A MIDDEN.
I STILL THINK IT WAS DAS DRAGOON...
BUT I GUESS IT WOULDN'T HURT LOOKING INTO THIS AS WELL.

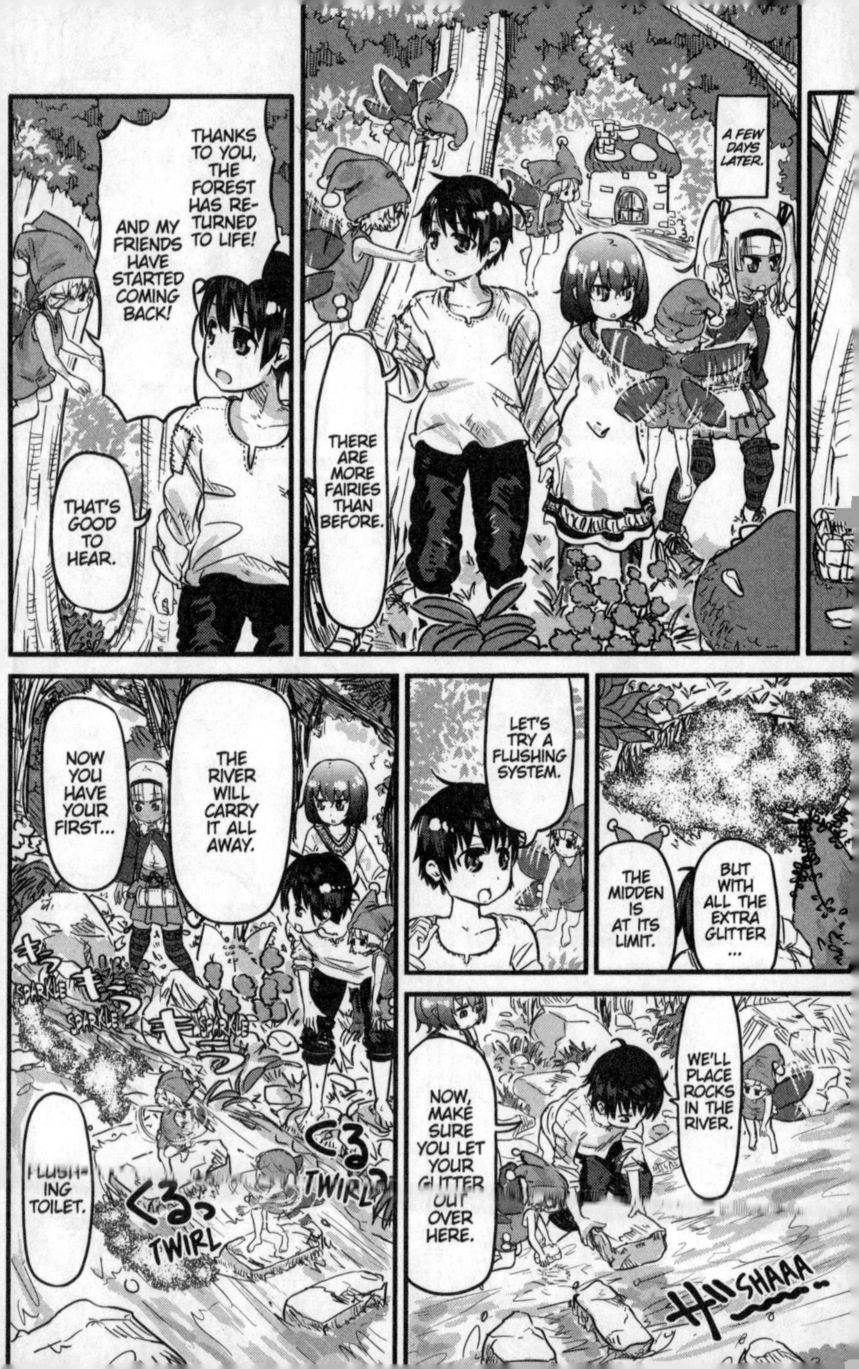
A FEW DAYS LATER.
THERE ARE MORE FAIRIES THAN BEFORE.
THANKS TO YOU, THE FOREST HAS RE-TURNED TO LIFE!
AND MY FRIENDS HAVE STARTED COMING BACK!
THAT'S GOOD TO HEAR.
BUT WITH ALL THE EXTRA GLITTER ...
THE MIDDEN IS AT ITS LIMIT.
LET'S TRY A FLUSHING SYSTEM.
WE'LL PLACE ROCKS IN THE RIVER.
NOW, MAKE SURE YOU LET YOUR GLITTER OUT OVER HERE.
SHAAA
THE RIVER WILL CARRY IT ALL AWAY.
NOW YOU HAVE YOUR FIRST...
FLUSH-ING TOILET.
SPARKLE
SPARKLE
SPARKLE
くる TWIRL
くるっ TWIRL

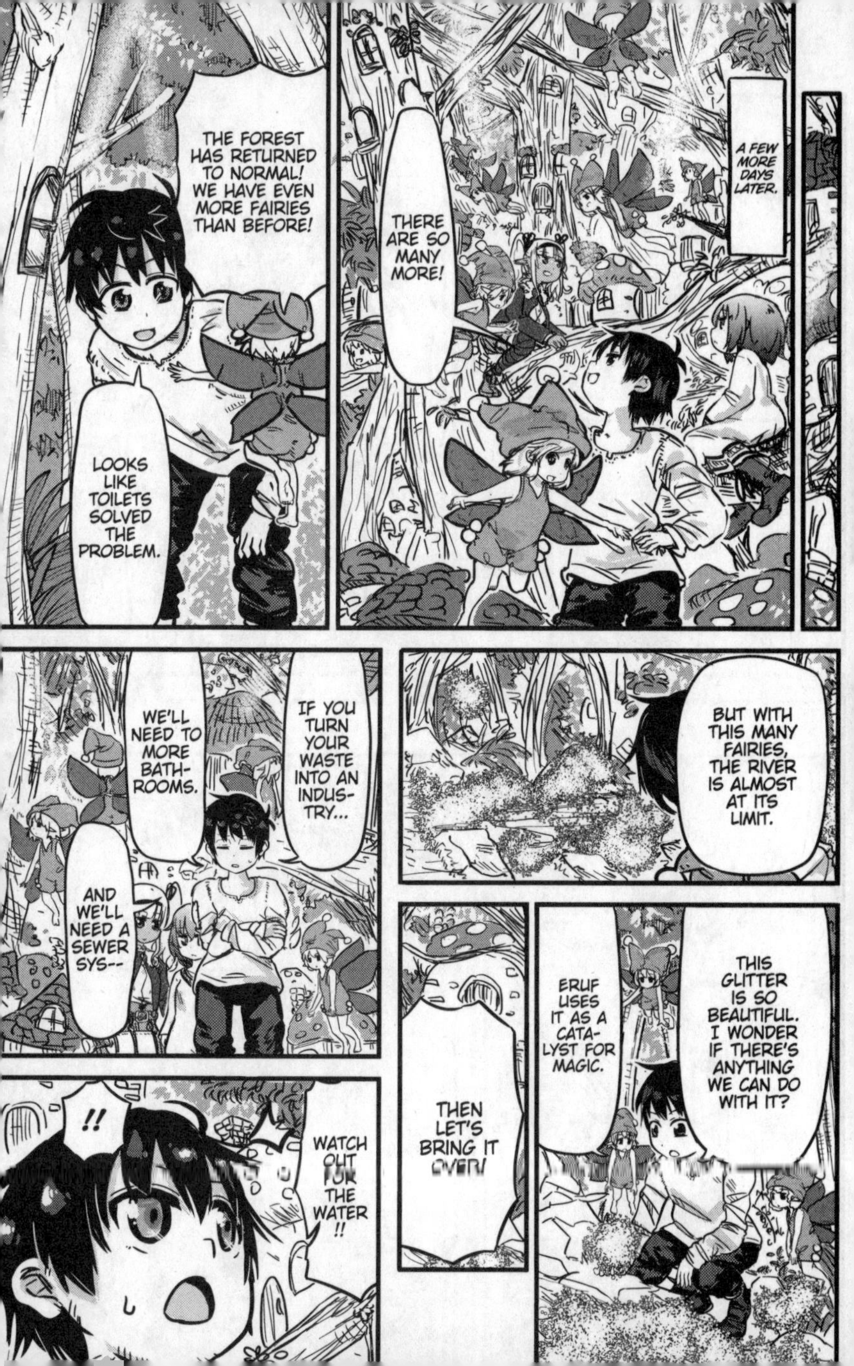
A FEW MORE DAYS LATER.
THERE ARE SO MANY MORE!
THE FOREST HAS RETURNED TO NORMAL! WE HAVE EVEN MORE FAIRIES THAN BEFORE!
LOOKS LIKE TOILETS SOLVED THE PROBLEM.
BUT WITH THIS MANY FAIRIES, THE RIVER IS ALMOST AT ITS LIMIT.
IF YOU TURN YOUR WASTE INTO AN INDUS-TRY...
WE'LL NEED TO MORE BATH-ROOMS.
AND WE'LL NEED A SEWER SYS--
THIS GLITTER IS SO BEAUTIFUL. I WONDER IF THERE'S ANYTHING WE CAN DO WITH IT?
ERUF USES IT AS A CATA-LYST FOR MAGIC.
THEN LET'S BRING IT OVER!
!!
WATCH OUT FOR THE WATER !!

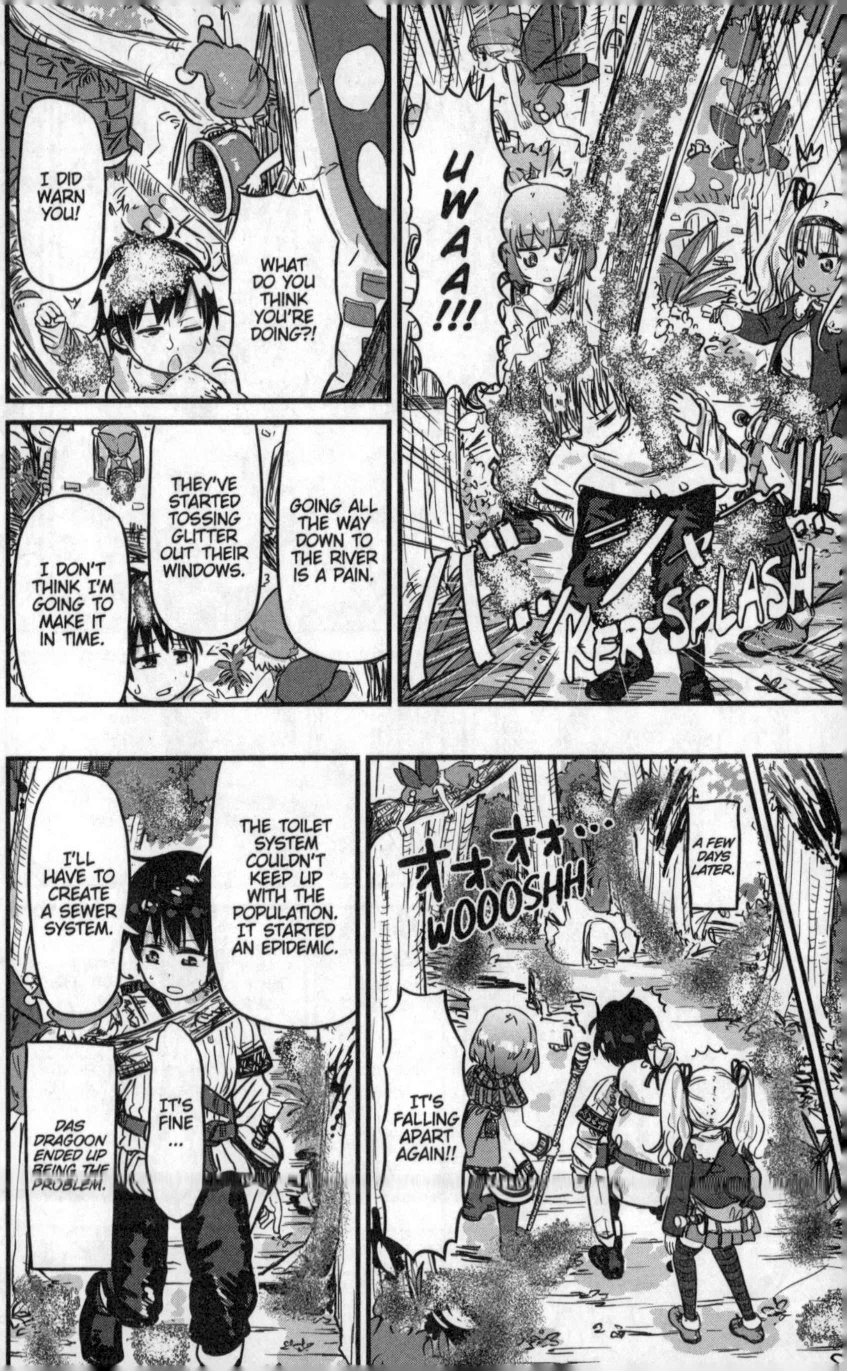
UWAAA!!!
KER-SPLASH
WHAT DO YOU THINK YOU'RE DOING?!
I DID WARN YOU!
GOING ALL THE WAY DOWN TO THE RIVER IS A PAIN.
THEY'VE STARTED TOSSING GLITTER OUT THEIR WINDOWS.
I DON'T THINK I'M GOING TO MAKE IT IN TIME.
A FEW DAYS LATER.
オォオ…
WOOOSHH
IT'S FALLING APART AGAIN!!
THE TOILET SYSTEM COULDN'T KEEP UP WITH THE POPULATION. IT STARTED AN EPIDEMIC.
I'LL HAVE TO CREATE A SEWER SYSTEM.
IT'S FINE…
DAS DRAGOON ENDED UP BEING THE PROBLEM.

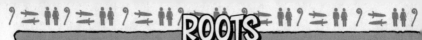

ROOTS

PEOPLE WHO DON'T VALUE TOILET TIME ARE NO GOOD.

FIFTH

TOILET TIME

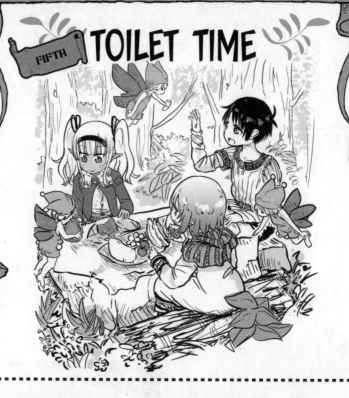

If we aim to dissect the history of humankind, we cannot do so without discussing the history of toilets. As populations increase, so does the need to manufacture and maintain an increasing number of toilets. It could even be said that humankind developed toilets in order to develop urban culture.

Let's talk about ancient times. When people came together in small settlements, they did their business without much concern for others. As populations grew, designated bathroom areas, such as riverbeds, became essential for both communal and sanitary reasons.

These could be called the first toilets, but the surprising truth is that during this time, Ancient Rome had already developed a system of sewers that used running water.

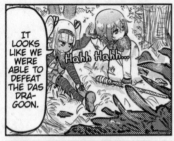

But in the Middle Ages, this technology was lost, and we returned to relieving ourselves in places like roads, which led to a rise in diseases as populations grew denser.

Even in Heiankyo (ancient Kyoto), we know from the Gakizoshi scroll that there was a designated area for people to take care of their business. As cities begin to develop, so did bathrooms. In medieval Europe, the French town of Troyes had Bois Street, which was outfitted not only with seated toilets, but also bedpans. When throwing their excrement out windows they would yell, "Gardez l'eau!" which means "Watch out for the water!" To protect themselves, the people below would wear silk hats, coats, and high heels.

This is how urban centers birthed toilets, and how those toilets in turn influenced the development of urban centers.

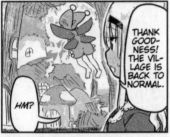

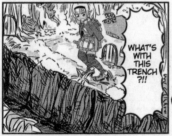

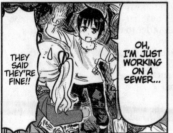

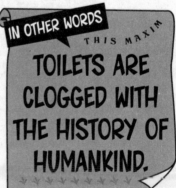

IN OTHER WORDS

THIS MAXIM

TOILETS ARE CLOGGED WITH THE HISTORY OF HUMANKIND.

Hahh Hahh...
IT LOOKS LIKE WE WERE ABLE TO DEFEAT THE DAS DRAGOON.
THANK GOODNESS! THE VILLAGE IS BACK TO NORMAL.
HM?
WHAT'S WITH THIS TRENCH?!!
OH, I'M JUST WORKING ON A SEWER...
THEY SAID THEY'RE FINE!!

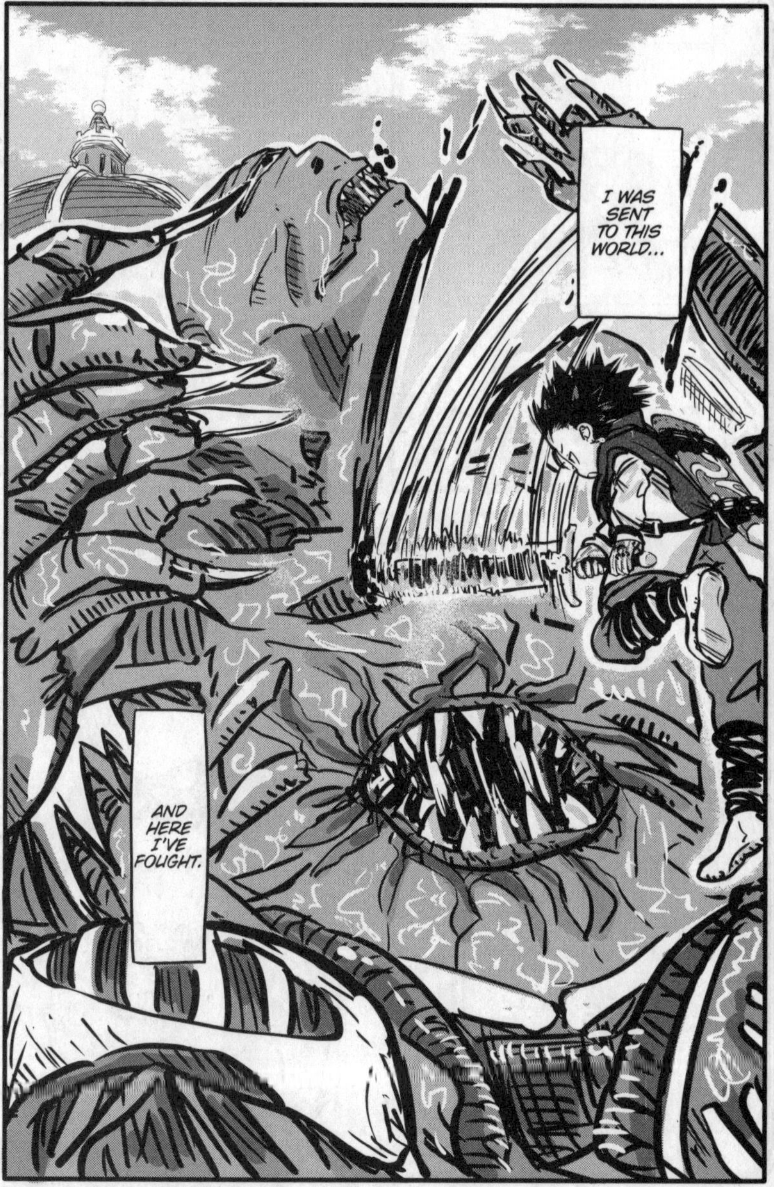
I WAS SENT TO THIS WORLD...
AND HERE I'VE FOUGHT.

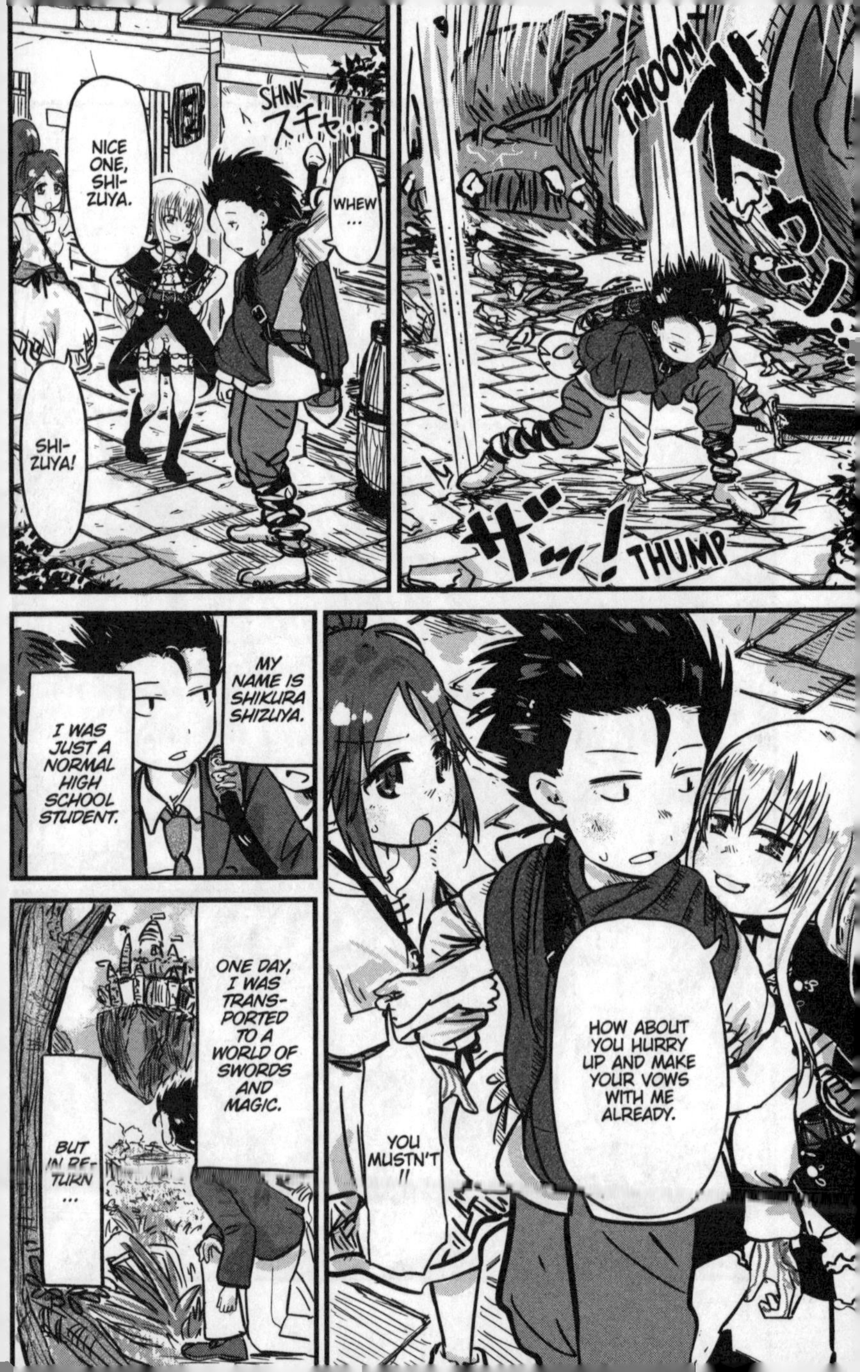
FWOOM
ザッ!
THUMP
SHNK
スチャ…
WHEW…
NICE ONE, SHI-ZUYA.
SHI-ZUYA!
HOW ABOUT YOU HURRY UP AND MAKE YOUR VOWS WITH ME ALREADY.
YOU MUSTN'T!!
MY NAME IS SHIKURA SHIZUYA.
I WAS JUST A NORMAL HIGH SCHOOL STUDENT.
ONE DAY, I WAS TRANS-PORTED TO A WORLD OF SWORDS AND MAGIC.
BUT IN RE-TURN…

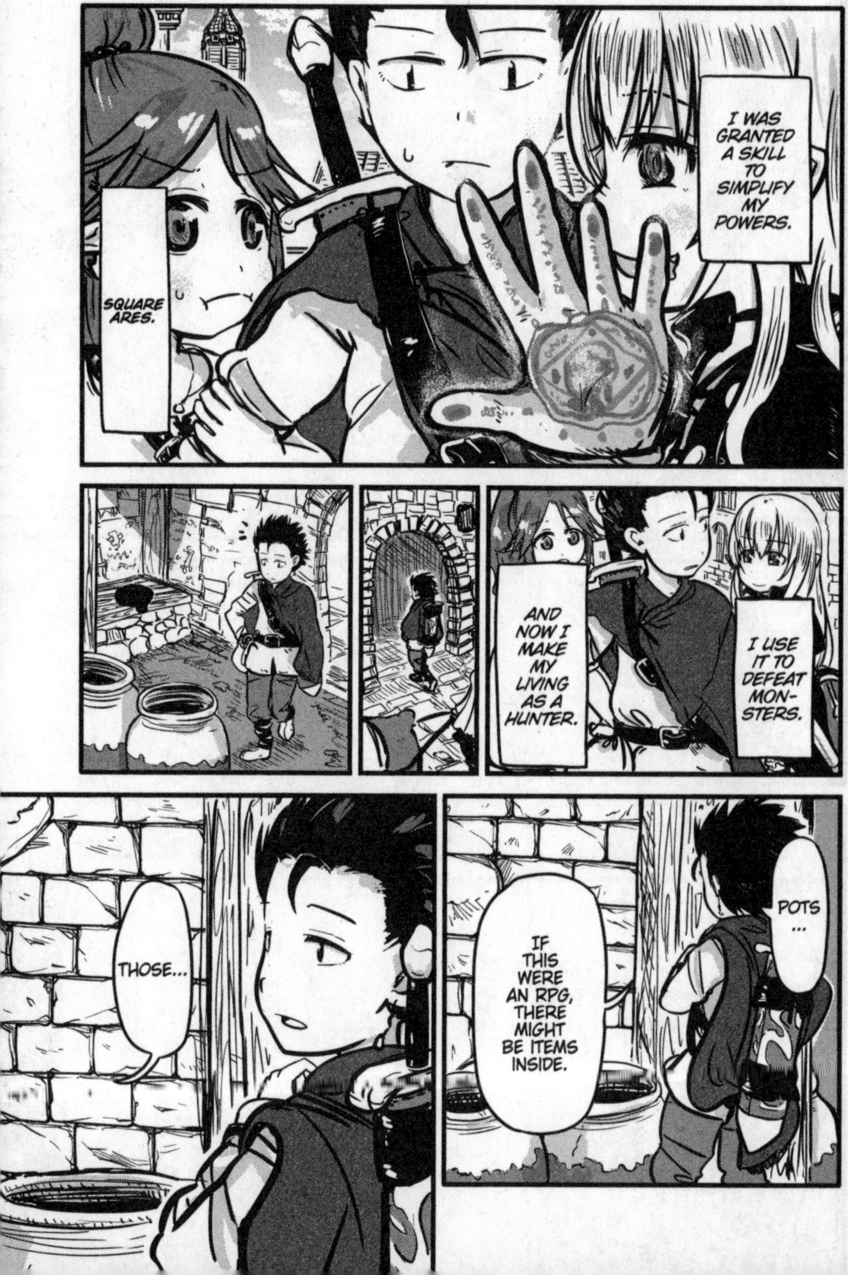
I WAS GRANTED A SKILL TO SIMPLIFY MY POWERS.
SQUARE ARES.
I USE IT TO DEFEAT MON-STERS.
AND NOW I MAKE MY LIVING AS A HUNTER.
POTS...
IF THIS WERE AN RPG, THERE MIGHT BE ITEMS INSIDE.
THOSE...

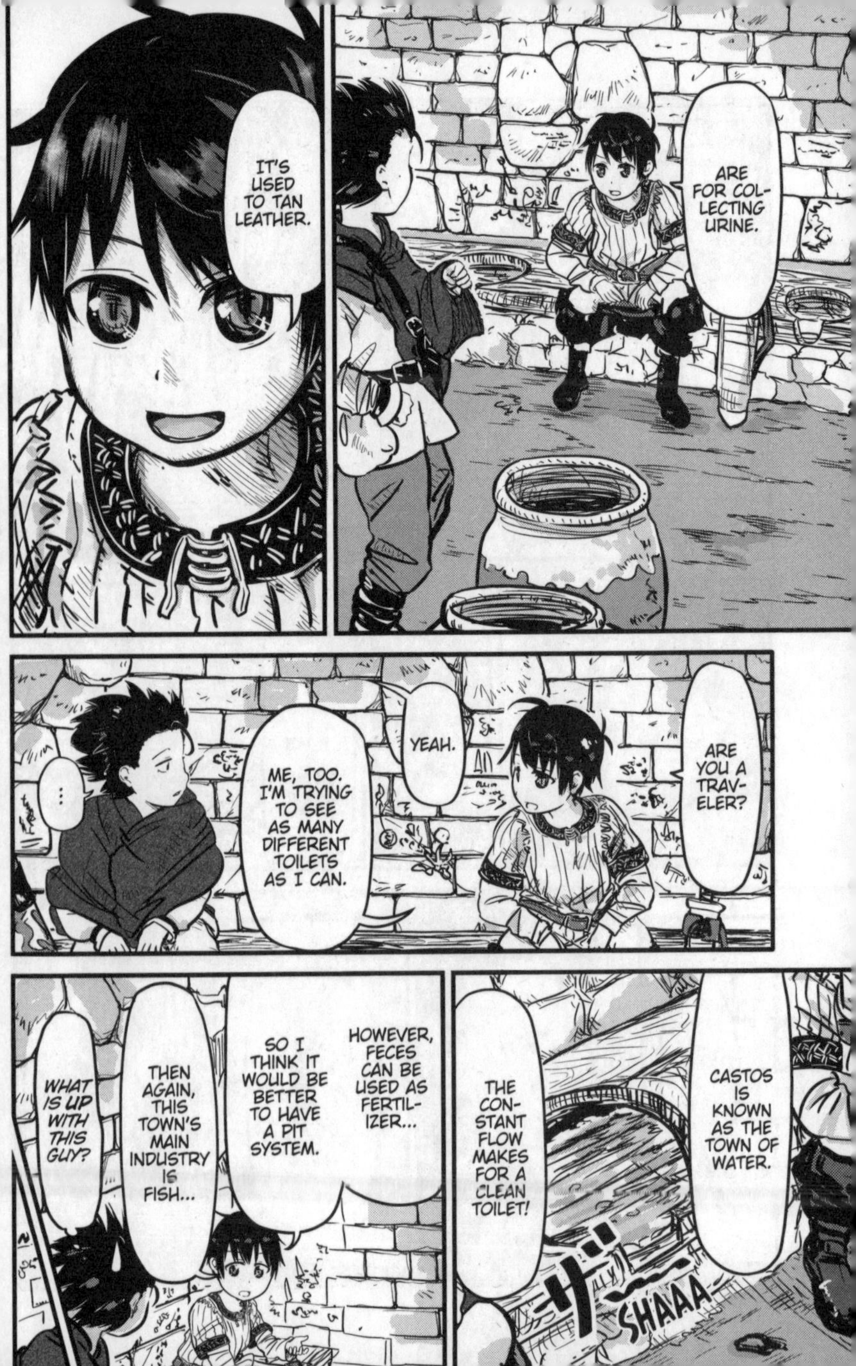
ARE FOR COLLECTING URINE.
IT'S USED TO TAN LEATHER.
ARE YOU A TRAVELER?
YEAH.
ME, TOO. I'M TRYING TO SEE AS MANY DIFFERENT TOILETS AS I CAN.
...
CASTOS IS KNOWN AS THE TOWN OF WATER.
THE CONSTANT FLOW MAKES FOR A CLEAN TOILET!
SHAAA
HOWEVER, FECES CAN BE USED AS FERTILIZER...
SO I THINK IT WOULD BE BETTER TO HAVE A PIT SYSTEM.
THEN AGAIN, THIS TOWN'S MAIN INDUSTRY IS FISH...
WHAT IS UP WITH THIS GUY?

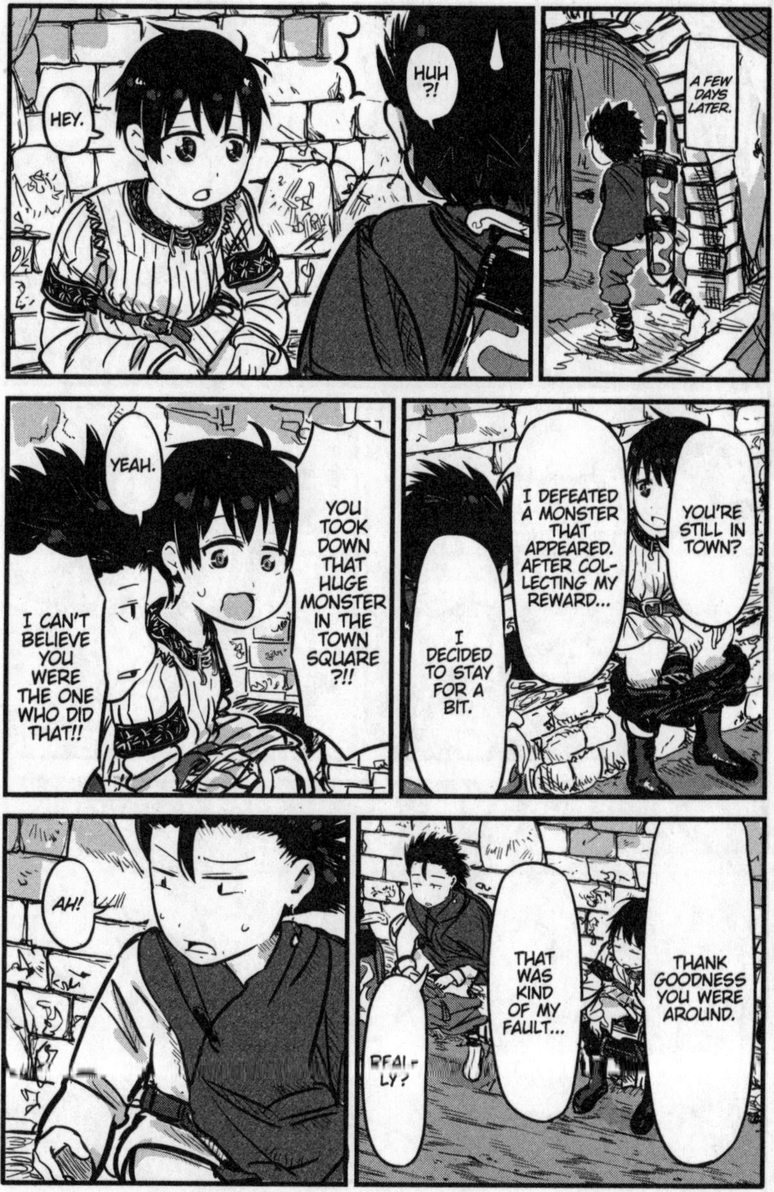
A FEW DAYS LATER.
HUH ?!
HEY.
YOU'RE STILL IN TOWN?
I DEFEATED A MONSTER THAT APPEARED. AFTER COL-LECTING MY REWARD...
I DECIDED TO STAY FOR A BIT.
YOU TOOK DOWN THAT HUGE MONSTER IN THE TOWN SQUARE ?!!
YEAH.
I CAN'T BELIEVE YOU WERE THE ONE WHO DID THAT!!
THANK GOODNESS YOU WERE AROUND.
THAT WAS KIND OF MY FAULT...
REAL-LY?
AH!

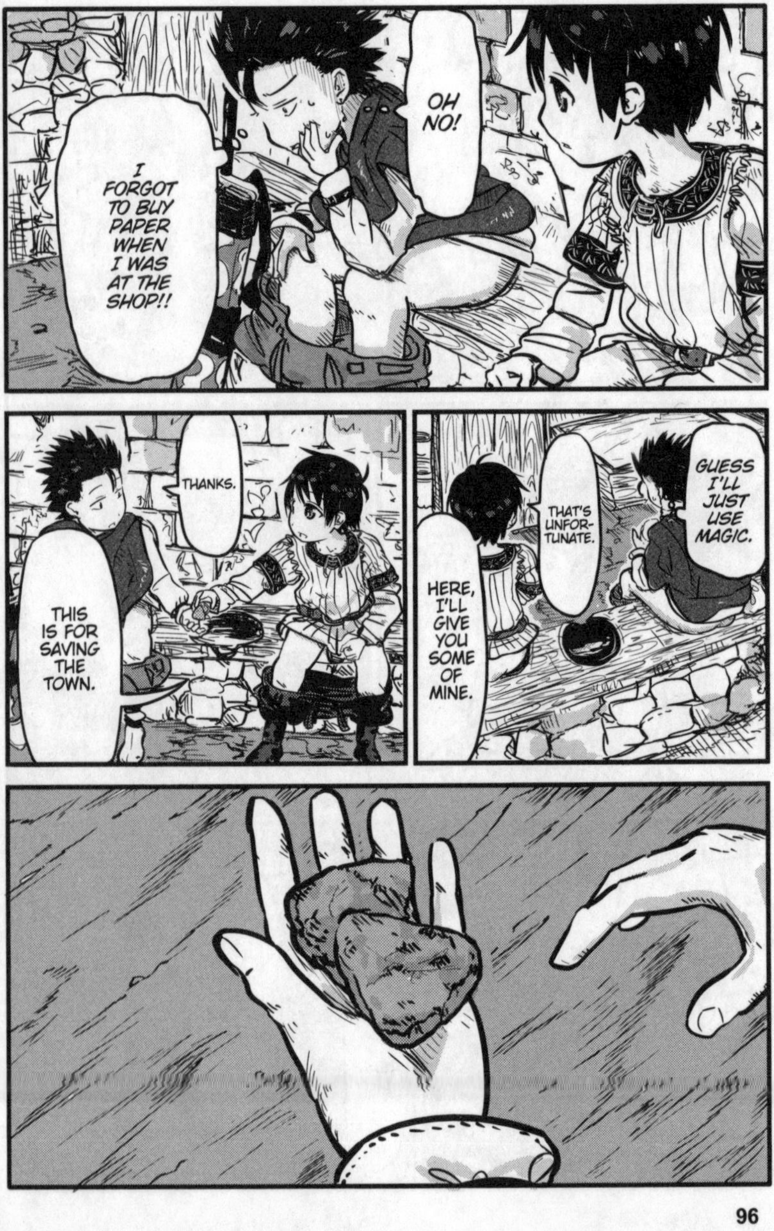
OH NO!
I FORGOT TO BUY PAPER WHEN I WAS AT THE SHOP!!
GUESS I'LL JUST USE MAGIC.
THAT'S UNFORTUNATE.
HERE, I'LL GIVE YOU SOME OF MINE.
THANKS.
THIS IS FOR SAVING THE TOWN.

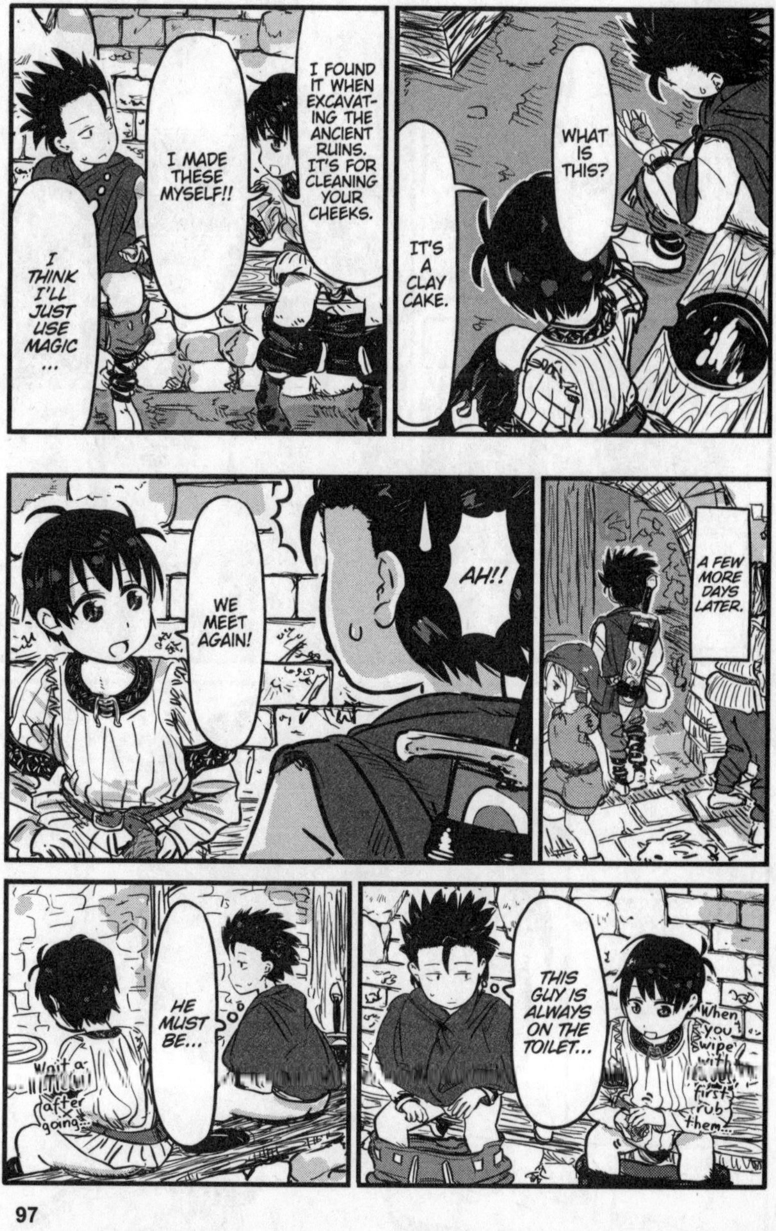
WHAT IS THIS?
IT'S A CLAY CAKE.
I FOUND IT WHEN EXCAVATING THE ANCIENT RUINS. IT'S FOR CLEANING YOUR CHEEKS.
I MADE THESE MYSELF!!
I THINK I'LL JUST USE MAGIC...
A FEW MORE DAYS LATER.
AH!!
WE MEET AGAIN!
When you swipe with first rub them...
THIS GUY IS ALWAYS ON THE TOILET...
HE MUST BE...
Wait a after going...

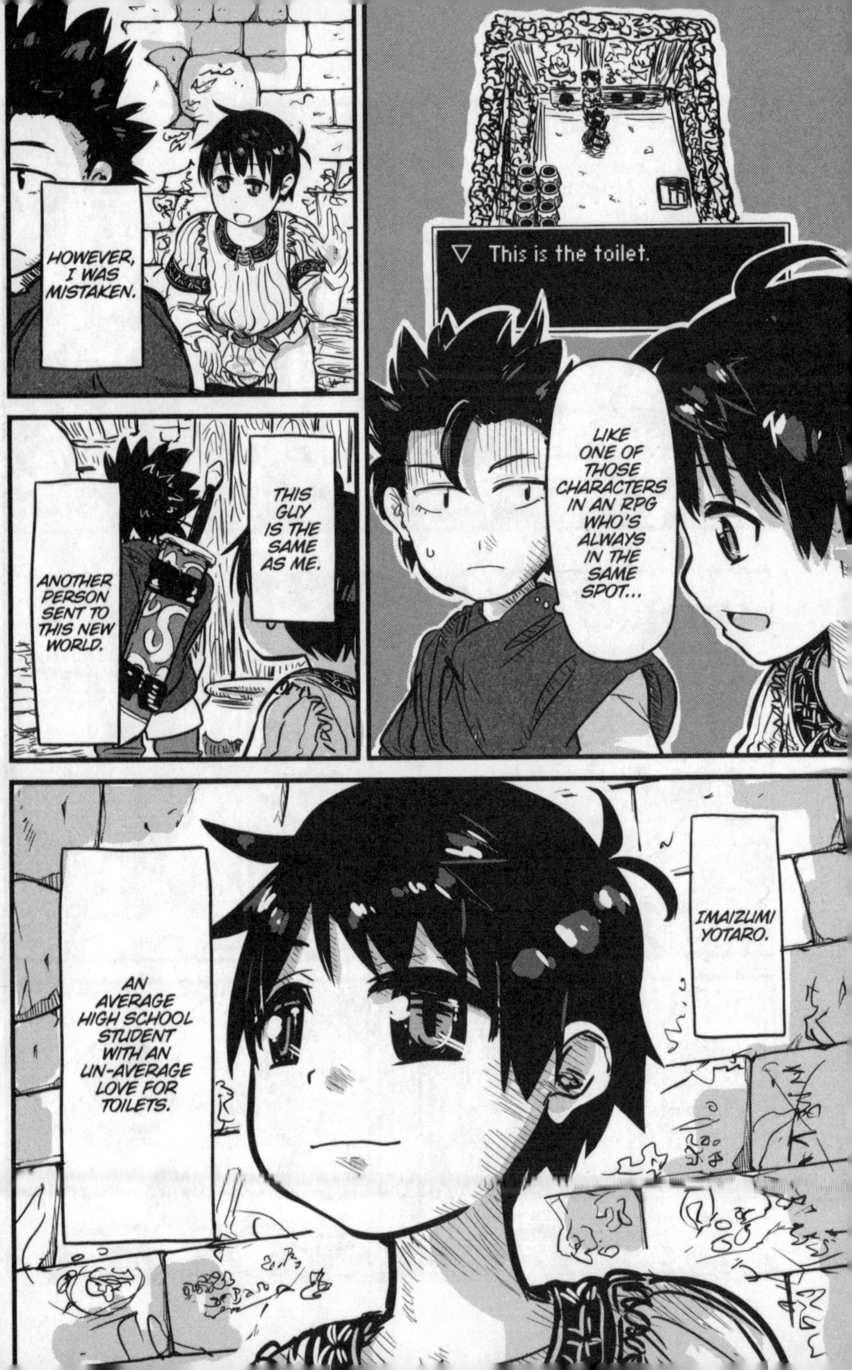
▽ This is the toilet.
LIKE ONE OF THOSE CHARACTERS IN AN RPG WHO'S ALWAYS IN THE SAME SPOT...
HOWEVER, I WAS MISTAKEN.
THIS GUY IS THE SAME AS ME.
ANOTHER PERSON SENT TO THIS NEW WORLD.
IMAIZUMI YOTARO.
AN AVERAGE HIGH SCHOOL STUDENT WITH AN UN-AVERAGE LOVE FOR TOILETS.

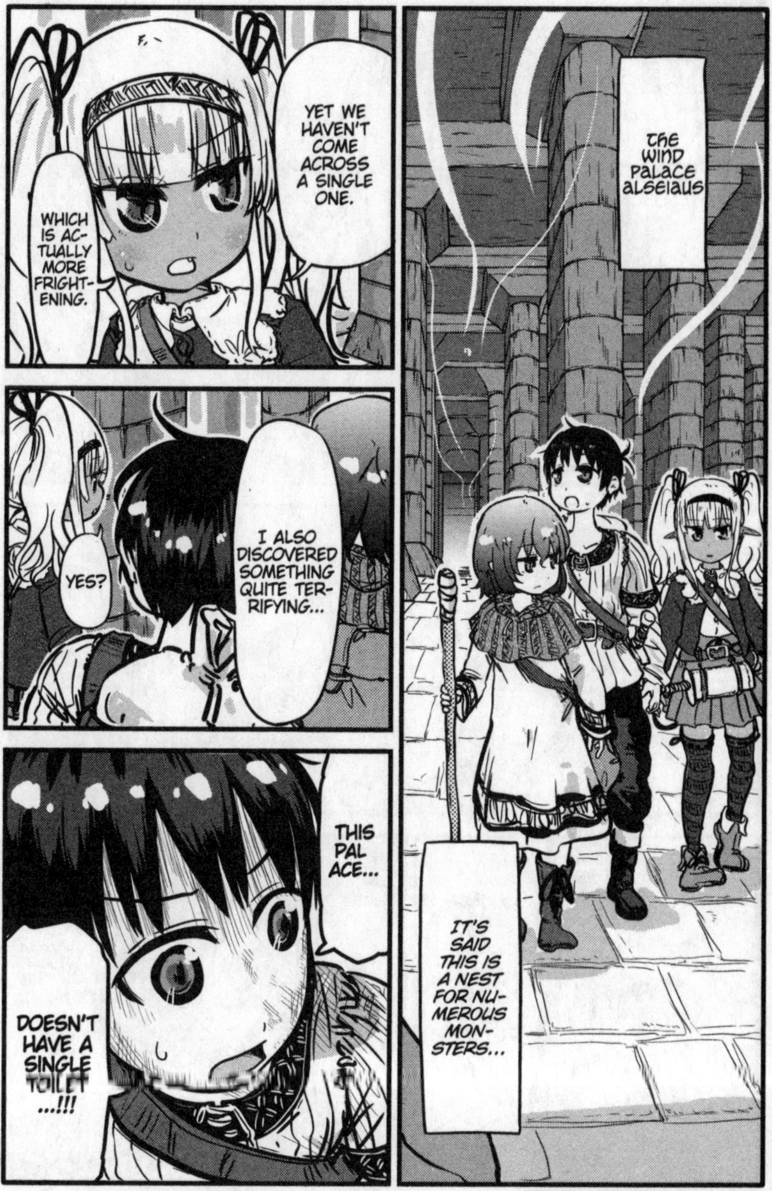
THE WIND PALACE ALSEIAUS
IT'S SAID THIS IS A NEST FOR NUMEROUS MONSTERS...
YET WE HAVEN'T COME ACROSS A SINGLE ONE.
WHICH IS ACTUALLY MORE FRIGHTENING.
I ALSO DISCOVERED SOMETHING QUITE TERRIFYING...
YES?
THIS PALACE...
DOESN'T HAVE A SINGLE TOILET ...!!!

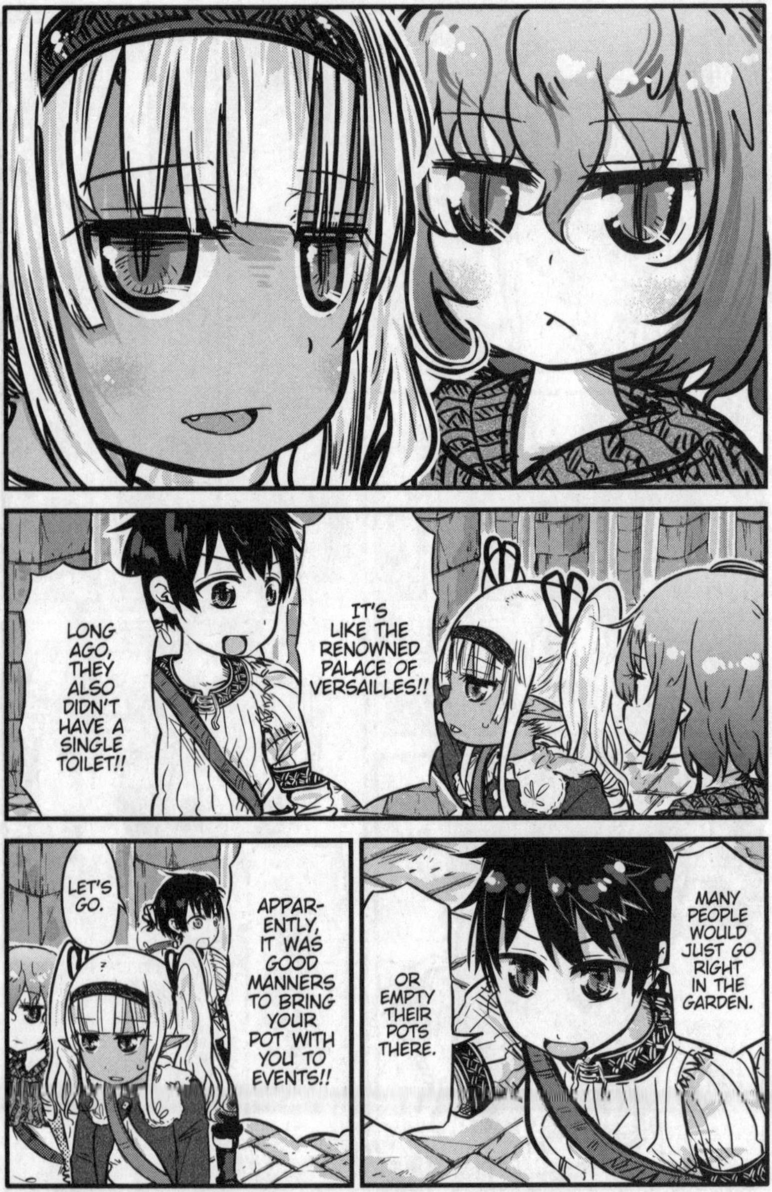
IT'S LIKE THE RENOWNED PALACE OF VERSAILLES!!
LONG AGO, THEY ALSO DIDN'T HAVE A SINGLE TOILET!!
MANY PEOPLE WOULD JUST GO RIGHT IN THE GARDEN.
OR EMPTY THEIR POTS THERE.
APPARENTLY, IT WAS GOOD MANNERS TO BRING YOUR POT WITH YOU TO EVENTS!!
LET'S GO.

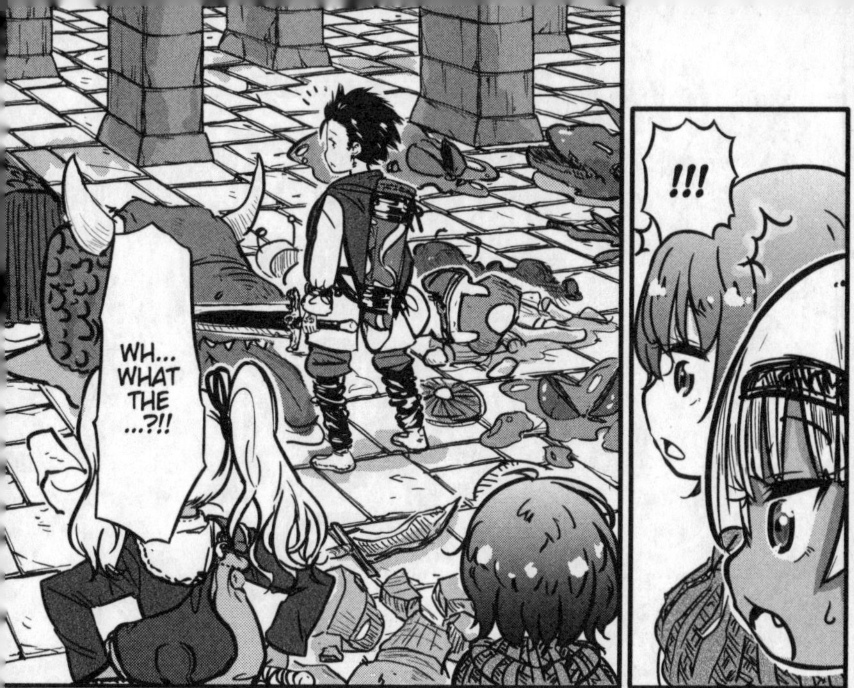
!!!
WH... WHAT THE ...?!!

*Non-player character.

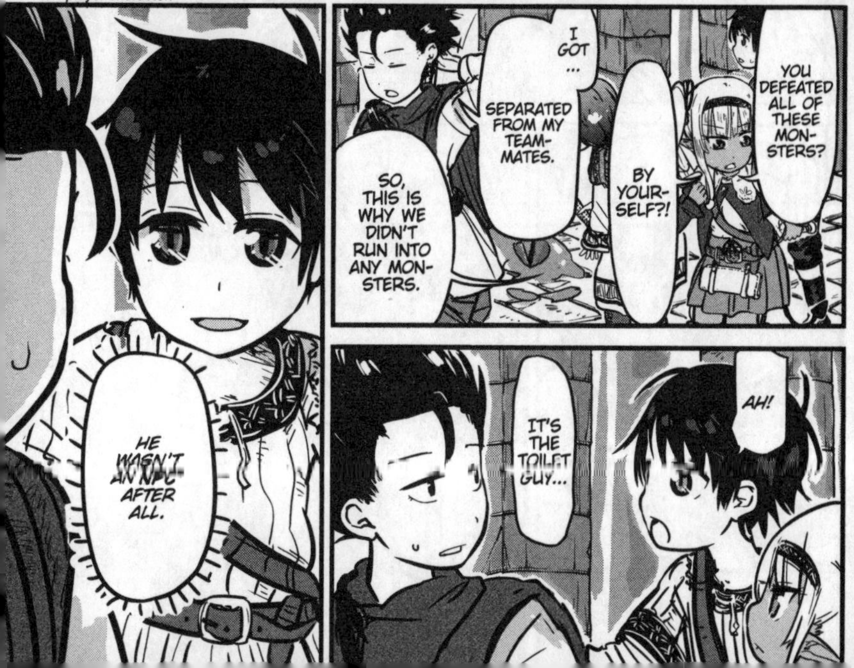
YOU DEFEATED ALL OF THESE MON- STERS?
BY YOUR- SELF?!
I GOT ...
SEPARATED FROM MY TEAM- MATES.
SO, THIS IS WHY WE DIDN'T RUN INTO ANY MON- STERS.
AH!
IT'S THE TOILET GUY...
HE WASN'T AN NPC AFTER ALL.

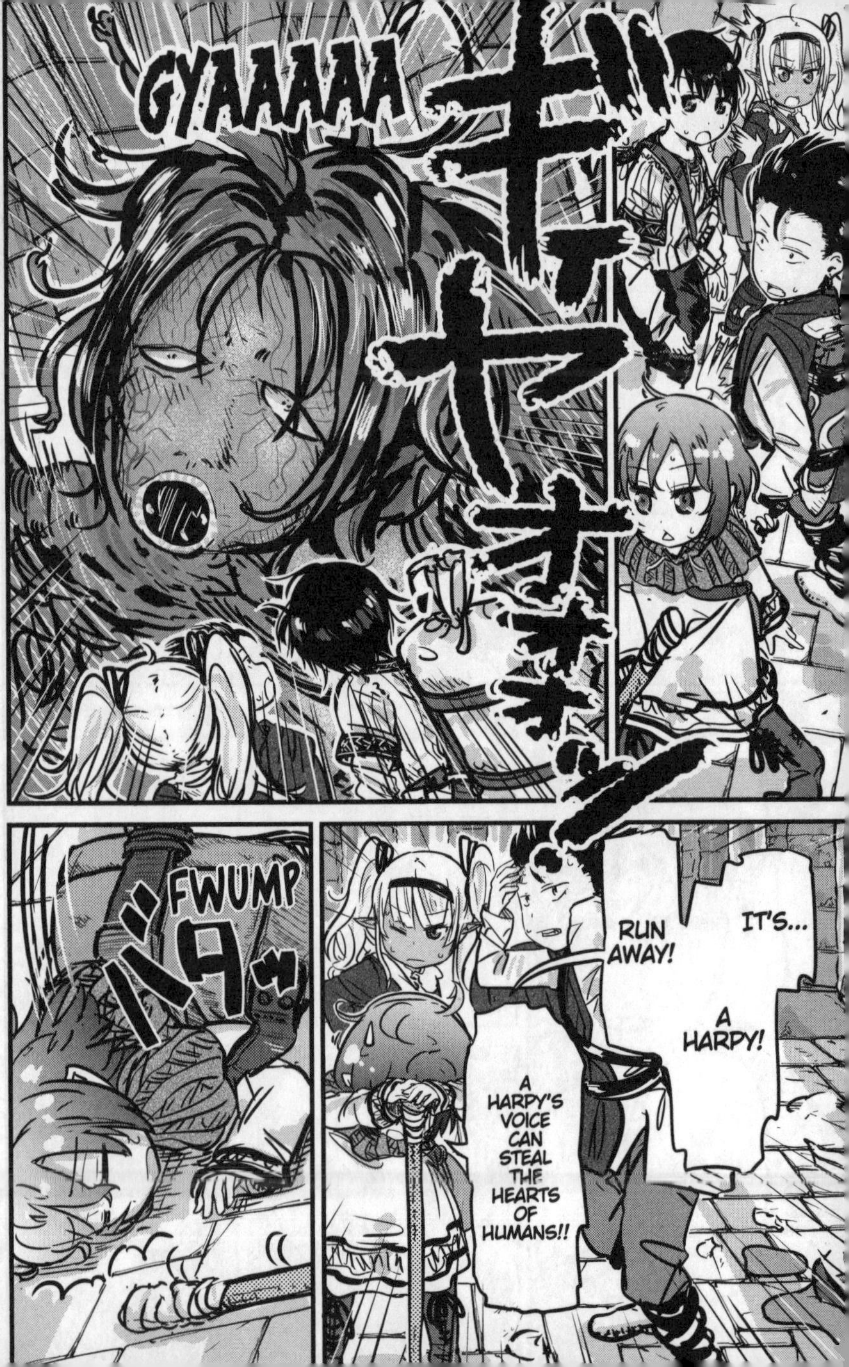
GYAAAAA
IT'S...
A HARPY!
RUN AWAY!
A HARPY'S VOICE CAN STEAL THE HEARTS OF HUMANS!!
FWUMP

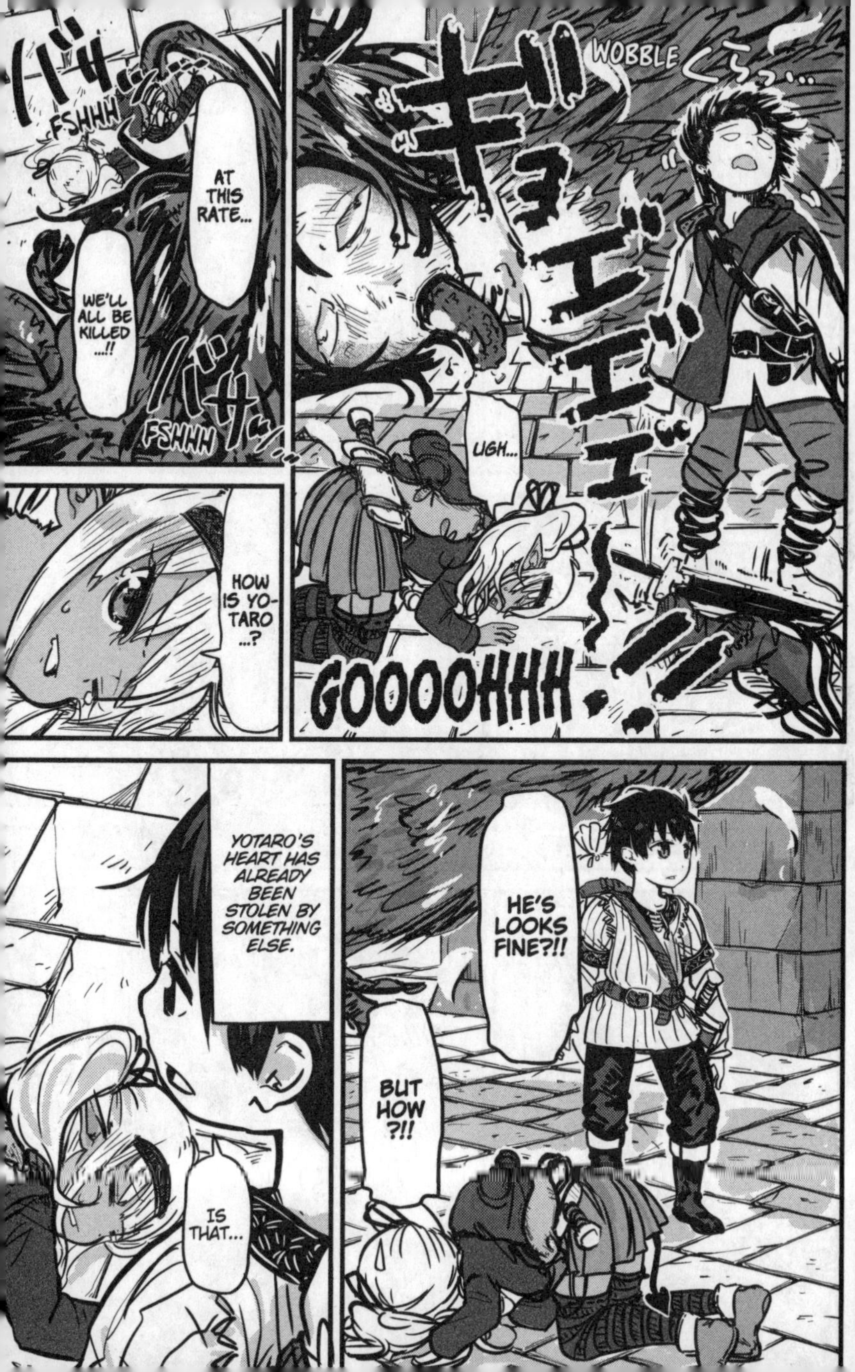
WOBBLE
くらっ…
ギョエエエ
UGH...
GOOOOHHH
バサッ
FSHHH
AT THIS RATE...
WE'LL ALL BE KILLED ...!!
バサッ
FSHHH
HOW IS YO-TARO ...?
HE'S LOOKS FINE?!!
BUT HOW ?!!
YOTARO'S HEART HAS ALREADY BEEN STOLEN BY SOMETHING ELSE.
IS THAT...

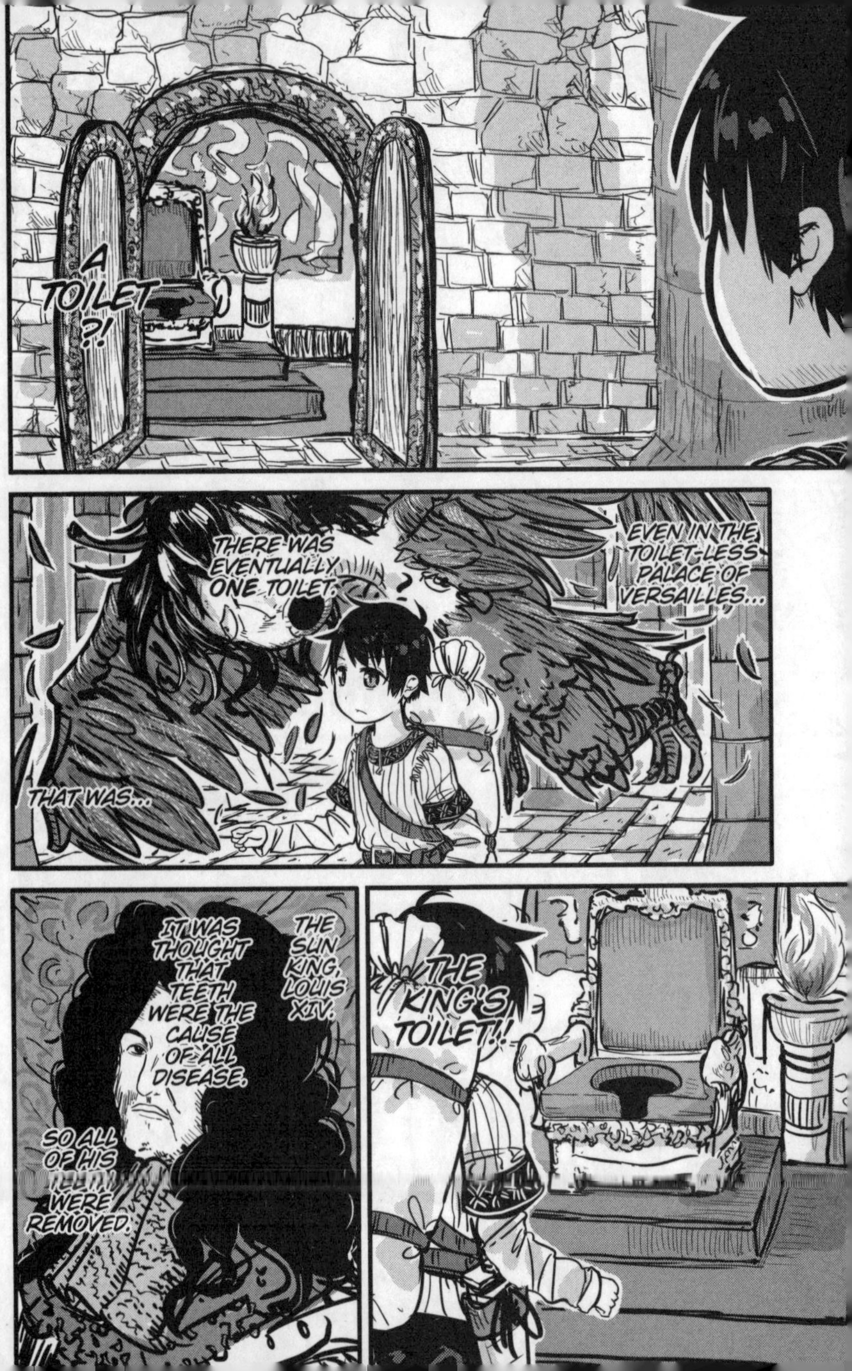
A TOILET?!
EVEN IN THE TOILET-LESS PALACE OF VERSAILLES...
THERE WAS EVENTUALLY ONE TOILET.
THAT WAS...
THE KING'S TOILET!!
THE SUN KING, LOUIS XIV.
IT WAS THOUGHT THAT TEETH WERE THE CAUSE OF ALL DISEASE.
SO ALL OF HIS
WERE REMOVED.

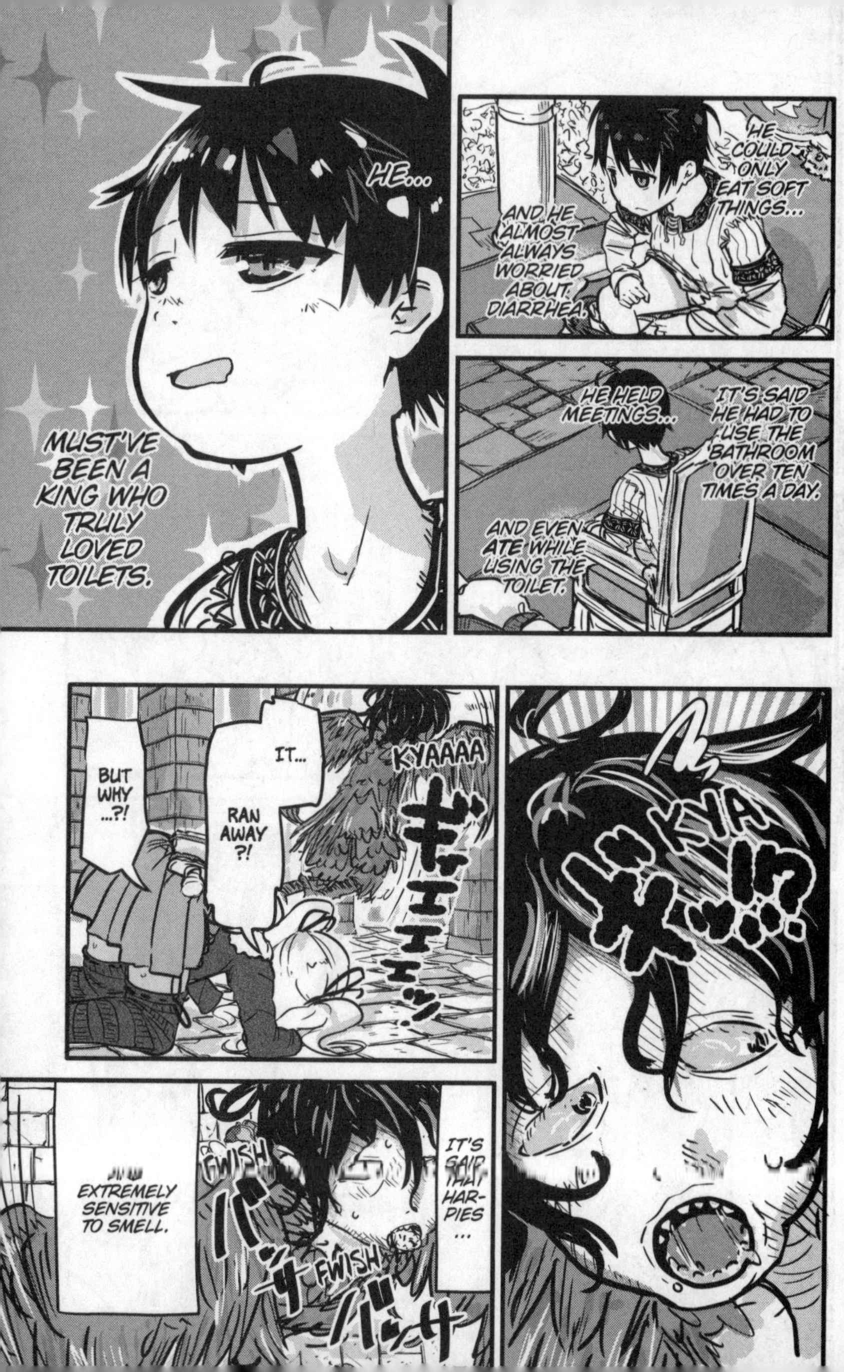
HE COULD ONLY EAT SOFT THINGS...
AND HE ALMOST ALWAYS WORRIED ABOUT DIARRHEA.
IT'S SAID HE HAD TO USE THE BATHROOM OVER TEN TIMES A DAY.
HE HELD MEETINGS...
AND EVEN ATE WHILE USING THE TOILET.
HE...
MUST'VE BEEN A KING WHO TRULY LOVED TOILETS.
KYA
KYAAAA
IT...
RAN AWAY?!
BUT WHY...?!
IT'S SAID THAT HARPIES...
EXTREMELY SENSITIVE TO SMELL.
FWISH
FWISH

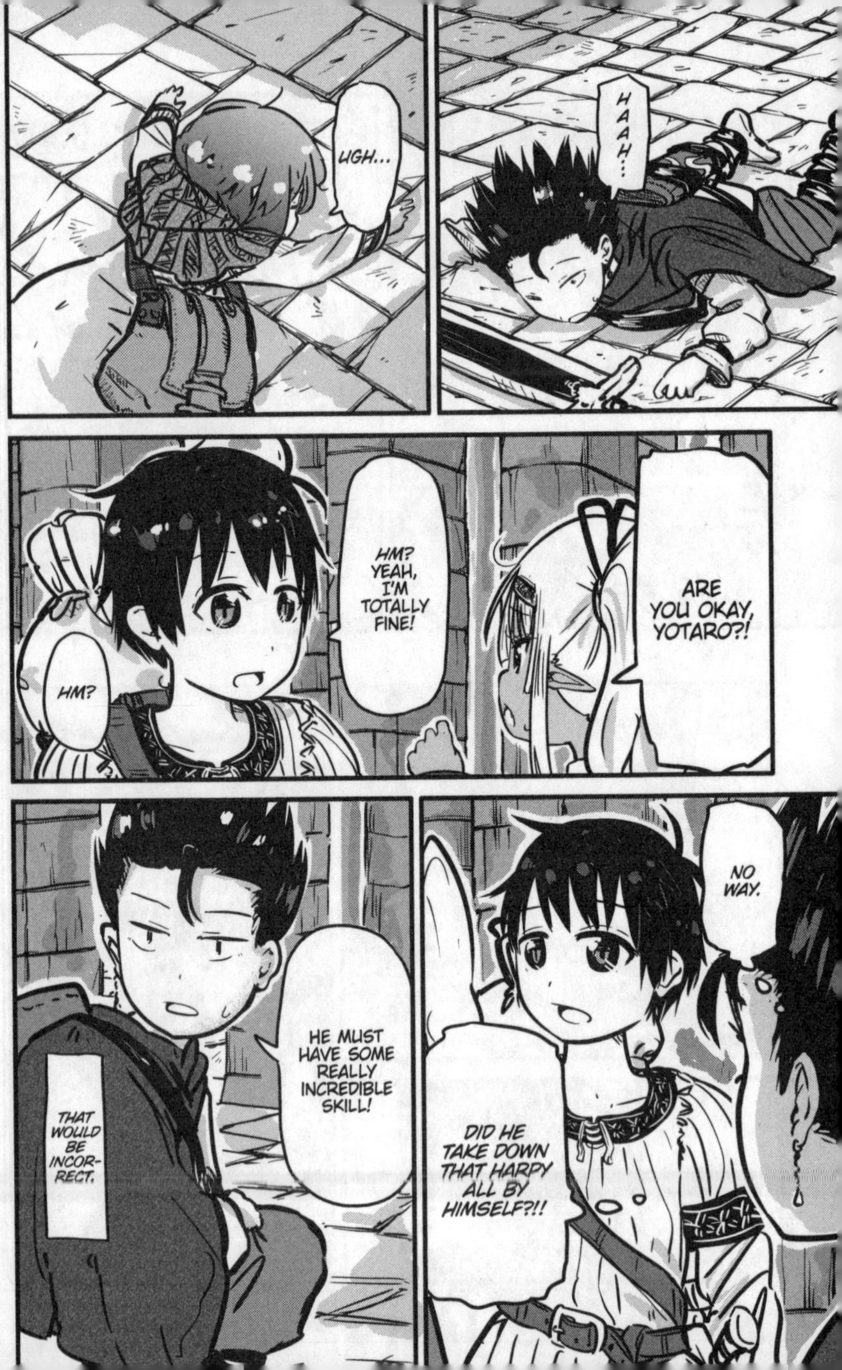
HAAAH...
UGH...
ARE YOU OKAY, YOTARO?!
HM? YEAH, I'M TOTALLY FINE!
HM?
NO WAY.
DID HE TAKE DOWN THAT HARPY ALL BY HIMSELF?!!
HE MUST HAVE SOME REALLY INCREDIBLE SKILL!
THAT WOULD BE INCORRECT.

ROOTS

PEOPLE WHO DON'T VALUE TOILET TIME ARE NO GOOD.

SIXTH TOILET TIME

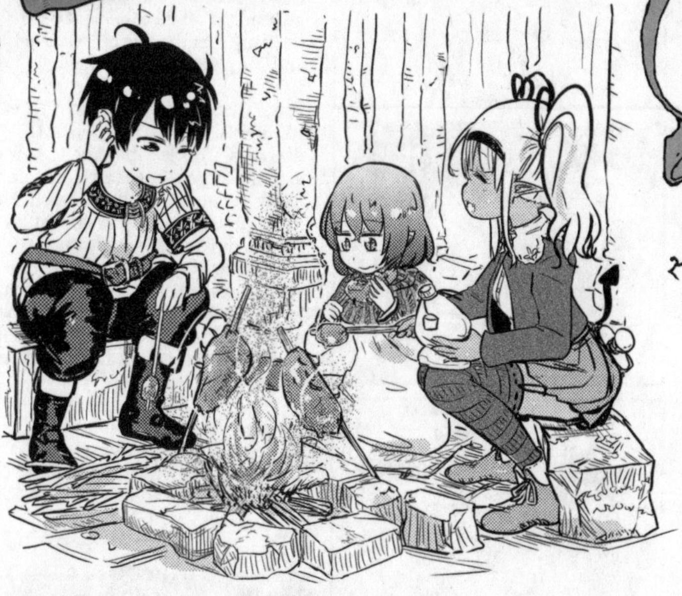

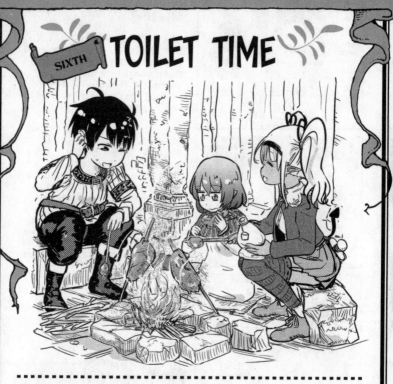

Toilets reflect the ingenuity of humanity.

For example, toilet paper. Many of us use this without a second thought, but the path to get here was riddled with trial and error. In desert areas there are many different ways to handle your business, like how Yotaro used sand to wipe. Small rocks were another option; however, rocks that have been basking in the sun all day are very hot on tender flesh.

This is how clay cakes came to be. Excavated from the Mohenjo-daro ruins, these are thought to be the world's first toilet paper. The clay triangle with rounded edges apparently wasn't too rough on skin.

Similarly, in the Japanese ruins, a spatula-like object called a "chugi" was discovered.

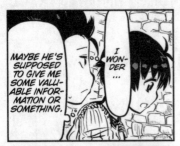

Eventually, these items led us to toilet paper.

When talking about ingenuity, King Louis XIV of France comes to mind. Louis' physician incorrectly stated that the teeth were the breeding ground for all diseases. Therefore, the king's teeth were all removed, and his palate was damaged.

From then on, Louis could only eat soft items. He was plagued with diarrhea. This led the king to carry around a chair-style portable toilet, using perfume to hide its smell. He sat on it while eating breakfast, as well as during his kingly duties. Following his example, many of his retainers started using seated toilets at the table as well. It must have been an interesting spectacle to see people do the royal squat and eat breakfast at the same time!

Despite these difficulties, King Louis XIV still lived a pleasant life. His ingenuity truly earns him his place in the annals of toilet history.

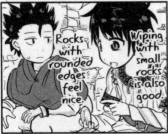

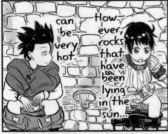

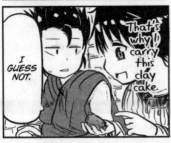

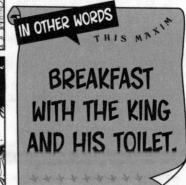

IN OTHER WORDS

THIS MAXIM

BREAKFAST WITH THE KING AND HIS TOILET.

I WONDER...
MAYBE HE'S SUPPOSED TO GIVE ME SOME VALUABLE INFORMATION OR SOMETHING.
Wiping with small rocks is also good.
Rocks with rounded edges feel nice.
However, rocks that have been lying in the sun...
can be very hot.
That's why I carry this clay cake.
I GUESS NOT.

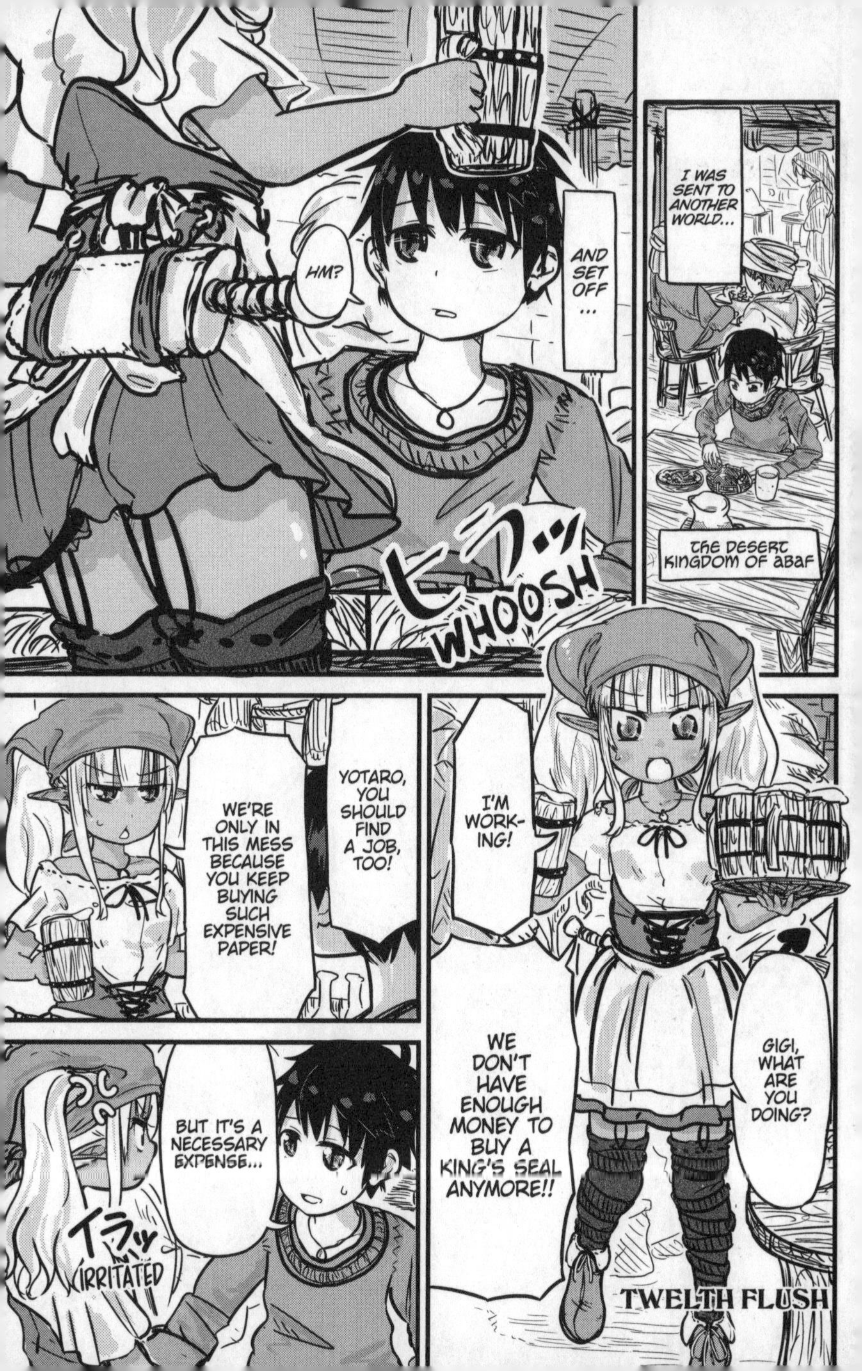
I WAS SENT TO ANOTHER WORLD...
THE DESERT KINGDOM OF ABAF
AND SET OFF...
HM?
ヒュッ
WHOOSH
GIGI, WHAT ARE YOU DOING?
WE DON'T HAVE ENOUGH MONEY TO BUY A KING'S SEAL ANYMORE!!
TWELTH FLUSH
I'M WORKING!
YOTARO, YOU SHOULD FIND A JOB, TOO!
WE'RE ONLY IN THIS MESS BECAUSE YOU KEEP BUYING SUCH EXPENSIVE PAPER!
BUT IT'S A NECESSARY EXPENSE...
イラッ
IRRITATED

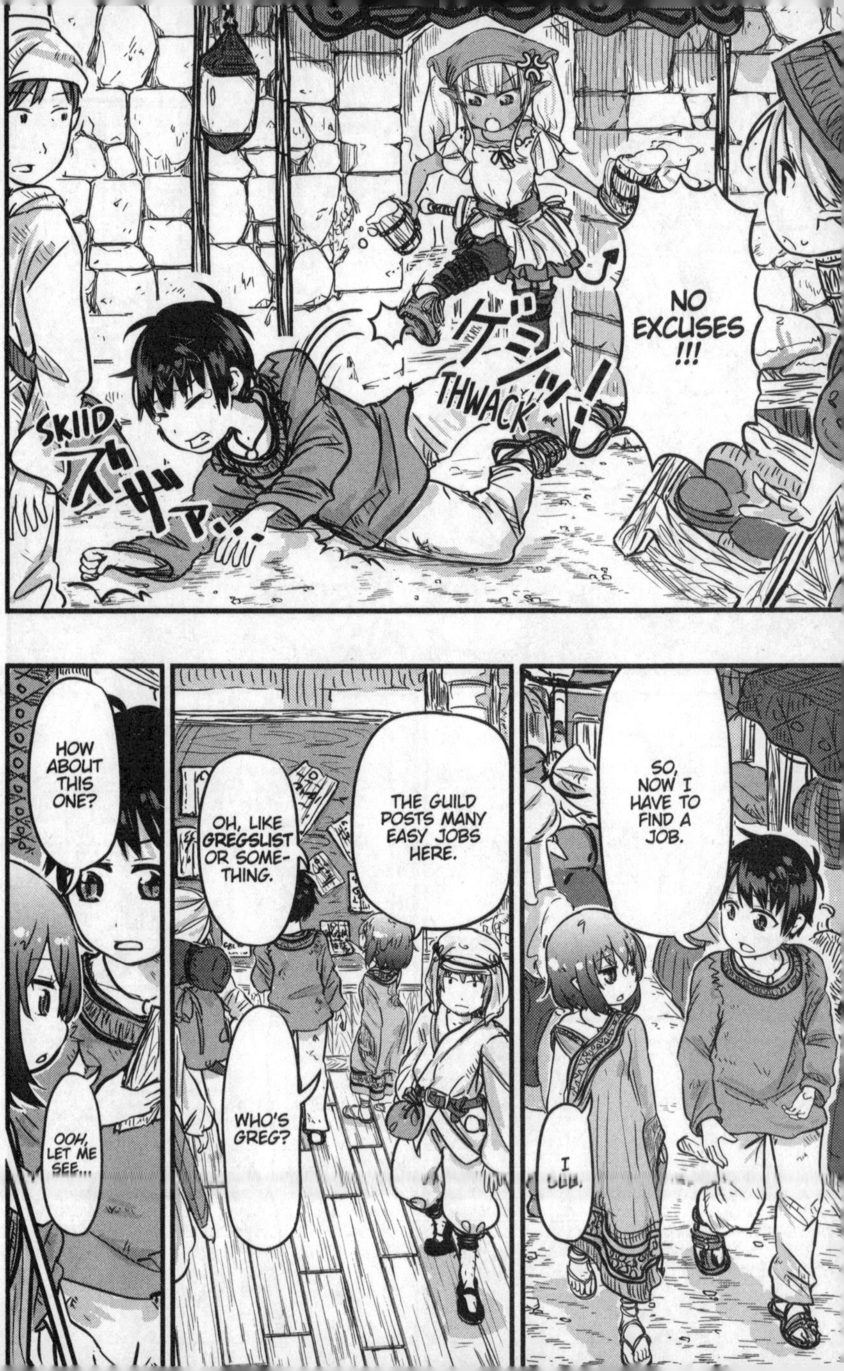
NO EXCUSES!!!
ゲシッッ!!
THWACK
ズザァ…
SKIID
SO, NOW I HAVE TO FIND A JOB.
I SEE.
THE GUILD POSTS MANY EASY JOBS HERE.
OH, LIKE GREGSLIST OR SOMETHING.
WHO'S GREG?
HOW ABOUT THIS ONE?
OOH, LET ME SEE...

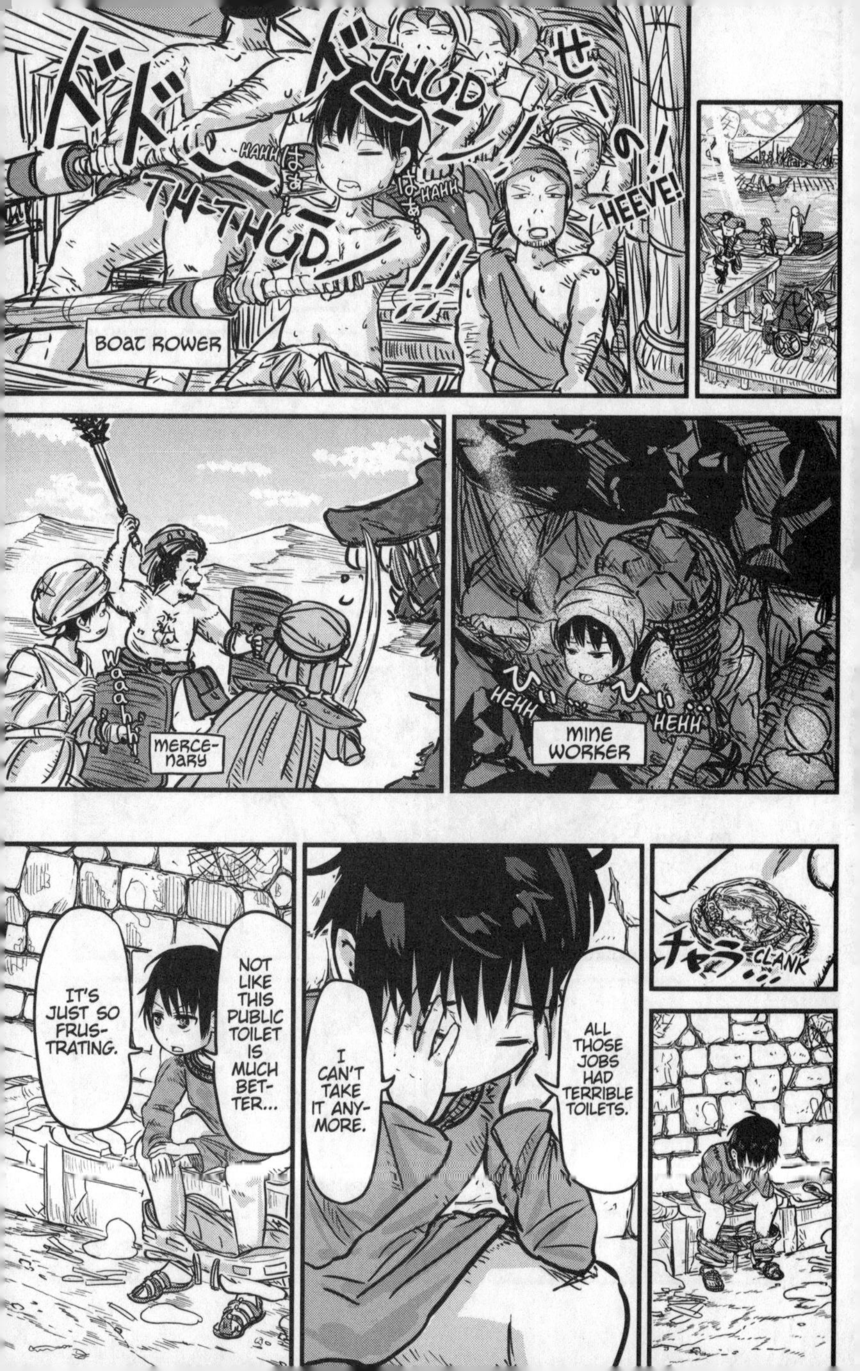

せーの!
HEEVE!
THUD
はぁ HAHH
はぁ HAHH
TH-THUD—!!
BOAT ROWER
HEHH
HEHH
MINE WORKER
Waaahh!
MERCE-NARY
チャラ CLANK
ALL THOSE JOBS HAD TERRIBLE TOILETS.
I CAN'T TAKE IT ANY-MORE.
NOT LIKE THIS PUBLIC TOILET IS MUCH BET-TER...
IT'S JUST SO FRUS-TRATING.

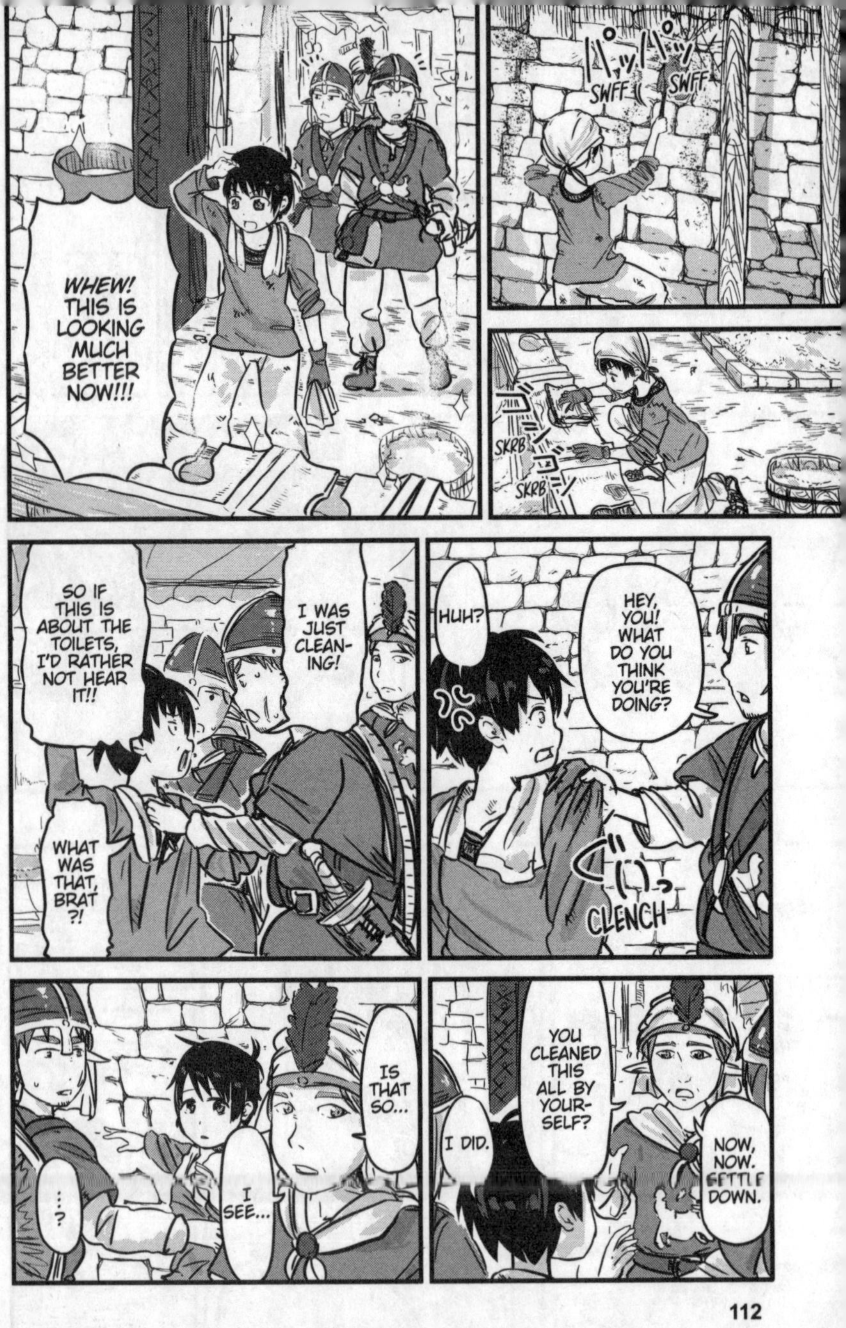
パッパッ
SWFF
SWFF
SKRB
SKRB
WHEW! THIS IS LOOKING MUCH BETTER NOW!!!
HUH?
HEY, YOU! WHAT DO YOU THINK YOU'RE DOING?
CLENCH
I WAS JUST CLEANING!
SO IF THIS IS ABOUT THE TOILETS, I'D RATHER NOT HEAR IT!!
WHAT WAS THAT, BRAT?!
NOW, NOW. SETTLE DOWN.
YOU CLEANED THIS ALL BY YOURSELF?
I DID.
IS THAT SO...
I SEE...
...?

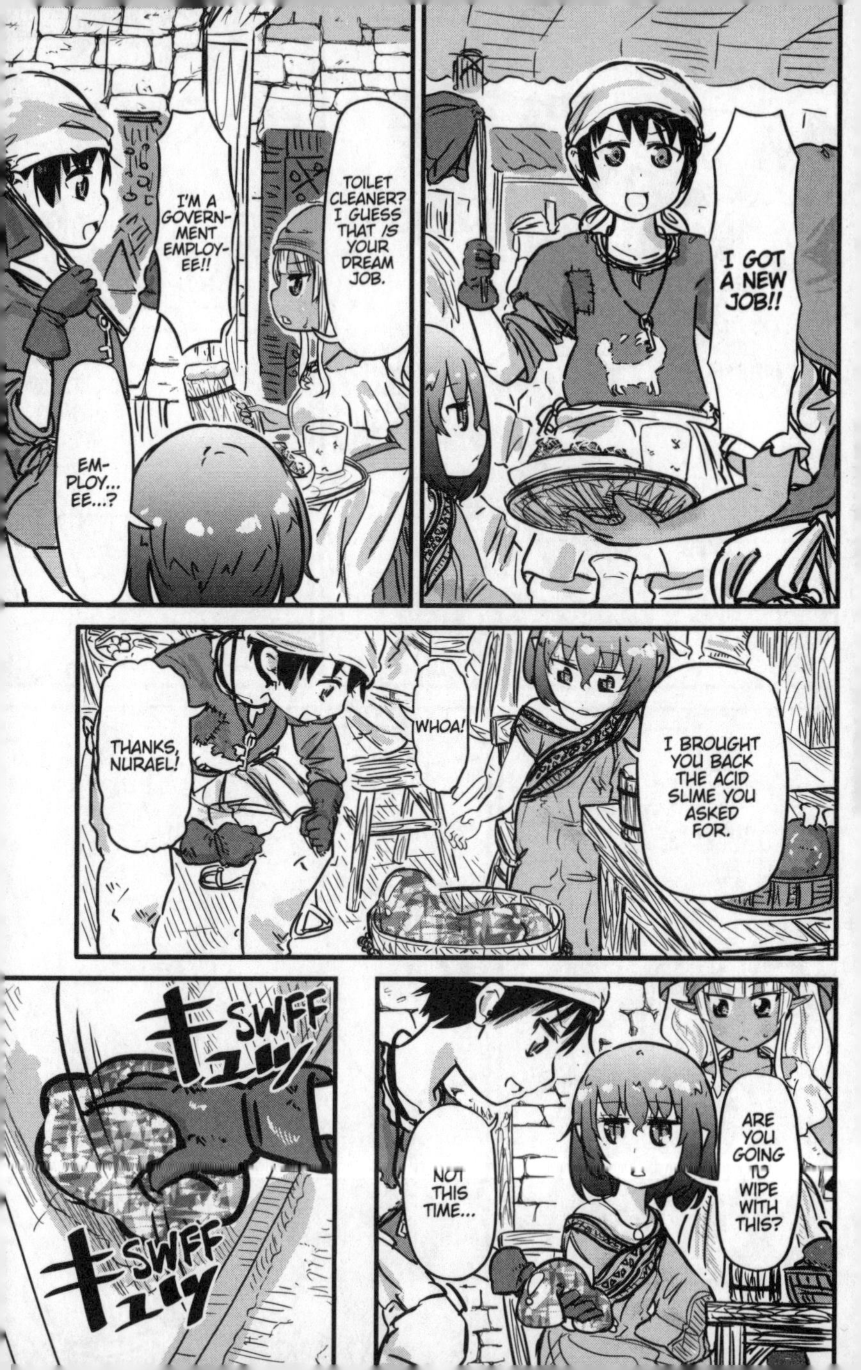
I GOT A NEW JOB!!
TOILET CLEANER? I GUESS THAT IS YOUR DREAM JOB.
I'M A GOVERNMENT EMPLOYEE!!
EMPLOY... EE...?
I BROUGHT YOU BACK THE ACID SLIME YOU ASKED FOR.
WHOA!
THANKS, NURAEL!
ARE YOU GOING TO WIPE WITH THIS?
NOT THIS TIME...
SWFF
SWFF

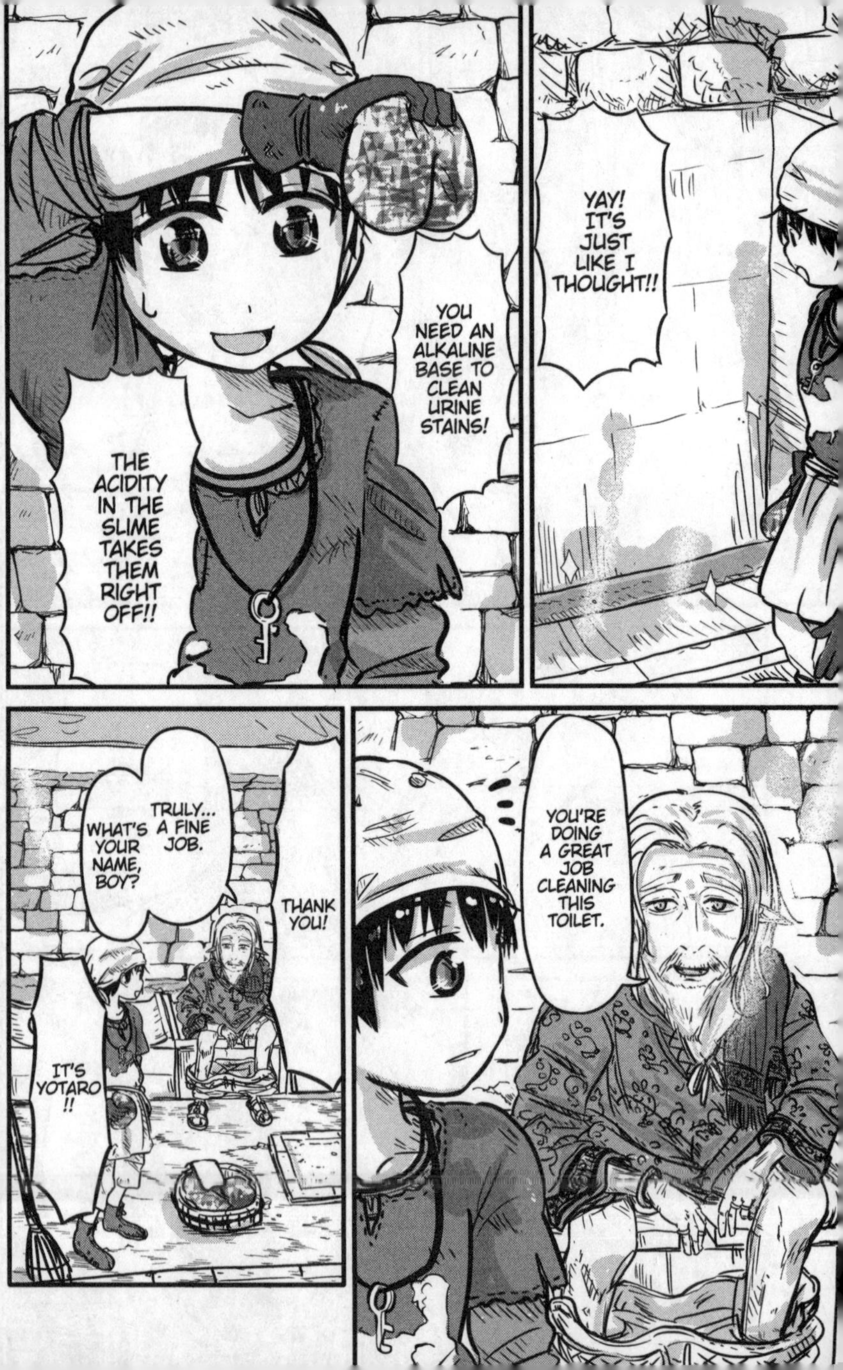
YAY! IT'S JUST LIKE I THOUGHT!!
YOU NEED AN ALKALINE BASE TO CLEAN URINE STAINS!
THE ACIDITY IN THE SLIME TAKES THEM RIGHT OFF!!
YOU'RE DOING A GREAT JOB CLEANING THIS TOILET.
THANK YOU!
TRULY... A FINE JOB. WHAT'S YOUR NAME, BOY?
IT'S YOTARO!!

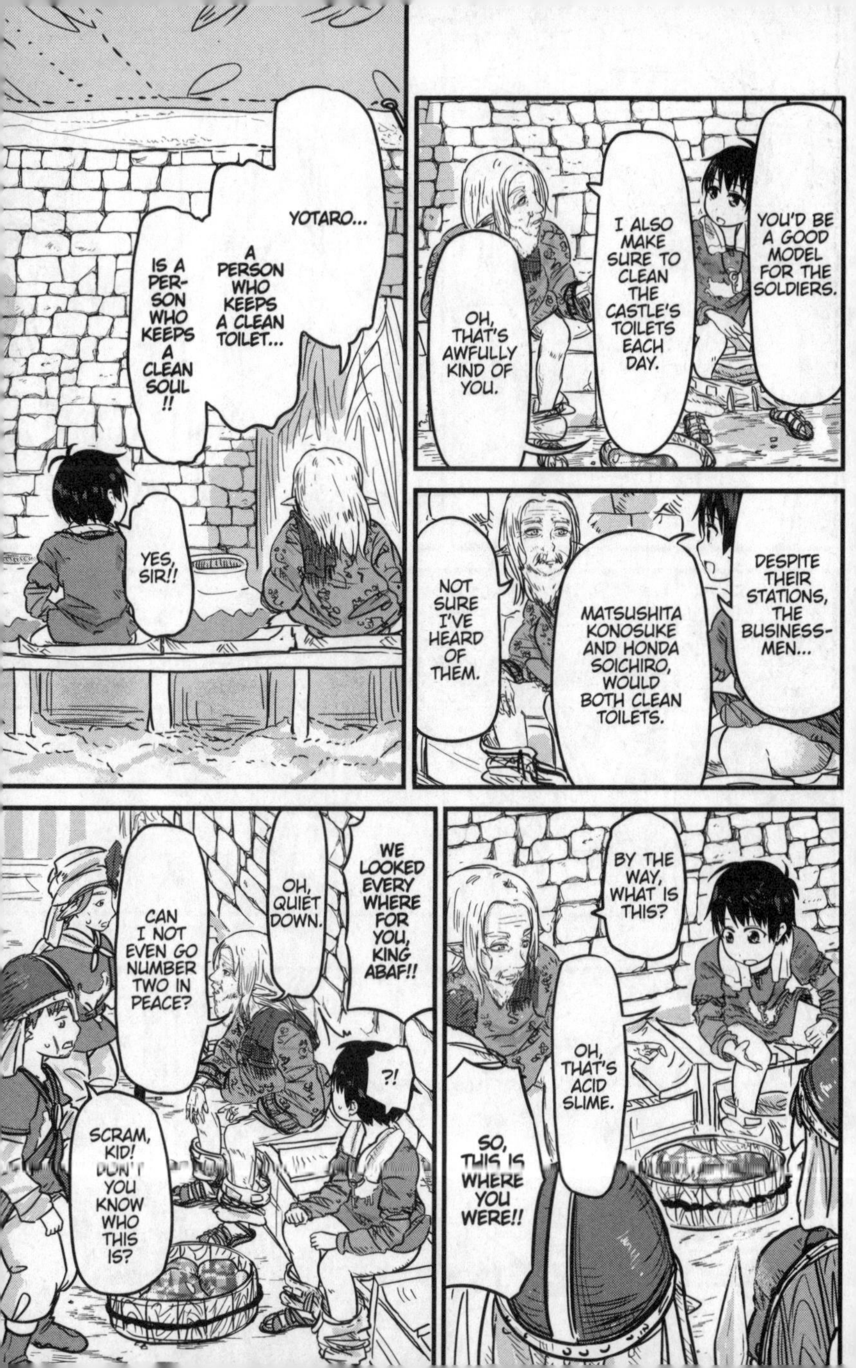
YOU'D BE A GOOD MODEL FOR THE SOLDIERS.
I ALSO MAKE SURE TO CLEAN THE CASTLE'S TOILETS EACH DAY.
OH, THAT'S AWFULLY KIND OF YOU.
DESPITE THEIR STATIONS, THE BUSINESS-MEN...
MATSUSHITA KONOSUKE AND HONDA SOICHIRO, WOULD BOTH CLEAN TOILETS.
NOT SURE I'VE HEARD OF THEM.
YOTARO...
A PERSON WHO KEEPS A CLEAN TOILET...
IS A PER-SON WHO KEEPS A CLEAN SOUL!!
YES, SIR!!
BY THE WAY, WHAT IS THIS?
OH, THAT'S ACID SLIME.
SO, THIS IS WHERE YOU WERE!!
WE LOOKED EVERY WHERE FOR YOU, KING ABAF!!
OH, QUIET DOWN.
CAN I NOT EVEN GO NUMBER TWO IN PEACE?
?!
SCRAM, KID! DON'T YOU KNOW WHO THIS IS?

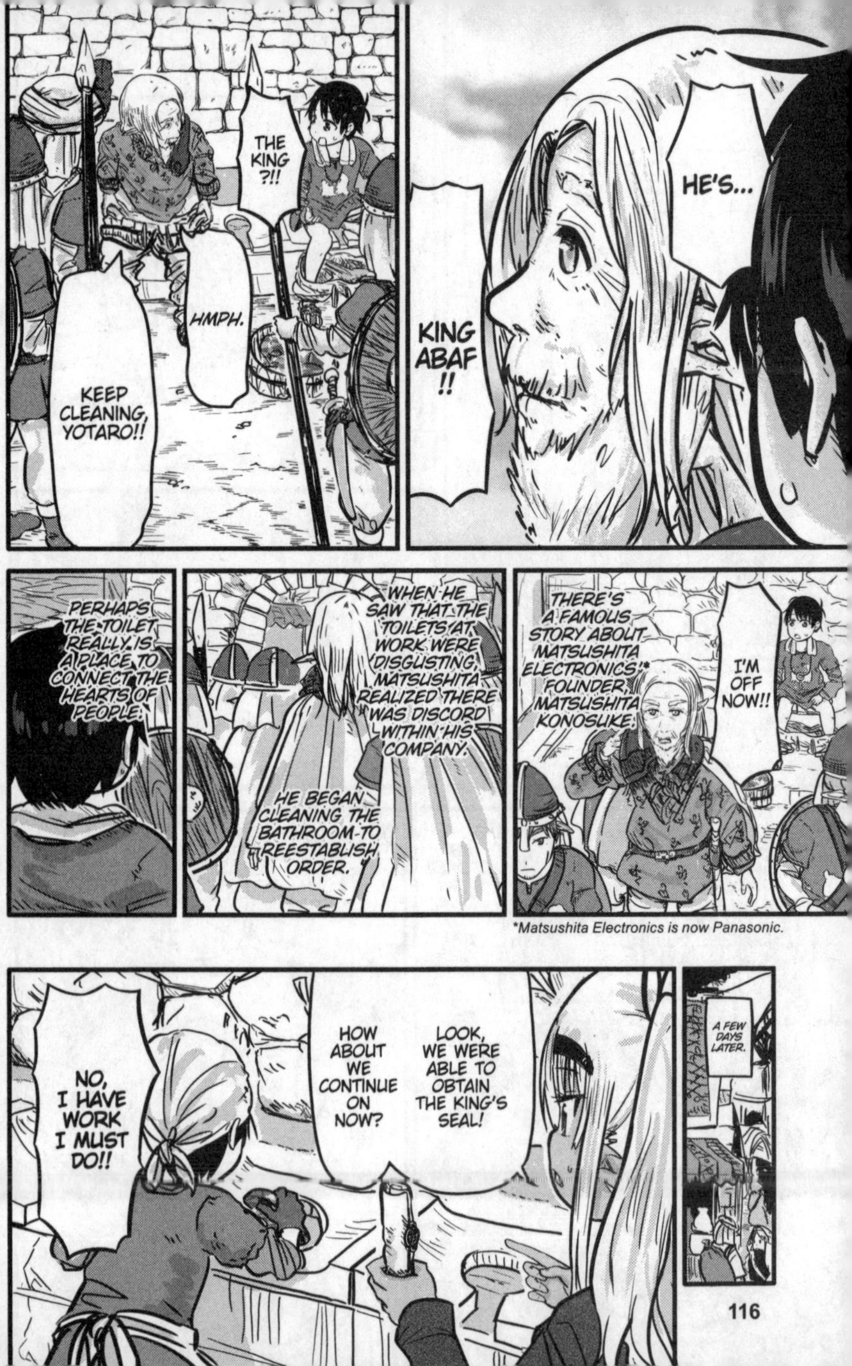
HE'S...
KING ABAF!!
THE KING?!!
HMPH.
KEEP CLEANING, YOTARO!!
I'M OFF NOW!!
THERE'S A FAMOUS STORY ABOUT MATSUSHITA ELECTRONICS'* FOUNDER, MATSUSHITA KONOSUKE.
WHEN HE SAW THAT THE TOILETS AT WORK WERE DISGUSTING, MATSUSHITA REALIZED THERE WAS DISCORD WITHIN HIS COMPANY.
HE BEGAN CLEANING THE BATHROOM TO REESTABLISH ORDER.
PERHAPS THE TOILET REALLY IS A PLACE TO CONNECT THE HEARTS OF PEOPLE.
A FEW DAYS LATER.
LOOK, WE WERE ABLE TO OBTAIN THE KING'S SEAL!
HOW ABOUT WE CONTINUE ON NOW?
NO, I HAVE WORK I MUST DO!!

*Matsushita Electronics is now Panasonic.

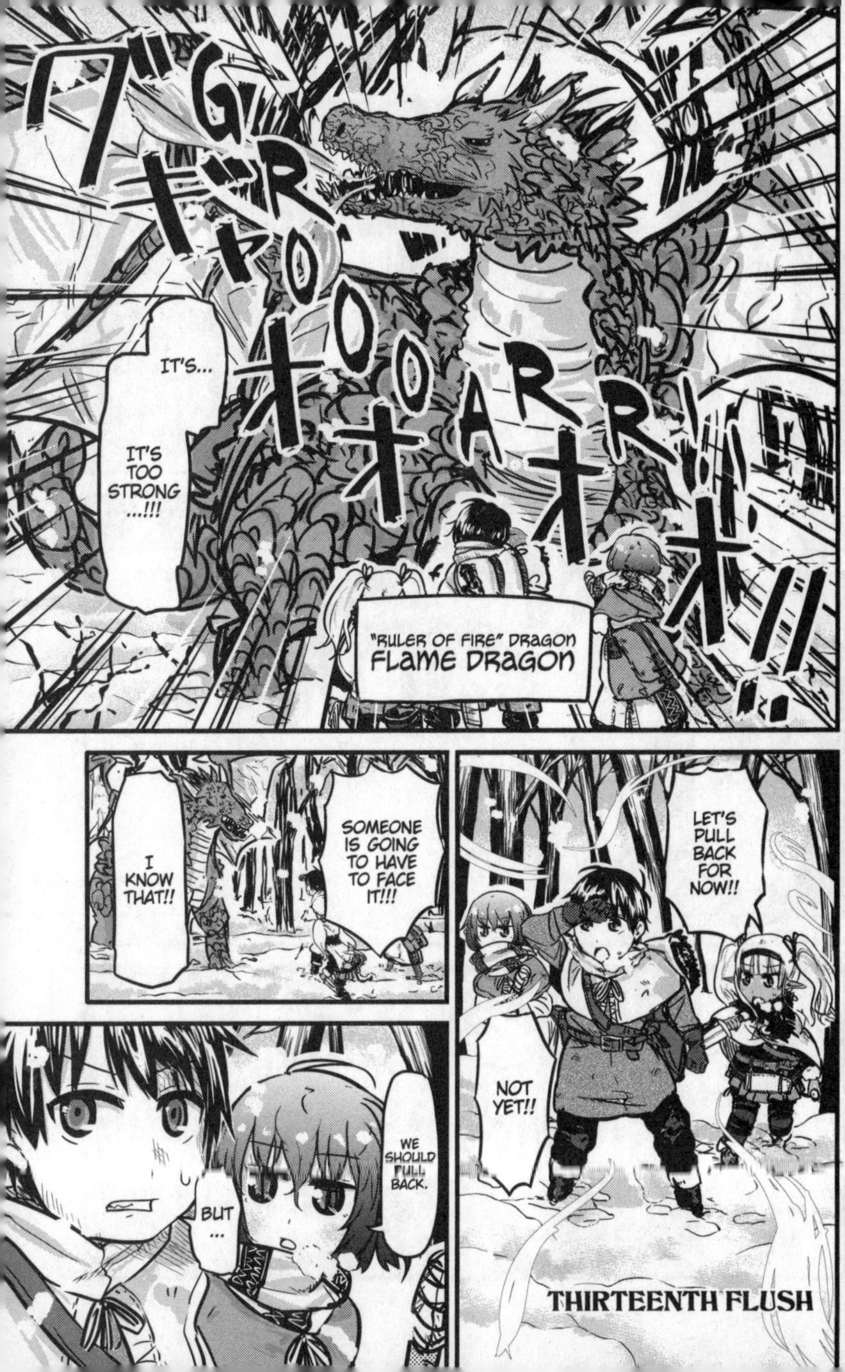

GROOOARR!!
IT'S...
IT'S TOO STRONG...!!!
"RULER OF FIRE" DRAGON
FLAME DRAGON
LET'S PULL BACK FOR NOW!!
NOT YET!!
THIRTEENTH FLUSH
SOMEONE IS GOING TO HAVE TO FACE IT!!!
I KNOW THAT!!
WE SHOULD PULL BACK.
BUT...

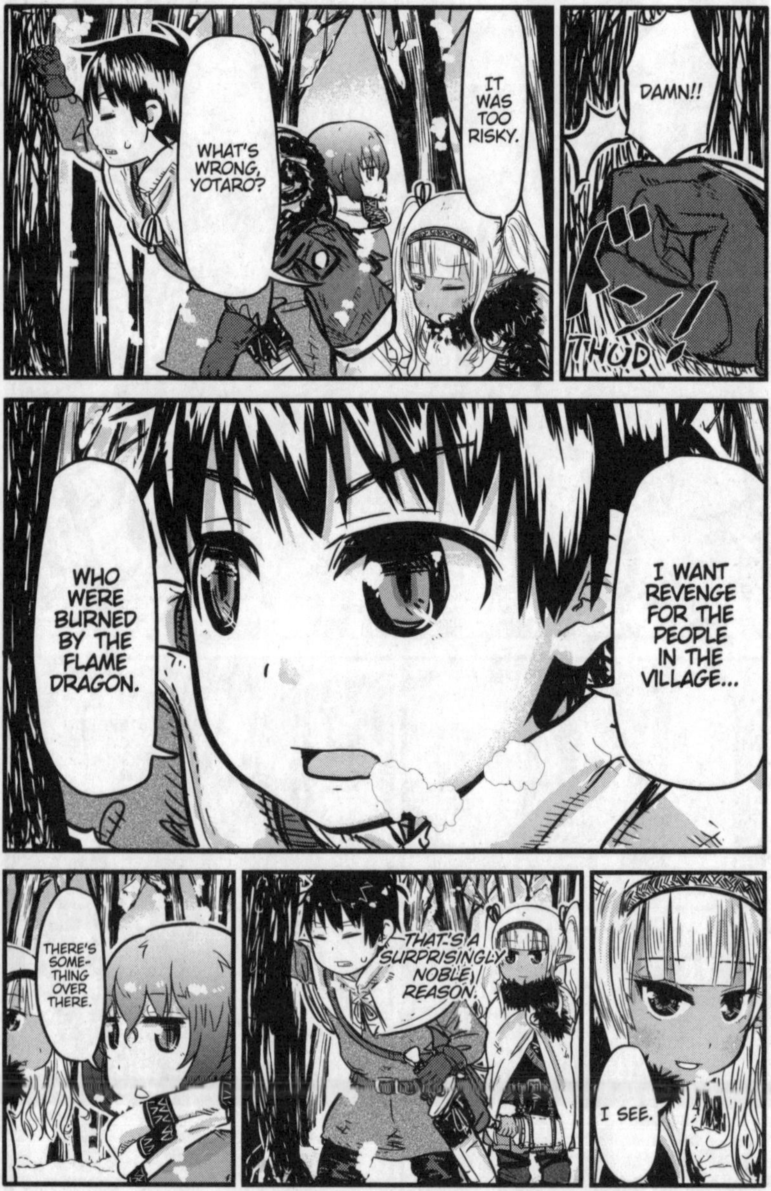
DAMN!!
THUD
IT WAS TOO RISKY.
WHAT'S WRONG, YOTARO?
I WANT REVENGE FOR THE PEOPLE IN THE VILLAGE...
WHO WERE BURNED BY THE FLAME DRAGON.
I SEE.
THAT'S A SURPRISINGLY NOBLE REASON.
THERE'S SOME-THING OVER THERE.

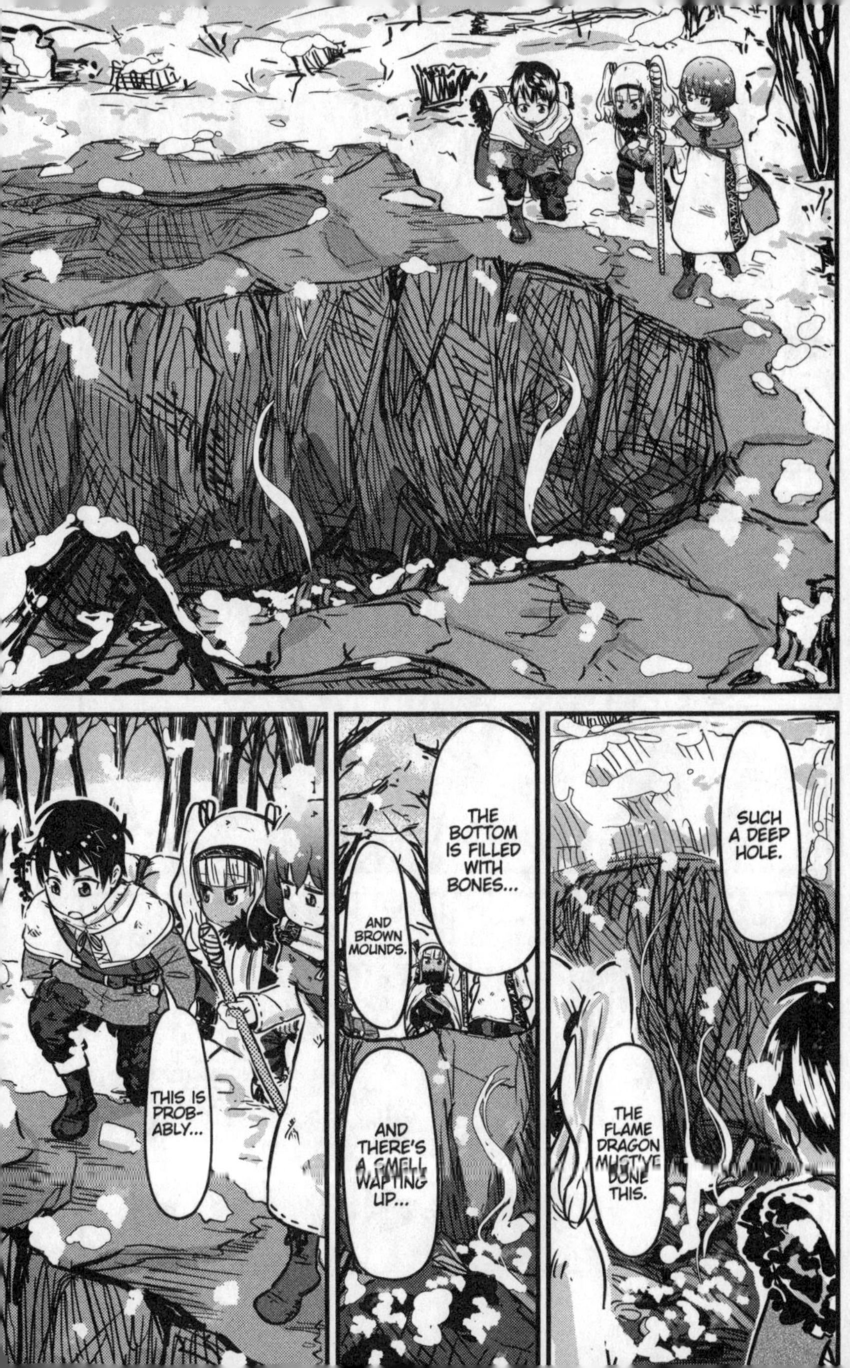
SUCH A DEEP HOLE.
THE FLAME DRAGON MUST'VE DONE THIS.
THE BOTTOM IS FILLED WITH BONES...
AND BROWN MOUNDS.
AND THERE'S A SMELL WAFTING UP...
THIS IS PROB-ABLY...

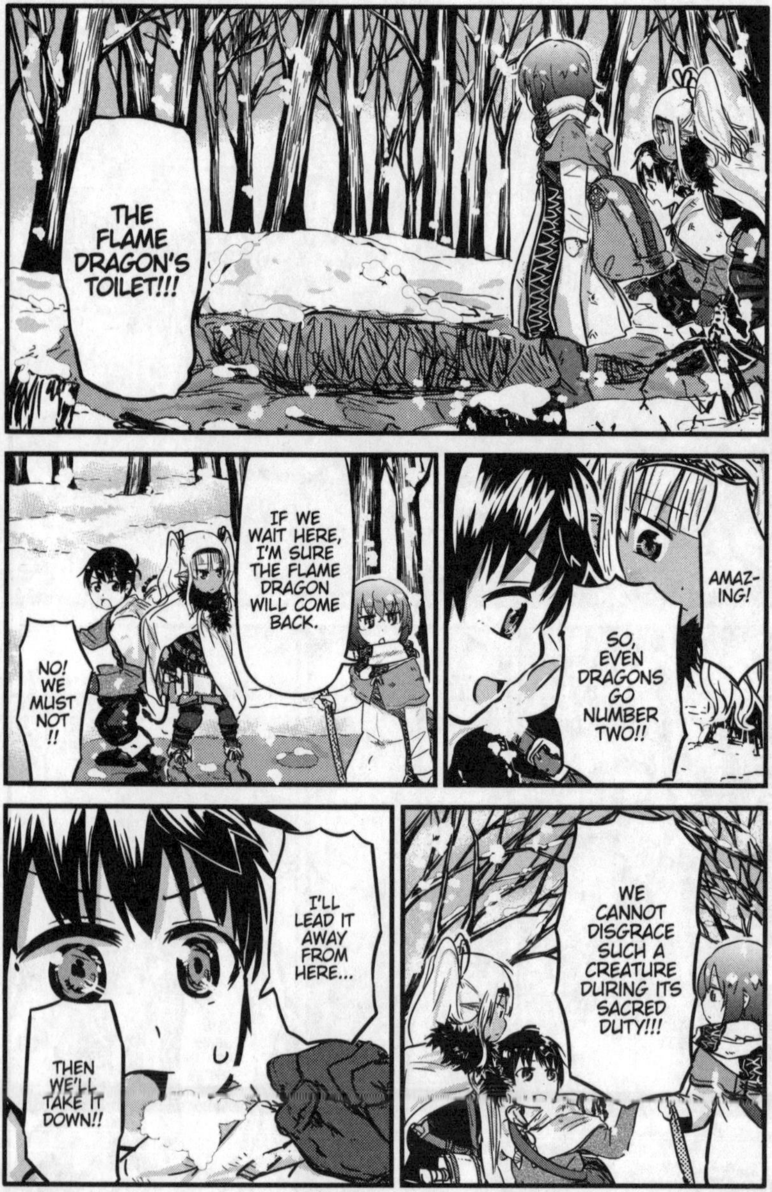
THE FLAME DRAGON'S TOILET!!!
AMAZ-ING!
SO, EVEN DRAGONS GO NUMBER TWO!!
IF WE WAIT HERE, I'M SURE THE FLAME DRAGON WILL COME BACK.
NO! WE MUST NOT!!
WE CANNOT DISGRACE SUCH A CREATURE DURING ITS SACRED DUTY!!!
I'LL LEAD IT AWAY FROM HERE...
THEN WE'LL TAKE IT DOWN!!

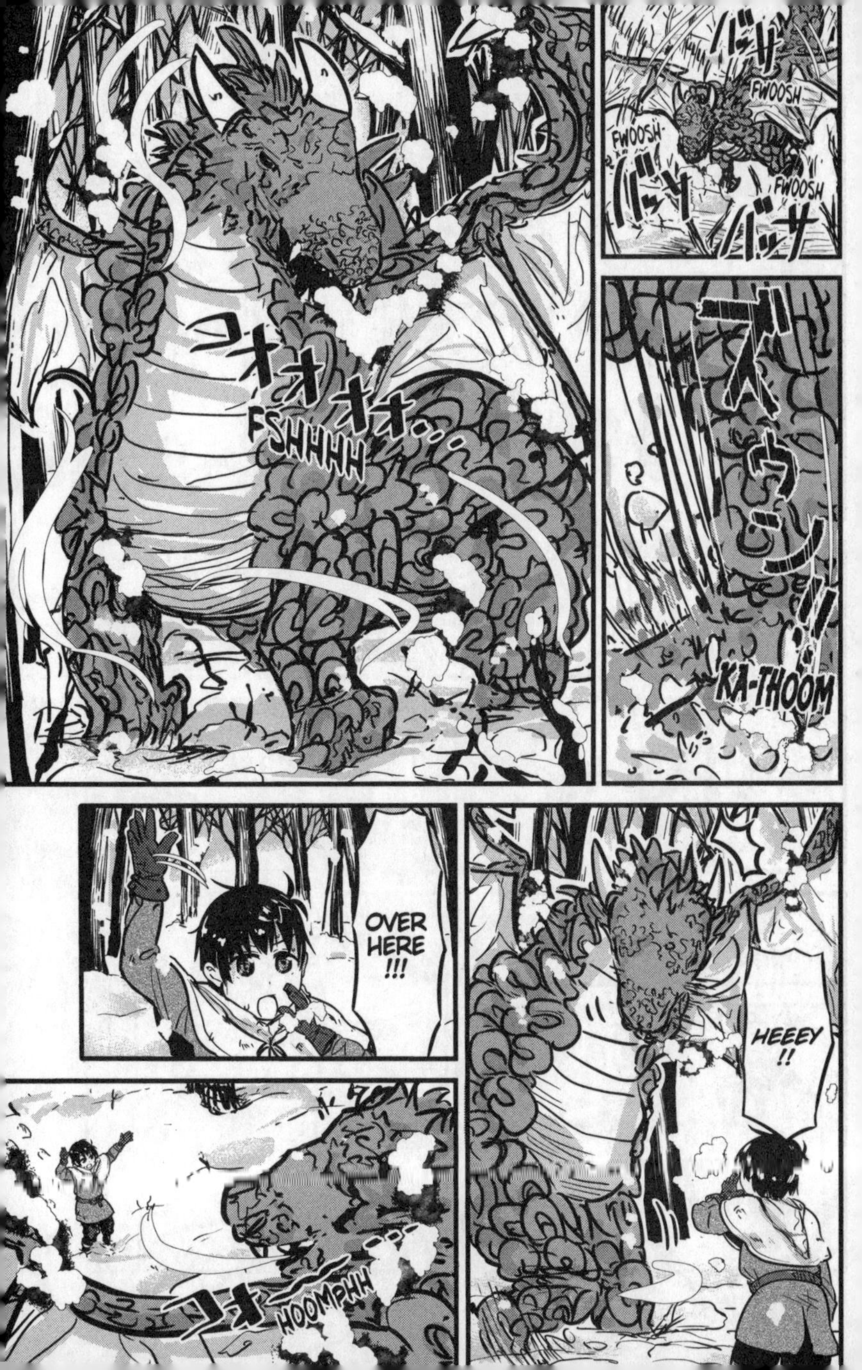
FWOOSH
FWOOSH
FWOOSH
KA-THOOM
FSHHHH
HEEEY!!
OVER HERE!!!
HOOMPHH

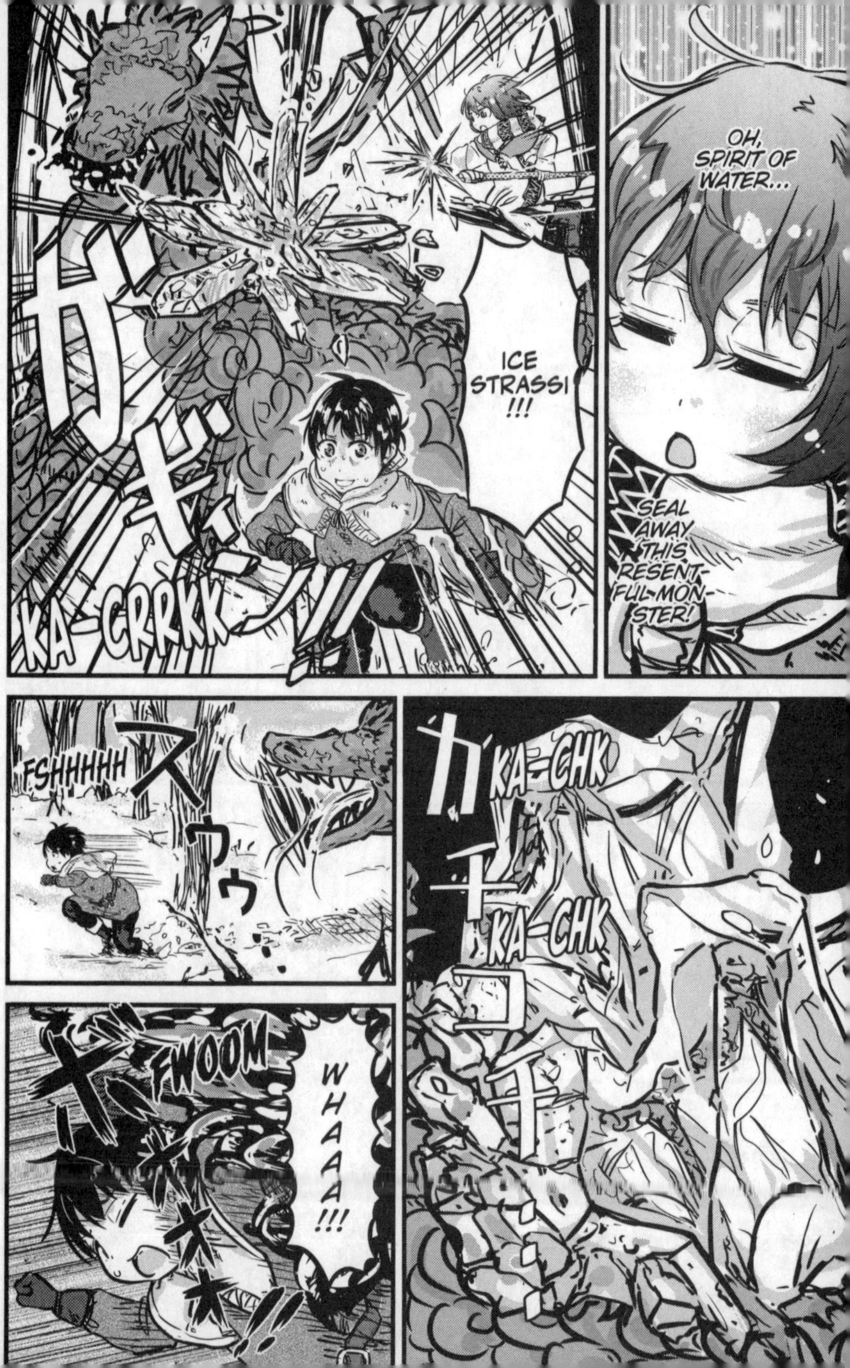
OH, SPIRIT OF WATER...
SEAL AWAY THIS RESENT-FUL MON-STER!
ICE STRASSI!!!
KA-CRRKK
KA-CHK
KA-CHK
FSHHHHH
FWOOM
WHAAAA!!!

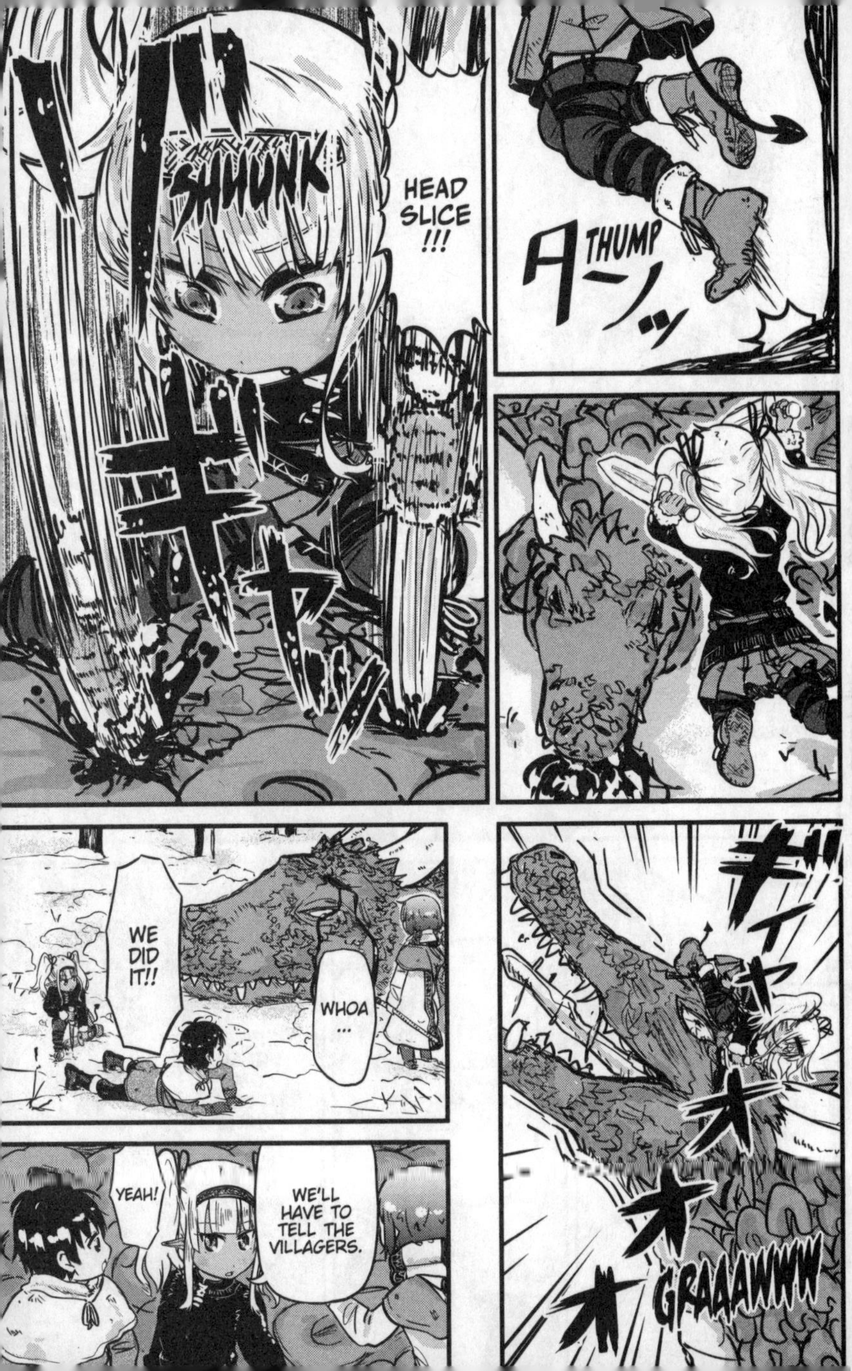
THUMP
HEAD SLICE !!!
SHUNK
GRAAAWWW
WE DID IT!!
WHOA ...
WE'LL HAVE TO TELL THE VILLAGERS.
YEAH!

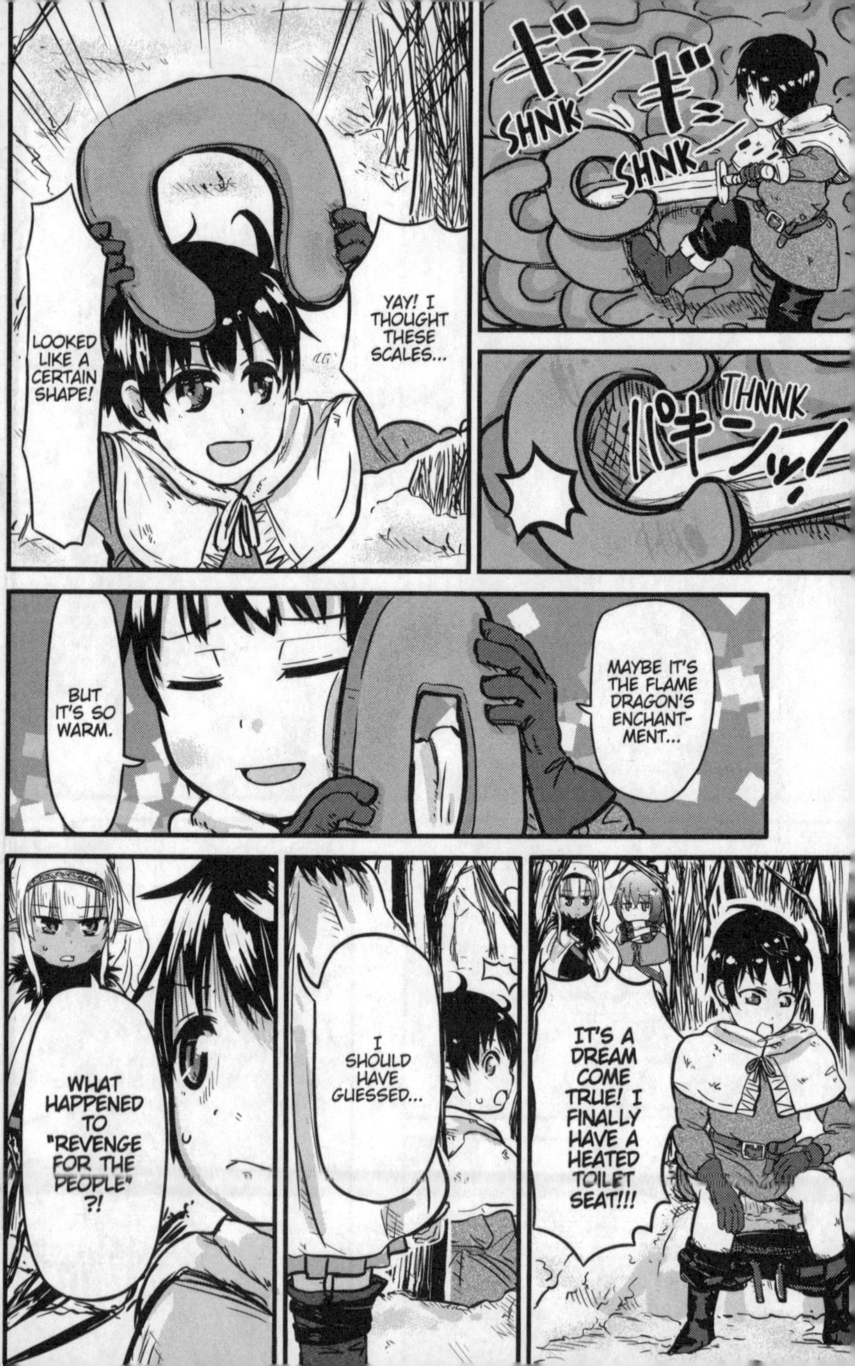

ギン
SHNK
ギン
SHNK
パキーンッ!
THNNK
YAY! I THOUGHT THESE SCALES...
LOOKED LIKE A CERTAIN SHAPE!
MAYBE IT'S THE FLAME DRAGON'S ENCHANT-MENT...
BUT IT'S SO WARM.
IT'S A DREAM COME TRUE! I FINALLY HAVE A HEATED TOILET SEAT!!!
I SHOULD HAVE GUESSED...
WHAT HAPPENED TO "REVENGE FOR THE PEOPLE"?!

ROOTS

PEOPLE WHO DON'T VALUE TOILET TIME ARE NO GOOD.

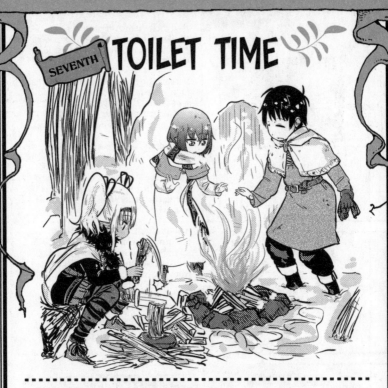

SEVENTH

TOILET TIME

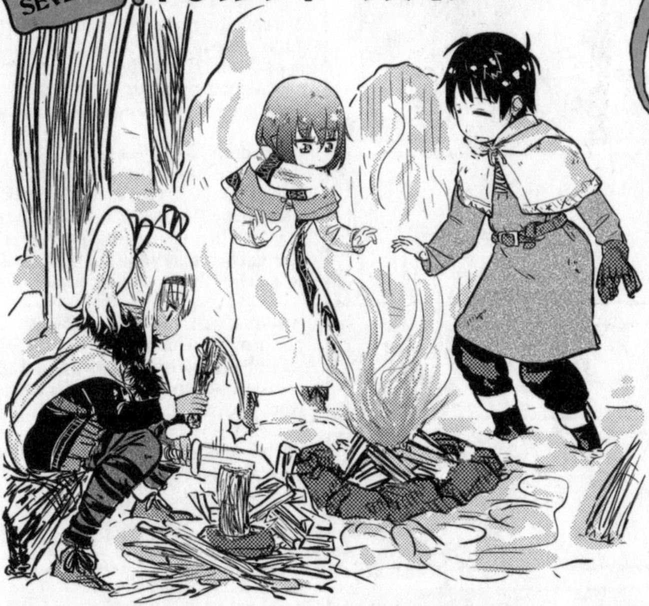

Just as the culture around toilets for humans varies from country to country, the way in which animals relieve themselves differs wildly. Some animals will go anywhere, some have a predetermined place, and some use it as an opportunity to mark their territory. In this article, I'd like to discuss how a few specific animals handle their business.

First, let's talk about the mole. Moles have a separate room in their nests specifically for dropping a load. This was determined after studying the increase in the number of mushrooms that grow from the bacteria attached to mole excrement.

Gorillas on the other hand will go right in their nests. In human terms, this would be like going number two in the middle of your living room. But fret not. Gorillas change their nests daily.

And then there's the animal most similar to humans, the chimpanzee. After taking a deuce, chimps use leaves to wipe themselves.

Raccoon dogs use a kind of communal toilet. One family will pass the same spot down through generations. It's like having your kids, parents, and grandparents all using the same toilet.

Apparently, koala feces smell quite nice, since eucalyptus has a very strong scent that doesn't disappear even after being expelled. Koalas also feed excrement to their young. This provides intestinal bacteria, allowing baby koalas to eat the otherwise toxic eucalyptus.

A similar procedure is now being performed on humans. It's called fecal microbiota transplantation, and it transfers healthy intestinal bacteria from one person to another.

There's much we can learn by studying animals' bathroom habits!

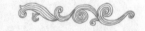

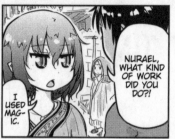

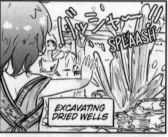

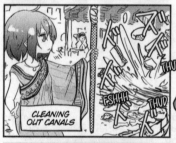

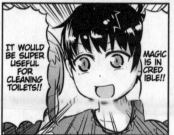

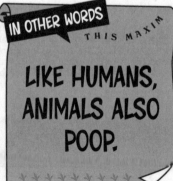

IN OTHER WORDS

THIS MAXIM

LIKE HUMANS, ANIMALS ALSO POOP.

NURAEL, WHAT KIND OF WORK DID YOU DO?!
I USED MAGIC.
SPLAASH
EXCAVATING DRIED WELLS
THUD
THUD
FSHHH
CLEANING OUT CANALS
MAGIC IS INCREDIBLE!!
IT WOULD BE SUPER USEFUL FOR CLEANING TOILETS!!

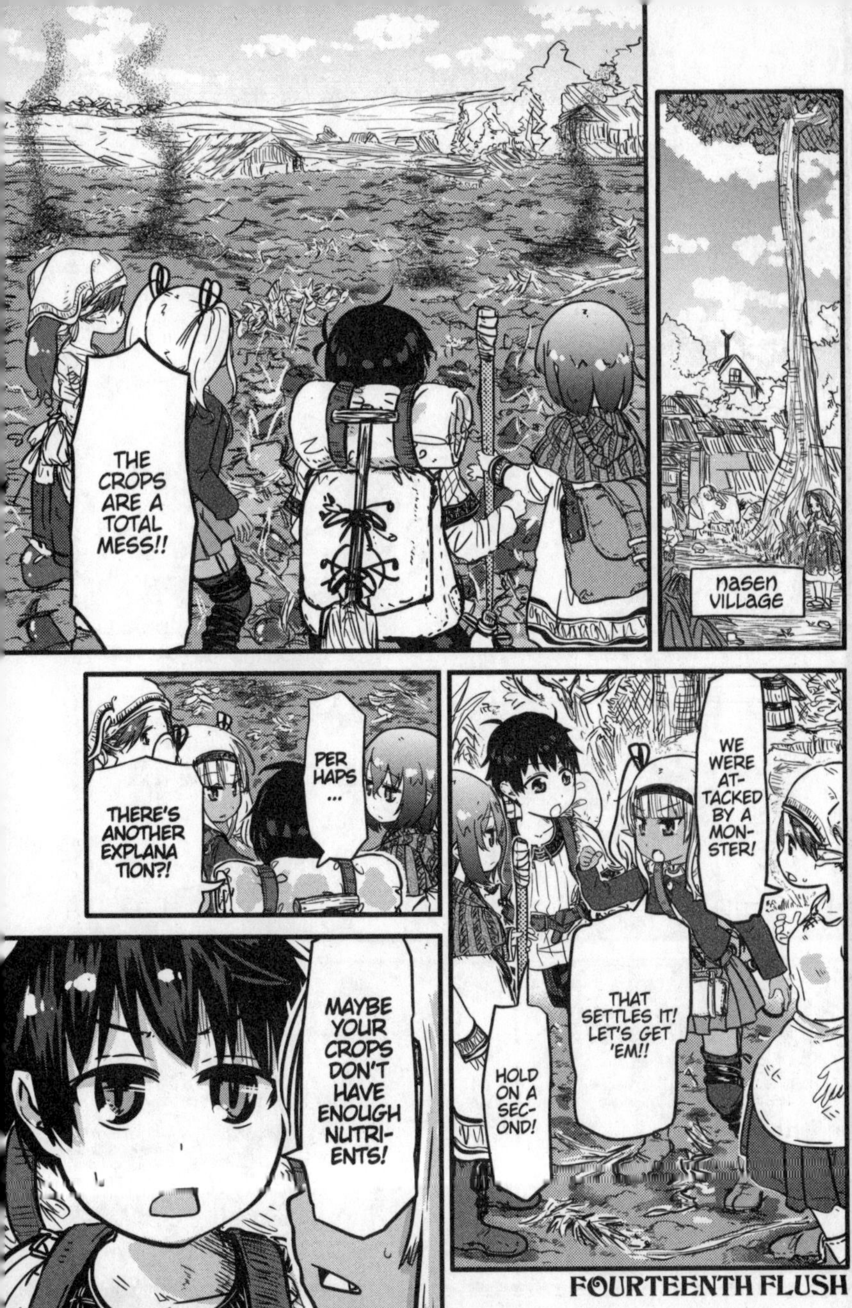
NASEN VILLAGE
THE CROPS ARE A TOTAL MESS!!
WE WERE ATTACKED BY A MONSTER!
THAT SETTLES IT! LET'S GET 'EM!!
HOLD ON A SECOND!
PERHAPS...
THERE'S ANOTHER EXPLANATION?!
MAYBE YOUR CROPS DON'T HAVE ENOUGH NUTRIENTS!

FOURTEENTH FLUSH

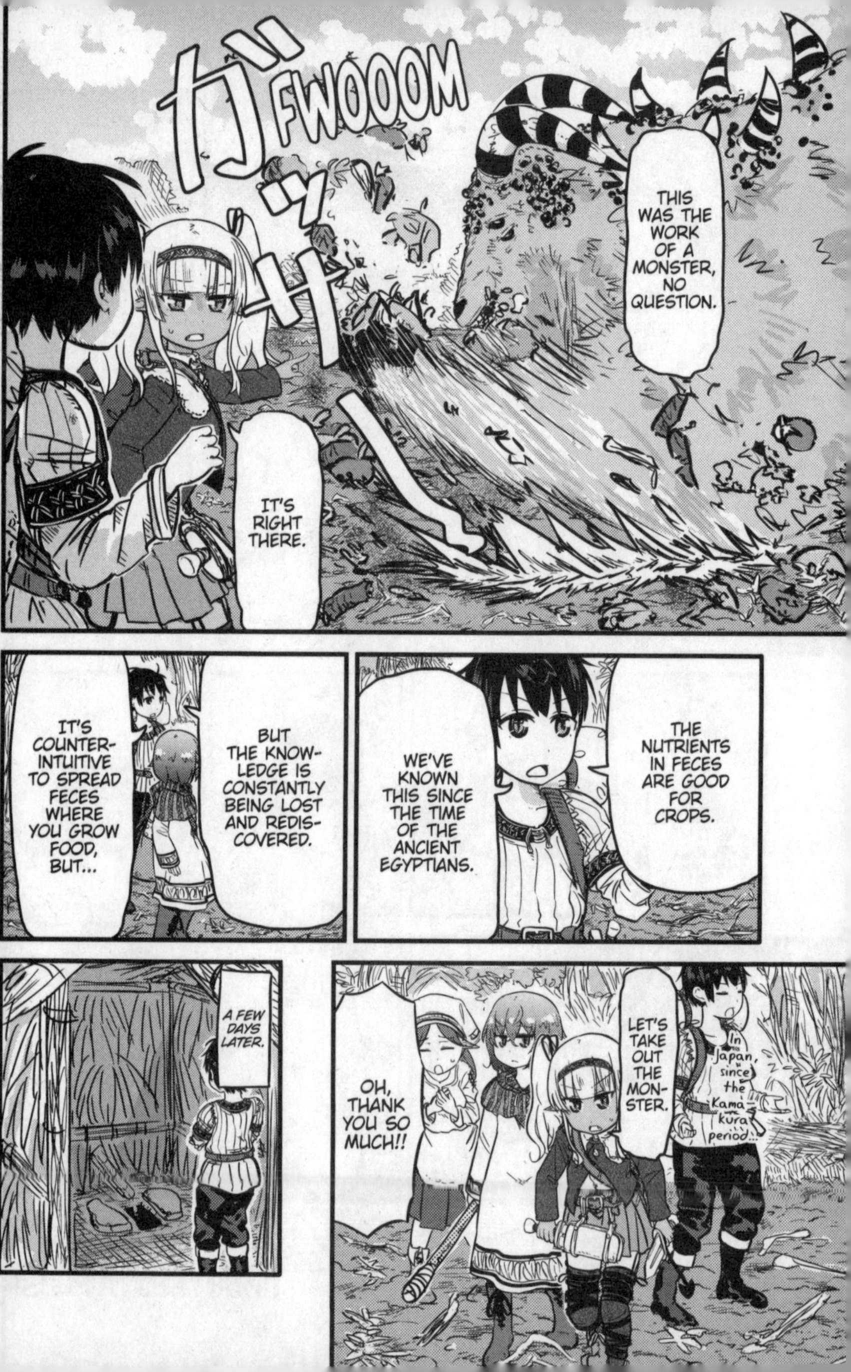
FWOOOM
THIS WAS THE WORK OF A MONSTER, NO QUESTION.
IT'S RIGHT THERE.
THE NUTRIENTS IN FECES ARE GOOD FOR CROPS.
WE'VE KNOWN THIS SINCE THE TIME OF THE ANCIENT EGYPTIANS.
BUT THE KNOWLEDGE IS CONSTANTLY BEING LOST AND REDISCOVERED.
IT'S COUNTER-INTUITIVE TO SPREAD FECES WHERE YOU GROW FOOD, BUT...
In Japan, since the Kamakura period...
LET'S TAKE OUT THE MONSTER.
OH, THANK YOU SO MUCH!!
A FEW DAYS LATER.

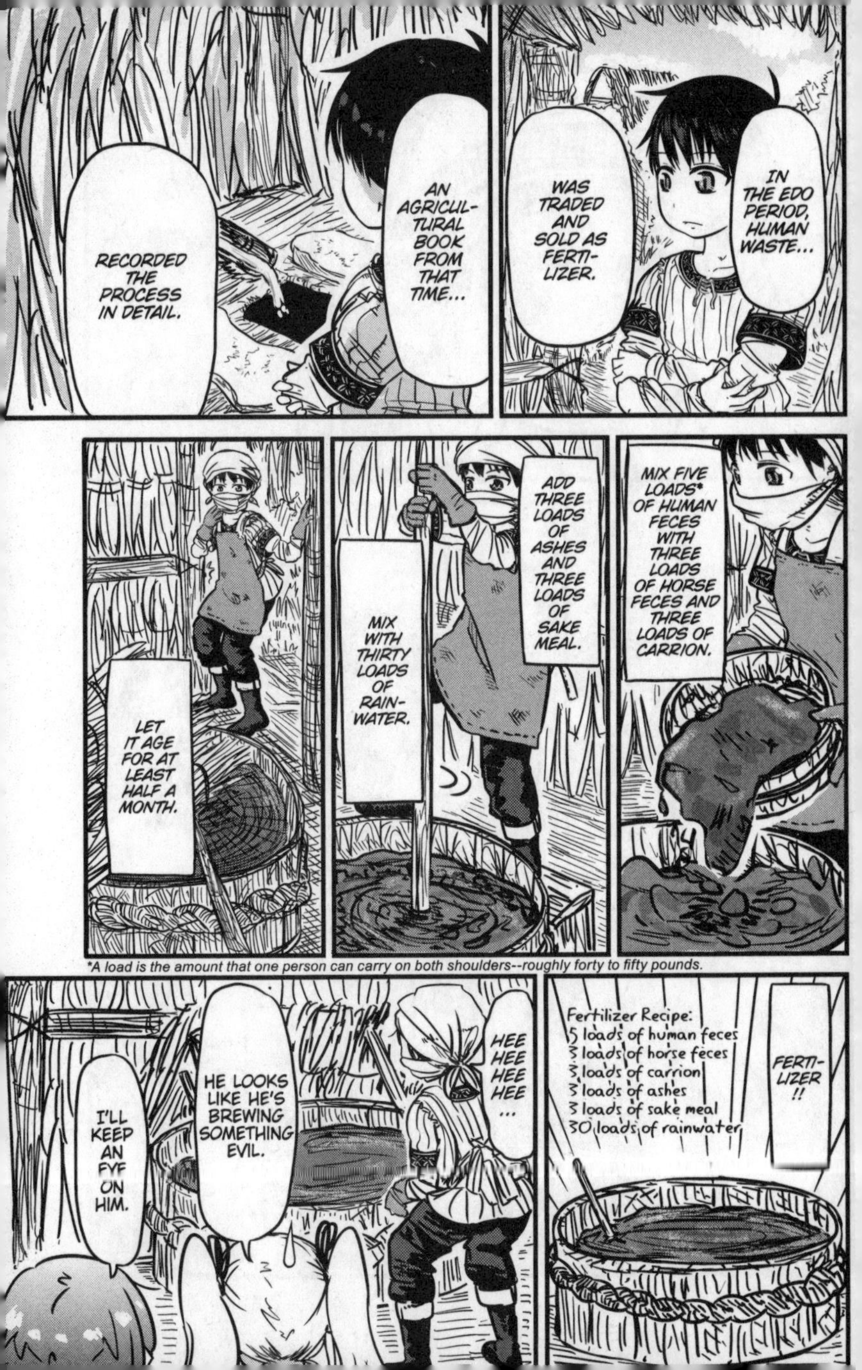
IN THE EDO PERIOD, HUMAN WASTE...
WAS TRADED AND SOLD AS FERTILIZER.
AN AGRICULTURAL BOOK FROM THAT TIME...
RECORDED THE PROCESS IN DETAIL.
MIX FIVE LOADS* OF HUMAN FECES WITH THREE LOADS OF HORSE FECES AND THREE LOADS OF CARRION.
ADD THREE LOADS OF ASHES AND THREE LOADS OF SAKE MEAL.
MIX WITH THIRTY LOADS OF RAINWATER.
LET IT AGE FOR AT LEAST HALF A MONTH.
FERTILIZER!!
Fertilizer Recipe:
5 loads of human feces
3 loads of horse feces
3 loads of carrion
3 loads of ashes
3 loads of sake meal
30 loads of rainwater
HEE HEE HEE HEE...
HE LOOKS LIKE HE'S BREWING SOMETHING EVIL.
I'LL KEEP AN EYE ON HIM.

*A load is the amount that one person can carry on both shoulders--roughly forty to fifty pounds.

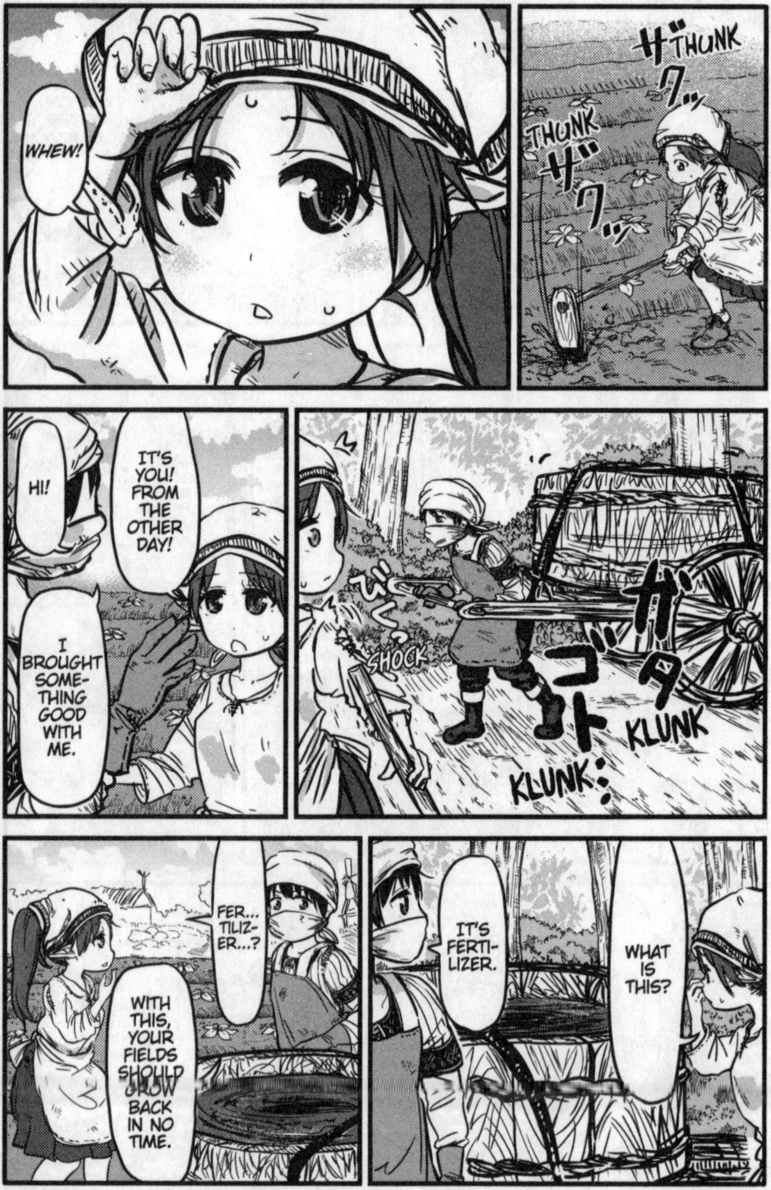

ザク THUNK
ザクッ THUNK
WHEW!
びくっ SHOCK
ガタ KLUNK
ゴト KLUNK
IT'S YOU! FROM THE OTHER DAY!
HI!
I BROUGHT SOMETHING GOOD WITH ME.
WHAT IS THIS?
IT'S FERTILIZER.
FER... TILIZER...?
WITH THIS, YOUR FIELDS SHOULD GROW BACK IN NO TIME.

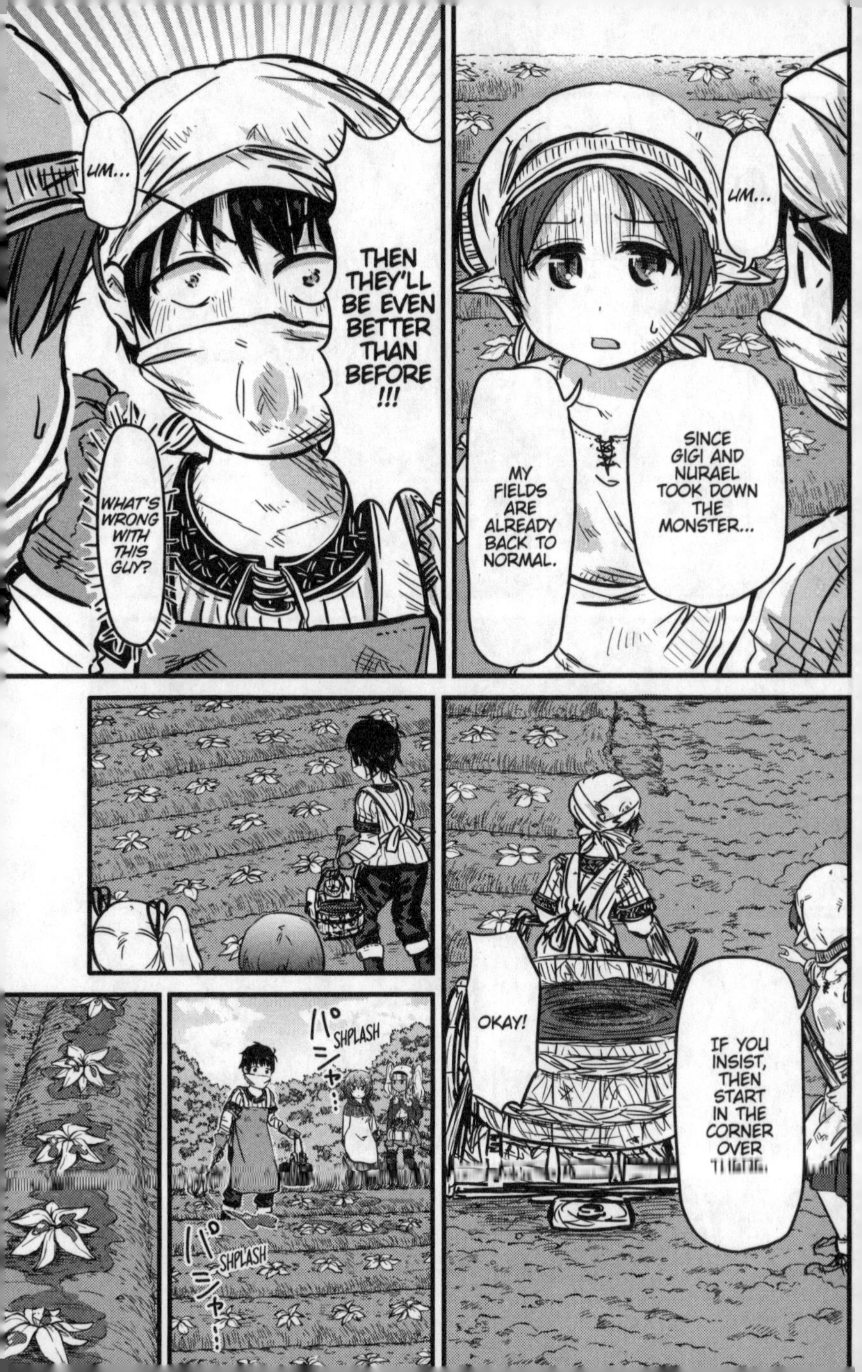
UM...
SINCE GIGI AND NURAEL TOOK DOWN THE MONSTER...
MY FIELDS ARE ALREADY BACK TO NORMAL.
UM...
THEN THEY'LL BE EVEN BETTER THAN BEFORE!!!
WHAT'S WRONG WITH THIS GUY?
IF YOU INSIST, THEN START IN THE CORNER OVER
OKAY!
パシャ...
SHPLASH
パシャ...
SHPLASH

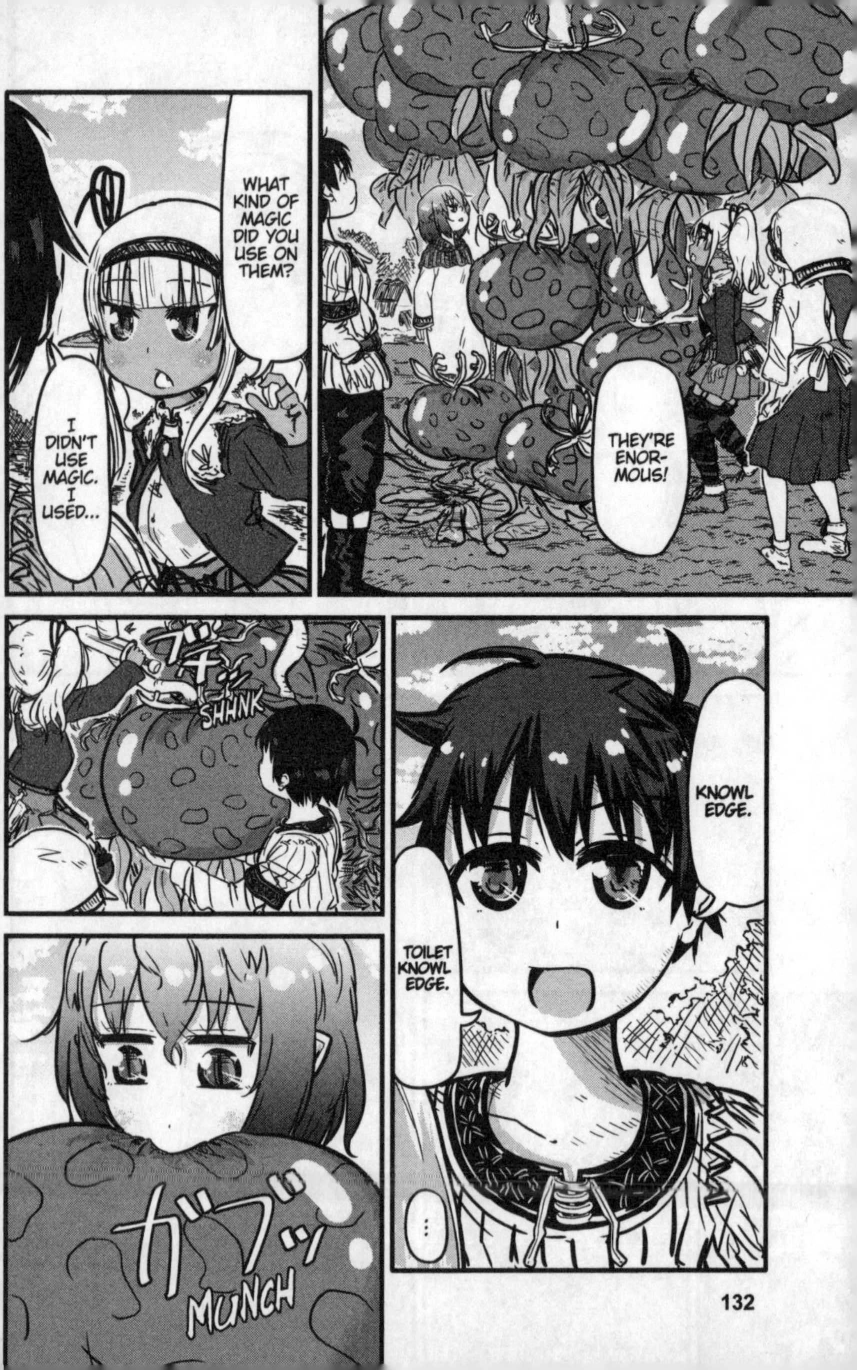
THEY'RE ENORMOUS!
WHAT KIND OF MAGIC DID YOU USE ON THEM?
I DIDN'T USE MAGIC. I USED...
KNOWL EDGE.
TOILET KNOWL EDGE.
...
ブチッ
SHHNK
ガブッ
MUNCH

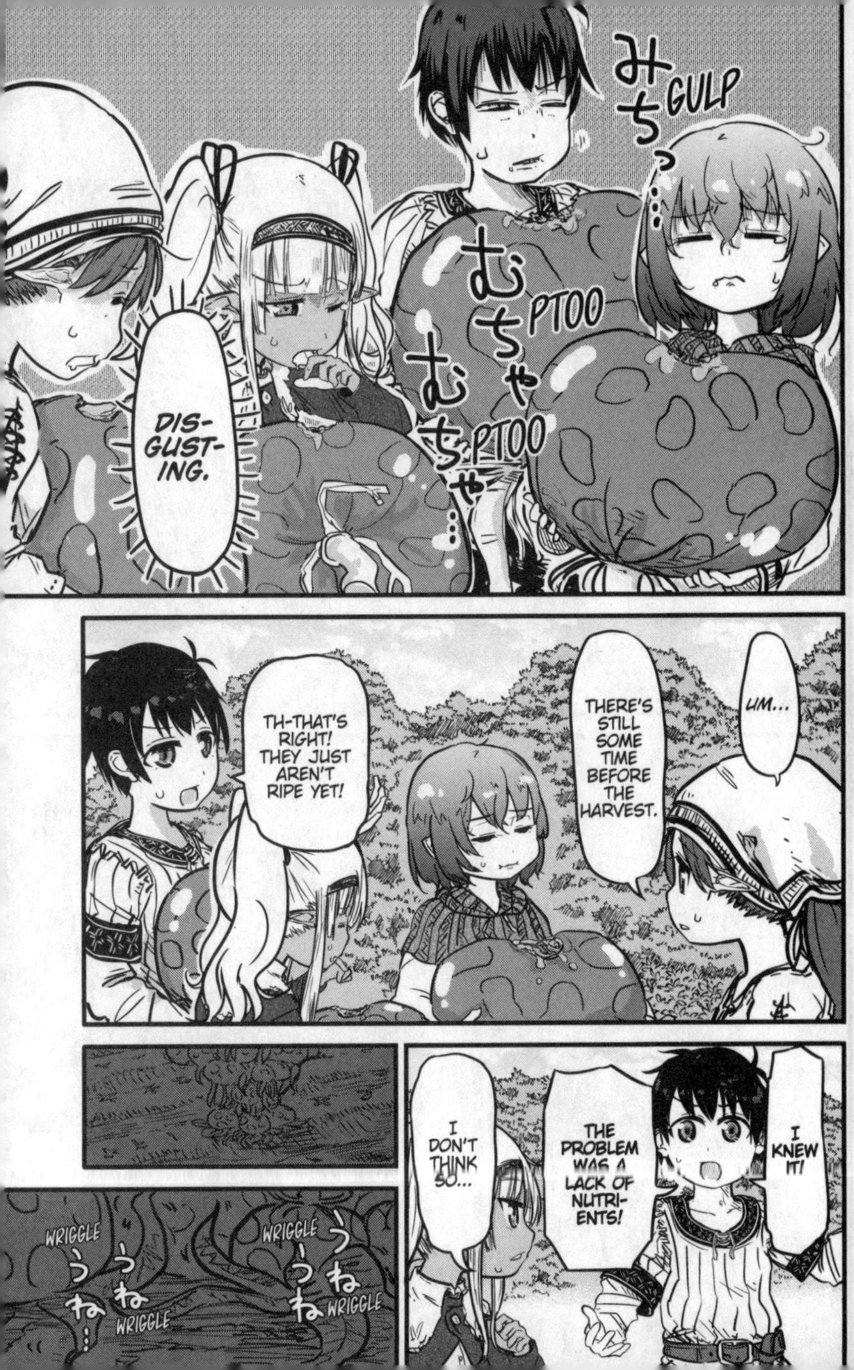

みちっ
GULP
むちゃむちゃ
PTOO
PTOO
DIS-GUSTING.
UM...
THERE'S STILL SOME TIME BEFORE THE HARVEST.
TH-THAT'S RIGHT! THEY JUST AREN'T RIPE YET!
I KNEW IT!
THE PROBLEM WAS A LACK OF NUTRI-ENTS!
I DON'T THINK SO...
うねうね
WRIGGLE
うねうね
WRIGGLE
うねうね…
WRIGGLE
WRIGGLE

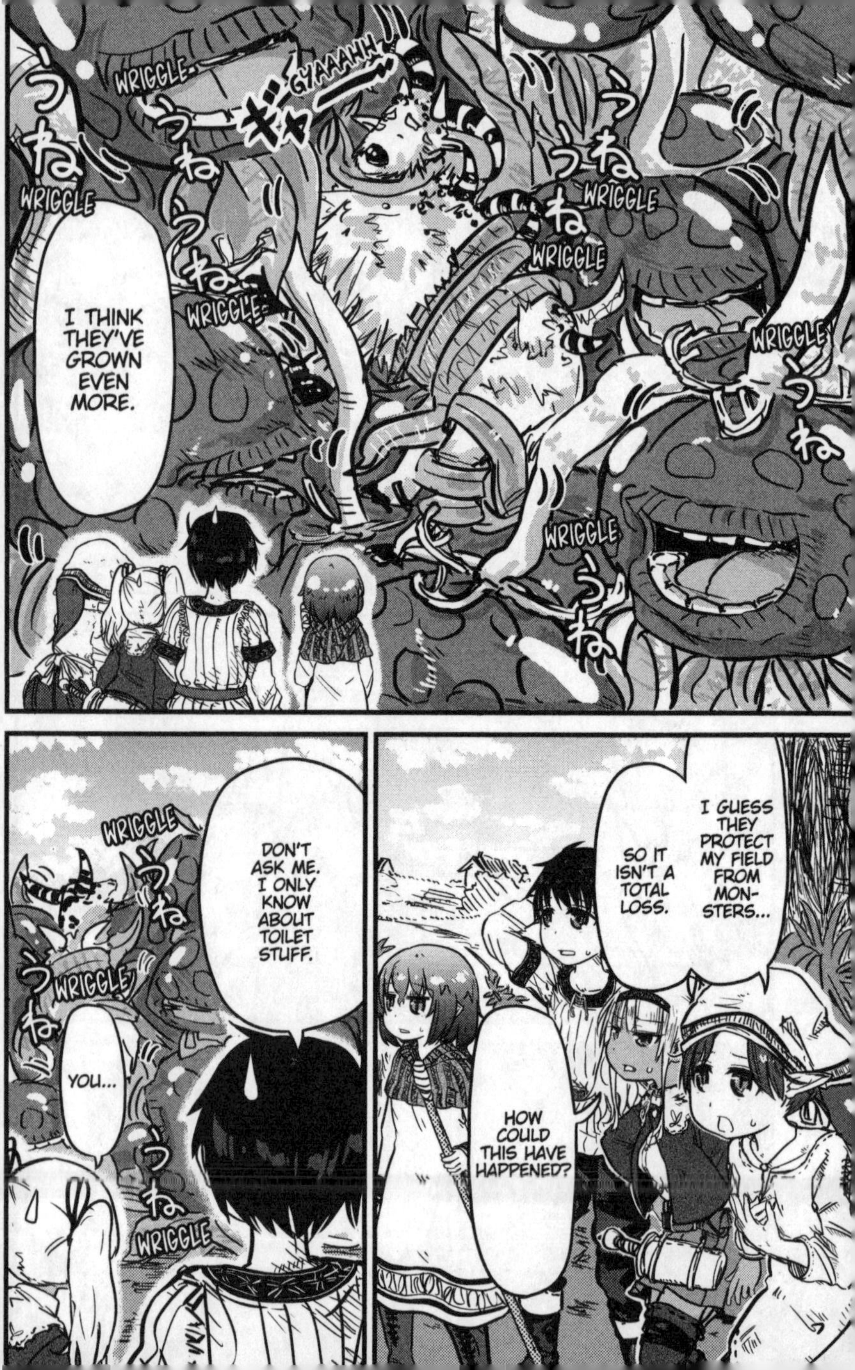
うね
WRIGGLE
うね
WRIGGLE
ね
WRIGGLE
GYAAAHH
ギャー
WRIGGLE
うね
うね
WRIGGLE
うね
WRIGGLE
I THINK THEY'VE GROWN EVEN MORE.
WRIGGLE
うね
I GUESS THEY PROTECT MY FIELD FROM MON-STERS...
SO IT ISN'T A TOTAL LOSS.
HOW COULD THIS HAVE HAPPENED?
WRIGGLE
うね
DON'T ASK ME. I ONLY KNOW ABOUT TOILET STUFF.
WRIGGLE
うね
YOU...
うね
WRIGGLE

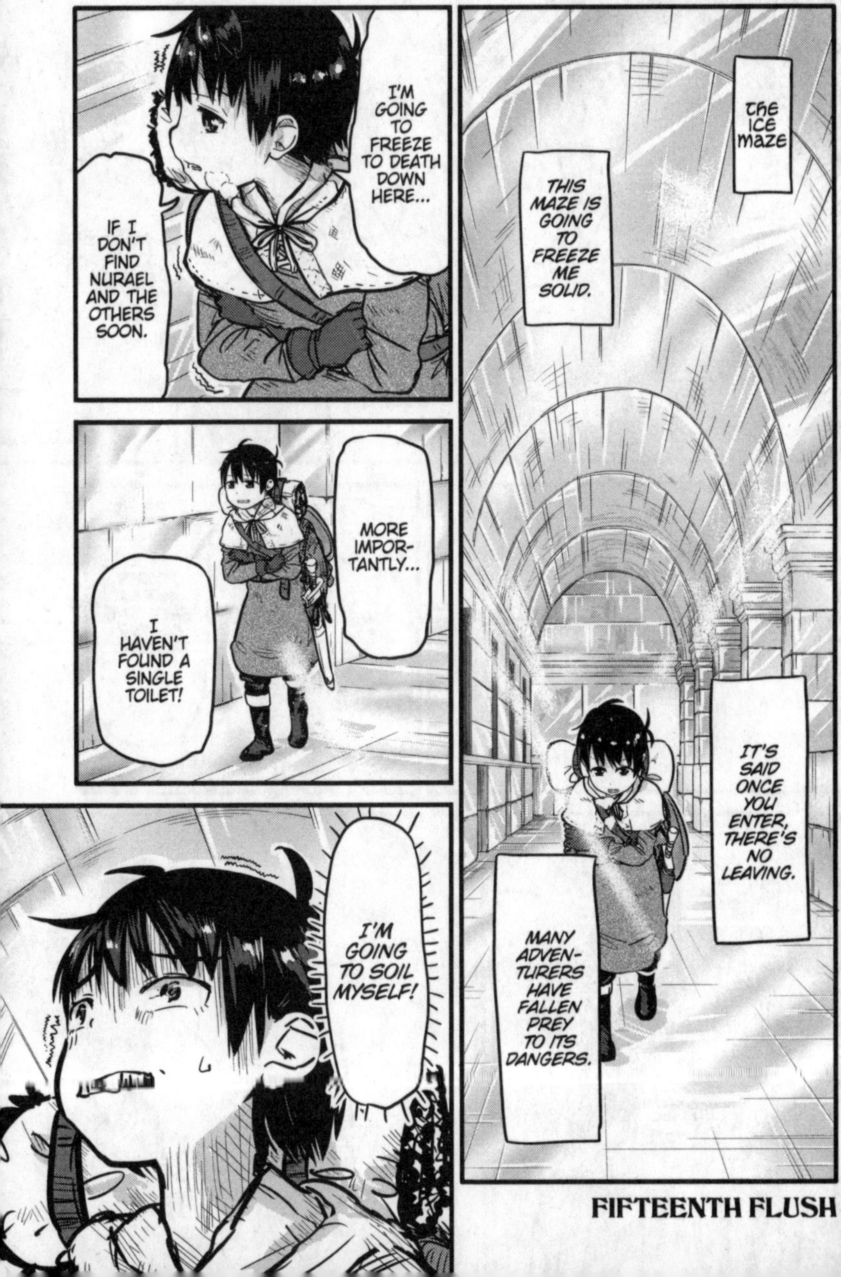
THE ICE MAZE
THIS MAZE IS GOING TO FREEZE ME SOLID.
IT'S SAID ONCE YOU ENTER, THERE'S NO LEAVING.
MANY ADVENTURERS HAVE FALLEN PREY TO ITS DANGERS.
I'M GOING TO FREEZE TO DEATH DOWN HERE...
IF I DON'T FIND NURAEL AND THE OTHERS SOON.
MORE IMPORTANTLY...
I HAVEN'T FOUND A SINGLE TOILET!
I'M GOING TO SOIL MYSELF!

FIFTEENTH FLUSH

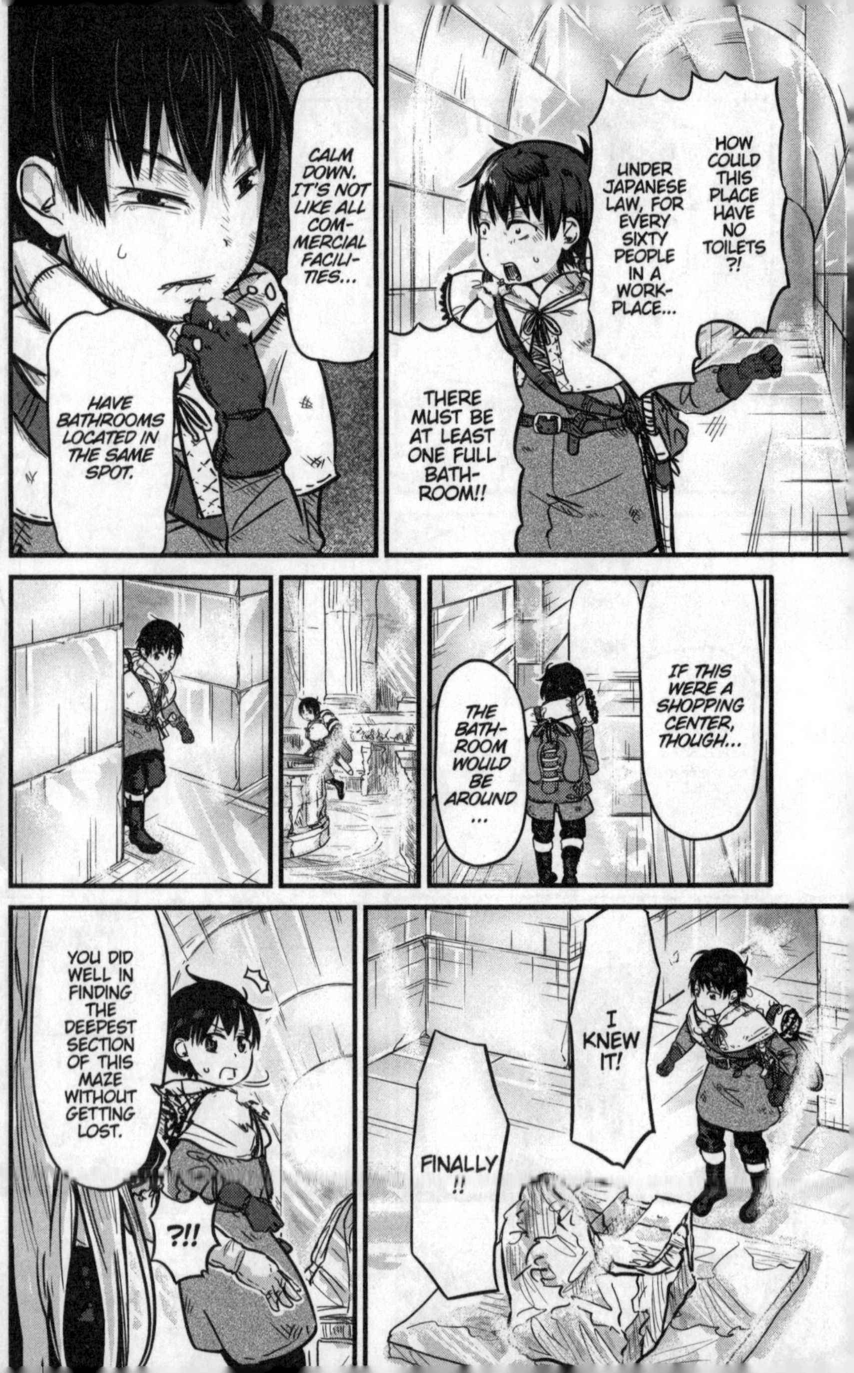
HOW COULD THIS PLACE HAVE NO TOILETS?!
UNDER JAPANESE LAW, FOR EVERY SIXTY PEOPLE IN A WORKPLACE...
THERE MUST BE AT LEAST ONE FULL BATHROOM!!
CALM DOWN. IT'S NOT LIKE ALL COMMERCIAL FACILITIES...
HAVE BATHROOMS LOCATED IN THE SAME SPOT.
IF THIS WERE A SHOPPING CENTER, THOUGH...
THE BATHROOM WOULD BE AROUND...
I KNEW IT!
FINALLY!!
YOU DID WELL IN FINDING THE DEEPEST SECTION OF THIS MAZE WITHOUT GETTING LOST.
?!!

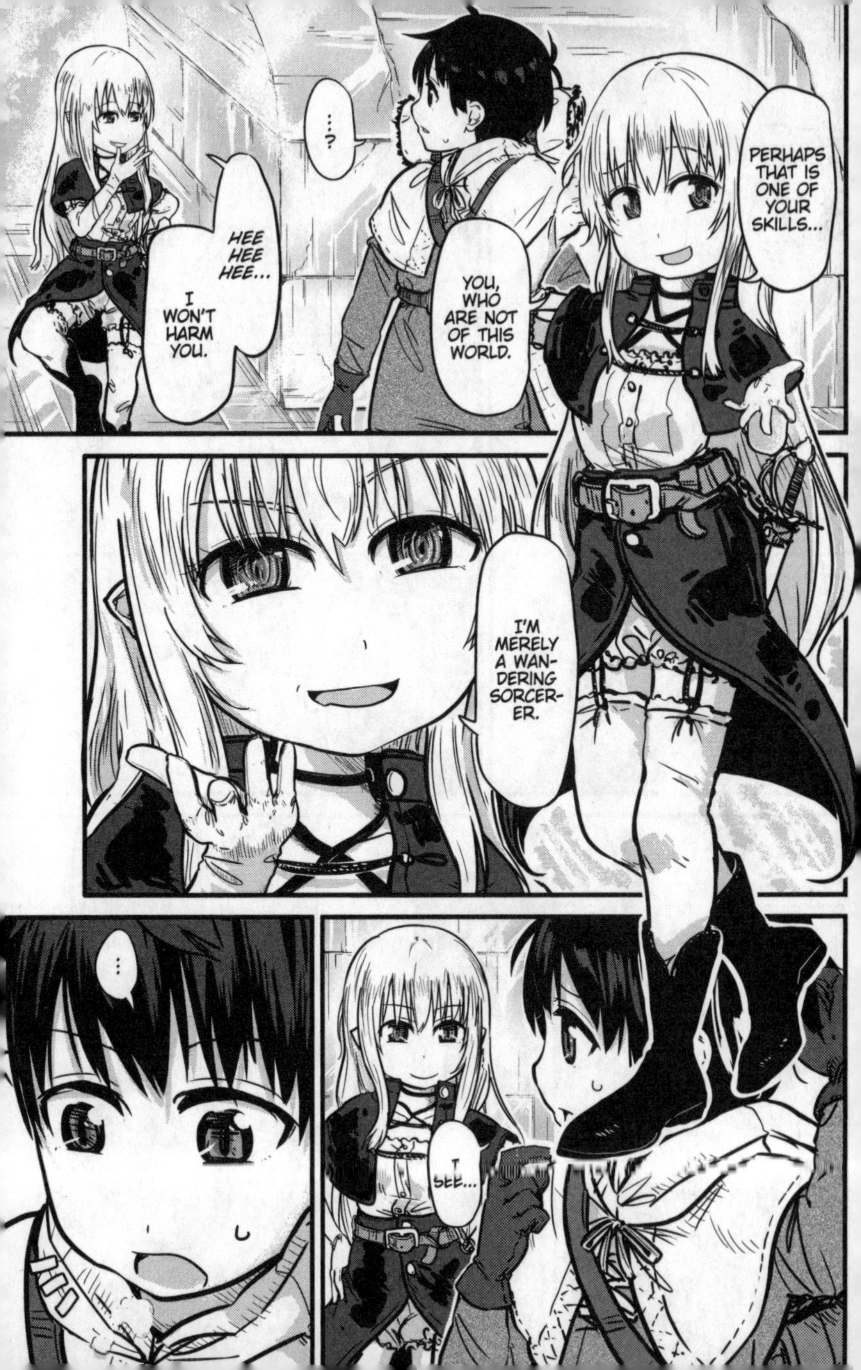
PERHAPS THAT IS ONE OF YOUR SKILLS...
YOU, WHO ARE NOT OF THIS WORLD.
...?
HEE HEE HEE...
I WON'T HARM YOU.
I'M MERELY A WAN-DERING SORCERER-ER.
I SEE...
...

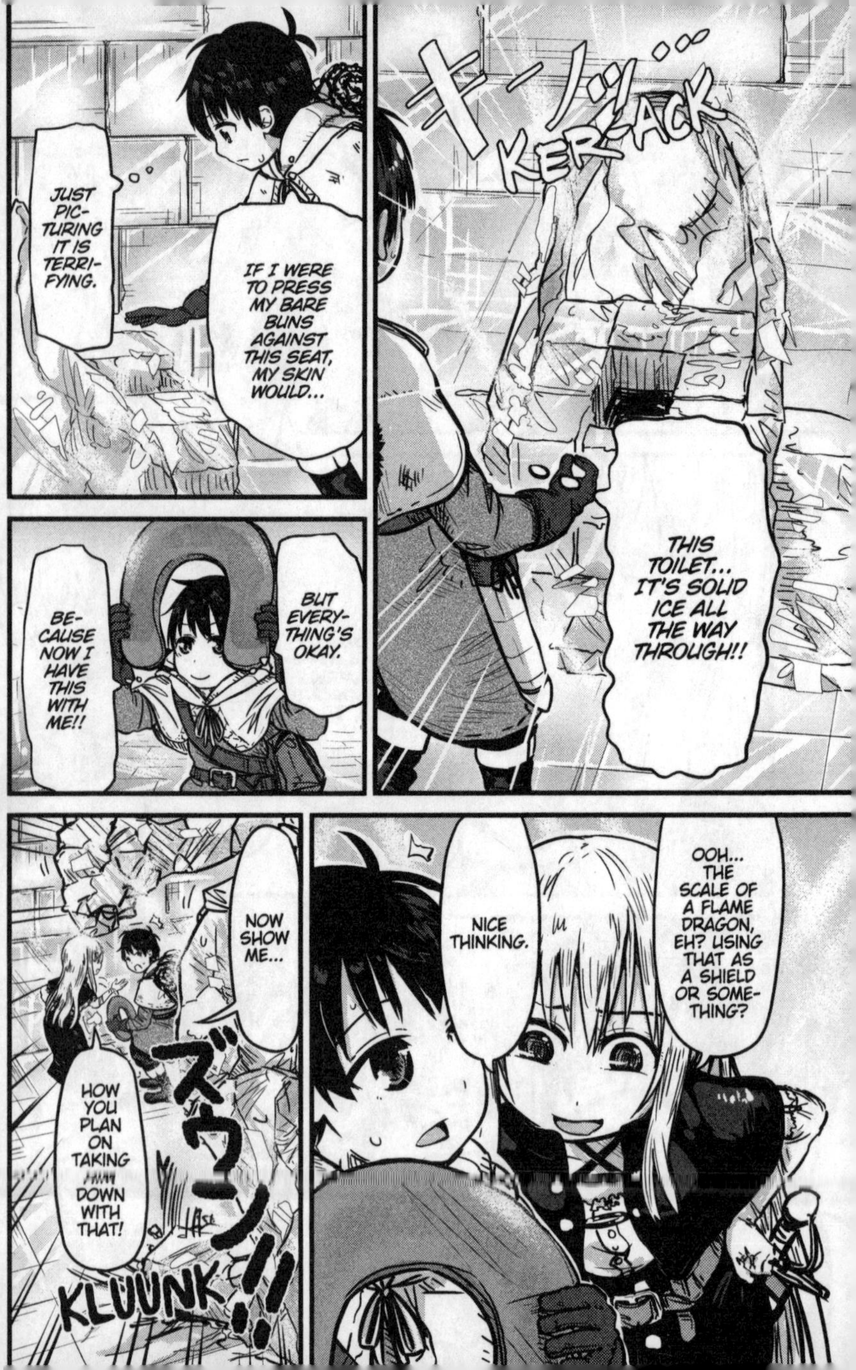
KER-ACK
THIS TOILET... IT'S SOLID ICE ALL THE WAY THROUGH!!
IF I WERE TO PRESS MY BARE BUNS AGAINST THIS SEAT, MY SKIN WOULD...
JUST PIC-TURING IT IS TERRI-FYING.
BUT EVERY-THING'S OKAY.
BE-CAUSE NOW I HAVE THIS WITH ME!!
OOH... THE SCALE OF A FLAME DRAGON, EH? USING THAT AS A SHIELD OR SOME-THING?
NICE THINKING.
NOW SHOW ME...
HOW YOU PLAN ON TAKING DOWN WITH THAT!
ズウーン
KLUUNK!!

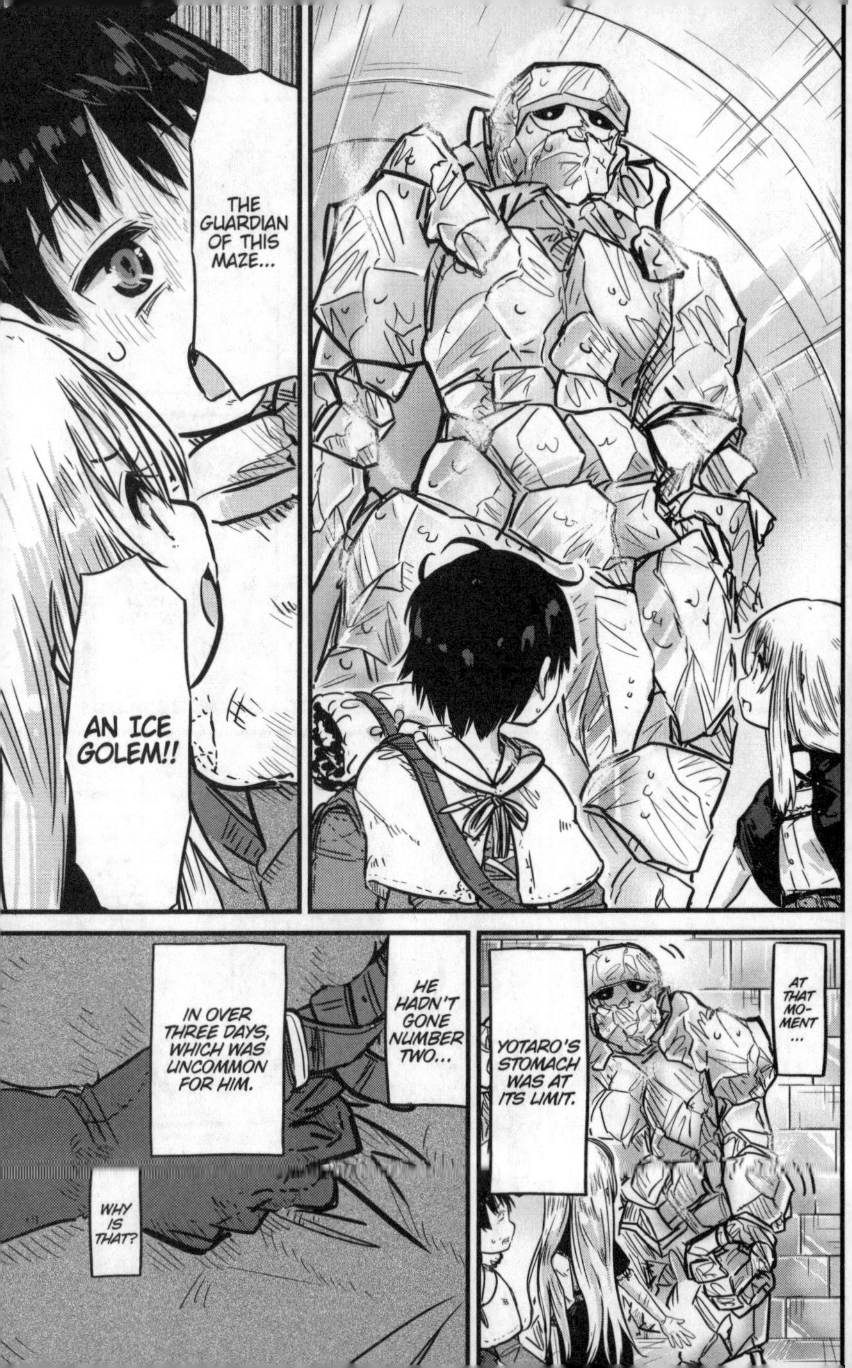
THE GUARDIAN OF THIS MAZE...
AN ICE GOLEM!!
AT THAT MOMENT...
YOTARO'S STOMACH WAS AT ITS LIMIT.
HE HADN'T GONE NUMBER TWO...
IN OVER THREE DAYS, WHICH WAS UNCOMMON FOR HIM.
WHY IS THAT?

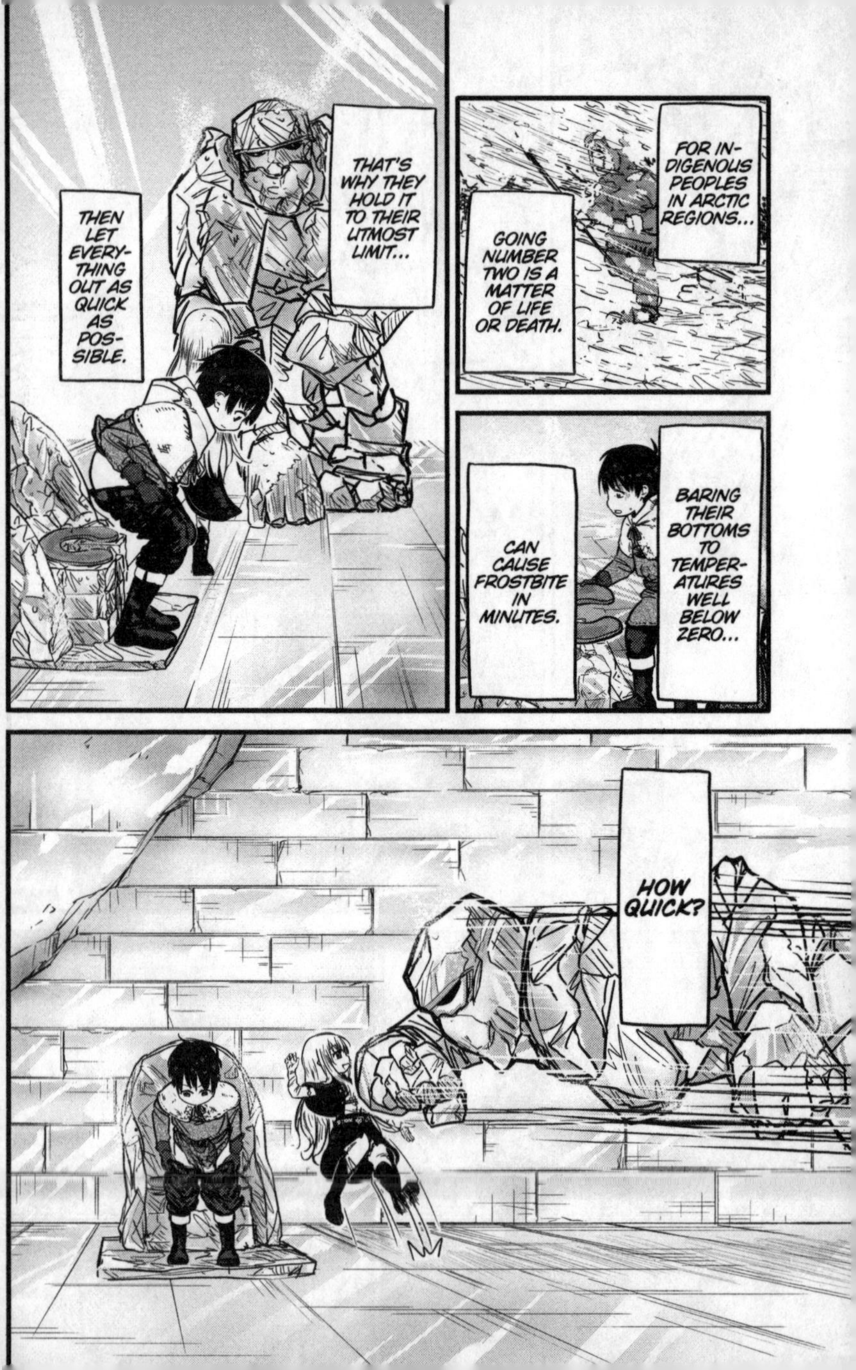
FOR INDIGENOUS PEOPLES IN ARCTIC REGIONS...
GOING NUMBER TWO IS A MATTER OF LIFE OR DEATH.
BARING THEIR BOTTOMS TO TEMPERATURES WELL BELOW ZERO...
CAN CAUSE FROSTBITE IN MINUTES.
THAT'S WHY THEY HOLD IT TO THEIR UTMOST LIMIT...
THEN LET EVERYTHING OUT AS QUICK AS POSSIBLE.
HOW QUICK?

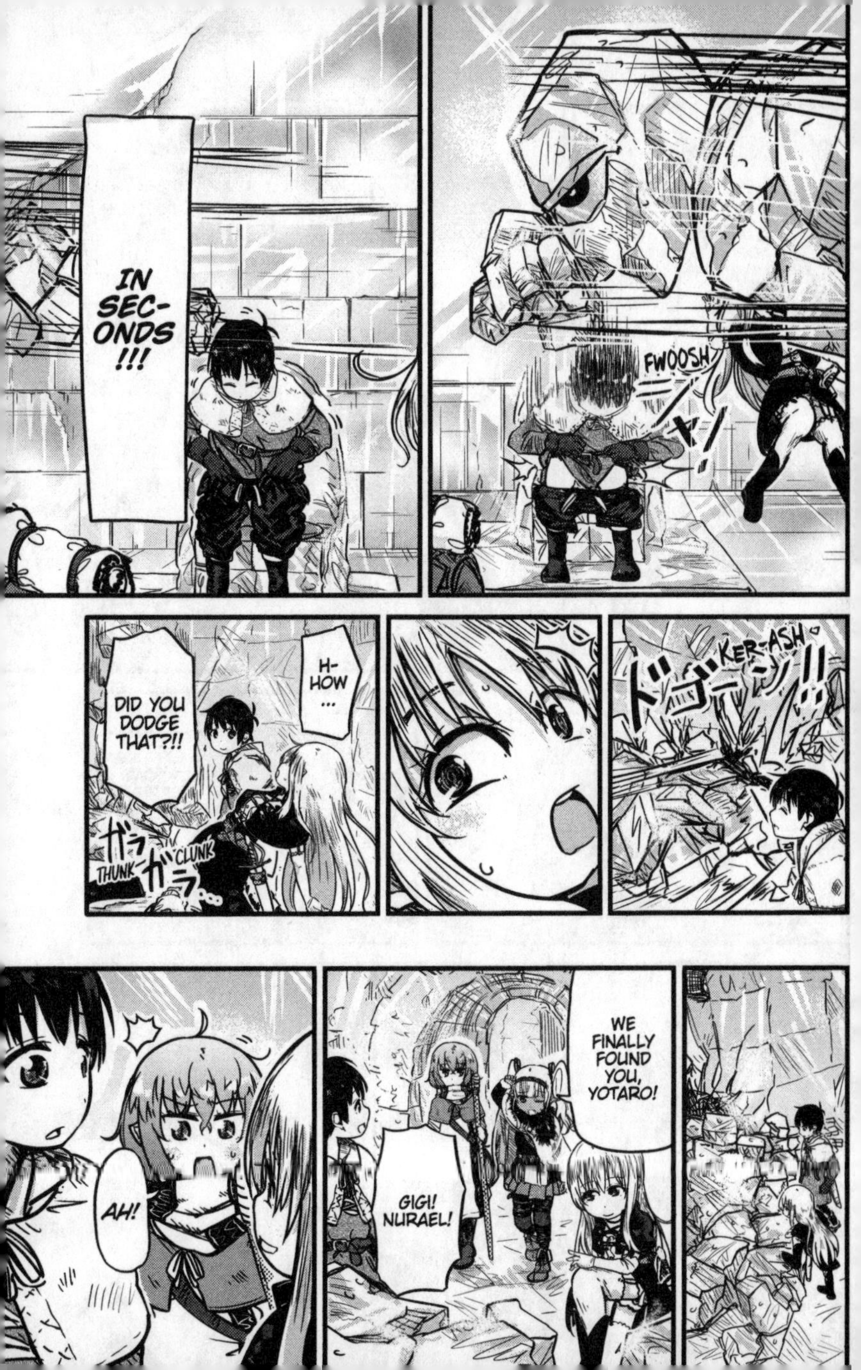
FWOOSH
IN SEC-ONDS !!!
KER-ASH
H-HOW...
DID YOU DODGE THAT?!!
CLUNK
THUNK
WE FINALLY FOUND YOU, YOTARO!
GIGI! NURAEL!
AH!

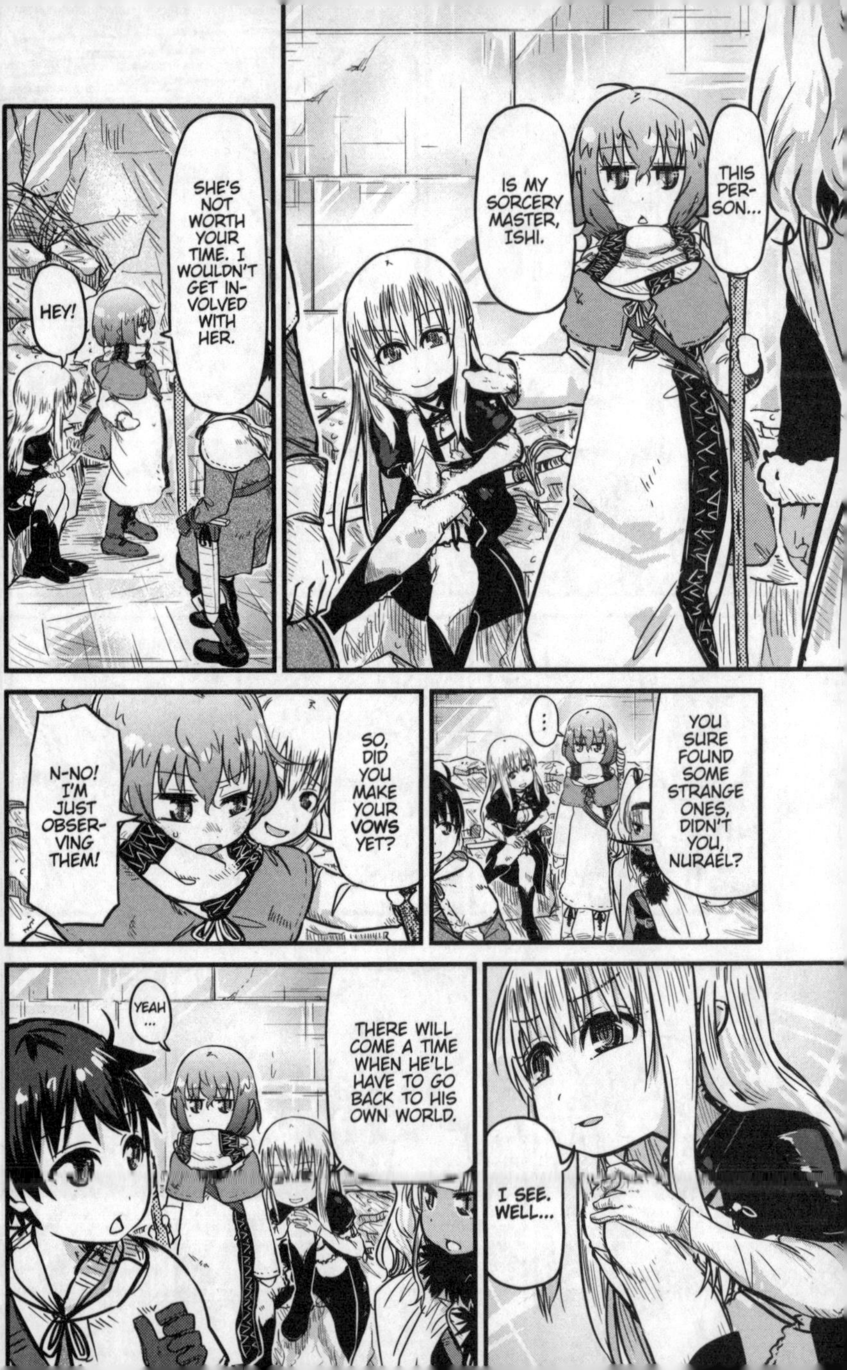
THIS PER-SON...
IS MY SORCERY MASTER, ISHI.
SHE'S NOT WORTH YOUR TIME. I WOULDN'T GET IN-VOLVED WITH HER.
HEY!
YOU SURE FOUND SOME STRANGE ONES, DIDN'T YOU, NURAEL?
...
SO, DID YOU MAKE YOUR VOWS YET?
N-NO! I'M JUST OBSER-VING THEM!
I SEE. WELL...
THERE WILL COME A TIME WHEN HE'LL HAVE TO GO BACK TO HIS OWN WORLD.
YEAH ...

ROOTS
PEOPLE WHO DON'T VALUE TOILET TIME ARE NO GOOD.

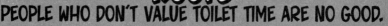

EIGHTH TOILET TIME

Today, I want all of you passive poopers to take a moment and understand the importance of what you do each and every day.

In the Edo period, human excrement was sold as a product. That's because fecal matter could be used as fertilizer. Koeoke referred to the buckets a person would use to collect feces from people's homes and carry it to farms.

Koeoke

Waste even had a ranking system: high, mid, and low quality. Compared to average homes, houses with a more plentiful diet, such as nobles or samurai, were thought to have better quality excrement, and it would sell for a higher price.

Since it was such a valuable commodity, the excrement in public toilets was considered the property of the landlord, and citizens could even pay a portion of their rent with their own feces.

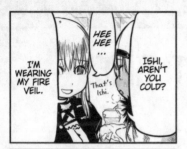

ISHI, AREN'T YOU COLD?
That's Ishi.
HEE HEE ...
I'M WEARING MY FIRE VEIL.
YOU ARE!
PAT
SO WARM.
SQUEEZE
SQUEEZE
WHAT ARE YOU TWO ...?
※ Closing the lid on a heated toilet seat will help you reduce your electricity bill.

The price of fecal matter was even known to start disputes between different cities. So while you go about your business, playing on your phone without a care in the world, I hope you take this to heart.

I have another story for all of you passive poopers about going number two in Arctic regions around the world.

In those areas, it really is a matter of life or death. It isn't just your tush that's in danger. You use a surprising amount of energy when going number two. Doing it incorrectly can cause you to freeze and even die the moment that dung golem leaves your body.

That is why some indigenous peoples will go days without having a movement, only to release it quickly, all at once. This way of pooping is apparently quite nice, but if you decide to do it, please do so responsibly.

I hope that by sharing these interesting facts with you, I'll help you improve your own toilet time.

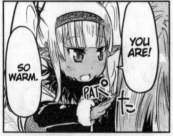

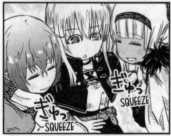

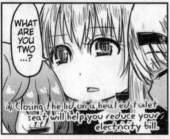

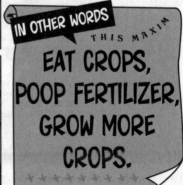

IN OTHER WORDS

THIS MAXIM

EAT CROPS, POOP FERTILIZER, GROW MORE CROPS.

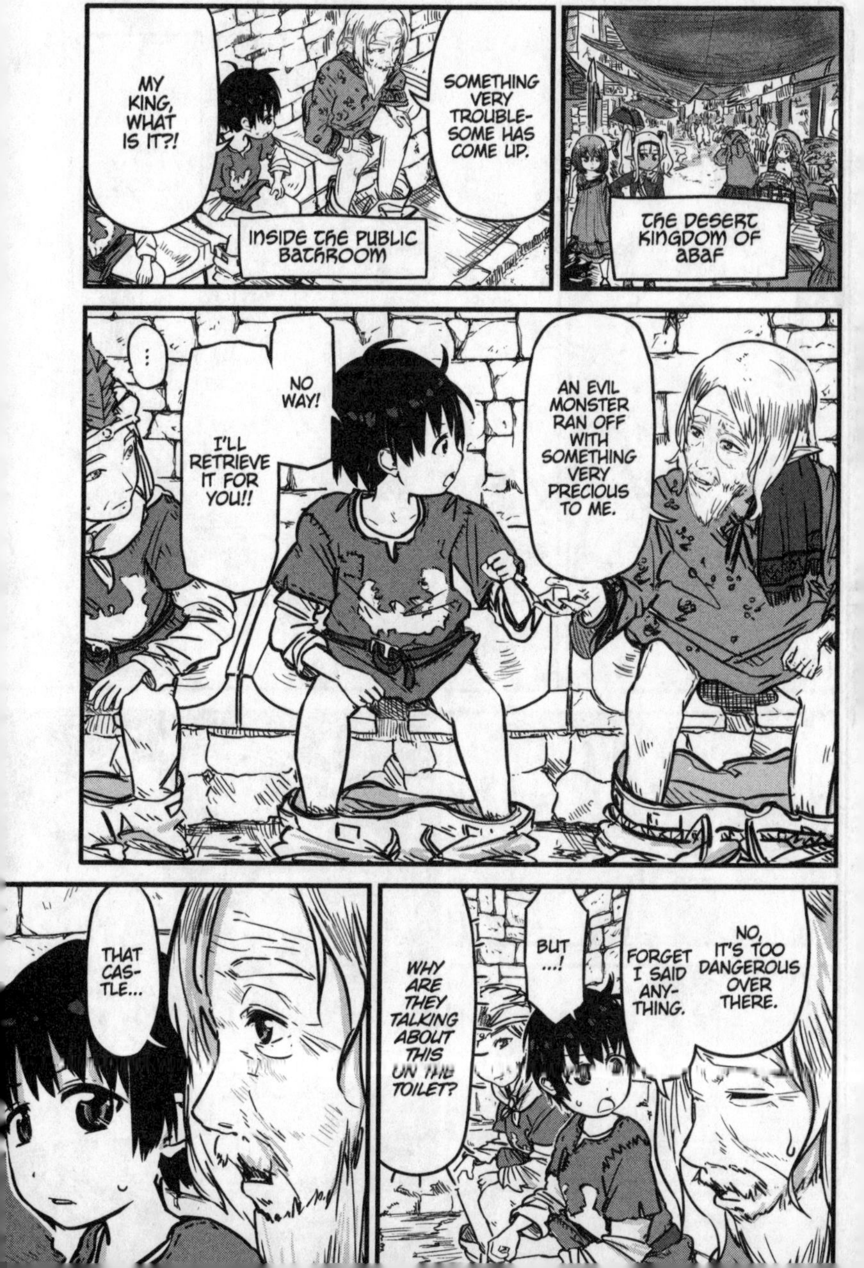
THE DESERT KINGDOM OF ABAF
INSIDE THE PUBLIC BATHROOM
SOMETHING VERY TROUBLE-SOME HAS COME UP.
MY KING, WHAT IS IT?!
AN EVIL MONSTER RAN OFF WITH SOMETHING VERY PRECIOUS TO ME.
NO WAY!
I'LL RETRIEVE IT FOR YOU!!
...
NO, IT'S TOO DANGEROUS OVER THERE.
FORGET I SAID ANY-THING.
BUT ...!
WHY ARE THEY TALKING ABOUT THIS ON THE TOILET?
THAT CAS-TLE...

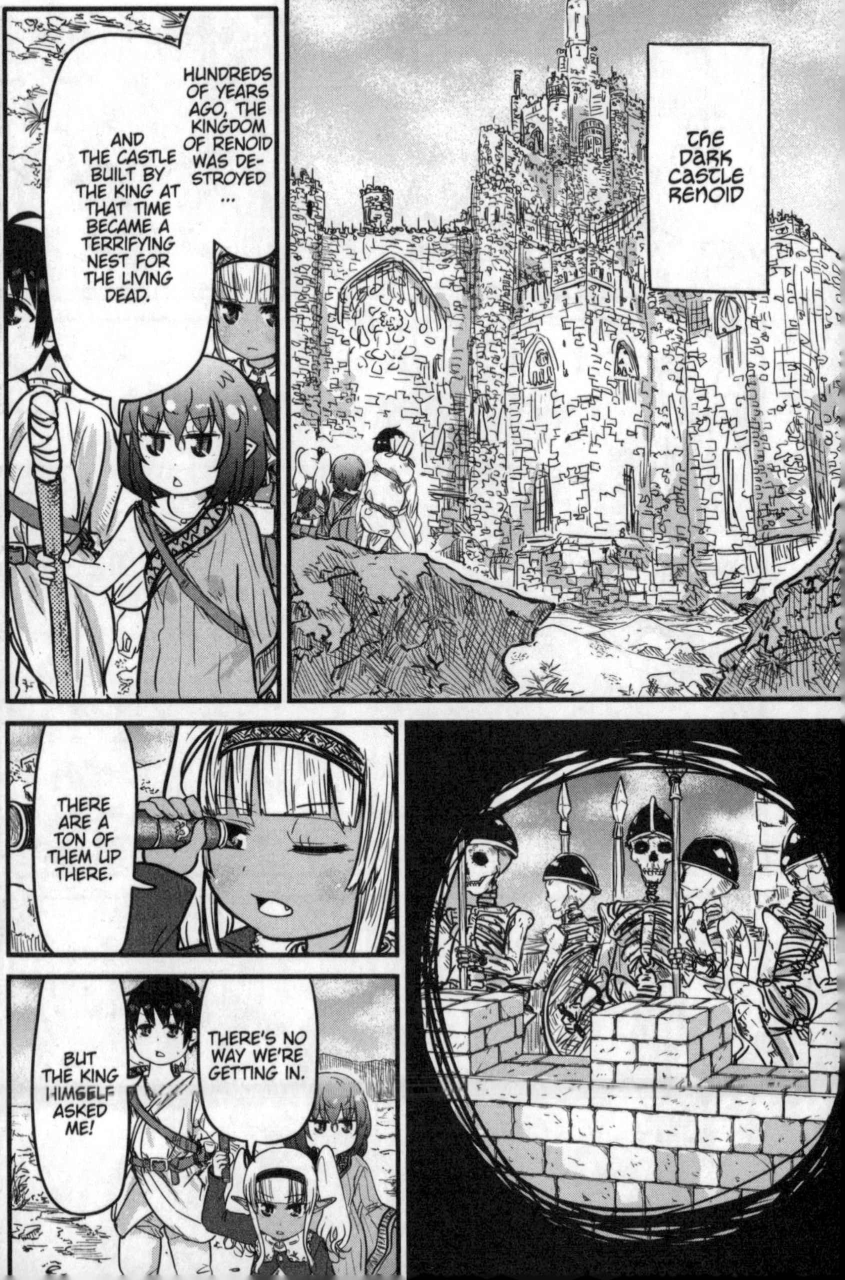
THE DARK CASTLE RENOID
HUNDREDS OF YEARS AGO, THE KINGDOM OF RENOID WAS DE-STROYED ...
AND THE CASTLE BUILT BY THE KING AT THAT TIME BECAME A TERRIFYING NEST FOR THE LIVING DEAD.
THERE ARE A TON OF THEM UP THERE.
THERE'S NO WAY WE'RE GETTING IN.
BUT THE KING HIMSELF ASKED ME!

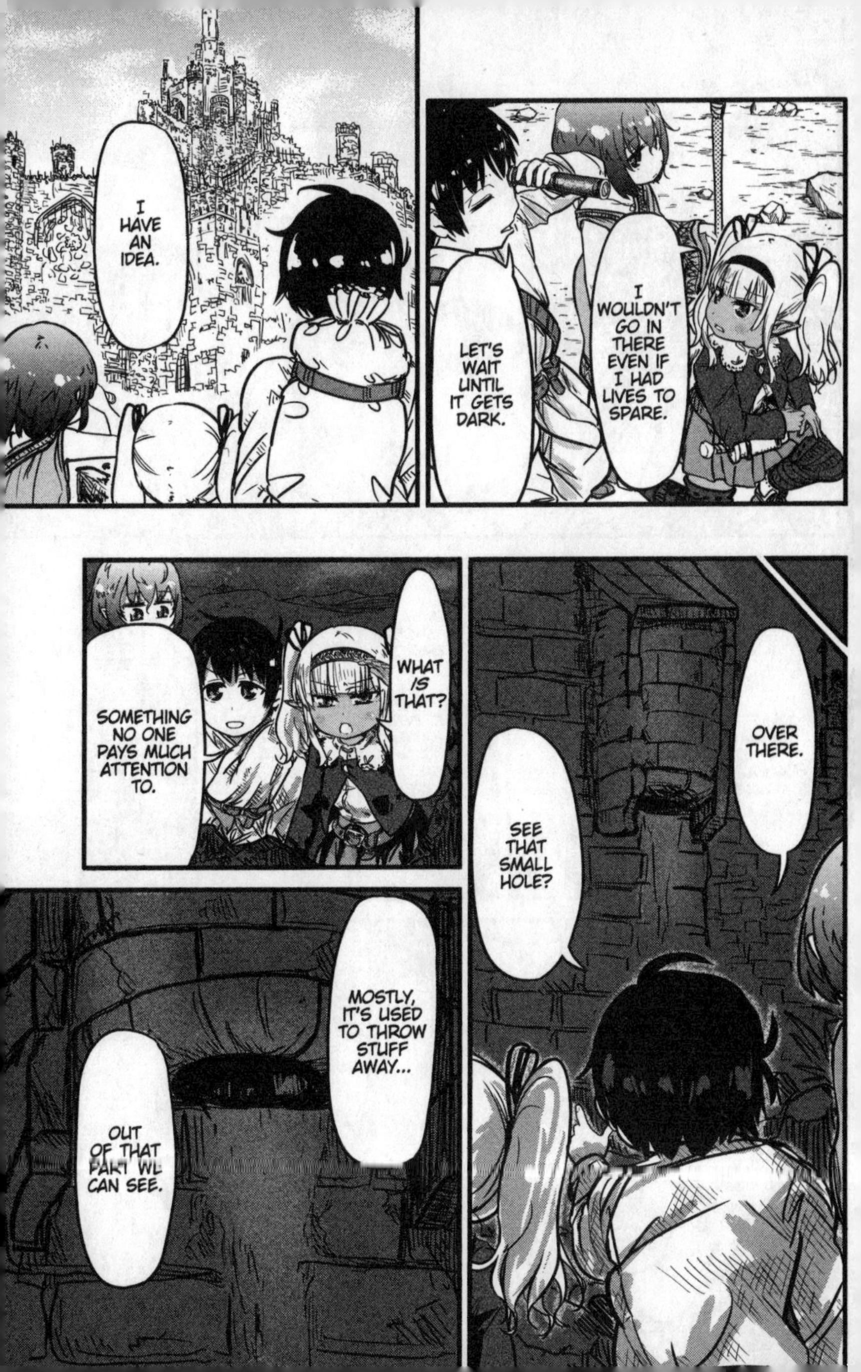
I WOULDN'T GO IN THERE EVEN IF I HAD LIVES TO SPARE.
LET'S WAIT UNTIL IT GETS DARK.
I HAVE AN IDEA.
OVER THERE.
SEE THAT SMALL HOLE?
WHAT IS THAT?
SOMETHING NO ONE PAYS MUCH ATTENTION TO.
MOSTLY, IT'S USED TO THROW STUFF AWAY...
OUT OF THAT PART WE CAN SEE.

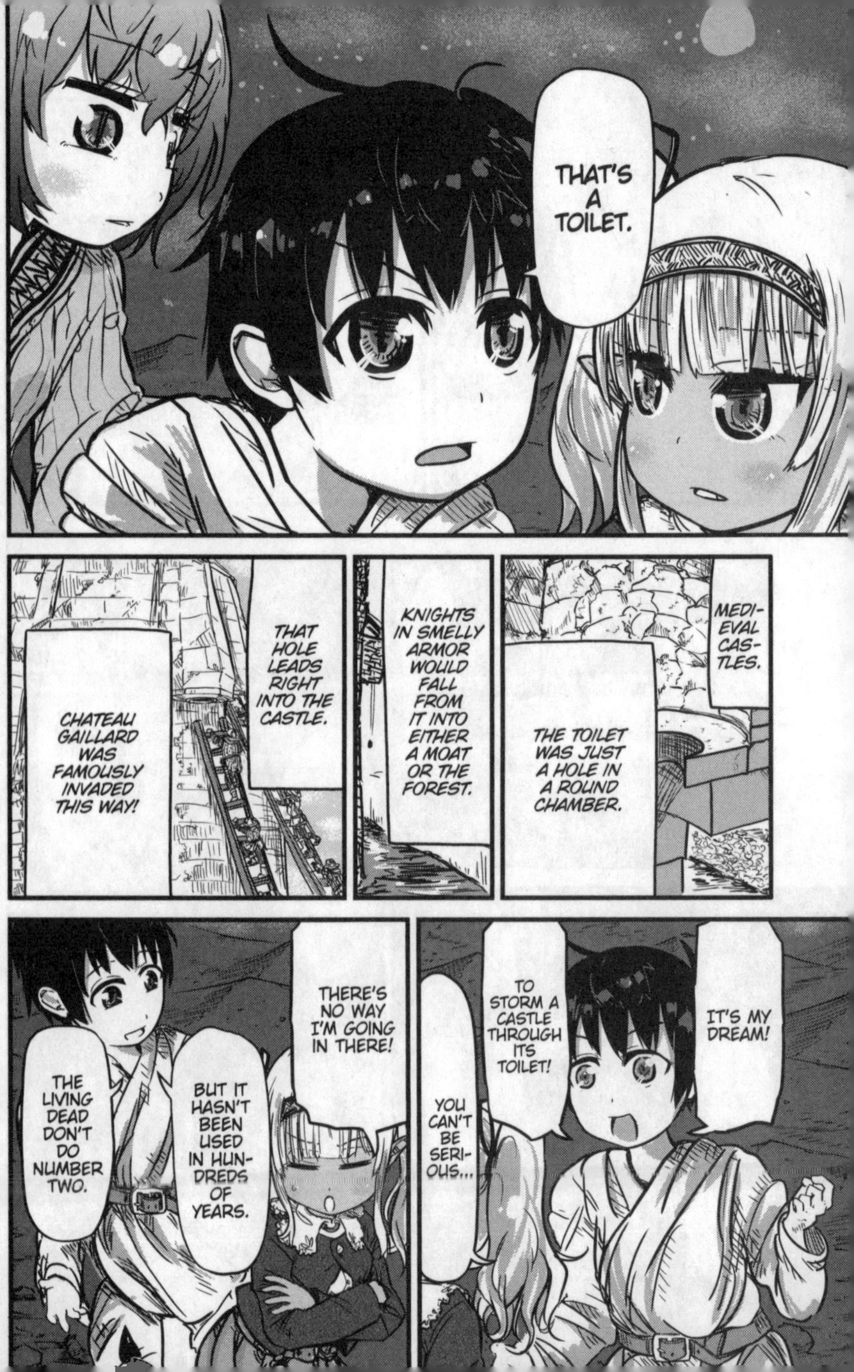
THAT'S A TOILET.
MEDIEVAL CASTLES.
THE TOILET WAS JUST A HOLE IN A ROUND CHAMBER.
KNIGHTS IN SMELLY ARMOR WOULD FALL FROM IT INTO EITHER A MOAT OR THE FOREST.
THAT HOLE LEADS RIGHT INTO THE CASTLE.
CHATEAU GAILLARD WAS FAMOUSLY INVADED THIS WAY!
IT'S MY DREAM!
TO STORM A CASTLE THROUGH ITS TOILET!
YOU CAN'T BE SERIOUS...
THERE'S NO WAY I'M GOING IN THERE!
BUT IT HASN'T BEEN USED IN HUNDREDS OF YEARS.
THE LIVING DEAD DON'T DO NUMBER TWO.

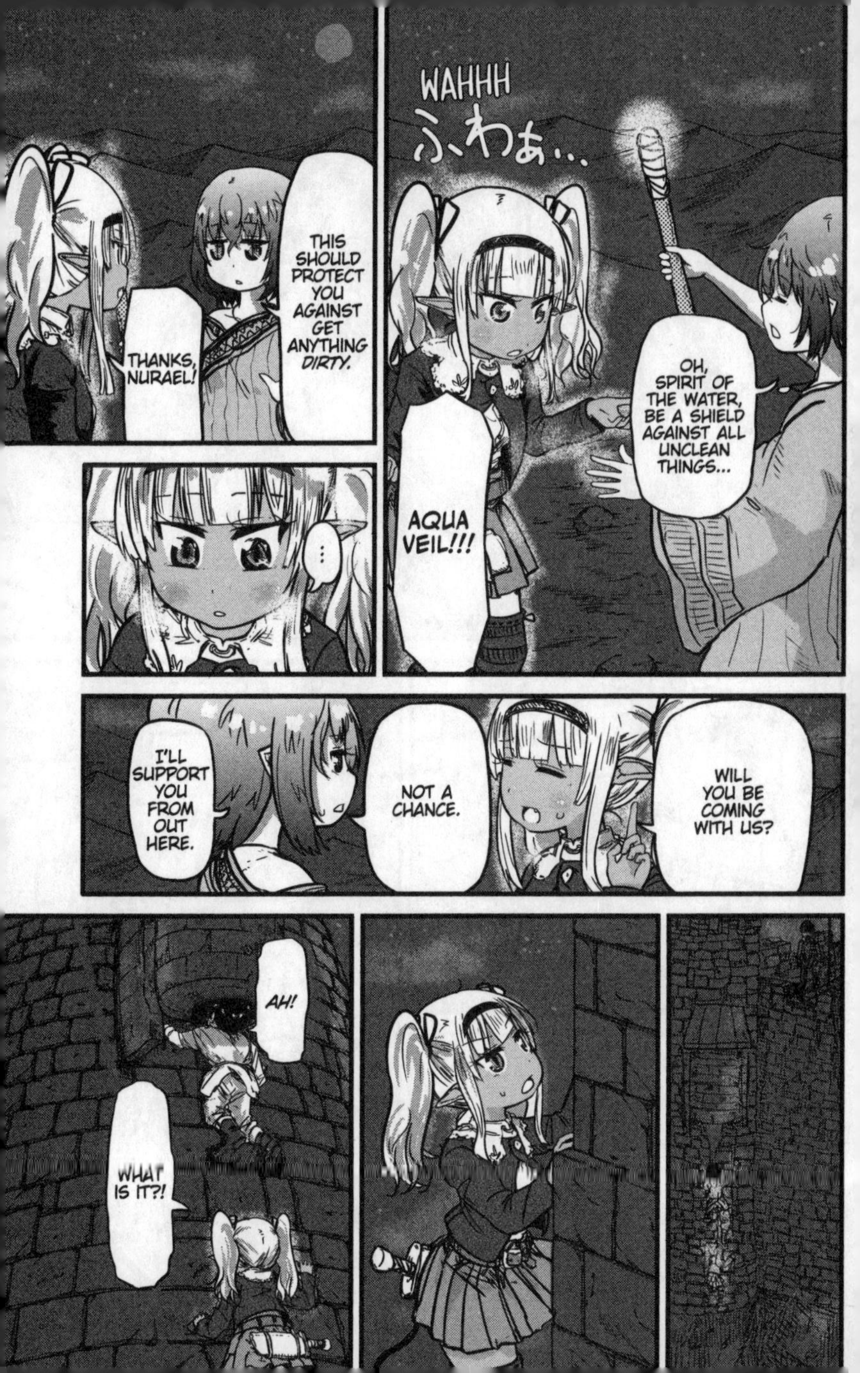
WAHHH
ふわぁ...
OH, SPIRIT OF THE WATER, BE A SHIELD AGAINST ALL UNCLEAN THINGS...
AQUA VEIL!!!
THIS SHOULD PROTECT YOU AGAINST GET ANYTHING DIRTY.
THANKS, NURAEL!
...
WILL YOU BE COMING WITH US?
NOT A CHANCE.
I'LL SUPPORT YOU FROM OUT HERE.
AH!
WHAT IS IT?!

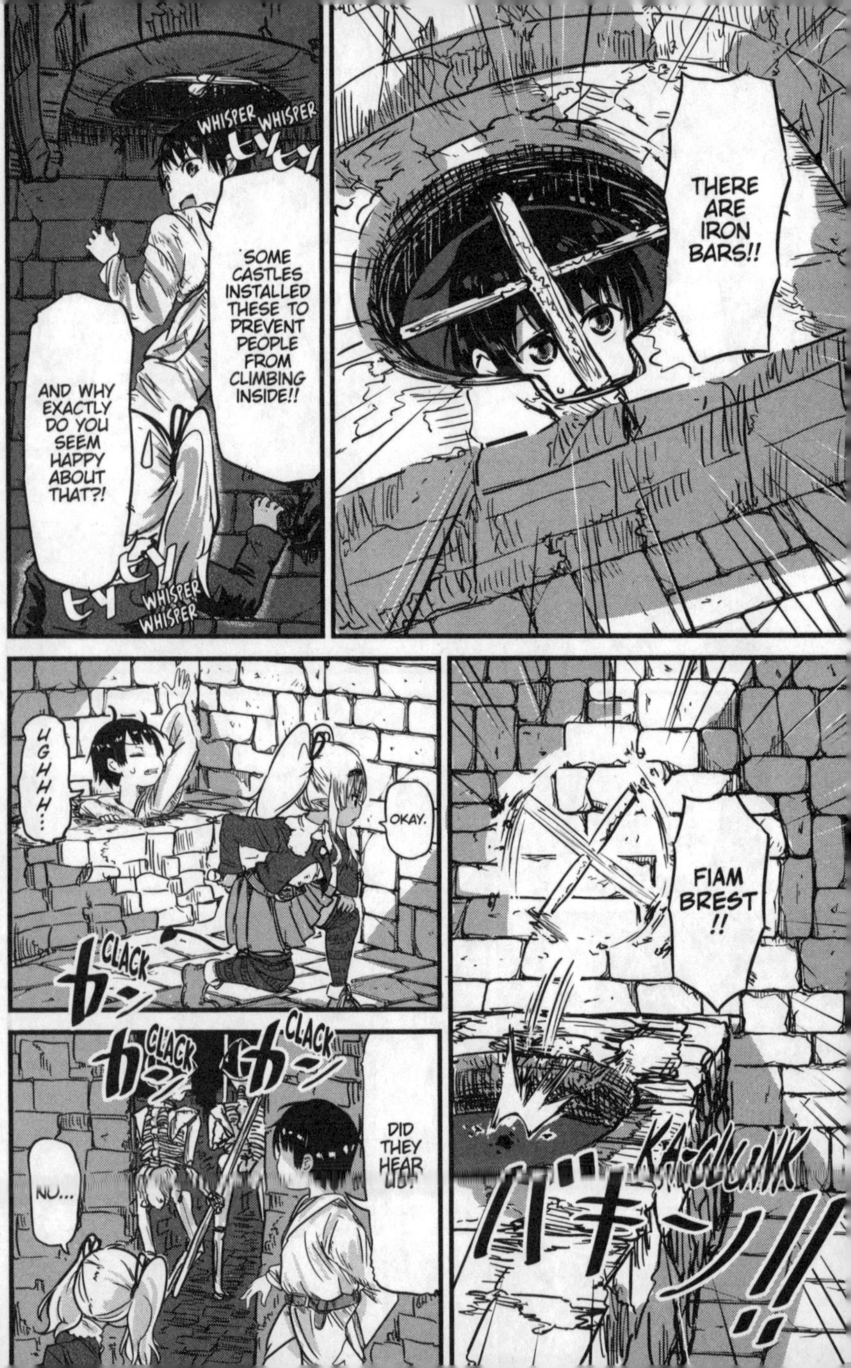
THERE ARE IRON BARS!!
WHISPER WHISPER
ヒソヒソ
SOME CASTLES INSTALLED THESE TO PREVENT PEOPLE FROM CLIMBING INSIDE!!
AND WHY EXACTLY DO YOU SEEM HAPPY ABOUT THAT?!
ヒソヒソ
WHISPER WHISPER
FIAM BREST!!
KA-CLUNK
バキーン!!
UGHHH...
OKAY.
CLACK
カーン
CLACK
CLACK
DID THEY HEAR US?
NU...

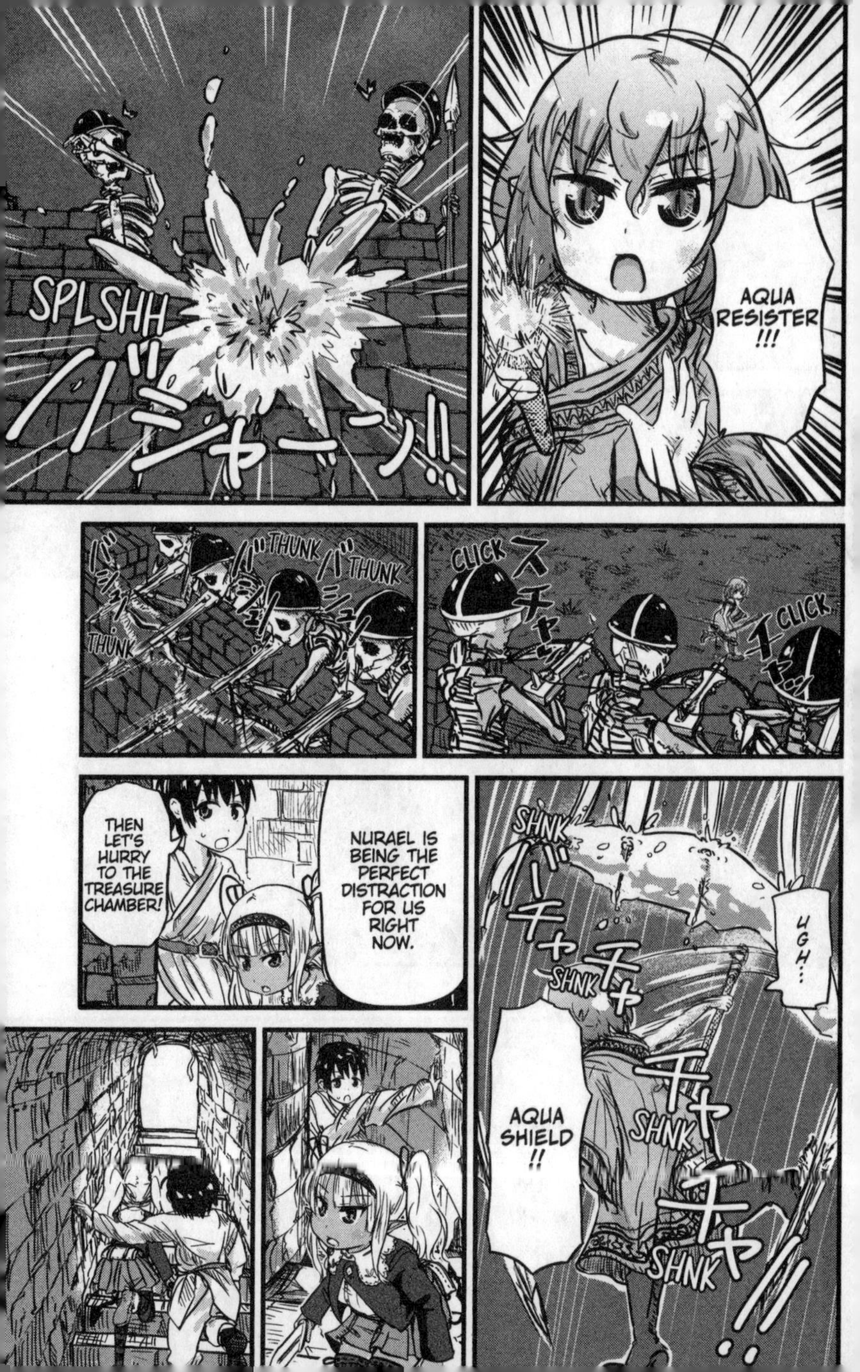
AQUA RESISTER!!!
SPLSHH
バシャーン!!
CLICK
スチャ
CLICK
チャ
THUNK
バシュ
THUNK
バシュ
THUNK
バシュ
UGH...
SHNK
バーチャ
SHNK
チャ
AQUA SHIELD!!
SHNK
チャ
SHNK
チャ!!
NURAEL IS BEING THE PERFECT DISTRACTION FOR US RIGHT NOW.
THEN LET'S HURRY TO THE TREASURE CHAMBER!

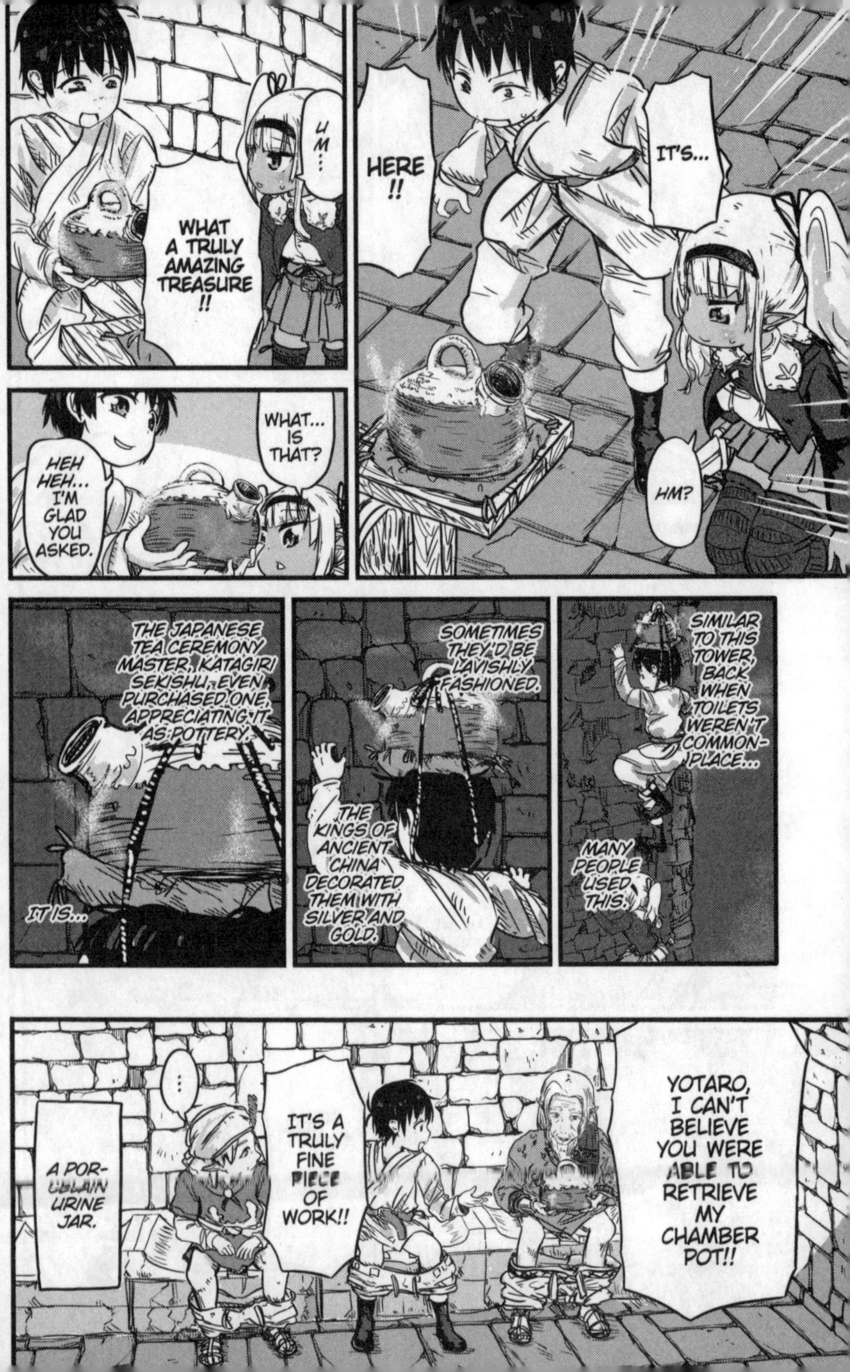
IT'S...
HERE!!
HM?
UM...
WHAT A TRULY AMAZING TREASURE!!
WHAT... IS THAT?
HEH HEH... I'M GLAD YOU ASKED.
SIMILAR TO THIS TOWER, BACK WHEN TOILETS WEREN'T COMMON-PLACE...
MANY PEOPLE USED THIS.
SOMETIMES THEY'D BE LAVISHLY FASHIONED.
THE KINGS OF ANCIENT CHINA DECORATED THEM WITH SILVER AND GOLD.
THE JAPANESE TEA CEREMONY MASTER, KATAGIRI SEKISHU, EVEN PURCHASED ONE, APPRECIATING IT AS POTTERY.
IT IS...
YOTARO, I CAN'T BELIEVE YOU WERE ABLE TO RETRIEVE MY CHAMBER POT!!
IT'S A TRULY FINE PIECE OF WORK!!
...
A POR-CELAIN URINE JAR.

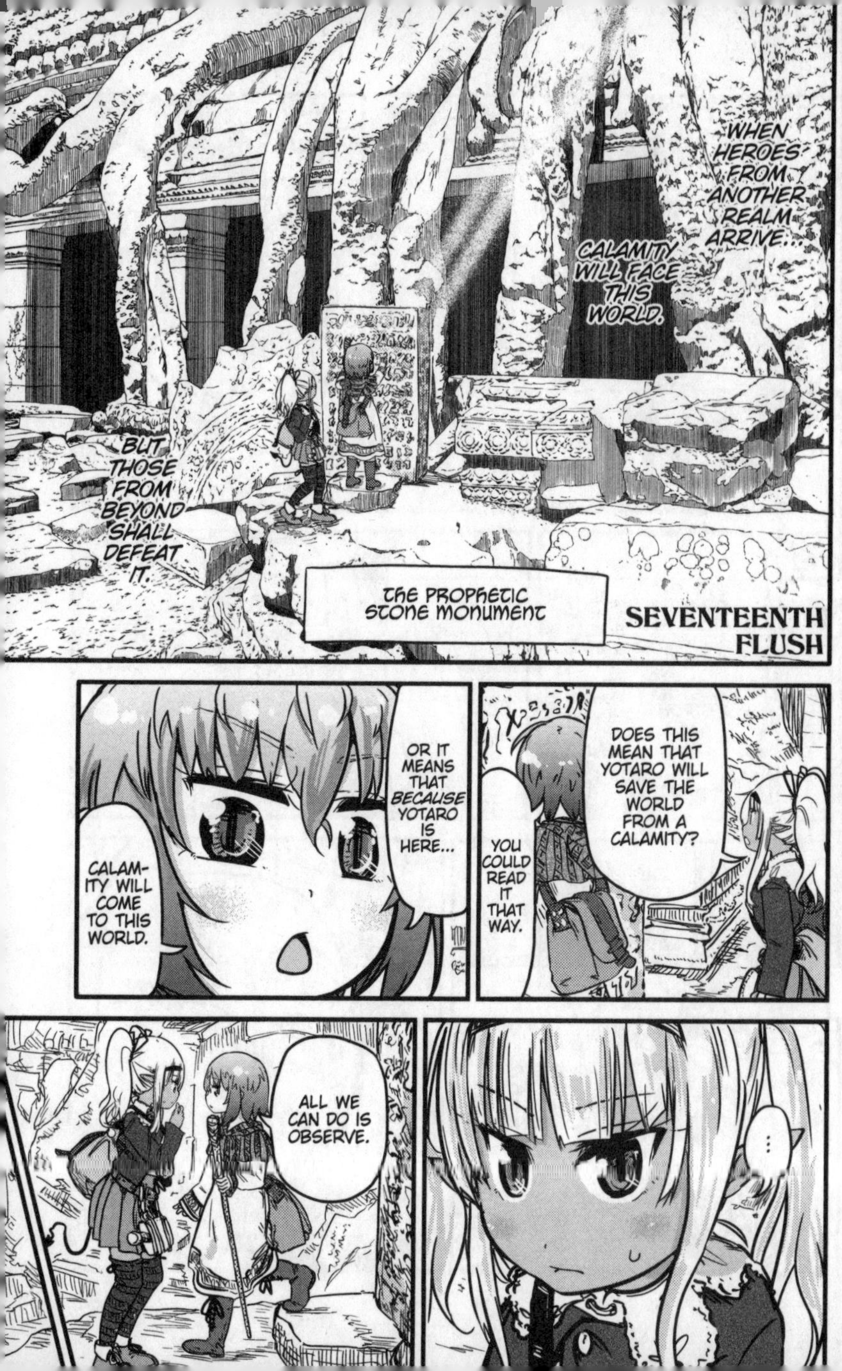
WHEN HEROES FROM ANOTHER REALM ARRIVE...
CALAMITY WILL FACE THIS WORLD.
BUT THOSE FROM BEYOND SHALL DEFEAT IT.
THE PROPHETIC STONE MONUMENT
SEVENTEENTH FLUSH
DOES THIS MEAN THAT YOTARO WILL SAVE THE WORLD FROM A CALAMITY?
YOU COULD READ IT THAT WAY.
OR IT MEANS THAT *BECAUSE* YOTARO IS HERE...
CALAMITY WILL COME TO THIS WORLD.
...
ALL WE CAN DO IS OBSERVE.

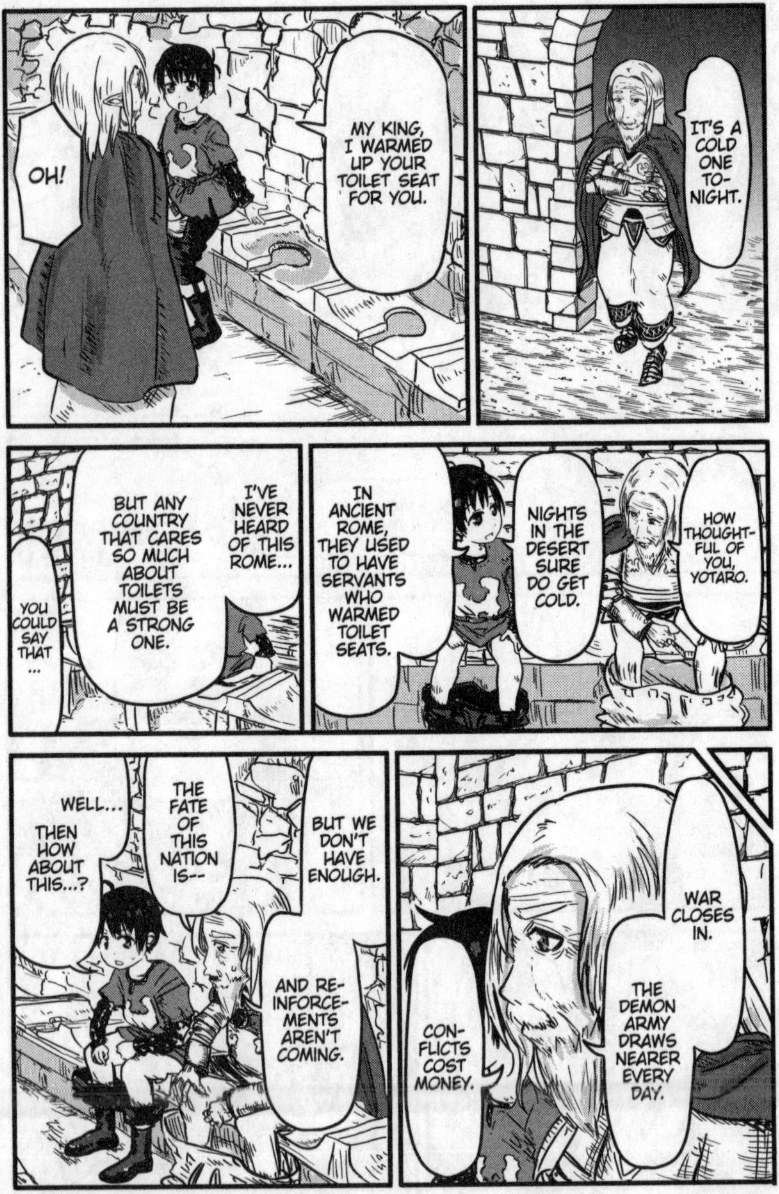
IT'S A COLD ONE TO-NIGHT.
MY KING, I WARMED UP YOUR TOILET SEAT FOR YOU.
OH!
HOW THOUGHT-FUL OF YOU, YOTARO.
NIGHTS IN THE DESERT SURE DO GET COLD.
IN ANCIENT ROME, THEY USED TO HAVE SERVANTS WHO WARMED TOILET SEATS.
I'VE NEVER HEARD OF THIS ROME...
BUT ANY COUNTRY THAT CARES SO MUCH ABOUT TOILETS MUST BE A STRONG ONE.
YOU COULD SAY THAT ...
WAR CLOSES IN.
THE DEMON ARMY DRAWS NEARER EVERY DAY.
CON-FLICTS COST MONEY.
BUT WE DON'T HAVE ENOUGH.
AND RE-INFORCE-MENTS AREN'T COMING.
THE FATE OF THIS NATION IS--
WELL...
THEN HOW ABOUT THIS...?

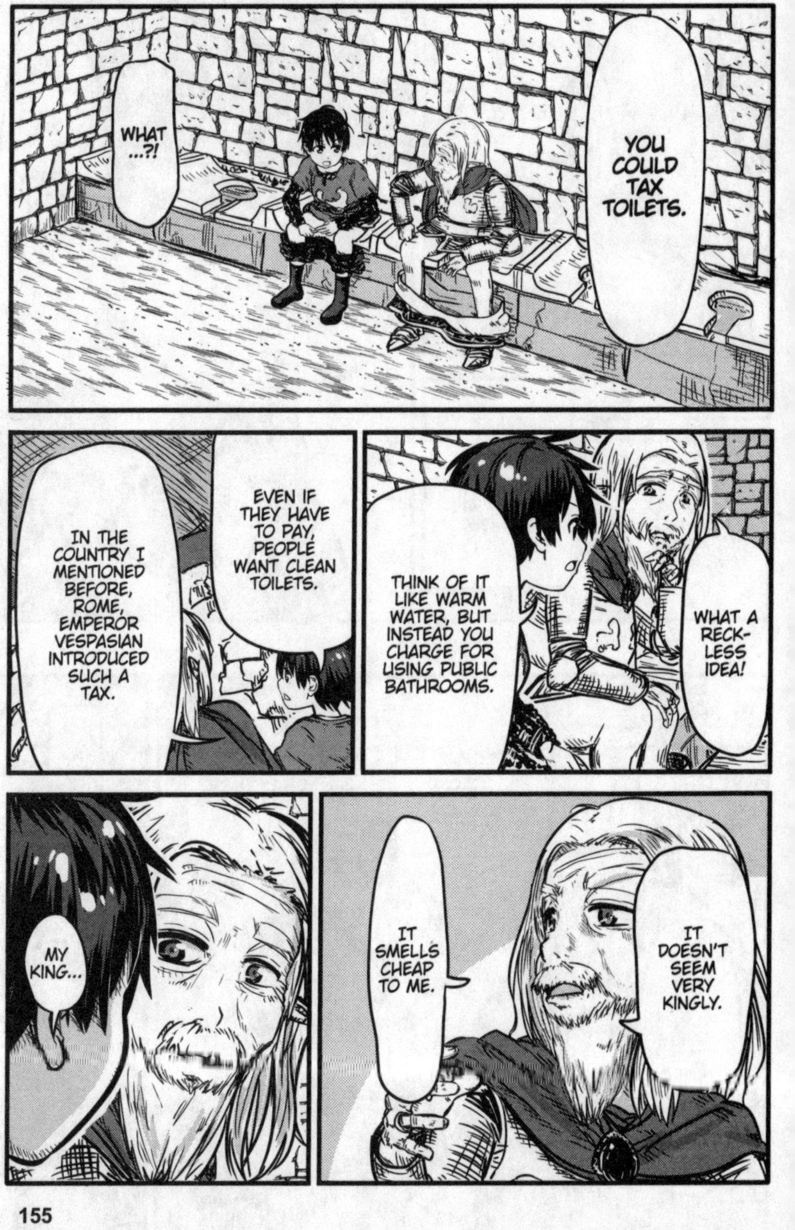
YOU COULD TAX TOILETS.
WHAT ...?!
WHAT A RECK-LESS IDEA!
THINK OF IT LIKE WARM WATER, BUT INSTEAD YOU CHARGE FOR USING PUBLIC BATHROOMS.
EVEN IF THEY HAVE TO PAY, PEOPLE WANT CLEAN TOILETS.
IN THE COUNTRY I MENTIONED BEFORE, ROME, EMPEROR VESPASIAN INTRODUCED SUCH A TAX.
IT DOESN'T SEEM VERY KINGLY.
IT SMELLS CHEAP TO ME.
MY KING...

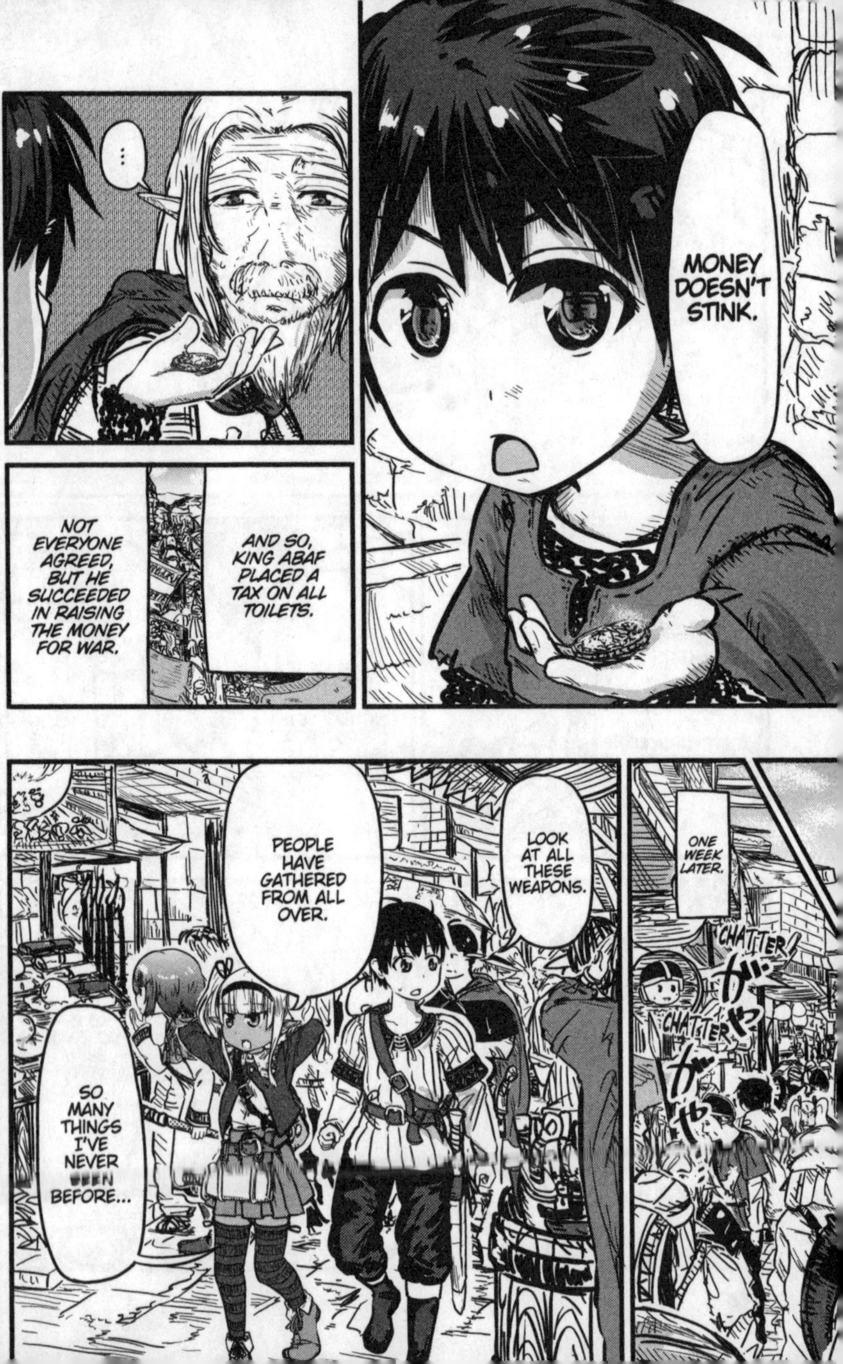
MONEY DOESN'T STINK.
...
AND SO, KING ABAF PLACED A TAX ON ALL TOILETS.
NOT EVERYONE AGREED, BUT HE SUCCEEDED IN RAISING THE MONEY FOR WAR.
ONE WEEK LATER.
CHATTER
CHATTER
LOOK AT ALL THESE WEAPONS.
PEOPLE HAVE GATHERED FROM ALL OVER.
SO MANY THINGS I'VE NEVER SEEN BEFORE...

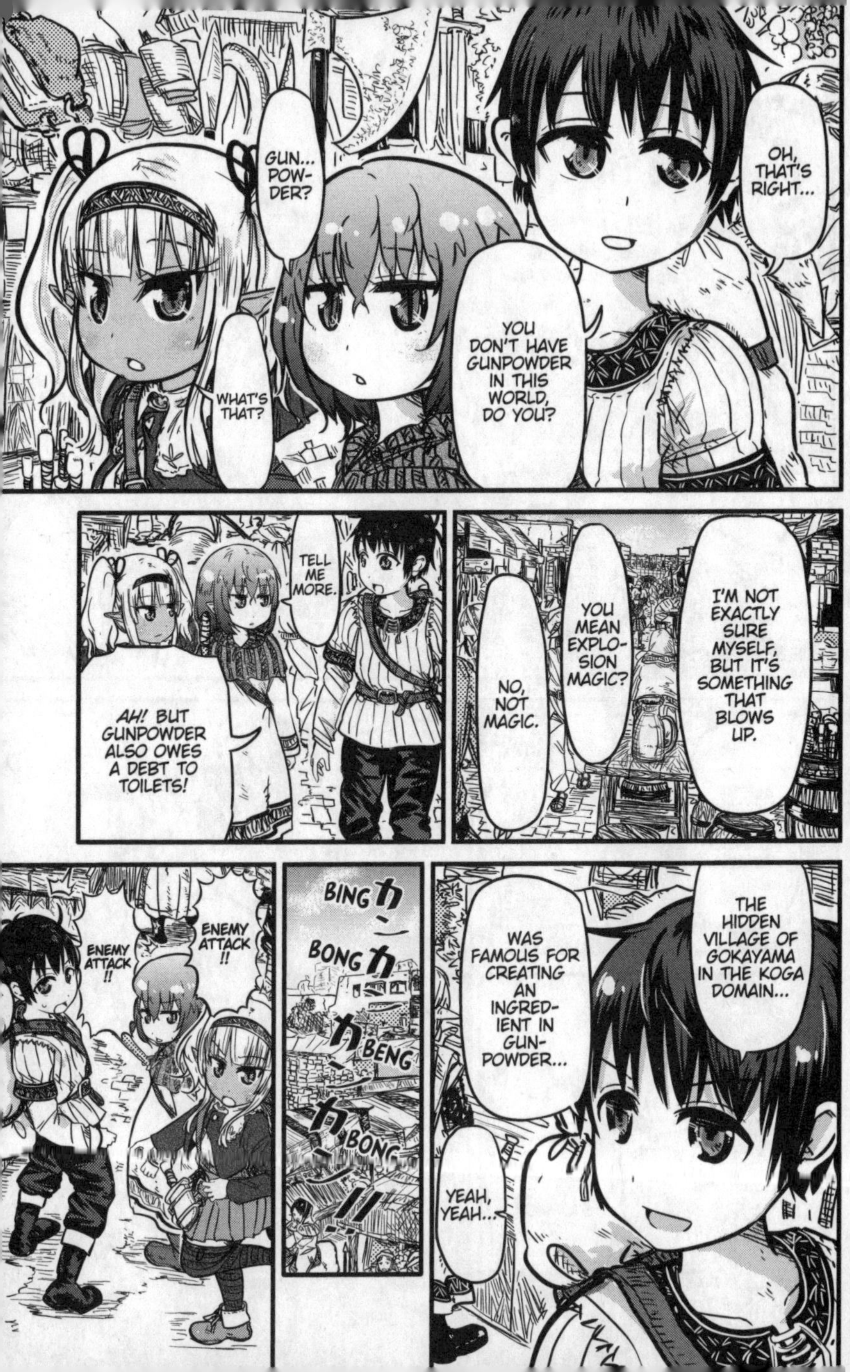
OH, THAT'S RIGHT...
YOU DON'T HAVE GUNPOWDER IN THIS WORLD, DO YOU?
GUN... POWDER?
WHAT'S THAT?
I'M NOT EXACTLY SURE MYSELF, BUT IT'S SOMETHING THAT BLOWS UP.
YOU MEAN EXPLOSION MAGIC?
NO, NOT MAGIC.
TELL ME MORE.
AH! BUT GUNPOWDER ALSO OWES A DEBT TO TOILETS!
THE HIDDEN VILLAGE OF GOKAYAMA IN THE KOGA DOMAIN...
WAS FAMOUS FOR CREATING AN INGREDIENT IN GUNPOWDER...
YEAH, YEAH...
BING
BONG
BENG
BONG!!
ENEMY ATTACK!!
ENEMY ATTACK!!

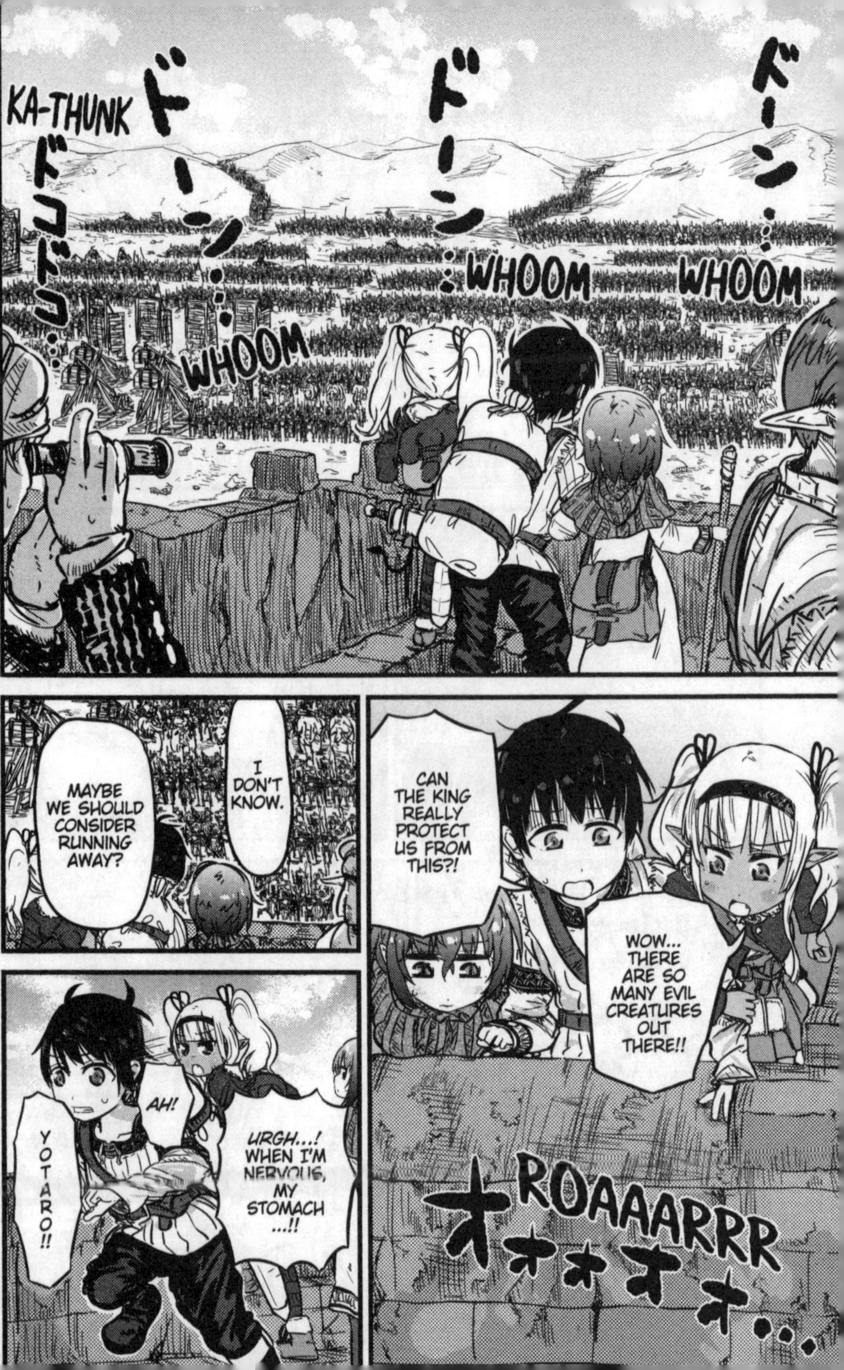
ドーン……
WHOOM
ドーン……
WHOOM
ドーン……
WHOOM
ゴトッ…
KA-THUNK
WOW... THERE ARE SO MANY EVIL CREATURES OUT THERE!!
CAN THE KING REALLY PROTECT US FROM THIS?!
I DON'T KNOW.
MAYBE WE SHOULD CONSIDER RUNNING AWAY?
オォォォォ…
ROAAARRR
URGH...! WHEN I'M NERVOUS, MY STOMACH ...!!
AH!
YOTARO!!

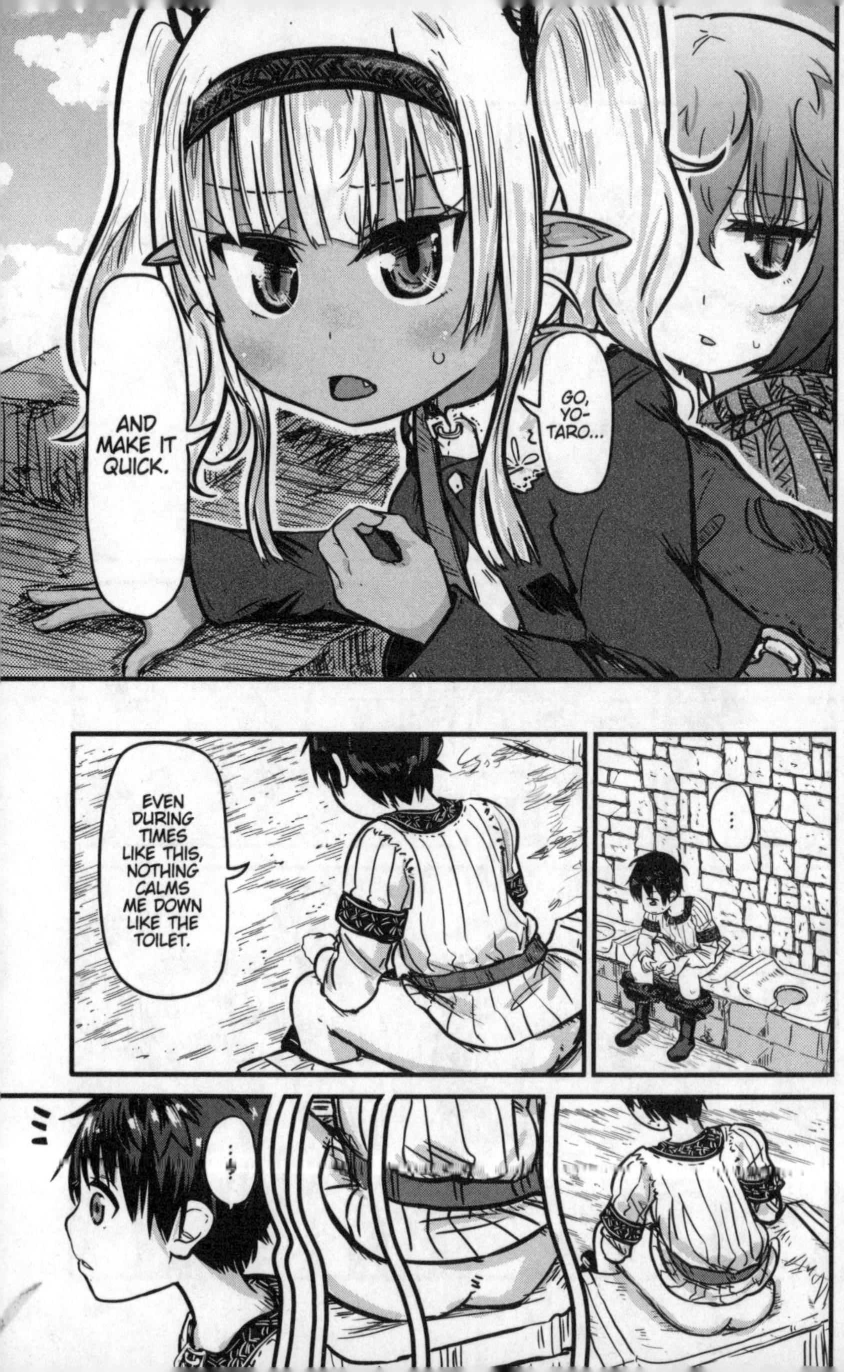
GO, YO-TARO...
AND MAKE IT QUICK.
...
EVEN DURING TIMES LIKE THIS, NOTHING CALMS ME DOWN LIKE THE TOILET.
...!

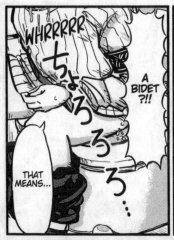

WH-WHERE AM I ?!!
WHRRRRR
ちょろろろ…
A BIDET ?!!
THAT MEANS...
I'VE RETURNED TO MY WORLD!!
NOTHING COM-PARES TO A MODERN JAPANESE TOILET!
AHH ...
IT'S GOOD TO BE BACK.
...
GIGI...
NURAEL...

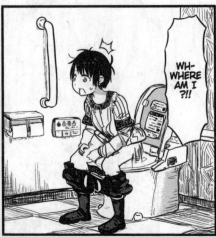

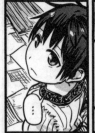

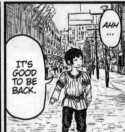

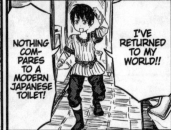

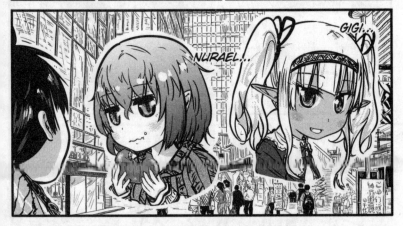

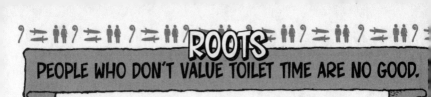

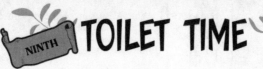

ROOTS

PEOPLE WHO DON'T VALUE TOILET TIME ARE NO GOOD.

NINTH

TOILET TIME

Outstanding people tend to think about toilets more.

This isn't some famous saying. It's merely an observation that those who make history tend to think more about toilets. From that illustrious group, there are two I'd like to introduce.

Toilets in medieval castles were undeniably terrible things. They were just protuberances in walls with a hole to let everything out. They were cold, smelly, and dark. The worst kind of environment to be in. Of course, castles were built for war, so you could say that the engineers had more important things to consider.

But there were also many developments during this period, such as the urine bottle. Today, urine bottles are mostly used in hospitals. However, back when toilets weren't as useful as they are now, these bottles were the perfect tool for going number one. This is why urine bottles developed into high-quality commodities. In ancient China, they were speckled with gold and silver, and there are terrifying stories of monarchs urinating in the skulls of conquered kings. In museums, you'll often see them labeled as flower vases or teapots, when in reality they were used to drain the dragon.

The Edo period tea ceremony master Katagiri Sekishu even developed a fondness for these urine bottles. He originally purchased one from a lodge he'd often visit, thinking it was a beautiful vase he could use as decoration. Later, when he discovered their true purpose, he destroyed his entire collection, to protect the aesthetics of the tea ceremony. As a result, these bottles lost a lot of their cultural significance.

In the Roman Empire, the emperor Vespasian became the first person in history to charge people to use public restrooms. (He would then sell the collected urine to laundry workers or hair dyers.) He was actually laughed at for collecting money for something everyone produced for free.

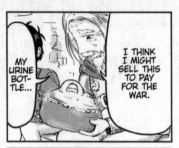

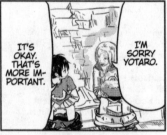

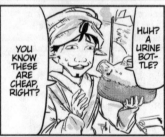

When Vespasian's son complained about the nature of this tax, the emperor held a coin up to his son's nose and said:

Pecunia non olet.
Money doesn't stink.

Vespasian's name still forms the root word for public bathrooms in many European countries.

Emperor Vespasian and Katagiri Sekishu both held toilets in high regard, and both became huge figures in the history of the world. It may seem like a stretch, but my conclusion is that these two things are related.

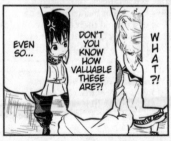

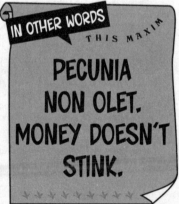

IN OTHER WORDS
THIS MAXIM

PECUNIA NON OLET. MONEY DOESN'T STINK.

I THINK I MIGHT SELL THIS TO PAY FOR THE WAR.
MY URINE BOT-TLE...
I'M SORRY YOTARO.
IT'S OKAY. THAT'S MORE IM-PORTANT.
HUH? A URINE BOT-TLE?
YOU KNOW THESE ARE CHEAP, RIGHT?
WHAT?!
DON'T YOU KNOW HOW VALUABLE THESE ARE?!
EVEN SO...

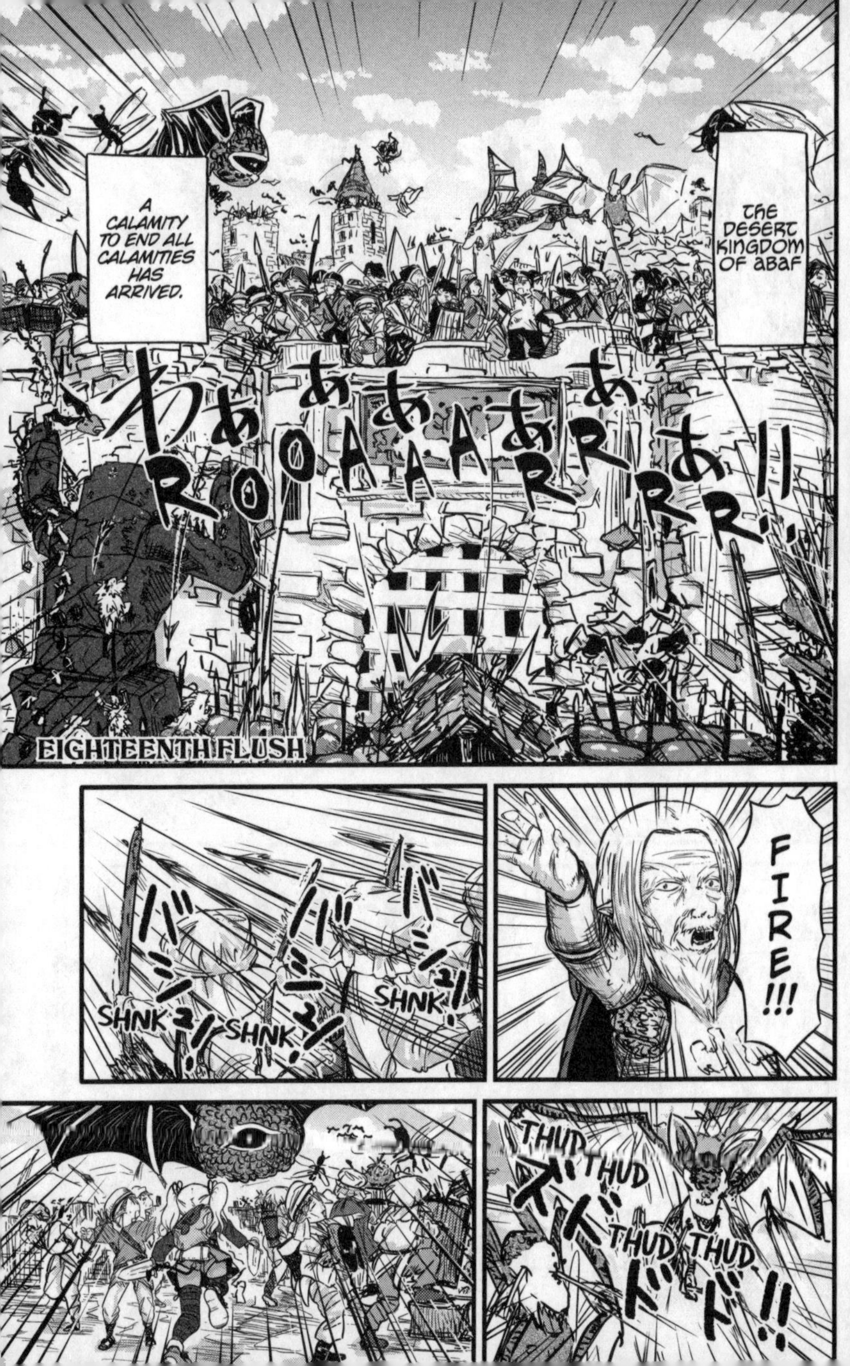
THE DESERT KINGDOM OF ABAF
A CALAMITY TO END ALL CALAMITIES HAS ARRIVED.
ROOAAARRRR!!
EIGHTEENTH FLUSH
FIRE!!!
SHNK! SHNK! SHNK!
THUD THUD THUD THUD!!

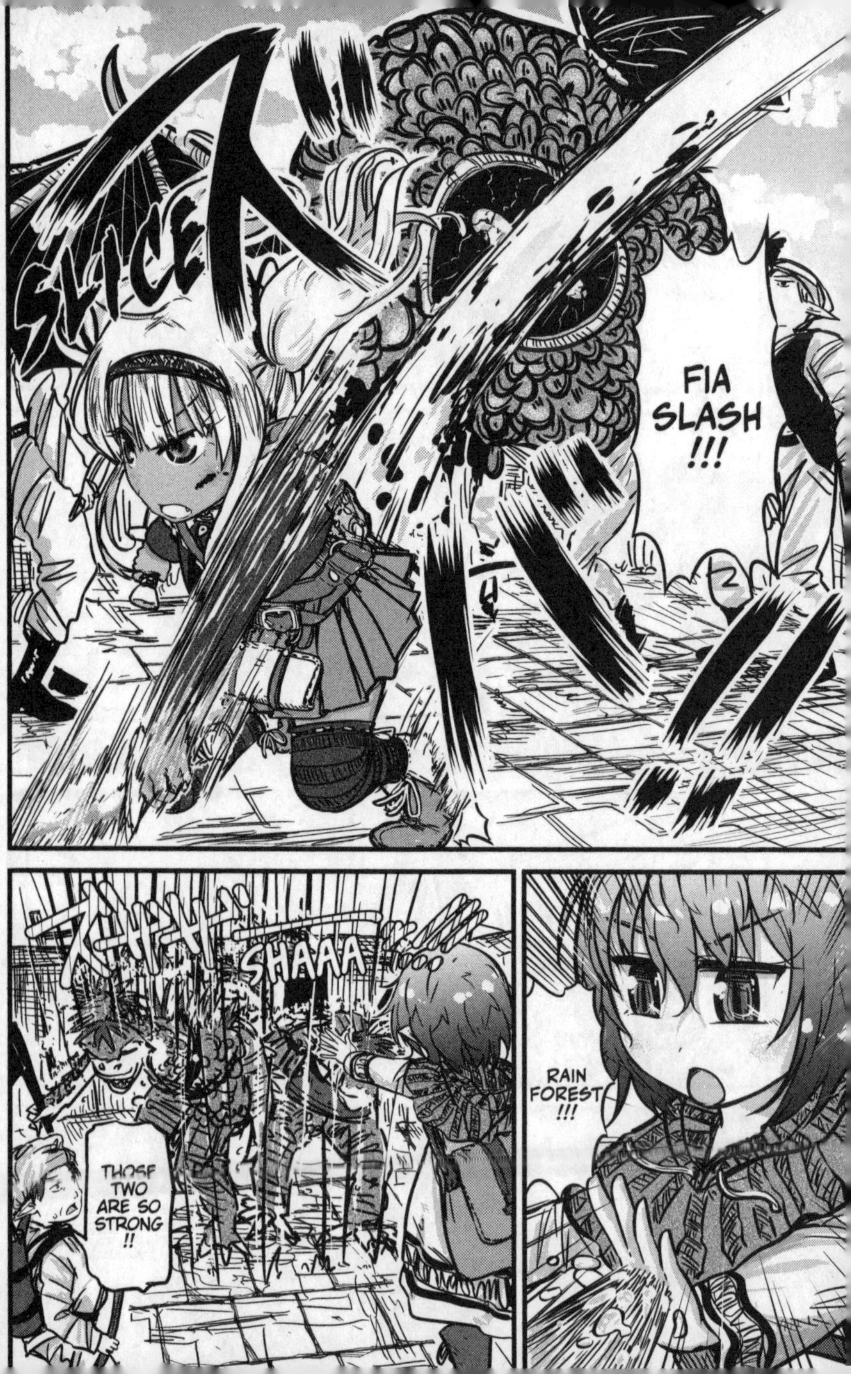
FIA SLASH!!!
SLICE
RAIN FOREST!!!
SHAAA
THOSE TWO ARE SO STRONG!!

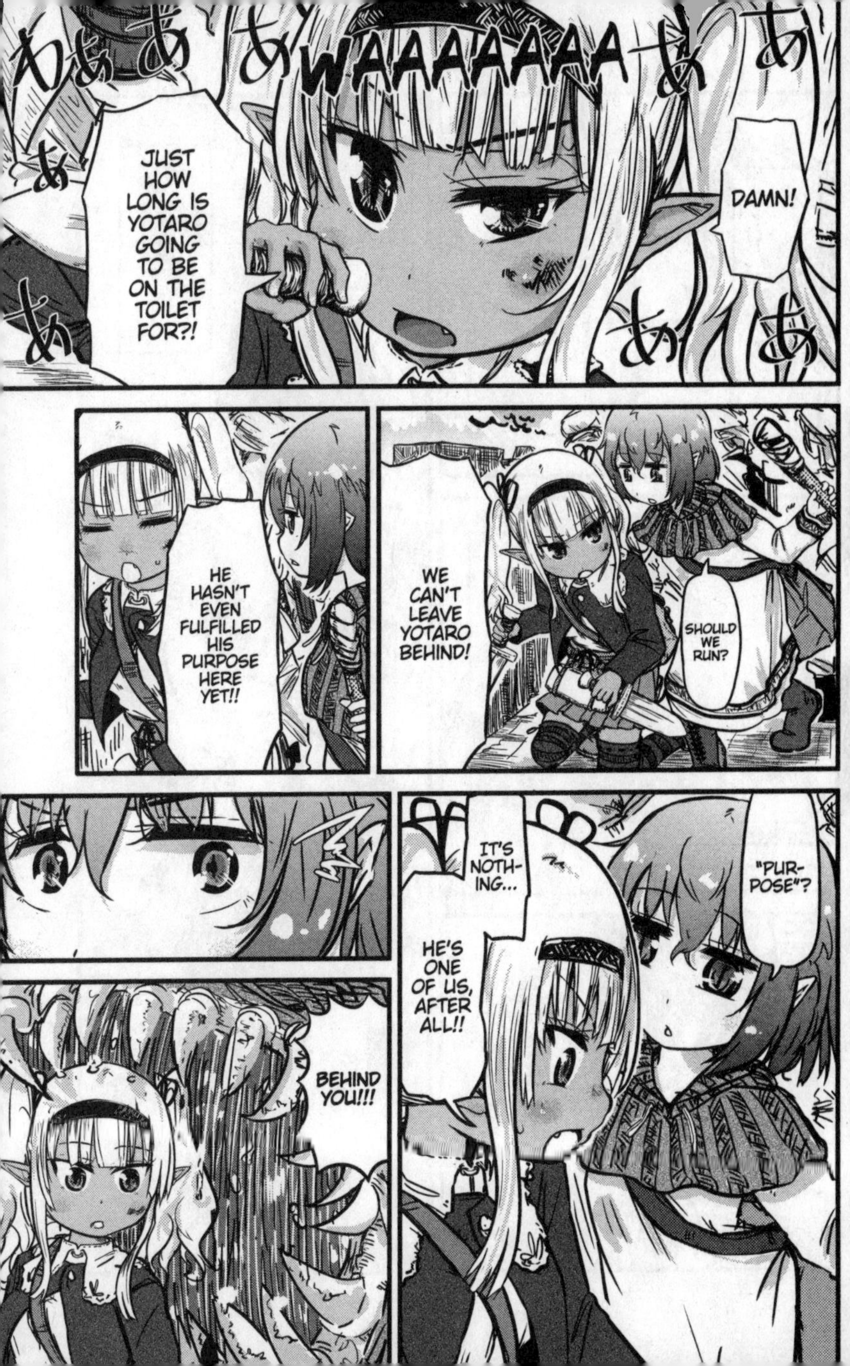
WAAAAAAA
DAMN!
JUST HOW LONG IS YOTARO GOING TO BE ON THE TOILET FOR?!
SHOULD WE RUN?
WE CAN'T LEAVE YOTARO BEHIND!
HE HASN'T EVEN FULFILLED HIS PURPOSE HERE YET!!
"PUR-POSE"?
IT'S NOTH-ING...
HE'S ONE OF US, AFTER ALL!!
BEHIND YOU!!!

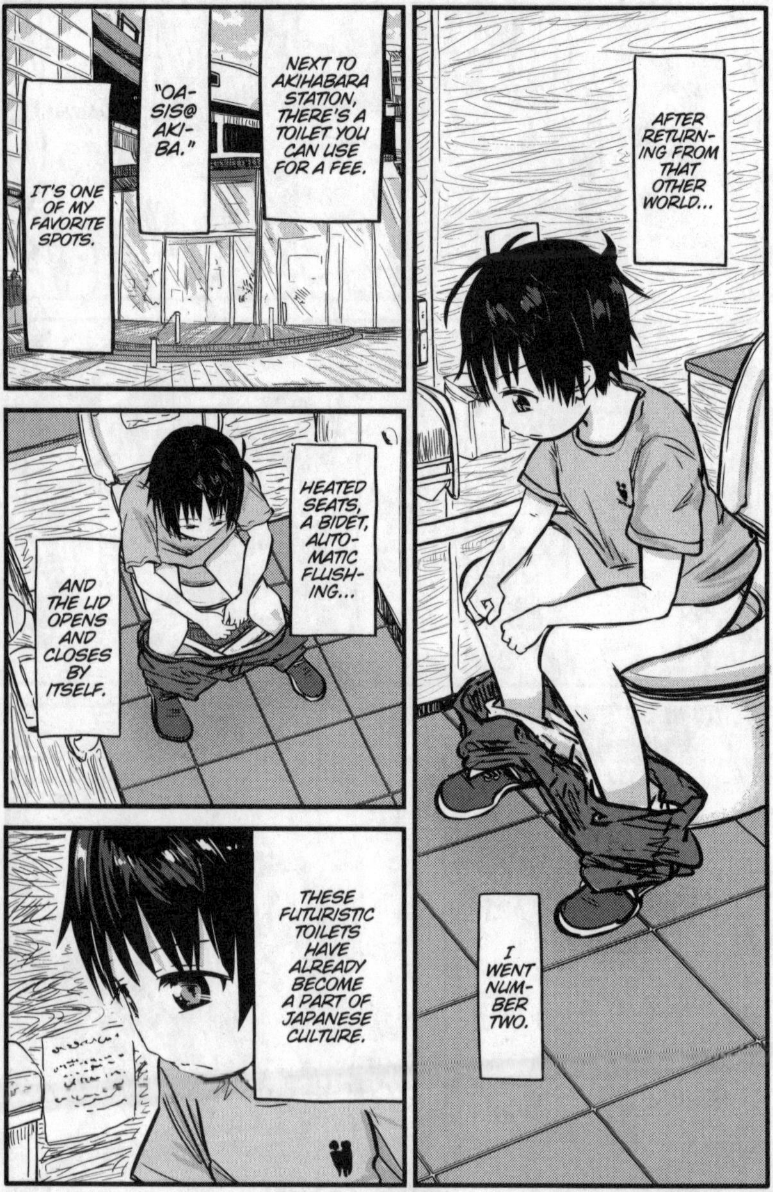
AFTER RETURNING FROM THAT OTHER WORLD...
I WENT NUMBER TWO.
NEXT TO AKIHABARA STATION, THERE'S A TOILET YOU CAN USE FOR A FEE.
"OASIS@AKIBA."
IT'S ONE OF MY FAVORITE SPOTS.
HEATED SEATS, A BIDET, AUTOMATIC FLUSHING...
AND THE LID OPENS AND CLOSES BY ITSELF.
THESE FUTURISTIC TOILETS HAVE ALREADY BECOME A PART OF JAPANESE CULTURE.

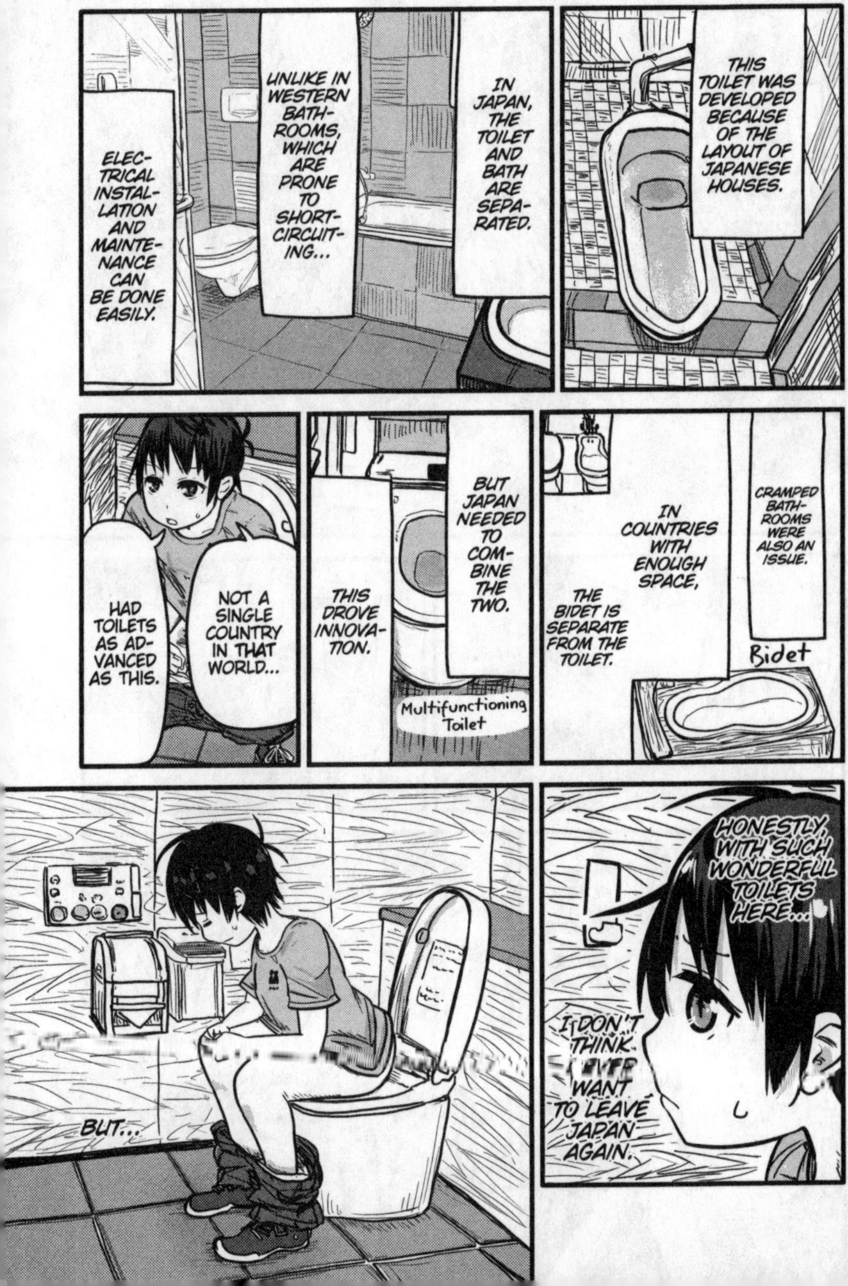
THIS TOILET WAS DEVELOPED BECAUSE OF THE LAYOUT OF JAPANESE HOUSES.
IN JAPAN, THE TOILET AND BATH ARE SEPARATED.
UNLIKE IN WESTERN BATHROOMS, WHICH ARE PRONE TO SHORT-CIRCUITING...
ELECTRICAL INSTALLATION AND MAINTENANCE CAN BE DONE EASILY.
CRAMPED BATHROOMS WERE ALSO AN ISSUE.
IN COUNTRIES WITH ENOUGH SPACE,
THE BIDET IS SEPARATE FROM THE TOILET.
Bidet
BUT JAPAN NEEDED TO COMBINE THE TWO.
THIS DROVE INNOVATION.
Multifunctioning Toilet
NOT A SINGLE COUNTRY IN THAT WORLD...
HAD TOILETS AS ADVANCED AS THIS.
HONESTLY, WITH SUCH WONDERFUL TOILETS HERE...
I DON'T THINK I'LL EVER WANT TO LEAVE JAPAN AGAIN.
BUT...

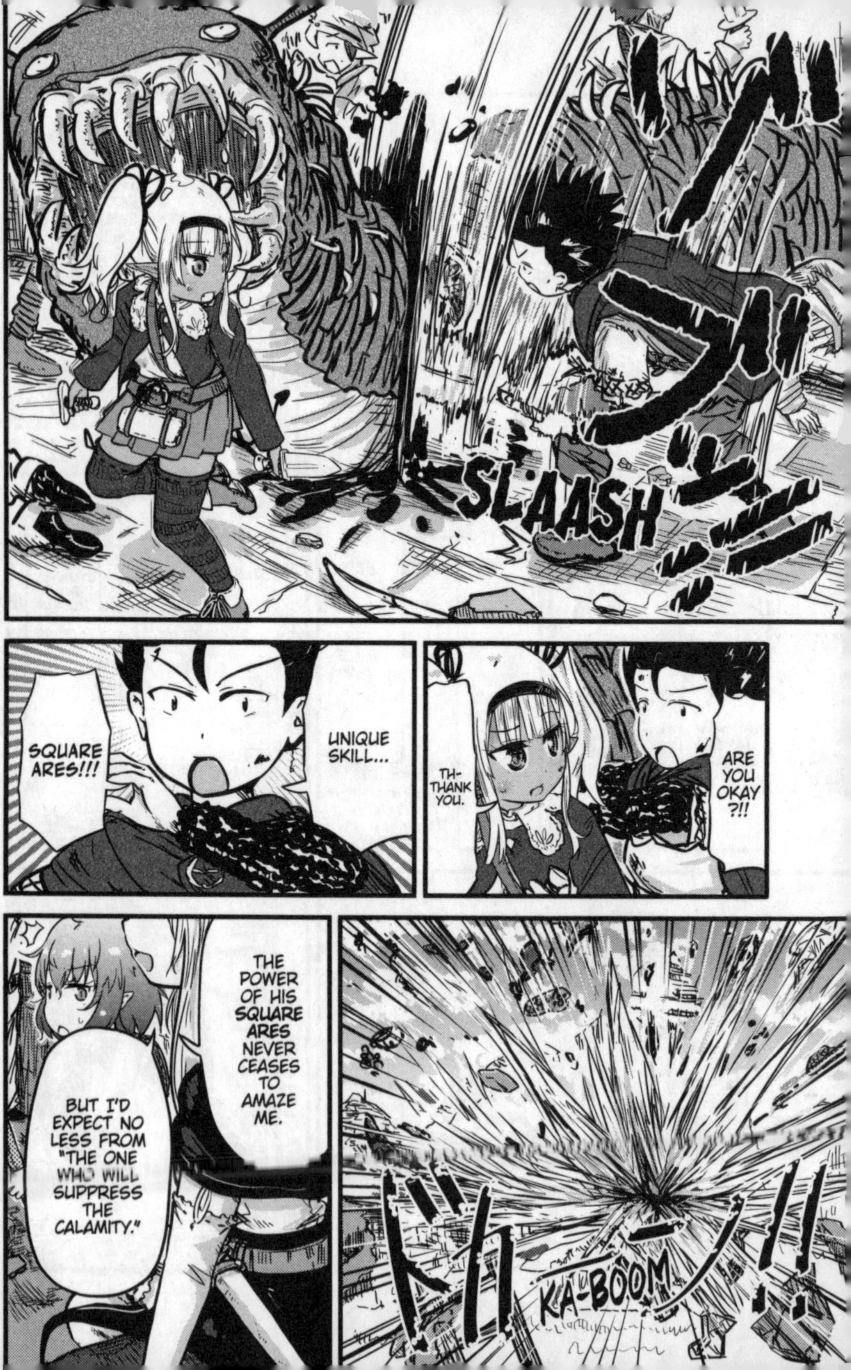
SLAASH
UNIQUE SKILL...
SQUARE ARES!!!
ARE YOU OKAY?!!
TH-THANK YOU.
KA-BOOM
THE POWER OF HIS SQUARE ARES NEVER CEASES TO AMAZE ME.
BUT I'D EXPECT NO LESS FROM "THE ONE WHO WILL SUPPRESS THE CALAMITY."

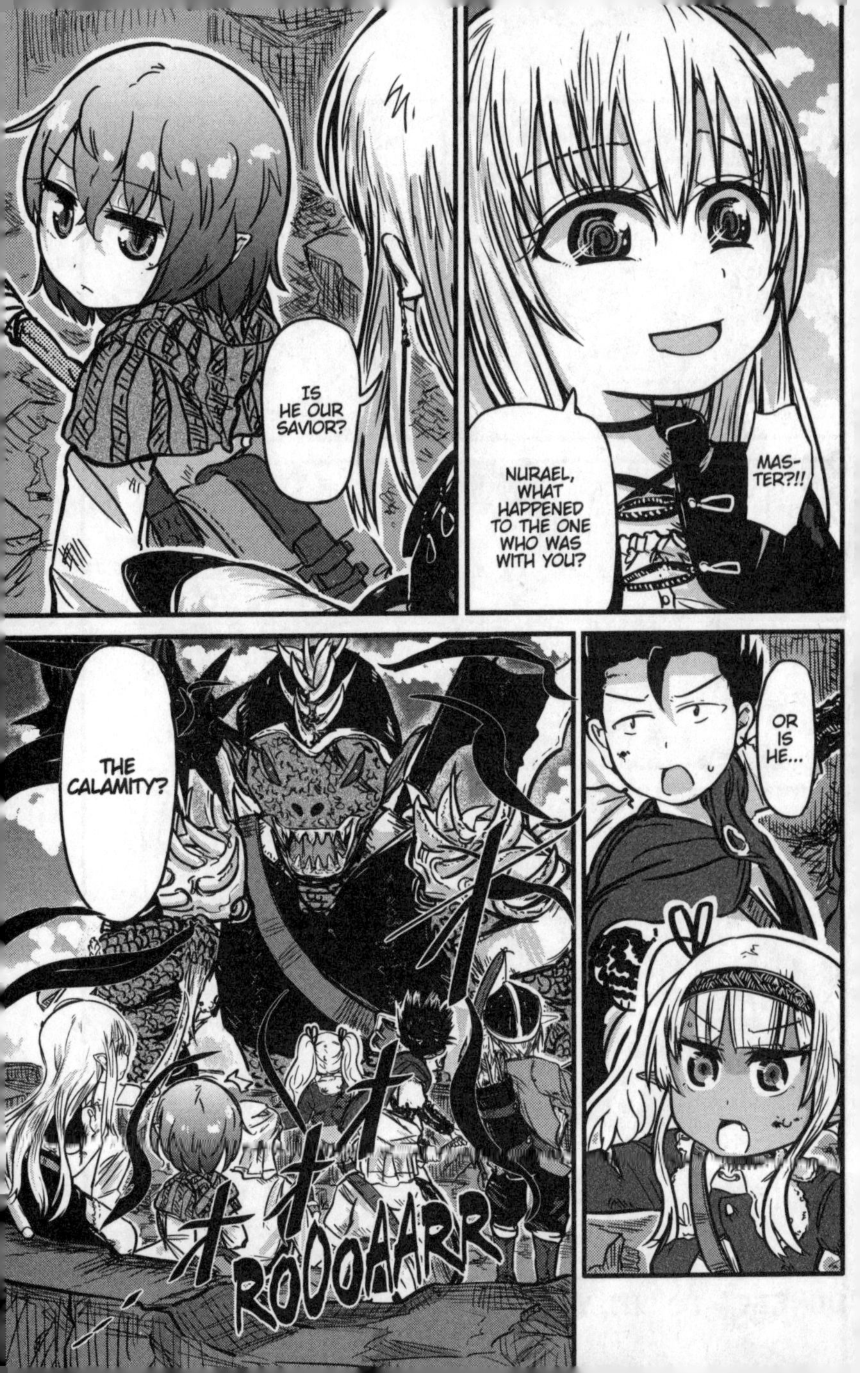
MAS-TER?!!
NURAEL, WHAT HAPPENED TO THE ONE WHO WAS WITH YOU?
IS HE OUR SAVIOR?
OR IS HE...
THE CALAMITY?
ROOOAARR

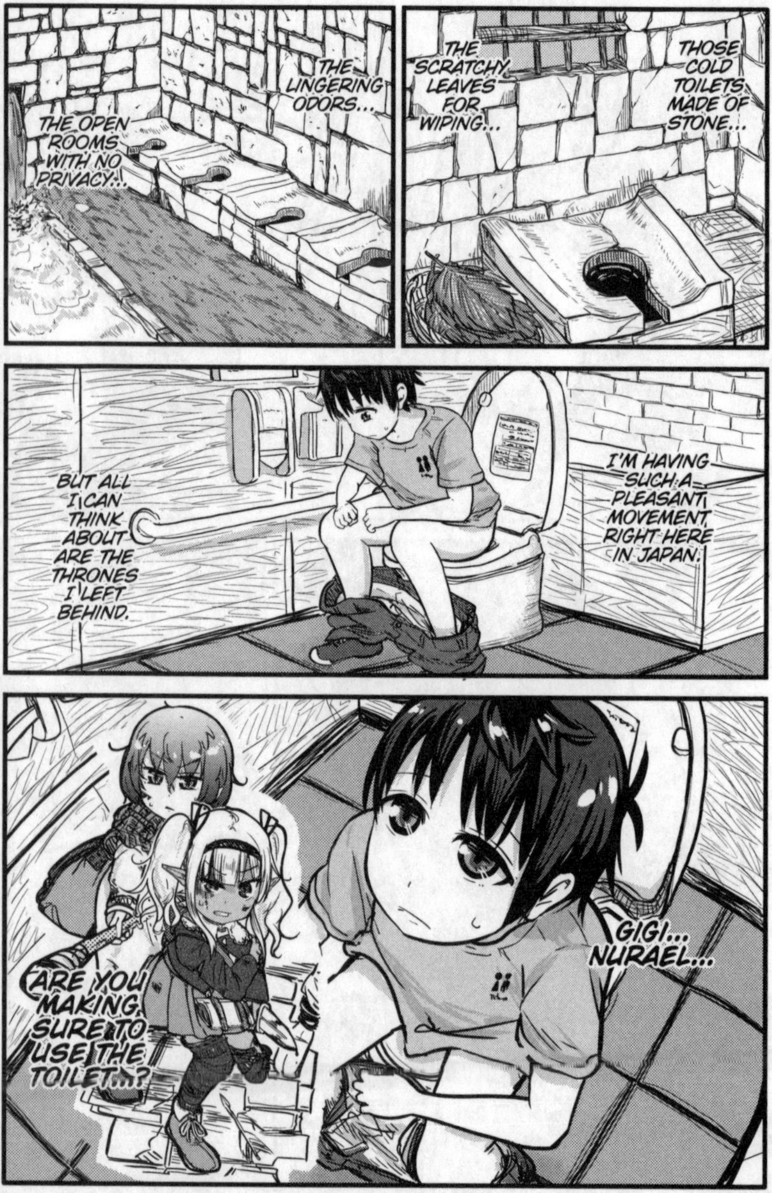
THOSE COLD TOILETS MADE OF STONE...
THE SCRATCHY LEAVES FOR WIPING...
THE LINGERING ODORS...
THE OPEN ROOMS WITH NO PRIVACY..!
I'M HAVING SUCH A PLEASANT MOVEMENT RIGHT HERE IN JAPAN.
BUT ALL I CAN THINK ABOUT ARE THE THRONES I LEFT BEHIND.
GIGI... NURAEL...
ARE YOU MAKING SURE TO USE THE TOILET...?

DUNGEON TOILET, VOL. 1 / THE END

Bibliography

Kawaya Kou by Rinoie Masafumi

Toilet Study Encyclopedia by the Japan Toilet Association

A Book of Funny Facts About Toilets by Planning OM

Let's Talk About Toilets: A Problem Spanning 6.5 Billion People
by Rose George; translated by Ozawa Akiko

*Water Flushing Toilets Have Been Around Since Ancient Times:
An Introduction to Ancient Toilet Studies* by Kurosaki Tadashi

*Architecture Picture Book, Household Fire and Water: The History of the Kitchen,
Bathroom, and Toilet* by Mitsufuji Toshio and Nakayama Shigenobu

Bath Toilet Eulogy by Lawrence Wright

Toilet Studies with Sato Mitsuharu by Sato Mitsuharu

Let's Talk about Toilets: Dialogues with Rinoie Masafumi by Rinoie Masafumi

Manure and Culture of Life: Scatology in the 21st Century by Rinoie Masafumi

Toilet Cultural History by Roger-Henri Guerrand; translated by Ooya Takayasu

Diagram of the Privy Mandala by Rinoie Masafumi, Muramatsu Teijiro,
Otomasu Shigetaka, Mitsuoka Tomotari, Miyazaki Akira, Fukuzumi Haruo,
and INAX Gallery Planning Committee

Compost Philosophy Will Save the World: Let's Start Pooping in the Leaves
by Izawa Masana

Everyone Poops by Gomi Taro

A Story About the World's Best Washlet Toilet by Hayashi Ryoyu

European Toilet Natural History by Unno Hiroshi,
Nimi Ryu, and Fritz Lischka

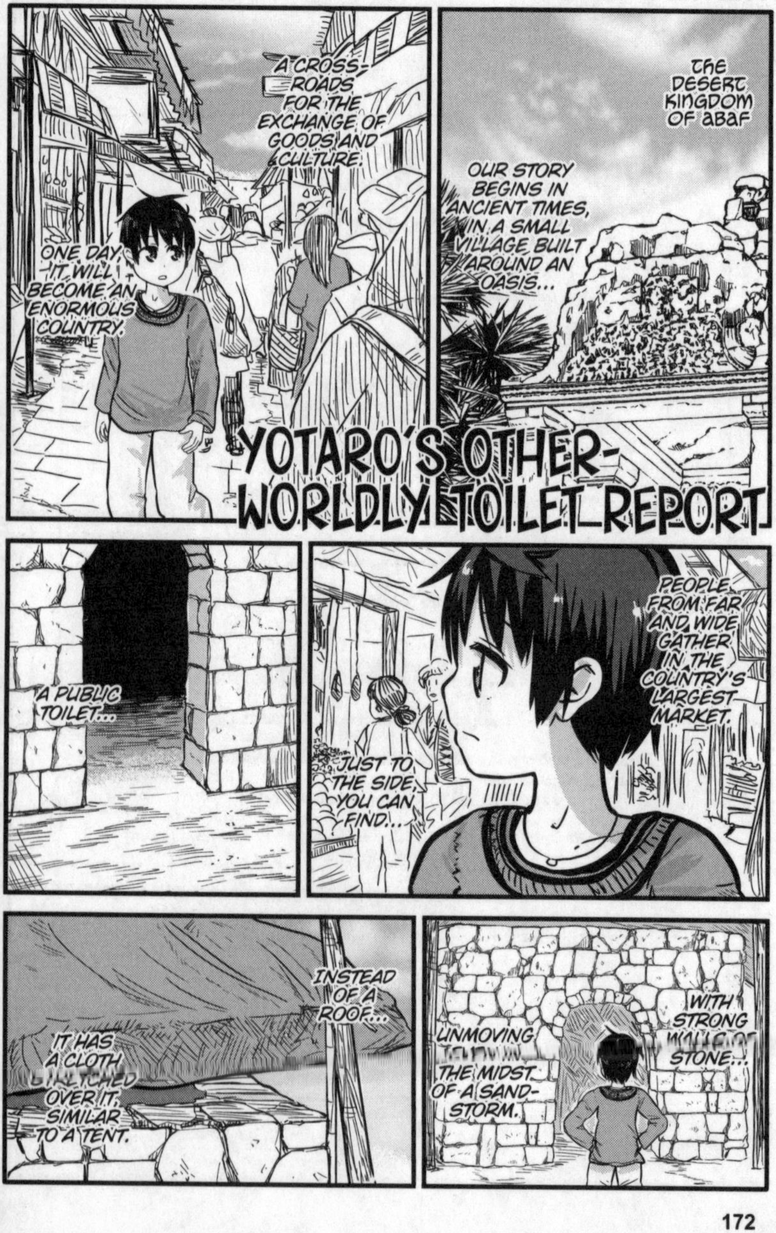
THE DESERT KINGDOM OF ABAF
OUR STORY BEGINS IN ANCIENT TIMES, IN A SMALL VILLAGE BUILT AROUND AN OASIS...
A CROSS-ROADS FOR THE EXCHANGE OF GOODS AND CULTURE.
ONE DAY, IT WILL BECOME AN ENORMOUS COUNTRY.
YOTARO'S OTHER-WORLDLY TOILET REPORT
PEOPLE FROM FAR AND WIDE GATHER IN THE COUNTRY'S LARGEST MARKET.
JUST TO THE SIDE, YOU CAN FIND...
A PUBLIC TOILET...
WITH STRONG
STONE...
UNMOVING
THE MIDST OF A SAND-STORM.
INSTEAD OF A ROOF...
IT HAS A CLOTH
OVER IT, SIMILAR TO A TENT.

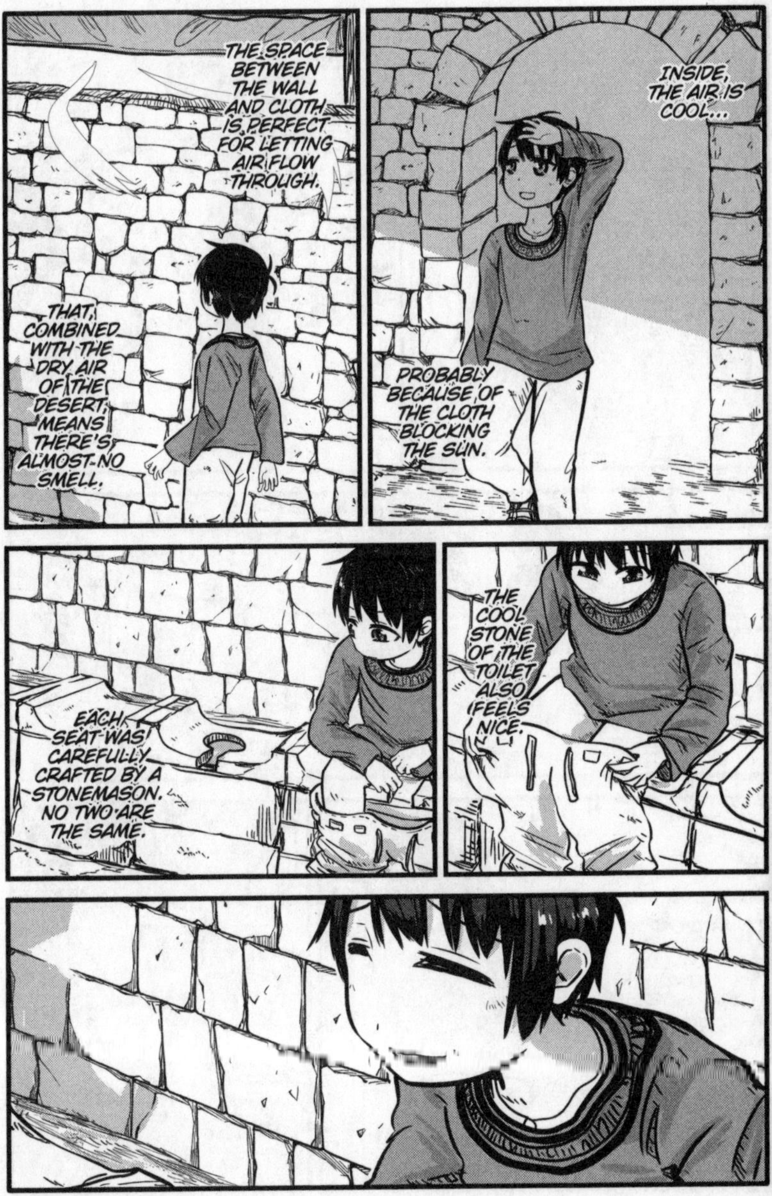
INSIDE, THE AIR IS COOL...
PROBABLY BECAUSE OF THE CLOTH BLOCKING THE SUN.
THE SPACE BETWEEN THE WALL AND CLOTH IS PERFECT FOR LETTING AIR FLOW THROUGH.
THAT, COMBINED WITH THE DRY AIR OF THE DESERT, MEANS THERE'S ALMOST NO SMELL.
THE COOL STONE OF THE TOILET ALSO FEELS NICE.
EACH SEAT WAS CAREFULLY CRAFTED BY A STONEMASON. NO TWO ARE THE SAME.

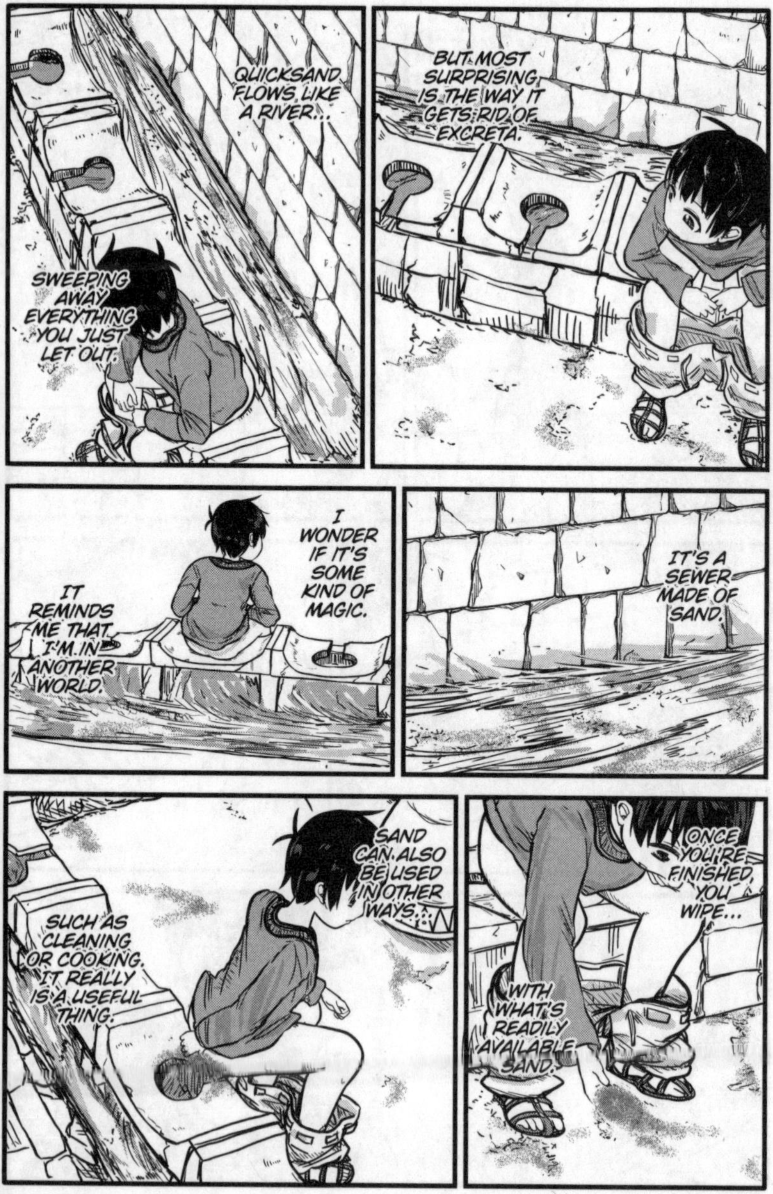
BUT MOST SURPRISING IS THE WAY IT GETS RID OF EXCRETA.
QUICKSAND FLOWS LIKE A RIVER...
SWEEPING AWAY EVERYTHING YOU JUST LET OUT.
IT'S A SEWER MADE OF SAND.
I WONDER IF IT'S SOME KIND OF MAGIC.
IT REMINDS ME THAT I'M IN ANOTHER WORLD.
ONCE YOU'RE FINISHED, YOU WIPE...
WITH WHAT'S READILY AVAILABLE SAND.
SAND CAN ALSO BE USED IN OTHER WAYS...
SUCH AS CLEANING OR COOKING. IT REALLY IS A USEFUL THING.

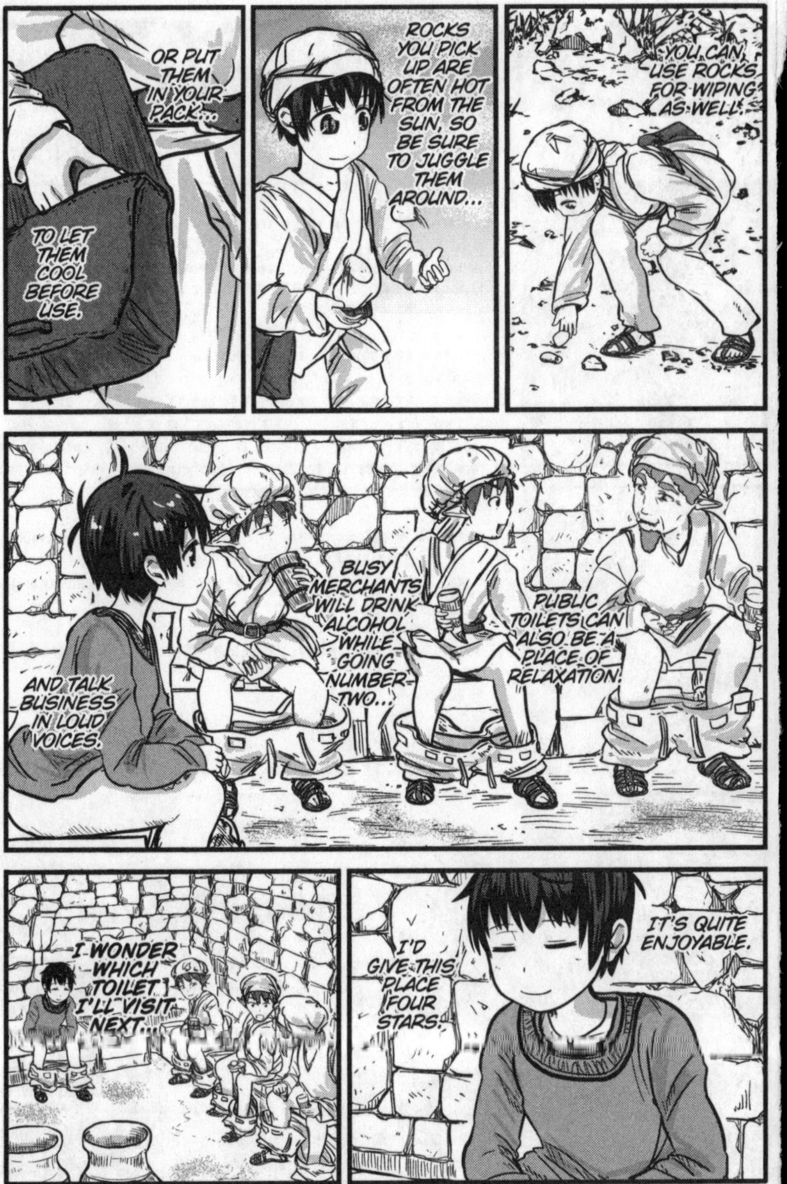
YOU CAN USE ROCKS FOR WIPING AS WELL.
ROCKS YOU PICK UP ARE OFTEN HOT FROM THE SUN, SO BE SURE TO JUGGLE THEM AROUND...
OR PUT THEM IN YOUR PACK...
TO LET THEM COOL BEFORE USE.
PUBLIC TOILETS CAN ALSO BE A PLACE OF RELAXATION!
BUSY MERCHANTS WILL DRINK ALCOHOL WHILE GOING NUMBER TWO...
AND TALK BUSINESS IN LOUD VOICES.
IT'S QUITE ENJOYABLE.
I'D GIVE THIS PLACE FOUR STARS.
I WONDER WHICH TOILET I'LL VISIT NEXT...

PLEASE LOOK FORWARD TO THE NEXT VOLUME!

SEVEN SEAS ENTERTAINMENT PRESENTS

DUNGEON TOILET

story and art by ROOTS

VOLUME 1

TRANSLATION
Thomas Zimmerman

ADAPTATION
Peter Adrian Behravesh

LETTERING
Chris Burgener

COVER DESIGN
Kris Aubin

COPY EDITOR
Dawn Davis
Meg van Huygen

EDITOR
Matthew Birkenhauer

PREPRESS TECHNICIAN
annon Rasmussen-Silverstein

PRODUCTION ASSISTANT
Christa Miesner

PRODUCTION MANAGER
Lissa Pattillo

MANAGING EDITOR
Julie Davis

ASSOCIATE PUBLISHER
Adam Arnold

PUBLISHER
Jason DeAngelis

ISEKAI NO TOILET DE DAI WO SURU Volume 1
© Roots 2019
Originally published in Japan in 2019 by Akita Publishing Co., Ltd.
English translation rights arranged with Akita Publishing Co., Ltd. through
TOHAN CORPORATION, Tokyo.

Seven Seas press and purchase enquiries can be sent to Marketing Manager Lianne
Sentar at press@gomanga.com. Information regarding the distribution and purchase of
digital editions is available from Digital Manager CK Russell at digital@gomanga.com.

ISBN: 978-1-64505-944-8
Printed in Canada
First Printing: May 2021
10 9 8 7 6 5 4 3 2 1

//// READING DIRECTIONS ////

This book reads from *right to left*,
Japanese style. If this is your first time
reading manga, you start reading from
the top right panel on each page and
take it from there. If you get lost, just
follow the numbered diagram here.
It may seem backwards at first,
but you'll get the hang of it! Have fun!!

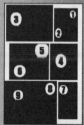

Follow us online: www.SevenSeasEntertainment.com